Malware Detection

Advances in Information Security

Sushil Jajodia
Consulting Editor
Center for Secure Information Systems
George Mason University
Fairfax, VA 22030-4444
email: jajodia@gmu.edu

The goals of the Springer International Series on ADVANCES IN INFORMATION SECURITY are, one, to establish the state of the art of, and set the course for future research in information security and, two, to serve as a central reference source for advanced and timely topics in information security research and development. The scope of this series includes all aspects of computer and network security and related areas such as fault tolerance and software assurance.

ADVANCES IN INFORMATION SECURITY aims to publish thorough and cohesive overviews of specific topics in information security, as well as works that are larger in scope or that contain more detailed background information than can be accommodated in shorter survey articles. The series also serves as a forum for topics that may not have reached a level of maturity to warrant a comprehensive textbook treatment.

Researchers, as well as developers, are encouraged to contact Professor Sushil Jajodia with ideas for books under this series.

Additional titles in the series:

Additional information about this series can be obtained from
http://www.springer.com

Malware Detection

edited by

Mihai Christodorescu
Somesh Jha
University of Wisconsin, USA

Douglas Maughan
Department of Homeland Security, USA

Dawn Song
Carnegie Mellon University, USA

Cliff Wang
Army Research Office, USA

 Springer

Mihai Christodorescu
Computer Sciences Department
University of Wisconsin
1210 W Dayton St
Madison, WI 53706-1685
mihai@cs.wisc.edu

Somesh Jha
Computer Sciences Department
University of Wisconsin
1210 W Dayton St
Madison, WI 53706-1685
jha@cs.wisc.edu

Douglas Maughan
Dept. of Homeland Security
Washington, D.C. 20528
Douglas.Maughan@dhs.gov

Dawn Song
CIC 2122
Carnegie Mellon University
4720 Forbes Ave
Pittsburgh, PA 15213
dawnsong@cmu.edu

Cliff Wang
Computing and Information Science Div.
U.S. Army Research Office
P.O. Box 12211
Research Triangle Park, NC 27709-2211
cliff.wang@us.army.mil

Malware Detection *edited by* Mihai Christodorescu, Somesh Jha, Douglas Maughan, Dawn Song, and Cliff Wang

ISBN 978-1-4419-4095-7   e-ISBN-10: 0-387-44599-4
                                e-ISBN-13: 978-0-387-44599-1

Printed on acid-free paper.

9 8 7 6 5 4 3 2 1

springer.com

Preface

Malicious programs present an increasing threat to the privacy of sensitive data and the availability of critical services. As Internet connectivity exploded and online services have become omnipresent, malware has targeted all aspects of the cyberworld. Driven by profit, malware authors have sharpened their skills to attack all online services, from banking to social networking to instant messaging, with increased frequency and sophistication.

This book captures recent advances in the defense against all types of threats, and the chapters reflect a diversity of defensive techniques. Chapter 1 presents a detailed view of the threat landscape and analyzes the malware trends. The remaining chapters are organized into themes corresponding to the various malware threats.

Chapters 2–5 present techniques for analyzing existing programs to determine their trustworthiness, as well as techniques for armoring programs against remote attacks. Chapter 2 introduces robust approaches to the disassembly and static analysis of obfuscated binaries, including obfuscated malware, while Chapter 3 describes a static analysis to recover high-level variables and data structures from binaries. Techniques that characterize the behavioral and structural properties of binary code are used to generate semantically-rich descriptions of malware in Chapter 4. New approaches for the detection and prevention of SQL injection attacks against database-driven web applications are presented in Chapter 5.

The second part of the book (chapters 6–9) tackles the problem of distributed threats and the challenge of distributed detection. Network containment of worms (Chapter 6) complements the host-based self-healing architecture of Sting (Chapter 7) to provide end-to-end defenses against fast Internet-scale worm attacks. Chapter 8 presents the inner workings of botnets, the large networks of infected hosts under the control of a remote attacker. Chapter 9 analyzes the benefits of cooperation between network-based and host-based intrusion detectors and provides practical guidelines for obtaining the maximum detection rate out of a cooperative setup.

Targeted and stealthy threats meet their match in Chapters 10 and 11. Shadow honeypots in Chapter 10 combine the power of anomaly detectors with the precision of honeypots to detect targeted attacks. Statistical methods for binary content analysis are then used in Chapter 11 to detect malware hiding in document files.

The last part of the book presents new techniques for constructing trustworthy services and applications from the ground up. Pioneer in Chapter 12 can verify the correct execution of a program on an untrusted remote host. Chapter 13 explains the principles of secure information flow analysis, with the goal of proving that a program does not leak sensitive information.

We are grateful to the authors appearing in this edited volume for their contributions to the field of malware detection, in all of its aspects, and for striving to make the Internet a safer, more trustworthy place.

Mihai Christodorescu
Somesh Jha
Douglas Maughan
Dawn Song
Cliff Wang

Contents

Introduction

Shared resources, such as the Internet, have created a highly interconnected cyber-infrastructure. Critical infrastructures in domains such as medical, power, telecommunications, and finance are highly dependent on information systems. These two factors have exposed our critical infrastructures to malicious attacks and accidental failures. Disruption of services caused by such undesirable events can have catastrophic effects, including loss of human life, disruption of essential services, and huge financial losses. For example, the outbreak of the CodeRed virus infected more than 359,000 hosts, resulting in financial losses of approximately 2.6 billion dollars [10]. Given the devastating effect malicious code can have on our cyber infrastructure, identifying and containing malicious programs is an important goal.

A *malware* is a program that has malicious intent. Examples of malware are viruses, trojans, and worms. Malware is usually classified [9] according to its propagation method and goal into the following categories:

- *viruses* are programs that self-replicate within a host by attaching themselves to programs and/or documents that become carriers of the malicious code;
- *worms* self-replicate across a network;
- *trojan horses* masquerade as useful programs, but contain malicious code to attack the system or leak data;
- *back doors* open the system to external entities by subverting the local security policies to allow remote access and control over a network;
- *spyware* is a useful software package that also transmits private user data to an external entity.

A *malware detector* is a system that attempts to identify malware. A virus scanner uses signatures and other heuristics to identify malware, and thus is an example of a malware detector. Given the havoc that can be caused by malware [4], malware detection is an important goal.

The goal of an malware writer (hacker) is to modify or morph their malware to evade detection by a malware detector. A common technique used by malware writers for evading detection is program obfuscation [11]. Polymorphism and metamorphism are two common obfuscation techniques used by malware writers. In order to evade detection, a virus morphs itself by encrypting its malicious payload and decrypting it during execution. A polymorphic virus obfuscates its decryption loop using several transformations, such as nop-insertion, code transposition (changing the order of instructions and placing jump instructions to maintain the original semantics), and register reassignment (permuting the register allocation). *Metamorphic viruses* attempt to evade detection by obfuscating the entire virus. When they replicate, these viruses change their code in a variety of ways, such as code transposition, substitution of equivalent instruction sequences, change of conditional jumps, and register reassignment [8, 12, 13].

Addition of new behaviors to existing malware is another favorite technique used by malware writers. For example, the *Sobig.A* through *Sobig.F* worm variants (widespread during the summer of 2003) were developed iteratively, with each successive iteration adding or changing small features [5, 6, 7]. Each new variant manages to evade detection either through the use of obfuscations or through adding more behavior. The recent recurrence of the Netsky and Beagle worms (both active in the first half of 2004) are also examples of how adding new code or changing existing code creates new undetectable and more malicious variants [2, 3]. For example, the Beagle worm shows a series of "upgrades" from version A to version C that include the addition of a backdoor, code to disable local security mechanisms, and functionality to better hide the worm within existing processes. A quote from [3] summarizes the challenges worm families pose to malware detectors:

> Arguably the most striking aspect of Beagle is the dedication of the author or authors to refining the code. New pieces are tested, perfected, and then deployed with great forethought as to how to evade antivirus scanners and how to defeat network edge protection devices.

Commercial malware detectors (such as virus scanners) use a simple pattern matching approach to malware detection, i.e., a program is declared as malware if it contains a sequence of instructions that is matched by a regular expression. A recent study demonstrated that such malware detectors can be easily defeated using simple program obfuscations [1], which are already being used by hackers. The basic deficiency in the "pattern matching" approach to malware detection is that *they ignore the semantics of instructions*. Since the pattern-matching algorithm is not very resilient to slight variations, these malware detectors have to use different patterns for detecting two malware that are slight variations of each other. This is the reason that the signature database of a commercial virus scanner has to be updated frequently. The paper by Christodorescu and Jha [1] demonstrates that in the field of malware detection a fundamental shift in direction is required. If malware detectors keep relying on simple techniques (such as pattern matching), they are bound to fall behind in the "arms race".

In order to address these challenges in malware detection, a workshop on Malware Detection was held on August 10-11, 2005 at SRI International, Arlington,

Virginia.[1] The workshop was co-sponsored by the Army Research Office (ARO) and Department of Homeland Security (DHS). Several experts in the field of malware detection attended the workshop. Presentations covered various topics, such static analysis, distributed threat detection, and novel techniques for building trustworthy services. The papers in this edited volume represent the cutting edge techniques in detection malware.

References

1. M. Christodorescu and S. Jha. Testing malware detectors. In *Proceedings of the ACM SIGSOFT International Symposium on Software Testing and Analysis 2004 (ISSTA'04)*, pages 34–44, Boston, MA, USA, July 2004. ACM Press.
2. M. Ciubotariu. Netsky: a conflict starter? *Virus Bulletin*, pages 4–8, May 2004.
3. J. Gordon. Lessons from virus developers: The Beagle worm history through april 24, 2004. In *SecurityFocus Guest Feature Forum*. SecurityFocus, May 2004. Published on-line at http://www.securityfocus.com/guest/24228. Last accessed: 9 Sep. 2004.
4. L. A. Gordon, M. P. Loeb, W. Lucyshyn, and R. Richardson. 2004 CSI/FBI computer crime and security survey. Technical report, Computer Security Institute, 2004.
5. LURHQ Threat Intelligence Group. Sobig.a and the spam you received today. Technical report, LURHQ, 2003. Published online at http://www.lurhq.com/sobig.html. Last accessed on 16 Jan. 2004.
6. LURHQ Threat Intelligence Group. Sobig.e - Evolution of the worm. Technical report, LURHQ, 2003. Published online at http://www.lurhq.com/sobig-e.html. Last accessed on 16 Jan. 2004.
7. LURHQ Threat Intelligence Group. Sobig.f examined. Technical report, LURHQ, 2003. Published online at http://www.lurhq.com/sobig-f.html. Last accessed on 16 Jan. 2004.
8. A. Marinescu. Russian doll. *Virus Bulletin*, pages 7–9, Aug. 2003.
9. G. McGraw and G. Morrisett. Attacking malicious code: report to the Infosec research council. *IEEE Software*, 17(5):33 – 41, Sept./Oct. 2000.
10. D. Moore, C. Shannon, and J. Brown. Code-Red: a case study on the spread and victims of an internet worm. In *Proceedings ot the Internet Measurement Workshop 2002, Marseille, France*, November 6-8 2002.
11. C. Nachenberg. Computer virus-antivirus coevolution. *Commun. ACM*, 40(1):46–51, Jan. 1997.
12. P. Ször and P. Ferrie. Hunting for metamorphic. In *Proceedings of the 2001 Virus Bulletin Conference (VB2001)*, pages 123 – 144, September 2001.
13. z0mbie. z0mbie's homepage. Published online at http://z0mbie.host.sk. Last accessed: 16 Jan. 2004.

---

[1] Details about the workshop can be found at
http://www.cs.wisc.edu/malwareworkshop2005/.

Part I

Overview

Malware Evolution: A Snapshot of Threats and Countermeasures in 2005

Brian Witten and Carey Nachenberg

[1] Symantec Corporation, 12801 Worldgate Drive, Suite 800, Herndon, VA
20170
bwitten@symantec.com

[2] Symantec Corporation, 2500 Broadway, Suite 200, Santa Monica, CA
90404
cnachenberg@symantec.com

1.1 Overview

Speed, stealth, and purpose of malware [1] threats and countermeasures are
evolving quickly. This chapter describes these three facets of current malware threats, and describes a few countermeasures emerging to better address such threats.

1.2 Evolution of Threats

Defenders currently have a much smaller window from discovery of a
vulnerability to release of malware exploiting that vulnerability. Further, a
number of malware threats released within the last five years have been
effectively designed to propagate far faster than threats released in previous
periods. Yet more disconcerting, malware authors and distributors are increasingly focused on collection of private and directly valuable information, both in spyware [2] and other forms of malware, and they have a
growing number of techniques for hiding themselves.

1.2.1 Evolution of Threat Speed

The average time between announcement of a computer system security flaw and appearance of malicious code that takes advantage of the flaw declined from 281 days in 1999 to 10 days in 2004 [15]. Recent threats are also faster in propagation rate. By way of example, on January 25, 2003 an SQL based worm commonly referred to as Slammer [18] infected 90% of vulnerable servers within the first 10 minutes of propagation [37]. Similarly, on July 19, 2001 in less than 14 hours more than 359,000 computers were infected with a variant of the Code-Red worm [32]. In contrast, the Morris Worm of 1988 [6] spread over the course of days [26]. Given that the current average time between the disclosure of a vulnerability and the release of an associated exploit is 6 days, and that the average patch-release time is 54 days [44], patching is largely ineffective against new threats.

1.2.2 Evolution of Threat Purpose

Malicious code for profit remains on the rise [44], as are spyware and other threats to confidential information. Between January 1 and June 30, 2005, malicious code that exposed confidential information represented 74% of the top 50 malicious code samples reported to Symantec, up from 54% during the previous six months [44], and 44% between January 1 and June 30, 2004 [43]. Spyware is now among the most pervasive and fastest growing forms of malware. In a recent study by NCSA and AOL, 80% of systems scanned were infected by spyware [12]. Even by conservative standards of cataloging spyware, Symantec now lists 221 families of spyware that have appeared in and since 2003 [7]. To contrast the spyware threat with viruses and worms, although thousands of variants of viruses and worms are found each quarter, only 830 families of viruses and worms were discovered between January 1, 2003 and June 30, 2005 [44]. In short, although anti-spyware offerings did not appear until 2000 [8], the rate at which new families of spyware are being created is now nearing the rate at which new viruses are being created. Moreover, by laying in waiting at well advertised sites and bundling itself with desirable downloads such as Browser Helper Objects, and other software that users intentionally or unintentionally download, it's easier to broadcast some forms spyware to very broad distributions of victims immediately, rather than waiting through the first portion of s-shaped infection growth curves experienced by viruses and worms. Given these propagation vectors and threat speeds described above, along with the number of unprotected systems and systems that update their defenses infrequently, malware authors have succeeded in compromising countless systems. In fact, police recently arrested three people accused of compromising 100,000 systems [21]. Moreover, given the changing motives described above, it is very common to establish a persistent presence called a "bot" on such compromised machines for financial gain. Once such a bot is installed, its owner can steal confidential information, use the machine for spam distribution, falsely increasing hit rates on advertisements to increase hit rate-based ad revenue, or simply sell the bot to others for such illicit uses. We recently reported evidence of underground selling of bot networks and reported identifying an average of over 10,000 bots per day over a six month period [44].

1.2.3 Evolution of Threat Stealth

Such financial motives give direct financial value to the ability to hide a persistent presence to prevent detection. Rootkits [9] are among the tools which malware may use to persistently hide itself as well as installed bots. This is a growing area of interest for malware authors, and several techniques have recently been published showing how to more effectively hide persistent malware from detection by security software [10, 41]. Further, as the number of variants of viruses and worms continues to nearly double every six months [44], the risk of previously unseen malware evading detection continues to increase substantially each quarter. Moreover, as the number of vulnerabilities continues to grow so does the risk that someone might quietly and non-publicly find a new, unpublished vulnerability and create malware exploiting the vulnerability on large scale before most defenders are able to find and mitigate the vulnerability. Last, as defenses and detection schemes have evolved to better protect operating systems and standard services, many malware authors have focused their attention on higher level web applications where fewer defenses have existed historically, resulting in a countless number of incidents with sweeping loss of privacy [31, 45].

1.3 Evolution of Countermeasures

This section describes a sampling of recently emerging countermeasures for fast spreading and previously unseen threats, as well as spyware. Since emergence of fast spreading threats such as Slammer and Code Red, techniques and technologies have emerged to better mitigate risks from such fast spreading threats. Various forms of rate-limiting, such as Virus Throttling [50], were among early countermeasures proposed to slow such rapid and potentially entirely-unknown threats. Other countermeasures, however, don't merely slow the threat but rather completely block previously unseen threats from actually infecting protected machines. Given the strong industry emphasis on signature-based detection for intrusion detection and anti-virus, malware authors and distributors have found great value in leveraging previously unseen threats to evade detection. For this reason, proactive approaches will grow to be an increasingly important tool in the security arsenal. However, broadening and generalizing protection against many classes of previously unseen threats is not sufficient for all threats. More and more spyware threats are employing self-updating to add functionality and change their signature faster than security vendors can respond with traditional techniques; moreover, they have distribution vectors that are vastly different from traditional malware, Thus, security firms are having to devote substantial effort addressing these unique behaviors, including building farms of spyware to rapidly harvest new spyware variants as they update themselves. Further, when threats such as rootkits, which are becoming increasingly stealthy in establishing and maintaining covert and persistent presence, are coupled with either a previously unseen threat or the exceptionally broad distribution vectors of spyware, the result is a blended threat that is exceedingly difficult to detect at time of compromise, and can be exceedingly difficult to detect and remove after compromise. For these reasons, the next sections focus on countermeasures for previously unseen malware threats in general, then specific attention to countermeasures for rootkits and spyware.

1.3.1 Countermeasures for Previously Unseen Threats

Countermeasures for previously unseen threats are addressed below first for detecting previously unseen threats against already known vulnerabilities and identifying previously unknown vulnerabilities, and then for detecting previously unseen threats without foreknowledge of the vulnerability.

Blocking Previously Unseen Threats Against Already Known Vulnerabilities

Techniques such as Generic Exploit Blocking (GEB) [33] and Microsoft's Shield effort [47] were conceived to provide protection against previously unseen threats. These techniques use analysis of a known vulnerability to produce a signature that is not specific to any single instance of malware exploiting the vulnerability. Thus, such a properly written signature can properly detect all potential attacks against a given vulnerability. This is in contrast with traditional antivirus and IDS heuristics which may be able to detect a percentage of new threats, but cannot guarantee complete detection. However, these approaches include a number of challenges in implementation, including the following three challenges.

- First, the signatures must be specified in a language and processed by a scanning engine that facilitate "performant" scanning, either in the sense of high line-speeds, as is the constraint for traditional intrusion detection and network level anti-virus systems, or in the sense of low CPU burden.
- Second, the system must maintain low false positives while producing high true positives.
- Third, even though these approaches do not require prior knowledge of the malware, they still require prior knowledge of the vulnerability. The luxury of that prior knowledge is not always available.

The next two sections describe techniques for identifying previously unknown vulnerabilities, and techniques for detecting previously unseen threats without the luxury of knowledge of the vulnerability.

Identifying Previously Unknown Vulnerabilities

Given that the above techniques rely on prior knowledge of vulnerabilities, they would be substantially more valuable if it was possible to better identify vulnerabilities in software before malware was created to exploit those vulnerabilities. A form of random test case generation known as Fuzzing [5] is among the most common techniques for finding vulnerabilities. More recently, static analysis of the target software itself has been used to intelligently generate test cases more efficiently identifying vulnerabilities likely to exist near corner cases in target software execution [16, 23]. Although these techniques currently require source code, substantial progress has been made in extracting models from executable code for model checking and other static analysis without source code [13, 14]. However, in discussing static analysis of binaries, it is important to note that such tools can be used very effectively by creators of malware just as easily as they can be used by the security community [30].

Identifying Previously Unseen Threats without Prior Knowledge of Vulnerabilities

In this section we describe several emerging techniques that do not require prior knowledge of vulnerabilities for identifying previously unseen threats. These techniques include behavior based techniques, honeypots, anomaly detection, fault analysis, and correlation. Dynamic analysis of program behavior within a host is not new [11]. Behavior analysis was extended with various forms of anomaly detection [25] to improve generalization to previously unseen attacks while reducing false positives. However, some of these techniques are vulnerable to evasion [30]. More recent techniques include:

Model Extraction:
- Machine learning of packet payload statistical profiles to model normality for anomaly correlation
- Machine learning of state models of run-time behavior to detect run-time deviation from model
- Using static analysis to extract models for run-time monitors that detect deviation from model

Automated Signature Inference, extracting signatures:
- From static samples in controlled environments
- From taint analysis of fault inducing inputs in production systems
- From correlation of fault inducing inputs in production systems
- From analysis of fault inducing inputs in honeypots shadowing production systems
- Via correlation for longest common byte sequences in honeypot traffic and other inputs given above
- Via correlation for trees of token subsequences to reduce false positives

Model Extraction

Having a model of how a system should behave can be helpful in detecting new threats that cause misbehavior. Even if there is no prior knowledge of the threat, such models make detection of the misbehavior possible, therein facilitating potential remedies.

One approach for modeling how a system should behave involves learning the statistical composition of traffic coming and going from a system. With such statistical models, anomalies are detectable, and it may even be possible to correlate commonality between anomalies occurring at a distributed set of sites [48].

For stateful systems, including many software applications that query database systems, it is possible to build more precise models of normal behavior by modeling the behavior in terms of state machines. This works best when a full set of normal queries can be learned quickly so that after such a learning period, the system can alert on any anomalies in different fields of queries via statistical approaches without intolerable false positives. Recent progress demonstrated this possible for at least one web based database application [46].

However, not all anomalies are misbehaviors. Since some rare and anomalous behaviors are legitimate behaviors, there are advantages in applying static analysis to the software to build a model of how the software should behave, and detecting deviations from such models [24].

Automated Signature Inference

Once a new, previously unseen threat is detected, extracting a signature of that threat and disseminating that signature to others may help others better protect themselves. Of course, automated signature extraction is not new in controlled environments [27], and there has been tremendous progress recently in automated signature extraction in the "wild" of less controlled environments such as production systems, honeypots, and other threat collection systems.

One technique for automatically extracting signatures from production systems leverages analysis of fault inducing inputs. By using tainting, it is possible to trace backwards from a fault to the fault inducing input [35].

Similarly, without runtime tracing, it is possible to capture the set of inputs preceding a fault or disallowed state, and send those inputs to other parties for correlation with other inputs preceding and not preceding faults [19].

Moreover, a third approach to fault handling leverages parallel execution of inputs on production systems and more controlled systems to provide the ability to not only detect previously unseen threats, but to dynamically generate and dynamically apply curative patches and allow the system to continue operation despite receipt of what would have been fault inducing input [38, 39]. In this model, the more controlled system, is a honeypot shadowing the production system. The honeypot executes the inputs first, and if a fault occurs, an overarching control system attempts to mutate the executable around the region of the fault to produce a variant of the executable that does not fault on the input. Once such a curative patch is generated and applied to the production system, the production system is allowed to process the input which caused the fault in the controlled system but does not cause faults in the dynamically patched system.

Automated signature extraction has also been developed for less controlled honeypot environments to function without requiring either faults as triggers or production systems to shadow. One version of this approach works by using longest common sequences in message exchanges [28].

Such techniques have been improved in systems such as Polygraph by using trees of token sequences to reduce false positives [34]. Moreover, such techniques have been further improved in a similar system, Earlybird, to support processing traffic at speeds up to 200 Mbps [40]. More recently, a similar system, "DACODA" demonstrated detection of more than a dozen worms, with no prior knowledge of the worms and no false positives over a six month period [20]. Maintaining negligible false positives is critical since preventing threats so rapidly propagating as Warhol Worms [42] requires both rapid signature inference and rapid blocking, and system owners and operators have little tolerance for blockage of legitimate traffic. Regrettably though, DACODA does not have the line speed scalability of Earlybird.

1.3.2 Countermeasures for Rootkit Detection

As described in the "Evolution of Threats," above, malware authors and distributors currently have many vectors for establishing access to a system, and direct financial motives for establishing and maintaining undetected persistent presence on compromised systems, effectively hiding themselves indefinitely. Recently, some techniques have begun to emerge for detecting the stealth threats by searching for side effects of the stealthing mechanism (e.g. changes made to various operating system structures, checking for unusual hooks in the operating system kernel, etc.). One technique uses static analysis of the operating system to identify critical regions of memory and valid values for those regions, and provides those results to a run time kernel integrity monitor [22, 36]. Another technique uses static analysis to construct a model of a module's programmed behavior to determine at load time whether or not the module will behave like a rootkit at runtime [29]. Though not mentioned by the authors, similar techniques may also have utility in detection and classification of spyware.

1.3.3 Countermeasures for Spyware

However, spyware also requires technologies orthogonal to load time analysis, categorization, and run time rootkit detection. Perhaps most importantly, the rate of spyware evolution, the rate of spyware distribution, and the means of spyware distribution broadcast from thousands to millions of websites to countless unsuspecting users, practically all require the security industry to more actively seek out these threats on the internet. Such techniques have been proposed and implemented by Microsoft [49], WebRoot [3], and others. Moreover, spyware defenses are now in or entering the market as either standalone offerings, or as offerings integrated with anti-virus and other product offerings.

1.4 Summary

The speed, stealth, and purpose of malware are evolving rapidly. Over recent years, substantial technology has emerged to help mitigate risks of fast spreading threats, and a variety of technologies have emerged to begin to help mitigate risks from previously unseen threats. However, malware is becoming both increasingly stealthy, and increasingly malicious in the sense of collection of private and directly valuable personal information. Gone are the relatively innocent glory days where fame and infamy were primary motivators behind construction of most malware seen. We've now entered the era where malicious collection of private and directly valuable personal information from unsuspecting users is a billion dollar [4] illicit industry.

References

1. http://en.wikipedia.org/wiki/Malware
2. http://en.wikipedia.org/wiki/Malware#Spyware
3. http://www.webroot.com/resources/phileas/
4. http://www.gartner.com/DisplayDocument?doc_cd=120804
5. ftp://ftp.cs.wisc.edu/paradyn/technical_papers/fuzz.pdf
6. http://en.wikipedia.org/wiki/Morris_worm
7. http://securityresponse.symantec.com/avcenter/expanded_threats/spyware/index.html
8. http://en.wikipedia.org/wiki/Spyware
9. http://en.wikipedia.org/wiki/Rootkit
10. http://cme.mitre.org/data/list.html#589
11. http://en.wikipedia.org/wiki/Host-based_intrusion_detection_system
12. AOL/NCSA Online Safety Study, Conducted by America Online and the National Cyber Security Alliance, October 2004, http://www.staysafeonline.info/pdf/safety_study_v04.pdf
13. G. Balakrishnan, et. al, "Model checking x86 executables with Code-Surfer/x86 and WPDS++," (tool-demonstration paper). In Proc. Computer-Aided Verification, 2005. http://www.cs.wisc.edu/wpis/papers/CAV05-tool-demo.pdf
14. G. Balakrishnan, et. al, "WYSINWYX: What You See Is Not What You eXecute." To appear in Proc. IFIP Working Conference on Verified Software: Theories, Tools, Experiments, Zurich, Switzerland, Oct. 10-13, 2005. http://www.cs.wisc.edu/wpis/papers/wysinwyx05.pdf

15. D. Bank, "Computer Worm Is Turning Faster," The Wall Street Journal, May 27, 2004.
16. C. Cadar and D. Engler, "Execution Generated Test Cases: How to Make Systems Code Crash Itself," CSTR-2005-04, http://www.stanford.edu/~engler/cstr-3.25.5.pdf
17. CAN-2003-0533
18. CERT® Advisory CA-2003-04 MS-SQL Server Worm; http://www.cert.org/advisories/CA-2003-04.html
19. M. Costa, et. al, "Vigilante: End-to-End Containment of Internet Worms," ACM SIGOPS Operating Systems Review, Volume 39, Issue 5 (December 2005), http://research.microsoft.com/~manuelc/MS/VigilanteSOSP.pdf
20. J. Crandall, et. al, "On Deriving Unknown Vulnerabilities from Zero-Day Polymorphic and Metamorphic Worm Exploits," 12th ACM Conference on Computer and Communications Security (CCS). Alexandria, Virginia. November 2005, http://wwwcsif.cs.ucdavis.edu/~crandall/ccsdacoda.pdf
21. J. Evers, "Dutch police nab suspected 'bot herders," CNET, October 7, 2005, 3:41 PM PDT
22. T. Fraser, "Automatic Discovery of Integrity Constraints in Binary Kernel Modules," UMIACS TR-2005-02, December 2004, http://www.missl.cs.umd.edu/~tfraser/TRs/fraser-copilot-config.pdf
23. P. Godefroid, et. al, "DART: Directed Automated Random Testing," to appear in PLDI05, http://cm.bell-labs.com/who/god/public_psfiles/pldi2005.pdf
24. W. Halfond and A. Orso, "AMNESIA: Analysis and Monitoring for NEutralizing SQLInjection Attacks," http://www.cc.gatech.edu/grads/w/whalfond/papers/halfond.orso.ASE05.pdf
25. S. A. Hofmeyr, et. al, "Intrusion Detection using Sequences of System Calls," Journal of Computer Security Vol. 6, pp. 151-180 (1998). http://cs.unm.edu/~forrest/publications/int_decssc.pdf
26. M. W. Jon and J. A. Rochlis, "With Microscope and Tweezers: An Analysis of the Internet Virus of November 1988," http://web.mit.edu/eichin/www/virus/main.html
27. J. O. Kephart and W. C. Arnold, "Automatic Extraction of Computer Virus Signatures,"In Proceedings of teh 4th Virus Bulletin International Conference, R. Ford, ed., Virus Bulletin Ltd., Abingdon, England, 1994, pp. 178-184, http://www.research.ibm.com/antivirus/SciPapers/Kephart/VB94/vb94.html

28. C. Kreibich and J. Crowcroft, "Honeycomb: Creating Intrusion Detection Signatures Using Honeypots," In Proceedings of the USENIX/ACM Workshop on Hot Topics in Networking, Nov. 2003. http://citeseer.ist.psu.edu/cache/papers/cs/30348/http:zSzzSznms.lcs.m it.eduzSzHotNets-IIzSzpaperszSzhoneycomb.pdf/kreibich03honeycom b.pdf

29. C. Kruegel, et. al, "Detecting Kernel-Level Rootkits Through Binary Analysis," Proceedings of the Annual Computer Security Applications Conference (ACSAC) 91-100 Tucson, AZ December 2004, http://www.cs.ucsb.edu/~vigna/publications.html

30. C. Kruegel, et. al, "Automating Mimicry Attacks Using Static Binary Analysis," Proceedings of the USENIX Security Symposium Baltimore,   MD   August   2005, http://www.cs.ucsb.edu/~vigna/pub/2005_kruegel_kirda_robertson_m utz_vigna_USENIX05.pdf

31. L. Mearian, "System break-in nets hackers 8 million credit card numbers,"   COMPUTERWORLD,   February   24,   2003, http://www.computerworld.com/securitytopics/security/story/0,10801, 78747,00.html

32. D. Moore and C. Shannon, "The Spread of the Code-Red Worm (CRv2)," http://www.caida.org/analysis/security/code-red/coderedv2_analysis.x ml

33. C. Nachenberg, "Generic Exploit Blocking," Virus Bulletin, February, 2005

34. J. Newsome, et. al, "Automatically Generating Signatures for Polymorphic Worms," in the Proceedings of the IEEE Symposium on Security and Privacy (Oakland 2005), Oakland, CA, May, 2005. http://www.cs.ucl.ac.uk/staff/B.Karp/polygraph-oakland2005.pdf

35. J. Newsome and D. Song, "Dynamic Taint Analysis for Automatic Detection, Analysis, and Signature Generation of Exploits on Commodity Software," In Proceedings of the 12th Annual Network and Distributed System Security Symposium (NDSS '05), February 2005. http://www.ece.cmu.edu/~jnewsome/docs/taintcheck.pdf

36. N. L. Petroni, Jr., et. al, "Copilot - a Coprocessor-based Kernel Runtime Integrity Monitor," 13th Usenix Security Symposium 2004, http://www.jesusmolina.com/docs/copilot.pdf

37. J. Roculan, et. al, "DeepSight™ Threat Management System Threat Analysis: SQLExp   SQL   Server   Worm," http://securityresponse.symantec.com/avcenter/Analysis-SQLExp.pdf, January 25, 2003

38. S. Sidiroglou, et. al, "An EmailWorm Vaccine Architecture," In Proceedings of the 1st Information Security Practice and Experience Conference (ISPEC), pp. 97 - 108. April 2005, Singapore. http://www1.cs.columbia.edu/~angelos/Papers/2005/email-worm.pdf

39. S. Sidiroglou and A. Keromytis, "Countering Network Worms Through Automatic Patch Generation," In IEEE Security & Privacy, vol. 3, no. 6, pp. 52 - 60, November/December 2005, http://www1.cs.columbia.edu/~angelos/Papers/2005/j6ker3.pdf

40. S. Singh, "Automated Worm Fingerprinting," Proceedings of the ACM/USENIX Symposium on Operating System Design and Implementation, San Francisco, CA, December 2004. http://www.cs.ucsd.edu/~savage/papers/OSDI04.pdf

41. S. Sparks and J. Butler, "Shadow Walker - Raising The Bar For Rootkit Detection," DefCon 13, July 29-31, 2005, http://www.blackhat.com/presentations/bh-jp-05/bh-jp-05-sparks-butler.pdf

42. S. Staniford, et. al, "How to 0wn the Internet in Your Spare Time," Proceedings of the 11th USENIX Security Symposium (Security '02) http://www.cs.berkeley.edu/~nweaver/cdc.web/cdc.web.pdf

43. Symantec Internet Security Threat Report, Volume VII, Published March 2005

44. Symantec Internet Security Threat Report, Volume VIII, Published September 2005

45. J. Swartz, "40 million credit card holders may be at risk," USA TODAY, June 19, 2005, http://www.usatoday.com/money/perfi/general/2005-06-19-breach-usat_x.htm

46. F. Valeur, et. al, "A Learning-Based Approach to the Detection of SQL Attacks,"Proceedings of the Conference on Detection of Intrusions and Malware & Vulnerability Assessment (DIMVA) Vienna, Austria July 2005, http://www.cs.ucsb.edu/~vigna/publications.html

47. H. J. Wang, C. Guo, D. R. Simon, and A. Zugenmaier. Shield: Vulnerability-Driven Network Filters for Preventing Known Vulnerability Exploits. Proceedings of the ACM SIGCOMM Conference, Aug. 2004. http://citeseer.ist.psu.edu/cache/papers/cs2/162/http:zSzzSzresearch.micro-soft.comzSzresearchzSzshieldzSzpaperszSzshieldSigcomm04.pdf/wang04shield.pdf

48. K. Wang, et. al, "Anomalous Payload-based Worm Detection and Signature Generation," In Proceedings of the Eighth International Symposium on Recent Advances in Intrusion Detection, September 2005, http://worminator.cs.columbia.edu/papers/2005/raid-cut4.pdf

49. Y.-M. Wang, et. al, "Automated Web Patrol with Strider HoneyMonkeys: Finding Web Sites That Exploit Browser Vulnerabilities" MSR-TR-2005-72,   August   2005 ftp://ftp.research.microsoft.com/pub/tr/TR-2005-72.pdf
50. M. Williamson, et. al, "Virus Throttling," HPL-2003-69 20030430, Virus   Bulletin,   March   2003, http://www.hpl.hp.com/techreports/2003/HPL-2003-69.html

Software Analysis and Assurance

2

Static Disassembly and Code Analysis

Giovanni Vigna

Reliable Software Group, University of California, Santa Barbara
vigna@cs.ucsb.edu

Summary. The classification of an unknown binary program as malicious or benign requires two steps. In the first step, the stream of bytes that constitutes the program has to be transformed (or disassembled) into the corresponding sequence of machine instructions. In the second step, based on this machine code representation, static or dynamic code analysis techniques can be applied to determine the properties and function of the program.

Both the disassembly and code analysis steps can be foiled by techniques that obfuscate the binary representation of a program. Thus, robust techniques are required that deliver reliable results under such adverse circumstances. In this chapter, we introduce a disassemble technique that can deal with obfuscated binaries. Also, we introduce a static code analysis approach that can identify high-level semantic properties of code that are difficult to conceal.

2.1 Introduction

Code analysis takes as input a program and attempts to determine certain characteristics of this program. In particular, the goal of security analysis is to identify either malicious behavior or the presence of security flaws, which might be exploited to compromise the security of a system. In this chapter, we focus particularly on the security analysis of binary programs that use the Intel x86 instruction set. However, many of the concepts can also be applied to analyze code that exists in a different representation.

In the first step of the analysis, the code has to be disassembled. That is, we want to recover a symbolic representation of a program's machine code instructions from its binary representation. While disassembly is straightforward for regular binaries, the situation is different for malicious code. In particular, a number of techniques have been proposed that are effective in preventing a substantial fraction of a binary program from being disassembled correctly. This could allow an attacker to hide malicious code from the subsequent static program analysis. In Section 2.2, we present binary analysis techniques that substantially improve the success of the disassembly process when confronted with obfuscated binaries. Using control flow graph information and statistical methods, a large fraction of the program's instructions can be correctly identified.

Based on the program's machine code, the next step is to identify code sequences that are known to be malicious (or code sequences that violate a given specification of permitted behavior). Often, malicious code is defined at a very low level of abstraction. That is, a specification, or signature, of malicious code is expressed in terms of byte sequences or instruction sequences. While it is efficient and easy to search a program for the occurrence of specific byte strings, such *syntax-based* signatures can be trivially evaded. Therefore, specifications at a higher level are needed that can characterize the intrinsic properties of a program that are more difficult to disguise. Of course, suitable analysis techniques are required that can identify such higher-level properties. Moreover, these techniques have to be robust against deliberate efforts of an attacker to thwart analysis.

Code analysis techniques can be categorized into two main classes: dynamic techniques and static techniques. Approaches that belong to the first category rely on monitoring execution traces of an application to identify the executed instructions and their actions, or behavior. Approaches that belong to the second category analyze the binary structure statically, parsing the instructions as they are found in the binary image and attempting to determine a (possibly over-approximated) set of all possible behaviors.

Both static and dynamic approaches have advantages and disadvantages. Static analysis takes into account the complete program, while dynamic analysis can only operate on the instructions that were executed in a particular set of runs. Therefore, it is impossible to guarantee that the whole executable with all possible actions was covered when using dynamic analysis. On the other hand, dynamic analysis assures that only actual program behavior is considered. This eliminates possible incorrect results due to overly conservative approximations that are often necessary when performing static analysis.

In Section 2.3, we introduce our static analysis approach to find pieces of code that perform actions (i.e., behave) in a way that we have specified as malicious. More precisely, we describe our application of symbolic execution to the static analysis of binaries.

2.2 Robust Disassembly of Obfuscated Binaries

In this section, we introduce our approach to robust disassembly when facing obfuscated, malicious binaries. The term *obfuscation* refers to techniques that preserve the program's semantics and functionality while, at the same time, making it more difficult for the analyst to extract and comprehend the program's structures. In the context of disassembly, obfuscation refers to transformations of the binary such that the parsing of instructions becomes difficult.

In [13], Linn and Debray introduced novel obfuscation techniques that exploit the fact that the Intel x86 instruction set architecture contains variable length instructions that can start at arbitrary memory address. By inserting padding bytes at locations that cannot be reached during run-time, disassemblers can be confused to misinterpret large parts of the binary. Although their approach is limited to Intel x86 binaries, the obfuscation results against current state-of-the-art disassemblers are remarkable.

In general, disassemblers follow one of two approaches. The first approach, called linear sweep, starts at the first byte of the binary's text segment and proceeds from there, decoding one instruction after another. It is used, for example, by GNU's objdump [8]. The drawback of linear sweep disassemblers is that they are prone to errors that result from data embedded in the instruction stream. The second approach, called recursive traversal, fixes this problem by following the control flow of the program [4, 15]. This allows recursive disassemblers such as IDA Pro [7] to circumvent data that is interleaved with the program instructions. The problem with the second approach is that the control flow cannot always be reconstructed precisely. When the target of a control transfer instruction such as a jump or a call cannot be determined statically (e.g., in case of an indirect jump), the recursive disassembler fails to analyze parts of the program's code. This problem is usually solved with a technique called speculative disassembly [3], which uses a linear sweep algorithm to analyze unreachable code regions.

Linn and Debray's approach [13] to confuse disassemblers are based on two main techniques. First, junk bytes are inserted at locations that are not reachable at runtime. These locations can be found after control transfer instructions such as jumps where control flow does not continue. Inserting junk bytes at unreachable locations should not affect recursive disassemblers, but has a profound impact on linear sweep implementations.

The second technique relies on a branch function to change the way regular procedure calls work. This creates more opportunities to insert junk bytes and misleads both types of disassemblers. A normal call to a subroutine is replaced with a call to the branch function. This branch function uses an indirect jump to transfer control to the original subroutine. In addition, an offset value is added to the return address of the subroutine, which has been saved on the stack as part of the subroutine invocation. Therefore, when the subroutine is done, control is not transferred to the address directly after the call instruction. Instead, an instruction that is a certain number of bytes after the call instruction is executed. Because calls are redirected to the branch function, large parts of the binary become unreachable for the recursive traversal algorithm. As a result, recursive traversal disassemblers perform even worse on obfuscated binaries than linear sweep disassemblers.

When analyzing an obfuscated binary, one cannot assume that the code be generated by a well-behaved compiler. In fact, the obfuscation techniques introduced by Linn and Debray [13] precisely exploit the fact that standard disassemblers assume certain properties of compiler-generated code that can be violated without changing the program's functionality. However, in general, certain properties are easier to change than others and it is not straightforward to transform a binary into a functionally equivalent representation in which all the compiler-related properties of the original code are lost. When disassembling obfuscated binaries, we require that certain assumptions are valid.

First of all, we assume that valid instructions must not overlap. An instruction is denoted as *valid* if it belongs to the program, that is, it is reached (and executed) at run-time as part of some legal program execution trace. Two instructions *overlap* if one or more bytes in the executable are shared by both instructions. In other words, the start of one instruction is located at an address that is already used by another instruction. Overlapping instructions have been suggested to complicate disassembly in [5]. However, suitable candidate instructions for this type of transformation are difficult to find in real executables and the reported obfuscation effects were minimal [13].

The second assumption is that conditional jumps can be either taken or not taken. This means that control flow can continue at the branch target or at the instruction after the conditional branch. In particular, it is not possible to insert junk bytes at the branch target or at the address following the branch instruction. Linn and Debray [13] discuss the possibility to transform unconditional jumps into conditional branches using opaque predicates. Opaque predicates are predicates that always evaluate to either true or false, independent of the input. This would allow the obfuscator to insert junk bytes either at the jump target or in place of the fall-through instruction. However, it is not obvious how to generate opaque predicates that are not easily recognizable for the disassembler. Also, the obfuscator presented in [13] does not implement this transformation.

In addition to the assumptions above, we also assume that the code is not necessarily the output of a well-behaved compiler. That is, we assume that an arbitrary amount of junk bytes can be inserted at unreachable locations. Unreachable locations denote locations that are not reachable at run-time. These locations can be found after instructions that change the normal control flow. For example, most compilers arrange code such that the address following an unconditional jump contains a valid instruction. However, we assume that an arbitrary number of junk bytes can be inserted there. Also, the control flow does not have to continue immediately after a call instruction. Thus, an arbitrary number of padding bytes can be added after each call. This is different from the standard behavior where it is expected that the callee returns to the instruction following a call using the corresponding return instruction. More specifically, in the x86 instruction set, the `call` operation performs a jump to the call target and, in addition, pushes the address following the call instruction on the stack. This address is then used by the corresponding `ret` instruction, which performs a jump to the address currently on top of the stack. However, by redirecting calls to a branch function, it is trivial to change the return address.

Given the assumptions above, we have developed two classes of techniques: general techniques and tool-specific techniques. General techniques are techniques that do not rely upon any knowledge on *how* a particular obfuscator transforms the binary. It is only required that the transformations respect our assumptions. Our general techniques are based on the program's control flow, similar to a recursive traversal disassembler. However, we use a different approach to construct the control flow graph, which is more resilient to obfuscation attempts. Program regions that are not covered by the control flow graph are analyzed using statistical techniques.

An instance of an obfuscator that respects our assumptions is presented by Linn and Debray in [13]. By tailoring the static analysis process against a particular tool, it is often possible to reverse some of the performed transformations and improve the analysis results. For more information on how we can take advantage of tool-specific knowledge when disassembling binaries transformed with Linn and Debray's obfuscator, please refer to [11]. In the following, we only concentrate on the general disassembly techniques.

2.2.1 Function Identification

The first step when disassembling obfuscated programs is to divide the binary into functions that can then be analyzed independently. The main reason for doing so is run-time performance; it is necessary that the disassembler scale well enough such that the analysis of large real-world binaries is possible.

An important part of our analysis is the reconstruction of the program's control flow. When operating on the complete binary, the analysis does not scale well for large programs. Therefore, the binary is broken into smaller regions (i.e., functions) that can be analyzed consecutively. This results in a run-time overhead of the disassembly process that is linear in the number of instructions (roughly, the size of the code segment).

A straightforward approach to obtain a function's start addresses is to extract the targets of call instructions. When a linker generates an ordinary executable, the targets of calls to functions located in the binary's text segment are bound to the actual addresses of these functions. Given the call targets and assuming that most functions are actually referenced from others within the binary, one can obtain a fairly complete set of function start addresses. Unfortunately, this approach has two drawbacks. One problem is that this method requires that the call instructions are already identified. As the objective of our disassembler is precisely to provide that kind of information, the call instructions are not available at this point. Another problem is that an obfuscator can redirect all calls to a single branching function that transfers control to the appropriate targets. This technique changes all call targets to a single address, thus removing information necessary to identify functions.

We use a heuristic to locate function start addresses. More precisely, function start addresses are located by identifying byte sequences that implement typical function prologs. When a function is called, the first few instructions usually set up a new stack frame. This frame is required to make room for local variables and to be able restore the stack to its initial state when the function returns. In the current implementation, we scan the binary for byte sequences that represent instructions that push the frame pointer onto the stack and instructions that increase the size of the stack by decreasing the value of the stack pointer. The technique works very well for regular binaries and also for the obfuscated binaries used in our experiments. The reason is that the used obfuscation tool [13] does not attempt to hide function prologs. It is certainly possible to extend the obfuscator to conceal the function prolog. In this case, our function identification technique might require changes, possibly using tool-specific knowledge.

Note that the partitioning of the binary into functions is mainly done for performance reasons, and it is not crucial for the quality of the results that all functions are correctly identified. When the start point of a function is missed, later analysis simply has to deal with one larger region of code instead of two separate smaller parts. When a sequence of instructions within a function is misinterpreted as a function prolog, two parts of a single function are analyzed individually. This could lead to less accurate results when some intra-procedural jumps are interpreted as inter-procedural, making it harder to reconstruct the intra-procedural control flow graph as discussed in the following section.

2.2.2 Intra-Procedural Control Flow Graph

To find the valid instructions of a function (i.e., the instructions that belong to the program), we attempt to reconstruct the function's intra-procedural control flow graph. A control flow graph (CFG) is defined as a directed graph $G = (V, E)$ in which vertices $u, v \in V$ represent basic blocks and an edge $e \in E : u \rightarrow v$ represents a possible flow of control from u to v. A basic block describes a sequence of instructions without any jumps or jump targets in the middle. More formally, a basic block is defined as a sequence of instructions where the instruction in each position dominates, or always executes before, all those in later positions, and no other instruction executes between two instructions in the sequence. Directed edges between blocks represent jumps in the control flow, which are caused by control transfer instructions (CTIs) such as calls, conditional and unconditional jumps, or return instructions.

The traditional approach to reconstructing the control flow graph of a function works similar to a recursive disassembler. The analysis commences at the function's start address and instructions are disassembled until a control transfer instruction is encountered. The process is then continued, recursively, at all jump targets that are local to the procedure and, in case of a call instruction or a conditional jump, at the address following the instruction. In case of an obfuscated binary, however, the disassembler cannot continue directly after a call instruction. In addition, many local jumps are converted into non-local jumps to addresses outside the function to blur local control flow. In most cases, the traditional approach leads to a control flow graph that covers only a small fraction of the valid instructions of the function under analysis.

We developed an alternative technique to extract a more complete control flow graph. The technique is composed of two phases: in the first phase, an initial control flow graph is determined. In the following phase, conflicts and ambiguities in the initial CFG are resolved. The two phases are presented in detail in the following two sections.

2.2.3 Initial Control Flow Graph

To determine the initial control flow graph for a function, we first decode all possible instructions between the function's start and end addresses. This is done by treating each address in this address range as the beginning of a new instruction. Thus, one potential instruction is decoded and assigned to each address of the function. The reason for considering every address as a possible instruction start stems from the fact that x86 instructions have a variable length from one to fifteen bytes and do not have

```
          8048000 | 55             push   %ebp              : function func(int arg) {
          8048001 | 89 e5          mov    %esp, %ebp        :     int local_var, ret_val;
                  |                                         :
          8048003 | e8 00 00 74 11 call   19788008 <branch fnct>  :  local = other_func(arg);
          8048008 | 0a 05          (junk)                   :
                  |                                         :
          804800a | 3c 00          cmp    0, %eax           :     if (local_var == 0)
          804800c | 75 06          jne    8048014 <L1>      :
          804800e | b0 00          mov    0, %eax           :         ret_val = 0;
          8048010 | eb 07          jmp    8048019 <L2>      :     else
          8048012 | 0a 05          (junk)                   :
      L1: 8048014 | a1 00 00 74 01 mov    (1740000), %eax   :         ret_val = global_var;
                  |                                         :
      L2: 8048019 | 89 ec          mov    %ebp, %esp        :     return ret_val;
          804801b | 5d             pop    %ebp              :
          804801c | c3             ret                      :
          804801d | 90             nop                      : }
```

Disassembly of Obfuscated Function   C Function

Fig. 2.1. Example function.

to be aligned in memory (i.e., an instruction can start at an arbitrary address). Note that most instructions take up multiple bytes and such instructions overlap with other instructions that start at subsequent bytes. Therefore, only a subset of the instructions decoded in this first step can be valid. Figure 2.2 provides a partial listing of all instructions in the address range of the sample function (both in source and assembler format) that is shown in Figure 2.1. For the reader's reference, valid instructions are marked by an x in the "*Valid*" column. Of course, this information is not available to our disassembler. An example for the overlap between valid and invalid instructions can be seen between the second and the third instruction. The valid instruction at address 0×8048001 requires two bytes and thus interferes with the next (invalid) instruction at 0×8048002.

				Valid	Candidate
8048000	55	push	%ebp	x	
8048001	89 e5	mov	%esp, %ebp	x	
8048002	e5 e8	in	e8,%eax		
8048003	e8 00 00 74 11	call	19788008 <obfuscator>	x	
8048004	00 00	add	%al, %eax		
8048005	00 74	add			
8048006	74 11	je	8048019		x
...					
804800c	75 06	jne	8048014	x	x
...					
8048010	eb 07	jmp	8048019	x	x
...					
8048017	74 01	je	804801a		x
8048018	01 89 ec 5d c3 90	add	%dh,ffffff89(%ecx,%eax,1)		
8048019	89 ec	mov	%ebp, %esp	x	
804801a	ec	in	(%dx), %al		
804801b	5d	pop	%ebp		
...					

Fig. 2.2. Partial instruction listing.

The next step is to identify all intra-procedural control transfer instructions. For our purposes, an intra-procedural control transfer instruction is defined as a CTI with at least one known successor basic block in the same function. Remember that we assume that control flow only continues after conditional branches but not necessarily after call or unconditional branch instructions. Therefore, an instruction is an intra-procedural control transfer instruction if either (i) its target address can be determined and this address is in the range between the function's start and end addresses or (ii) it is a conditional jump. In the latter case, the address that immediately follows the conditional jump instruction is the start of a successor block.

Note that we assume that a function is represented by a contiguous sequence of instructions, with possible junk instructions added in between. This means that, it is not possible that the basic blocks of two different functions are intertwined. Therefore, each function has one start address and one end address (i.e., the last instruction of the last basic block that belongs to this function). However, it is possible that a function has multiple exit points.

To find all intra-procedural CTIs, the instructions decoded in the previous step are scanned for any control transfer instructions. For each CTI found in this way, we attempt to extract its target address. In the current implementation, only direct address modes are supported and no data flow analysis is performed to compute address values used by indirect jumps. However, such analysis could be later added to further improve the performance of our static analyzer. When the instruction is determined to be an intra-procedural control transfer operation, it is included in the set of *jump candidates*. The jump candidates of the sample function are marked in Figure 2.2 by an x in the "*Candidate*" column. In this example, the call at address 0x8048003 is not included into the set of jump candidates because the target address is located outside the function.

Given the set of jump candidates, an initial control flow graph is constructed. This is done with the help of a recursive disassembler. Starting with an initial empty CFG, the disassembler is successively invoked for all the elements in the set of jump candidates. In addition, it is also invoked for the instruction at the start address of the function.

The key idea for taking into account all possible control transfer instructions is the fact that the valid CTIs determine the skeleton of the analyzed function. By using *all* control flow instructions to create the initial CFG, we make sure that the real CFG is a subgraph of this initial graph. Because the set of jump candidates can contain both valid and invalid instructions, it is possible (and also frequent) that the initial CFG contains a superset of the nodes of the real CFG. These nodes are introduced as a result of argument bytes of valid instructions being misinterpreted as control transfer instructions. The Intel x86 instruction set contains 26 single-byte opcodes that map to control transfer instructions (out of 219 single-byte instruction opcodes). Therefore, the probability that a random argument byte is decoded as CTI is not negligible. In our experiments [11], we found that about one tenth of all decoded instructions are CTIs. Of those instructions, only two thirds were part of the real control flow graph. As a result, the initial CFG contains nodes and edges that represent invalid instructions. Most of the time, these nodes contain instructions that overlap with valid instructions of nodes that belong to the real CFG. The following section discusses mechanisms to remove these spurious nodes from the initial control flow graph. It is possible to distinguish spurious from valid nodes because invalid CTIs represent random jumps within the function while valid CTIs constitute a well-structured CFG with nodes that have no overlapping instructions.

Creating an initial CFG that includes nodes that are not part of the real control flow graph can been seen as the opposite to the operation of a recursive disassembler. A standard recursive disassembler starts from a known valid block and builds up the CFG by adding nodes as it follows the targets of control transfer instructions that are encountered. This technique seems favorable at a first glance, because it makes sure that no invalid instructions are incorporated into the CFG. However, most control flow graphs are partitioned into several unconnected subgraphs. This happens because there are control flow instructions such as indirect branches whose targets often cannot be determined statically. This leads to missing edges in the CFG and to the problem that only a fraction of the real control flow graph is reachable from a certain node. The situation is exacerbated when dealing with obfuscated binaries, as inter-procedural calls and jumps are redirected to a branching function that uses indirect jumps. This significantly reduces the parts of the control flow graph that are directly accessible to a recursive disassembler, leading to unsatisfactory results.

Although the standard recursive disassembler produces suboptimal results, we use a similar algorithm to extract the basic blocks to create the initial CFG. As mentioned before, however, the recursive disassembler is not only invoked for the start address of the function alone, but also for all jump candidates that have been identified. An initial control flow graph is then constructed.

There are two differences between a standard recursive disassembler and our prototype tool. First, we assume that the address after a call or an unconditional jump instruction does not have to contain a valid instruction. Therefore, our recursive disassembler cannot continue at the address following a call or an unconditional jump. Note, however, that we do continue to disassemble after a conditional jump (i.e., branch).

The second difference is due to the fact that it is possible to have instructions in the initial call graph that overlap. In this case, two different basic blocks in the call graph can contain overlapping instructions starting at slightly different addresses. When following a sequence of instructions, the disassembler can arrive at an instruction that is already part of a previously found basic block. Normally, this instruction is the first instruction of the existing block. The disassembler can then "close" the instruction sequence of the current block and create a link to the existing basic block in the control flow graph.

When instructions can overlap, it is possible that the current instruction sequence overlaps with another sequence in an existing basic block for some instructions before the two sequences eventually become identical. In this case, the existing basic block is split into two new blocks. One block refers to the overlapping sequence up to the instruction where the two sequences merge, the other refers to the instruction sequence that both have in common. All edges in the control flow graph that point to the original basic block are changed to point to the first block, while all outgoing edges of the original block are assigned to the second. In addition, the first block is connected to the second one.

The reason for splitting the existing block is the fact that a basic block is defined as a continuous sequence of instructions without a jump or jump target in the middle. When two different overlapping sequences merge at a certain instruction, this instruction has two predecessor instructions (one in each of the two overlapping sequences). Therefore, it becomes the first instruction of a new basic block. As an additional desirable side effect, each instruction appears at most once in a basic block of the call graph.

The fact that instruction sequences eventually "merge" is a common phenomenon when disassembling x86 binaries. The reason is called *self-repairing disassembly* and relates to the fact that two instruction sequences that start at slightly different addresses (that is, shifted by a few bytes) synchronize quickly, often after a few instructions. Therefore, when the disassembler starts at an address that does not correspond to a valid instruction, it can be expected to re-synchronize with the sequence of valid instructions after a few steps [13].

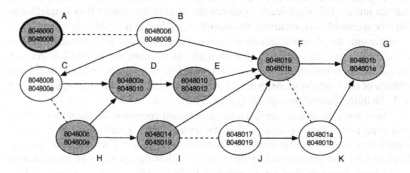

Fig. 2.3. Initial control flow graph.

The initial control flow graph generated for for our example function is shown in Figure 2.3. In this example, the algorithm is invoked for the function start at address 0x8048000 and the four jump candidates (0x8048006, 0x804800c, 0x8048010, and 0x8048017). The nodes in this figure represent basic blocks and are labeled with the start address of the first instruction and the end address of the last instruction in the corresponding instruction sequence. Note that the end address denotes the first byte *after* the last instruction and is not part of the basic block itself. Solid, directed edges between nodes represent the targets of control transfer instructions. A dashed line between two nodes signifies a *conflict* between the two corresponding blocks.

Two basic blocks are in conflict when they contain at least one pair of instructions that overlap. As discussed previously, our algorithm guarantees that a certain instruction is assigned to at most one basic block (otherwise, blocks are split appropriately). Therefore, whenever the address ranges of two blocks overlap, they must also contain different, overlapping instructions. Otherwise, both blocks would contain the same instruction, which is not possible. This is apparent in Figure 2.3, where the address ranges of all pairs of conflicting basic blocks overlap. To simplify the following discussion of the techniques used to resolve conflicts, nodes that belong to the real control flow graph are shaded. In addition, each node is denoted with an uppercase letter.

2.2.4 Block Conflict Resolution

The task of the block conflict resolution phase is to remove basic blocks from the initial CFG until no conflicts are present anymore. Conflict resolution proceeds in five steps. The first two steps remove blocks that are *definitely* invalid, given our assumptions. The last three steps are heuristics that choose *likely* invalid blocks. The conflict resolution phase terminates immediately after the last conflicting block is removed; it is not necessary to carry out all steps. The final step brings about a decision for any basic block conflict and the control flow graph is guaranteed to be free of any conflicts when the conflict resolution phase completes.

The five steps are detailed in the following paragraphs.

Step 1: We assume that the start address of the analyzed function contains a valid instruction. Therefore, the basic block that contains this instruction is valid. In addition, whenever a basic block is known to be valid, all blocks that are reachable from this block are also valid.

A basic block v is *reachable* from basic block u if there exists a path p from u to v. A path p from u to v is defined as a sequence of edges that begins at u and terminates at v. An edge is inserted into the control flow graph only when its target can be statically determined and a possible program execution trace exists that transfers control over this edge. Therefore, whenever a control transfer instruction is valid, its targets have to be valid as well.

We tag the node that contains the instruction at the function's start address and all nodes that are reachable from this node as valid. Note that this set of valid nodes contains exactly the nodes that a traditional recursive disassembler would identify when invoked with the function's start address. When the valid nodes are identified, any node that is in conflict with at least one of the valid nodes can be removed.

In the initial control flow graph for the example function in Figure 2.3, only node A (0x8048000) is marked as valid. That node is drawn with a stronger border in Figure 2.3. The reason is that the corresponding basic block ends with a call instruction at 0x8048003 whose target is not local. In addition, we do not assume that control flow resumes at the address after a call and thus the analysis cannot directly continue after the call instruction. In Figure 2.3, node B (the basic block at 0x8048006) is in conflict with the valid node and can be removed.

Step 2: Because of the assumption that valid instructions do not overlap, it is not possible to start from a valid block and reach two different nodes in the control flow graph that are in conflict. That is, whenever two conflicting nodes are both reachable from a third node, this third node cannot be valid and is removed from the CFG. The situation can be restated using the notion of a common ancestor node. A common ancestor node of two nodes u and v is defined as a node n such that both u and v are reachable from n.

In Step 2, all common ancestor nodes of conflicting nodes are removed from the control flow graph. In our example in Figure 2.3, it can be seen that the conflicting node F and node K share a common ancestor, namely node J. This node is removed from the CFG, resolving a conflict with node I. The resulting control flow graph after the first two steps is shown in Figure 2.4.

The situation of having a common ancestor node of two conflicting blocks is frequent when dealing with invalid conditional branches. In such cases, the branch target and the continuation after the branch instruction are often directly in conflict, allowing one to remove the invalid basic block from the control flow graph.

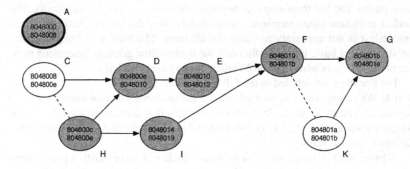

Fig. 2.4. CFG after two steps of conflict resolution.

Step 3: When two basic blocks are in conflict, it is reasonable to expect that a valid block is more tightly integrated into the control flow graph than a block that was created because of a misinterpreted argument value of a program instruction. That means that a valid block is often reachable from a substantial number of other blocks throughout the function, while an invalid block usually has only a few ancestors.

The degree of integration of a certain basic block into the control flow graph is approximated by the number of its predecessor nodes. A node u is defined as a *predecessor node* of v when v is reachable from u. In Step 3, the predecessor nodes for pairs of conflicting nodes are determined and the node with the smaller number is removed from the CFG.

In Figure 2.4, node K has no predecessor nodes while node F has five. Note that the algorithm cannot distinguish between real and spurious nodes and, thus, it includes node C in the set of predecessor nodes for node F. As a result, node K is removed. The number of predecessor nodes for node C and node H are both zero and no decision is made in the current step.

Step 4: In this step, the number of direct successor nodes of two conflicting nodes are compared. A node v is a *direct successor node* of node u when v can be directly reached through an outgoing edge from u. The node with less direct successor nodes is then removed. The rationale behind preferring the node with more outgoing edges is the fact that each edge represents a jump target within the function and it is more likely that a valid control transfer instruction has a target within the function than any random CTI.

In Figure 2.4, node C has only one direct successor node while node H has two. Therefore, node C is removed from the control flow graph. In our example, all conflicts are resolved at this point.

Step 5: In this step, all conflicts between basic blocks must be resolved. For each pair of conflicting blocks, one is chosen at random and then removed from the graph. No human intervention is required at this step, but it would be possible to create different alternative disassembly outputs (one output for each block that needs to be removed) that can be all presented to a human analyst.

It might also be possible to use statistical methods during Step 5 to improve the chances that the "correct" block is selected. However, this technique is not implemented and is left for future work.

The result of the conflict resolution step is a control flow graph that contains no overlapping basic blocks. The instructions in these blocks are considered valid and could serve as the output of the static analysis process. However, most control flow graphs do not cover the function's complete address range and gaps exist between some basic blocks.

2.2.5 Gap Completion

The task of the gap completion phase is to improve the results of our analysis by filling the gaps between basic blocks in the control flow graph with instructions that are likely to be valid. A *gap* from basic block b_1 to basic block b_2 is the sequence of addresses that starts at the first address after the end of basic block b_1 and ends at the last address before the start of block b_2, given that there is no other basic block in the control flow graph that covers any of these addresses. In other words, a gap contains bytes that are not used by any instruction in blocks the control flow graph.

Gaps are often the result of junk bytes that are inserted by the obfuscator. Because junk bytes are not reachable at run-time, the control flow graph does not cover such bytes. It is apparent that the attempt to disassemble gaps filled with junk bytes does not improve the results of the analysis. However, there are also gaps that do contain valid instructions. These gaps can be the result of an incomplete control flow graph, for example, stemming from a region of code that is only reachable through an indirect jump whose target cannot be determined statically. Another frequent cause for gaps that contain valid instructions are call instructions. Because the disassembler cannot continue after a call instruction, the following valid instructions are not immediately reachable. Some of these instructions might be included into the control flow graph because they are the target of other control transfer instructions. Those regions that are not reachable, however, cause gaps that must be analyzed in the gap completion phase.

The algorithm to identify the most probable instruction sequence in a gap from basic block b_1 to basic block b_2 works as follows. First, all possibly valid sequences in the gap are identified. A necessary condition for a valid instruction sequence is that its last instruction either (i) ends with the last byte of the gap or (ii) its last instruction is a non intra-procedural control transfer instruction. The first condition states that the last instruction of a valid sequence has to be directly adjacent to the first instruction of block b_2. This becomes evident when considering a valid instruction sequence in the gap that is executed at run-time. After the last instruction of the sequence is executed, the control flow has to continue at the first instruction of basic block b_2. The second condition states that a sequence does not need to end directly adjacent to block b_2 if the last instruction is a non intra-procedural control transfer. The restriction to non intra-procedural CTIs is necessary because all intra-procedural CTIs are included into the initial control flow graph. When an intra-procedural instruction appears in a gap, it must have been removed during the conflict resolution phase and should not be included again.

Instruction sequences are found by considering each byte between the start and the end of the gap as a potential start of a valid instruction sequence. Subsequent instructions are then decoded until the instruction sequence either meets or violates one of the necessary conditions defined above. When an instruction sequence meets a necessary condition, it is considered possibly valid and a *sequence score* is calculated for it. The sequence score is a measure of the likelihood that this instruction sequence appears in an executable. It is calculated as the sum of the *instruction scores* of all instructions in the sequence. The instruction score is similar to the sequence score and reflects the likelihood of an individual instruction. Instruction scores are always greater or equal than zero. Therefore, the score of a sequence cannot decrease when more instructions are added. We calculate instruction scores using statistical techniques and heuristics to identify improbable instructions.

The statistical techniques are based on instruction probabilities and digraphs. Our approach utilizes tables that denote both the likelihood of individual instructions appearing in a binary as well as the likelihood of two instructions occurring as a consecutive pair. The tables were built by disassembling a large set of common executables and tabulating counts for the occurrence of each individual instruction as well as counts for each occurrence of a pair of instructions. These counts were subsequently stored for later use during the disassembly of an obfuscated binary. It is important to note that only instruction opcodes are taken into account with this technique; operands are not considered. The basic score for a particular instruction is calculated as the sum of the probability of occurrence of this instruction and the probability of occurrence of this instruction followed by the next instruction in the sequence.

In addition to the statistical technique, a set of heuristics is used to identify improbable instructions. This analysis focuses on instruction arguments and observed notions of the validity of certain combinations of operations, registers, and accessing modes. Each heuristic is applied to an individual instruction and can modify the basic score calculated by the statistical technique. In our current implementation, the score of the corresponding instruction is set to zero whenever a rule matches. Examples of these rules include the following:

- operand size mismatches;
- certain arithmetic on special-purpose registers;
- unexpected register-to-register moves (e.g., moving from a register other than %ebp into %esp);
- moves of a register value into memory referenced by the same register.

When all possible instruction sequences are determined, the one with the highest sequence score is selected as the valid instruction sequence between b_1 and b_2.

8048000	55					55	push %ebp
8048001	89 e5					89 e5	mov %esp, %ebp
8048003	e8 00 00 74 11					e8 00 00 74 11	call 19788008
8048008	0a	0a					
8048009	05	05	05				
804800a	3c	3c	3c	3c		3c 00	cmp 0, %eax
804800b	00	00	00	00	00		
		75	75		75		
804800c	75 06	06	06		06	75 06	jne 8048014
804800e	b0 00					b0 00	mov 0, %eax
8048010	eb 07					eb 07	jmp 8048019
8048012	0a	0a					
8048013	05	05	05				
		a1	a1				
8048014	a1 00 00 74 01	00	00			a1 00 00 74 01	mov (1740000), %eax
		00	00				
8048019	89 ec	74	74			89 ec	mov %ebp, %esp
804801b	5d					5d	pop %ebp
804801c	c3					c3	ret
804801d	90					90	nop

Gap Sequences   Disassembler Output

Fig. 2.5. Gap completion and disassembler output.

The instructions that make up the control flow graph of our example function and the intermediate gaps are shown in the left part of Figure 2.5. It can be seen that only a single instruction sequence is valid in the first gap, while there is none in the second gap. The right part of Figure 2.5 shows the output of our disassembler. All valid instructions of the example function have been correctly identified.

Based on the list of valid instructions, the subsequent code analysis phase can attempt to detect malicious code. In the following Section 2.3, we present symbolic execution as one possible static analysis approach to identify higher-level properties of code.

2.3 Code Analysis

This section describes the use of symbolic execution [10], a static analysis technique to identify code sequences that exhibit certain properties. In particular, we aim at characterizing a code piece by its semantics, or, in other words, by its effect on the environment. The goal is to construct models that characterize malicious behavior, regardless of the particular sequence of instructions (and therefore, of bytes) used in the code. This allows one to specify more general and robust descriptions of malicious code that cannot be evaded by simple changes to the syntactic representation or layout of the code (e.g., by renaming registers or modify the execution order of instructions).

Symbolic execution is a technique that interpretatively executes a program, using symbolic expressions instead of real values as input. This also includes the execution environment of the program (data, stack, and heap regions) for which no initial value is known at the time of the analysis. Of course, for all variables for which concrete values are known (e.g., initialized data segments), these values are used. When the execution starts from the entry point in the program, say address s, a symbolic execution engine interprets the sequence of machine instructions as they are encountered in the program.

To perform symbolic execution of machine instructions (in our case, Intel x86 operations), it is necessary to extend the semantics of these instructions so that operands are not limited to real data objects but can also be symbolic expressions. The normal execution semantics of Intel x86 assembly code describes how data objects are represented, how statements and operations manipulate these data objects, and how control flows through the statements of a program. For symbolic execution, the definitions for the basic operators of the language have to be extended to accept symbolic operands and produce symbolic formulas as output.

2.3.1 Execution State

We define the execution state S of program p as a snapshot of the content of the processor registers (except the program counter) and all valid memory locations at a particular instruction of p, which is denoted by the program counter. Although it would be possible to treat the program counter like any other register, it is more intuitive to handle the program counter separately and to require that it contain a concrete value (i.e., it points to a certain instruction). The content of all other registers and memory locations can be described by symbolic expressions.

Before symbolic execution starts from address s, the execution state S is initialized by assigning symbolic variables to all processor registers (except the program counter) and memory locations for which no concrete value is known initially. Thus, whenever a processor register or a memory location is read for the first time, without any previous assignment to it, a new symbol is supplied from the list of variables $\{v_l, v_2, v_3, \dots\}$. Note that this is the only time when symbolic data objects are introduced.

In our current system, we do not support floating-point data objects and operations. Therefore, all symbols (variables) represent integer values. Symbolic expressions are linear combinations of these symbols (i.e., integer polynomials over the symbols). A symbolic expression can be written as $c_n * v_n + c_{n-1} * v_{n-1} + \cdots + c_1 * v_1 + c_0$ where the c_i are constants. In addition, there is a special symbol $\perp$ that denotes that no information is known about the content of a register or a memory location. Note that this is very different from a symbolic expression. Although there is no *concrete* value known for a symbolic expression, its value can be evaluated when concrete values are supplied for the initial execution state. For the symbol $\perp$, nothing can be asserted, even when the initial state is completely defined.

By allowing program variables to assume integer polynomials over the symbols v_i, the symbolic execution of assignment statements follows naturally. The expression on the right-hand side of the statement is evaluated, substituting symbolic expressions for source registers or memory locations. The result is another symbolic expression (an integer is the trivial case) that represents the new value of the left-hand side of the assignment statement. Because symbolic expressions are integer polynomials, it is possible to evaluate addition and subtraction of two arbitrary expressions. Also, it is possible to multiply or shift a symbolic expression by a constant value. Other instructions, such as the multiplication of two symbolic variables or a logic operation (e.g., and, or), result in the assignment of the symbol $\perp$ to the destination. This is because the result of these operations cannot (always) be represented as integer polynomial. The reason for limiting symbolic formulas to linear expressions will become clear in Section 2.3.3.

Whenever an instruction is executed, the execution state is changed. As mentioned previously, in case of an assignment, the content of the destination operand is replaced with the right-hand side of the statement. In addition, the program counter is advanced. In the case of an instruction that does not change the control flow of a program (i.e., an instruction that is not a jump or a conditional branch), the program counter is simply advanced to the next instruction. Also, an unconditional jump to a certain label (instruction) is performed exactly as in normal execution by transferring control from the current statement to the statement associated with the corresponding label.

Figure 2.6 shows the symbolic execution of a sequence of instructions. In addition to the x86 machine instructions, a corresponding fragment of C source code is shown. For each step of the symbolic execution, the relevant parts of the execution state are presented. Changes between execution states are shown in bold face. Note that the compiler (gcc 3.3) converted the multiplication in the C program into an equivalent series of add machine instructions.

2.3.2 Conditional Branches and Loops

To handle conditional branches, the execution state has to be extended to include a set of constraints, called the *path constraints*. In principle, a path constraint relates a symbolic expression L to a constant. This can be used, for example, to specify that the content of a register has to be equal to 0. More formally, a path constraint is a

```
int i, j, k;          8048364:   mov   0x8049588,%edx
                      804836a:   mov   %edx,%eax
void f()              804836c:   add   %eax,%eax
{                     804836e:   add   %edx,%eax
  i = 3*j + k;        8048370:   add   0x804958c,%eax
}                     8048376:   mov   %eax,0x8049590
                      804837b:
```

	Step 1	Step 2
eax:	$v0$	$v0$
edx:	$v1$	$v2$
8049588 (j) :	$v2$	$v2$
804958c (k):	$v3$	$v3$
8049590 (i) :	$v4$	$v4$
PC:	8048364	804836a

	Step 3	Step 4	Step 5	Step 6	Step 7
eax:	$v2$	$2*v2$	$3*v2$	$3*v2+v3$	$3*v2+v3$
edx:	$v2$	$v2$	$v2$	$v2$	$v2$
8049588 (j) :	$v2$	$v2$	$v2$	$v2$	$v2$
804958c (k):	$v3$	$v3$	$v3$	$v3$	$v3$
8049590 (i) :	$v4$	$v4$	$v4$	$v4$	$3*v2+v3$
PC:	804836c	804836e	8048370	8048376	804837b

Fig. 2.6. Symbolic execution.

boolean expression of the form $L \geq 0$ or $L = 0$, in which L is an integer polynomial over the symbols v_i. The set of path constraints forms a linear constraint system.

The symbolic execution of a conditional branch statement starts by evaluating the associated Boolean expression. The evaluation is done by replacing the instruction's operands with their corresponding symbolic expressions. Then, the inequality (or equality) is transformed and converted into the standard form introduced above. Let the resulting path constraint be called q.

To continue symbolic execution, both branches of the control path need to be explored. The symbolic execution forks into two "parallel" execution threads: one thread follows the *then* alternative, while the other one follows the *else* alternative. Both execution threads assume the execution state that existed immediately before the conditional statement, but proceed independently thereafter. Because the *then* alternative is only chosen if the conditional branch is taken, the corresponding path constraint q must be true. Therefore, we add q to the set of path constraints of this execution thread. The situation is reversed for the *else* alternative. In this case, the branch is not taken and q must be false. Thus, $\neg q$ is added to the path constraints of this execution.

After q (or $\neg q$) is added to a set of path constraints, the corresponding linear constraint system is immediately checked for satisfiability. When the set of path constraints has no solution, this implies that, independent of the choice of values for the initial configuration C, this path of execution can never occur. This allows us to immediately terminate impossible execution threads.

Each fork of execution at a conditional statement contributes a condition over the variables v_i that must hold for this particular execution thread. Thus, the set of path constraints determines which conditions the initial execution state must satisfy in order for an execution to follow the particular associated path. Each symbolic execution begins with an empty set of path constraints. As assumptions about the variables are made (in order to choose between alternative paths through the program as presented by conditional statements), those assumptions are added to the set. An example of

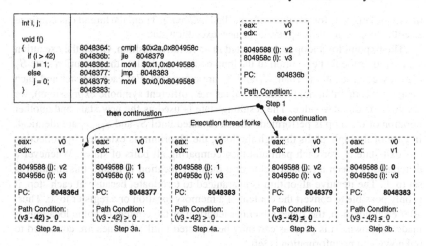

Fig. 2.7. Handling conditional branches during symbolic execution.

a fork into two symbolic execution threads as the result of an if-statement and the corresponding path constraints are shown in Figure 2.7. Note that the if-statement was translated into two machine instructions. Thus, special code is required to extract the condition on which a branch statement depends.

Because a symbolic execution thread forks into two threads at each conditional branch statement, loops represent a problem. In particular, we have to make sure that execution threads "make progress." The problem is addressed by requiring that a thread passes through the same loop at most three times. Before an execution thread enters a loop for the forth time, its execution is halted. Then, the effect of an arbitrary number of iterations of this loop on the execution state is approximated. This approximation is a standard static analysis technique [6, 14] that aims at determining value ranges for the variables that are modified in the loop body. Since the problem of finding exact ranges and relationships between variables is undecidable in the general case, the approximation naturally involves a certain loss of precision. After the effect of the loop on the execution thread is approximated, the thread can continue with the modified state after the loop. To determine loops in the control flow graph, we use the algorithm by Lengauer-Tarjan [12], which is based on dominator trees.

To approximate the effect of the loop body on an execution state, a *fixpoint* for this loop is constructed. For our purposes, a fixpoint is an execution state F that, when used as the initial state before entering the loop, is equivalent to the execution state after the loop termination. In other words, after the operations of the loop body are applied to the fixpoint state F, the resulting execution state is again F. Clearly, if there are multiple paths through the loop, the resulting execution states at each loop exit must be the same (and identical to F). Thus, whenever the effect of a loop on an execution state must be determined, we transform this state into a fixpoint for this loop. This transformation is often called *widening*. Then, the thread can continue after the loop using the fixpoint as its new execution state.

The fixpoint for a loop is constructed in an iterative fashion. Given the execution state S_1 after the first execution of the loop body, we calculate the execution state S_2 after a second iteration. Then, S_1 and S_2 are compared. For each register and each memory location that hold different values (i.e., different symbolic expressions), we assign $\perp$ as the new value. The resulting state is used as the new state and another iteration of the loop is performed. This is repeated until S_i and $S_{(i+1)}$ are identical. In case of multiple paths through the loop, the algorithm is extended by collecting one exit state S_i for each path and then comparing all pairs of states. Whenever a difference between a register value or a memory location is found, this location is set to $\perp$. The iterative algorithm is guaranteed to terminate, because at each step, it is only possible to convert the content of a memory location or a register to $\perp$. Thus, after each iteration, the states are either identical or the content of some locations is made unknown. This process can only be repeated until all values are converted to unknown and no information is left.

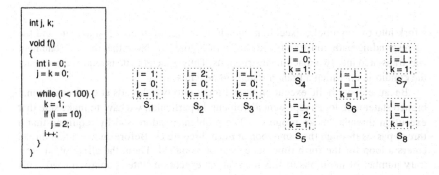

Fig. 2.8. Fixpoint calculation.

An example for a fixpoint calculation (using C code instead of x86 assembly) is presented in Figure 2.8. In this case, the execution state includes the values of the three variables i, j, and k. After the first loop iteration, the execution state S_1 is reached. Here, i has been incremented once, k has been assigned the constant 1, and j has not been modified. After a second iteration, S_2 is reached. Because i has changed between S_1 and S_2, its value is set to $\perp$ in S_3. Note that the execution has not modified j, because the value of i was known to be different from 10 at the if-statement. Using S_3 as the new execution state, two paths are taken through the loop. In one case (S_4), j is set to 2, in the other case (S_5), the variable j remains 0. The reason for the two different execution paths is the fact that i is no longer known at the if-statement and, thus, both paths have to be followed. Comparing S_3 with S_4 and S_5, the difference between the values of variable j leads to the new state S_6 in which j is set to $\perp$. As before, the new state S_6 is used for the next loop iteration.

Finally, the resulting states S_7 and S_8 are identical to S_6, indicating that a fixpoint is reached.

In the example above, we quickly reach a fixpoint. In general, by considering all modified values as unknown (setting them to $\perp$), the termination of the fixpoint algorithm is achieved very quickly. However, the approximation might be unnecessarily imprecise. For our current prototype, we use this simple approximation technique [14]. However, we plan to investigate more sophisticated fixpoint algorithms in the future.

2.3.3 Analyzing Effects of Code Sequences

As mentioned previously, the aim of the symbolic execution is to characterize the behavior of a piece of code. For example, symbolic execution could be used to determine if a system call is invoked with a particular argument. Another example is the assignment of a value to a certain memory address.

Consider a specification that defines a piece of code as malicious when it writes to an area in memory that should not be modified. Such a specification can be used to characterize kernel-level rootkits, which modify parts of the operating system memory (such as the system call table) that benign modules do not touch. To determine whether a piece of code can assign a value to a certain memory address t, the destination addresses of data transfer instructions (e.g., x86 mov) must be determined. Thus, whenever the symbolic execution engine encounters such an instruction, it checks whether this instruction can possibly access (or write to) address t. To this end, the symbolic expression that represents the destination of the data transfer instruction is analyzed. The reason is that if it were possible to force this symbolic expression to evaluate to t, then the attacker could achieve her goal.

Let the symbolic expression of the destination of the data transfer instruction be called s_t. To check whether it is possible to force the destination address of this instruction to t, the constraint $s_t = t$ is generated (this constraint simply expresses the fact that s_t should evaluate to the target address t). Now, we have to determine whether this constraint can be satisfied, given the current path constraints. To this end, the constraint $s_t = t$ is added to the path constraints, and the resulting linear inequality system is solved.

If the linear inequality system has a solution, then the sequence of code instructions that were symbolically executed so far can possibly write to t. Note that, since the symbolic expressions are integer polynomials over variables that describe the *initial state* of the system, the solution to the linear inequality system directly provides concrete values for the initial configuration that will eventually lead to a value being written to t. For example, in the case of kernel-level rootkit detection, a kernel module would be classified as malicious if a data transfer instruction (in its initialization routine) can be used to modify the address t of an entry in the system call table.

To solve the linear constraint systems, we use the Parma Polyhedral Library (PPL) [1]. In general, solving a linear constraint system is exponential in the number of inequalities. However, the number of inequalities is usually small, and PPL uses a number of optimizations to reduce the resources required at run time.

2.3.4 Memory Aliasing and Unknown Stores

In the previous discussion, two problems were ignored that considerably complicate the analysis for real programs: memory aliasing and store operations to unknown destination addresses.

Memory aliasing refers to the problem that two different symbolic expressions s_1 and s_2 might point to the same address. That is, although s_1 and s_2 contain different variables, both expressions evaluate to the same value. In this case, the assignment of a value to an address that is specified by s_1 has unexpected side effects. In particular, such an assignment simultaneously changes the content of the location pointed to by s_2.

Memory aliasing is a typical problem in the static analysis of high-level languages with pointers (such as C). Unfortunately, the problem is exacerbated at the machine code level. The reason is that, in a high-level language, only a certain subset of variables can be accessed via pointers. Also, it is often possible to perform alias analysis that further reduces the set of variables that might be subject to aliasing. Thus, one can often guarantee that certain variables are not modified by write operations through pointers. At machine level, the address space is uniformly treated as an array of storage locations. Thus, a write operation could potentially modify any other variable.

In our prototype, we take an optimistic approach and assume that different symbolic expressions refer to different memory locations. This approach is motivated by the fact that most C compilers address local and global variables so that a distinct expression is used for each access to a different variable. In the case of global variables, the address of the variable is directly encoded in the instruction, making the identification of the variable particularly easy. For each local variable, the access is performed by calculating a different offset with respect to the value of the base pointer register (%ebp).

A store operation to an unknown address is related to the aliasing problem as such an operation could potentially modify any memory location. Here, one can choose one of two options. A conservative and safe approach must assume that any variable could have been overwritten and no information remains. The other approach assumes that such a store operation does not interfere with any variable that is part of the solution of the linear inequality system. While this leads to the possibility of false negatives, it significantly reduces the number of false positives.

2.4 Conclusions

The analysis of an unknown program requires that the binary is first disassembled into its corresponding assembly code representation. Based on the code instructions, static or dynamic code analysis techniques can then be used to classify the program as malicious or benign.

In this chapter, we have introduced a robust disassembler that produces good results even when the malicious code employs tricks to resists analysis. This is crucial for many security tools, including virus scanners [2] and intrusion detection systems [9].

We also introduced symbolic execution as one possible static analysis technique to infer semantic properties of code. This allows us to determine the effects of the execution of a piece of code. Based on this knowledge, we can construct general and robust models of malicious code. These models do not describe particular instances of malware, but capture the properties of a whole class of malicious code. Thus, it is more difficult for an attacker to evade detection by applying simple changes to the syntactic representation of the code.

References

1. R. Bagnara, E. Ricci, E. Zaffanella, and P. M. Hill. Possibly not closed convex polyhedra and the Parma Polyhedra Library. In *9th International Symposium on Static Analysis*, 2002.
2. M. Christodorescu and S. Jha. Static Analysis of Executables to Detect Malicious Patterns. In *Proceedings of the 12th USENIX Security Symposium*, 2003.
3. C. Cifuentes and M. V. Emmerik. UQBT: Adaptable binary translation at low cost. *IEEE Computer*, 40(2-3), 2000.
4. C. Cifuentes and K. Gough. Decompilation of Binary Programs. *Software Practice & Experience*, 25(7):811–829, July 1995.
5. F. B. Cohen. Operating System Protection through Program Evolution. http://all.net/books/IP/evolve.html.
6. P. Cousot and R. Cousot. Abstract Interpretation: A Unified Lattice Model for Static Analysis of Programs by Construction or Approximation of Fixpoints. In *4th ACM Symposium on Principles of Programming Languages (POPL)*, 1977.
7. Data Rescure. IDA Pro: Disassembler and Debugger. http://www.datarescue.com/idabase/, 2004.
8. Free Software Foundation. *GNU Binary Utilities*, Mar 2002. http://www.gnu.org/software/binutils/manual/.
9. J. Giffin, S. Jha, and B. Miller. Detecting manipulated remote call streams. In *In Proceedings of 11th USENIX Security Symposium*, 2002.
10. J. King. Symbolic Execution and Program Testing. *Communications of the ACM*, 19(7), 1976.
11. C. Kruegel, F. Valeur, W. Robertson, and G. Vigna. Static Analysis of Obfuscated Binaries. In *Usenix Security Symposium*, 2004.
12. T. Lengauer and R. Tarjan. A Fast Algorithm for Finding Dominators in a Flowgraph. *ACM Transactions on Programming Languages and Systems*, 1(1), 1979.
13. C. Linn and S. Debray. Obfuscation of executable code to improve resistance to static disassembly. In *Proceedings of the 10th ACM Conference on Computer and Communications Security (CCS)*, pages 290–299, Washington, DC, October 2003.
14. F. Nielson, H. Nielson, and C. Hankin. *Principles of Program Analysis*. Springer Verlag, 1999.
15. R. Sites, A. Chernoff, M. Kirk, M. Marks, and S. Robinson. Binary Translation. *Digital Technical Journal*, 4(4), 1992.

3

A Next-Generation Platform for Analyzing Executables*

Thomas Reps[1,2], Gogul Balakrishnan[1], Junghee Lim[1], and Tim Teitelbaum[2]

[1] Department of Computer Sciences, University of Wisconsin, Madison
    {reps,bgogul,junghee}@cs.wisc.edu
[2] GrammaTech, Inc.
    tt@grammatech.com

Summary. In recent years, there has been a growing need for tools that an analyst can use to understand the workings of COTS components, plug-ins, mobile code, and DLLs, as well as memory snapshots of worms and virus-infected code. Static analysis provides techniques that can help with such problems; however, there are several obstacles that must be overcome:

- For many kinds of potentially malicious programs, symbol-table and debugging information is entirely absent. Even if it is present, it cannot be relied upon.
- To understand memory-access operations, it is necessary to determine the set of addresses accessed by each operation. This is difficult because
  - While some memory operations use explicit memory addresses in the instruction (easy), others use indirect addressing via address expressions (difficult).
  - Arithmetic on addresses is pervasive. For instance, even when the value of a local variable is loaded from its slot in an activation record, address arithmetic is performed.
  - There is no notion of type at the hardware level, so address values cannot be distinguished from integer values.
  - Memory accesses do not have to be aligned, so word-sized address values could potentially be cobbled together from misaligned reads and writes.

We have developed static-analysis algorithms to recover information about the contents of memory locations and how they are manipulated by an executable. By combining these analyses with facilities provided by the IDAPro and CodeSurfer toolkits, we have created CodeSurfer/x86, a prototype tool for browsing, inspecting, and analyzing x86 executables.

---

* This chapter is a slightly revised version of a paper that appeared in *Proceedings of the 3rd Asian Symposium on Programming Languages and Systems* [37]. Portions of the chapter also appeared in [3, 5, 36].

This work was supported in part by NSF under grant CCR-9986308, by ONR under contracts N00014-{01-1-0796,01-1-0708,03-C-0502,05-C-0357}, by ARFL under contract F30602-02-C-0051, and by HSARPA under contract FA8750-05-C-0179. The U.S. Government is authorized to reproduce and distribute reprints for Governmental purposes, notwithstanding any copyright notices affixed thereon. The views and conclusions contained herein are those of the authors, and should not be interpreted as necessarily representing the official policies or endorsements, either expressed or implied, of the above government agencies or the U.S. Government.

From an x86 executable, CodeSurfer/x86 recovers intermediate representations that are similar to what would be created by a compiler for a program written in a high-level language. CodeSurfer/x86 also supports a scripting language, as well as several kinds of sophisticated pattern-matching capabilities. These facilities provide a platform for the development of additional tools for analyzing the security properties of executables.

3.1 Introduction

Market forces are increasingly pushing companies to deploy COTS software when possible—for which source code is typically unavailable—and to out-source development when custom software is required. Moreover, a great deal of legacy code—for which design documents are usually out-of-date, and for which source code is sometimes unavailable and sometimes non-existent—will continue to be left deployed. An important challenge during the coming decade will be how to identify bugs and security vulnerabilities in such systems. Methods are needed to determine whether third-party and legacy application programs can perform malicious operations (or can be induced to perform malicious operations), and to be able to make such judgments in the absence of source code.

Recent research in programming languages, software engineering, and computer security has led to new kinds of tools for analyzing code for bugs and security vulnerabilities [26, 43, 21, 15, 9, 6, 11, 28, 18, 10]. In these tools, static analysis is used to determine a conservative answer to the question "Can the program reach a bad state?"[3] In principle, such tools would be of great help to an analyst trying to detect malicious code hidden in software, except for one important detail: the aforementioned tools all focus on analyzing *source code* written in a high-level language. Even if source code were available, there are a number of reasons why analyses that start from source code do not provide the right level of detail for checking certain kinds of properties, which can cause bugs, security vulnerabilities, and malicious behavior to be invisible to such tools. (See §3.2.)

In contrast, our work addresses the problem of finding bugs and security vulnerabilities in programs when source code is unavailable. Our goal is to create a platform that carries out static analysis on executables and provides information that an analyst can use to understand the workings of potentially malicious code, such as COTS components, plug-ins, mobile code, and DLLs, as well as memory snapshots of worms and virus-infected code. A second goal is to use this platform to create tools that an analyst can employ to determine such information as

- whether a program contains inadvertent security vulnerabilities

---

[3] Static analysis provides a way to obtain information about the possible states that a program reaches during execution, but without actually running the program on specific inputs. Static-analysis techniques explore the program's behavior for *all* possible inputs and *all* possible states that the program can reach. To make this feasible, the program is "run in the aggregate"—i.e., on descriptors that represent *collections* of memory configurations [16].

- whether a program contains deliberate security vulnerabilities, such as back doors, time bombs, or logic bombs. If so, the goal is to provide information about activation mechanisms, payloads, and latencies.

We have developed a tool, called CodeSurfer/x86, that serves as a prototype for a next-generation platform for analyzing executables. CodeSurfer/x86 provides a security analyst with a powerful and flexible platform for investigating the properties and possible behaviors of an x86 executable. It uses static analysis to recover intermediate representations (IRs) that are similar to those that a compiler creates for a program written in a high-level language. An analyst is able to use (i) CodeSurfer/x86's GUI, which provides mechanisms to understand a program's chains of data and control dependences, (ii) CodeSurfer/x86's scripting language, which provides access to all of the intermediate representations that CodeSurfer/x86 builds, and (iii) GrammaTech's Path Inspector, which is a model-checking tool that uses a sophisticated pattern-matching engine to answer questions about the flow of execution in a program.

Because CodeSurfer/x86 was designed to provide a platform that an analyst can use to understand the workings of potentially malicious code, a major challenge is that the tool must assume that the x86 executable is untrustworthy, and hence symbol-table and debugging information cannot be relied upon (even if it is present). The algorithms used in CodeSurfer/x86 provide ways to meet this challenge.

Although the present version of CodeSurfer/x86 is targeted to x86 executables, the techniques used [3, 35, 40, 33, 36] are language-independent and could be applied to other types of executables. In addition, it would be possible to extend CodeSurfer/x86 to use symbol-table and debugging information in situations where such information is available and trusted—for instance, if you have the source code for the program, you invoke the compiler yourself, and you trust the compiler to supply correct symbol-table and debugging information. Moreover, the techniques extend naturally if source code is available: one can treat the executable code as just another IR in the collection of IRs obtainable from source code. The mapping of information back to the source code would be similar to what C source-code tools already have to perform because of the use of the C preprocessor (although the kind of issues that arise when debugging optimized code [27, 46, 17] complicate matters).

The remainder of chapter is organized as follows: §3.2 illustrates some of the advantages of analyzing executables. §3.3 describes CodeSurfer/x86. §3.4 gives an overview of the model-checking facilities that have been coupled to CodeSurfer/x86. §3.5 discusses related work.

3.2 Advantages of Analyzing Executables

This section discusses why an analysis that works on executables can provide more accurate information than an analysis that works on source code.[4] An analysis that

---

[4] Terms like "an analysis that works on source code" and "source-level analyses" are used as a shorthand for "analyses that work on IRs built from the source code."

works on source code can fail to detect certain bugs and vulnerabilities due to the WYSINWYX phenomenon: "What You See Is Not What You eXecute" [5], which can cause there to be a mismatch between what a programmer intends and what is actually executed by the processor. The following source-code fragment, taken from a login program, illustrates the issue [30]:

```
memset(password, '\0', len);
free(password);
```

The login program temporarily stores the user's password—in clear text—in a dynamically allocated buffer pointed to by the pointer variable password. To minimize the lifetime of the password, which is sensitive information, the code fragment shown above zeroes-out the buffer pointed to by password before returning it to the free-storage pool. Unfortunately, a compiler that performs useless-code elimination may reason that the program never uses the values written by the call on memset, and therefore the call on memset can be removed—thereby leaving sensitive information exposed in the free-storage pool. This is not just hypothetical; a similar vulnerability was discovered during the Windows security push in 2002 [30]. This vulnerability is invisible in the source code; it can only be detected by examining the low-level code emitted by the optimizing compiler.

A second example where analysis of an executable does better than typical source-level analyses involves pointer arithmetic and an indirect call:

```
int (*f)(void);
int diff = (char*)&f2 - (char*)&f1; // The offset between f1 and f2
f = &f1;
f = (int (*)())((char*)f + diff); // f now points to f2
(*f)(); // indirect call;
```

Existing source-level analyses (that we know of) are ill-prepared to handle the above code. The conventional assumption is that arithmetic on function pointers leads to undefined behavior, so source-level analyses either (a) assume that the indirect function call might call any function, or (b) ignore the arithmetic operations and assume that the indirect function call calls f1 (on the assumption that the code is ANSI-C compliant). In contrast, the analysis described by Balakrishnan and Reps [3, 36] correctly identifies f2 as the invoked function. Furthermore, the analysis can detect when arithmetic on addresses creates an address that does not point to the beginning of a function; the use of such an address to perform a function "call" is likely to be a bug (or else a very subtle, deliberately introduced security vulnerability).

A third example involves a function call that passes fewer arguments than the procedure expects as parameters. (Many compilers accept such (unsafe) code as an easy way of implementing functions that take a variable number of parameters.) With most compilers, this effectively means that the call-site passes some parts of one or more local variables of the calling procedure as the remaining parameters (and, in effect, these are passed by reference—an assignment to such a parameter in the callee will overwrite the value of the corresponding local in the caller.) An analysis that works on executables can be created that is capable of determining what the extra parameters are [3, 36], whereas a source-level analysis must either make a cruder over-approximation or an unsound under-approximation.

A final example is shown in Fig. 3.1. The C code on the left uses an uninitialized variable (which triggers a compiler warning, but compiles successfully). A source-code analyzer must assume that local can have any value, and therefore the value of v in main is either 1 or 2. The assembly listings on the right show how the C code could be compiled, including two variants for the prolog of function callee. The Microsoft compiler (cl) uses the second variant, which includes the following strength reduction:

> The instruction sub esp, 4 that allocates space for local is replaced by
> a push instruction of an arbitrary register (in this case, ecx).

An analysis of the executable can determine that this optimization results in local being initialized to 5, and therefore v in main can only have the value 1.

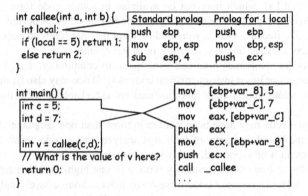

Fig. 3.1. Example of unexpected behavior due to compiler optimization. The box at the top right shows two variants of code generated by an optimizing compiler for the prolog of callee. Analysis of the second of these reveals that the variable local necessarily contains the value 5.

To summarize, the advantage of an analysis that works on executables is that an executable contains the actual instructions that will be executed, and hence provides information that reveals the actual behavior that arises during program execution. This information includes

- memory-layout details, such as (i) the positions (i.e., offsets) of variables in the runtime stack's activation records, and (ii) padding between structure fields.
- register usage
- execution order (e.g., of actual parameters)
- optimizations performed
- artifacts of compiler bugs

Access to such information can be crucial; for instance, many security exploits depend on platform-specific features, such as the structure of activation records. Vulnerabilities can escape notice when a tool does not have information about adjacency relationships among variables.

In contrast, there are a number of reasons why analyses based on source code do not provide the right level of detail for checking certain kinds of properties:

- Source-level tools are only applicable when source is available, which limits their usefulness in security applications (e.g., to analyzing code from open-source projects).
- Analyses based on source code typically make (unchecked) assumptions, e.g., that the program is ANSI-C compliant. This often means that an analysis does not account for behaviors that are allowed by the compiler (e.g., arithmetic is performed on pointers that are subsequently used for indirect function calls; pointers move off the ends of arrays and are subsequently dereferenced; etc.)
- Programs typically make extensive use of libraries, including dynamically linked libraries (DLLs), which may not be available in source-code form. Typically, source-level analyses are performed using code stubs that model the effects of library calls. Because these are created by hand they are likely to contain errors, which may cause an analysis to return incorrect results.
- Programs are sometimes modified subsequent to compilation, e.g., to perform optimizations or insert instrumentation code [44]. (They may also be modified to insert malicious code.) Such modifications are not visible to tools that analyze source.
- The source code may have been written in more than one language. This complicates the life of designers of tools that analyze source code because multiple languages must be supported, each with its own quirks.
- Even if the source code is primarily written in one high-level language, it may contain inlined assembly code in selected places. Source-level analysis tools typically either skip over inlined assembly code [14] or do not push the analysis beyond sites of inlined assembly code [1].

Thus, even if source code is available, a substantial amount of information is hidden from analyses that start from source code, which can cause bugs, security vulnerabilities, and malicious behavior to be invisible to such tools. Moreover, a source-level analysis tool that strives to have greater fidelity to the program that is actually executed would have to duplicate all of the choices made by the compiler and optimizer; such an approach is doomed to failure.

3.3 Analyzing Executables in the Absence of Source Code

To be able to apply techniques like the ones used in [26, 43, 21, 15, 9, 6, 11, 28, 18, 10], one already encounters a challenging program-analysis problem. From the perspective of the compiler community, one would consider the problem to be "IR recovery": one needs to recover *intermediate representations* from the executable that are similar to those that would be available had one started from source code. From the perspective of the model-checking community, one would consider the problem to be that of "model extraction": one needs to extract a suitable *model* from the executable. To solve the IR-recovery problem, several obstacles must be overcome:

- For many kinds of potentially malicious programs, symbol-table and debugging information is entirely absent. Even if it is present, it cannot be relied upon.
- To understand memory-access operations, it is necessary to determine the set of addresses accessed by each operation. This is difficult because
  - While some memory-access operations use explicit memory addresses in the instruction (easy), others use indirect addressing via address expressions (difficult).
  - Arithmetic on addresses is pervasive. For instance, even when the value of a local variable is loaded from its slot in an activation record, address arithmetic is performed.
  - There is no notion of type at the hardware level, so address values cannot be distinguished from integer values.
  - Memory accesses do not have to be aligned, so word-sized address values could potentially be cobbled together from misaligned reads and writes.

For the past few years, we have been working to create a prototype next-generation platform for analyzing executables. The tool set that we have developed extends static vulnerability-analysis techniques to work directly on executables, even in the absence of source code. The tool set builds on (i) recent advances in static analysis of program executables [3, 36], and (ii) new techniques for software model checking and dataflow analysis [8, 39, 40, 33]. The main components of the tool set are *CodeSurfer/x86*, *WPDS++*, and the *Path Inspector*:

- CodeSurfer/x86 recovers IRs from an executable that are similar to the IRs that source-code-analysis tools create—but, in many respects, the IRs that CodeSurfer/x86 builds are more precise. CodeSurfer/x86 also provides an API to these IRs.
- WPDS++ [32] is a library for answering generalized reachability queries on *weighted pushdown systems* (WPDSs) [8, 39, 40, 33]. This library provide a mechanism for defining and solving model-checking and dataflow-analysis problems. To extend CodeSurfer/x86's analysis capabilities, the CodeSurfer/x86 API can be used to extract a WPDS model from an executable and to run WPDS++ on the model.
- The Path Inspector is a software model checker built on top of CodeSurfer and WPDS++. It supports safety queries about a program's possible control configurations.

In addition, by writing scripts that traverse the IRs that CodeSurfer/x86 recovers, the tool set can be extended with further capabilities (e.g., decompilation, code rewriting, etc.).

Fig. 3.2 shows how these components fit together. CodeSurfer/x86 makes use of both IDAPro [31], a disassembly toolkit, and GrammaTech's CodeSurfer system [14], a toolkit originally developed for building program-analysis and inspection tools that analyze source code. These components are glued together by a piece called the Connector, which uses two static analyses—value-set analysis (VSA) [3, 36] and aggregate-structure identification (ASI) [35] to recover information about the contents of memory locations and how they are manipulated by an executable.[5]

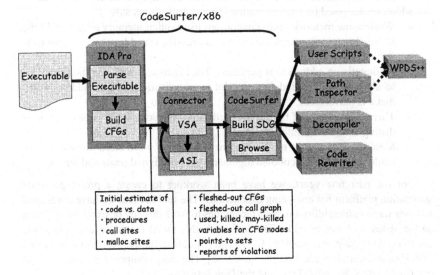

Fig. 3.2. Organization of CodeSurfer/x86 and companion tools.

An x86 executable is first disassembled using IDAPro. In addition to the disassembly listing, IDAPro also provides access to the following information:

Statically known memory addresses and offsets: IDAPro identifies the statically known memory addresses and stack offsets in the program, and renames all occurrences of these quantities with a consistent name. This database is used to define the set of data objects in terms of which (the initial run of) VSA is carried out; these objects are called *a-locs*, for "abstract locations". VSA is an analysis that, for each instruction, determines an over-approximation of the set of values that each a-loc could hold.

Information about procedure boundaries: X86 executables do not have information about procedure boundaries. IDAPro identifies the boundaries of most of the procedures in an executable.[6]

---

[5] VSA also makes use of the results of an additional static-analysis phase, called affine-relation analysis (ARA), which, for each program point, identifies affine relationships [34] that hold among the values of registers; see [3, 33].

[6] IDAPro does not identify the targets of all indirect jumps and indirect calls, and therefore the call graph and control-flow graphs that it constructs are not complete. However, the information computed during VSA is used to augment the call graph and control-flow graphs on-the-fly to account for indirect jumps and indirect calls.

Calls to library functions: IDAPro discovers calls to library functions using an algorithm called Fast Library Identification and Recognition Technology (FLIRT) [24].

IDAPro provides access to its internal resources via an API that allows users to create plug-ins to be executed by IDAPro. CodeSurfer/x86 uses a plug-in to IDAPro to read out information from IDAPro. This information is then used by the Connector to create the initial versions of its own intermediate representations (see Fig. 3.2); VSA and ASI are implemented using the intermediate representations created by the Connector. The IDAPro-plug-in/Connector combination is also able to create the same data structures for DLLs, and to link them into the data structures that represent the program itself. This infrastructure permits whole-program analysis to be carried out—including analysis of the code for all library functions that are called.

CodeSurfer/x86 makes no use of symbol-table or debugging information. Instead, the results of VSA and ASI provide a substitute for absent or untrusted symbol-table and debugging information. Initially, the set of a-locs is determined based on the static memory addresses and stack offsets that are used in instructions in the executable. Each run of ASI refines the set of a-locs used for the next run of VSA.

Because the IRs that CodeSurfer/x86 recovers are extracted directly from the executable code that is run on the machine, and because the entire program is analyzed—including any libraries that are linked to the program—this approach provides a "higher fidelity" platform for software model checking than the IRs derived from source code that other software model checkers use [26, 43, 21, 15, 9, 6, 11, 28, 18, 10].

CodeSurfer/x86 supports a scripting language that provides access to all of the IRs that CodeSurfer/x86 builds for the executable. This provides a way to connect CodeSurfer/x86 to other analysis tools, such as model checkers (see §3.4), as well as to implement other tools on top of CodeSurfer/x86, such as decompilers, code rewriters, etc. It also provides an analyst with a mechanism to develop any additional "one-off" analyses he needs to create.

3.3.1 Memory-Access Analysis in the Connector

The analyses in CodeSurfer/x86 are a great deal more ambitious than even relatively sophisticated disassemblers, such as IDAPro. At the technical level, CodeSurfer/x86 addresses the following problem:

Given a stripped executable E, identify the

- procedures, data objects, types, and libraries that it uses

and

- for each instruction I in E and its libraries
- for each interprocedural calling context of I
- for each machine register and a-loc A

statically compute an accurate over-approximation to

- the set of values that A may contain when I executes
- the instructions that may have defined the values used by I
- the instructions that may use the values defined by execution of I

and provide effective means to access that information both interactively and under program control.

Value-Set Analysis.   VSA [3, 36] is a combined numeric and pointer-analysis algorithm that determines an over-approximation of the set of numeric values and addresses (or *value set*) that each a-loc holds at each program point. The information computed during VSA is used to augment the call graph and control-flow graphs on-the-fly to account for indirect jumps and indirect function calls.

VSA is related to pointer-analysis algorithms that have been developed for programs written in high-level languages, which determine an over-approximation of the set of variables whose addresses each pointer variable can hold:

> *VSA determines an over-approximation of the set of addresses that each data object can hold at each program point.*

At the same time, VSA is similar to range analysis and other numeric static-analysis algorithms that over-approximate the integer values that each variable can hold:

> *VSA determines an over-approximation of the set of integer values that each data object can hold at each program point.*

The following insights shaped the design of VSA:

- A *non-aligned access* to memory—e.g., an access via an address that is not aligned on a 4-byte word boundary—spans parts of two words, and provides a way to forge a new address from *parts* of old addresses. It is important for VSA to discover information about the alignments and strides of memory accesses, or else most indirect-addressing operations appear to be possibly non-aligned accesses.
- To prevent most loops that traverse arrays from appearing to be possible stack-smashing attacks, the analysis needs to use relational information so that the values of a-locs assigned to within a loop can be related to the values of the a-locs used in the loop's branch condition (see [3, 34, 33]).
- It is desirable for VSA to track integer-valued and address-valued quantities *simultaneously*. This is crucial for analyzing executables because

- integers and addresses are indistinguishable at execution time, and
- compilers use address arithmetic and indirect addressing to implement such features as pointer arithmetic, pointer dereferencing, array indexing, and accessing structure fields.

Moreover, information about integer values can lead to improved tracking of address-valued quantities, and information about address values can lead to improved tracking of integer-valued quantities.

VSA produces information that is more precise than that obtained via several more conventional numeric analyses used in compilers, including constant propagation, range analysis, and integer-congruence analysis. At the same time, VSA provides an analog of pointer analysis that is suitable for use on executables.

Aggregate-Structure Identification. One of the major stumbling blocks in analysis of executables is the difficulty of recovering information about variables and types, especially for aggregates (i.e., structures and arrays). CodeSurfer/x86 uses an iterative strategy for recovering such information; with each round, it refines its notion of the program's variables and types.

Initially, VSA uses a set of variables ("a-locs") that are obtained from IDAPro. Because IDAPro has relatively limited information available at the time that it applies its variable-discovery heuristics (i.e., it only knows about statically known memory addresses and stack offsets), what it can do is rather limited, and generally leads to a very coarse-grained approximation of the program's variables.

Once a given run of VSA completes, the value sets for the a-locs at each instruction provide a way to identify an over-approximation of the memory accesses performed at that instruction. This information is used to refine the current set of a-locs by running a variant of the ASI algorithm [35], which identifies commonalities among accesses to different parts of an aggregate data value. ASI was originally developed for analysis of Cobol programs: in that context, ASI ignores all of the type declarations in the program, and considers an aggregate to be merely a sequence of bytes of a given length; an aggregate is then broken up into smaller parts depending upon how the aggregate is accessed by the program. In the context in which we use ASI—namely, analysis of x86 executables—ASI cannot be applied until the results of VSA are already in hand: ASI requires points-to, range, and stride information to be available; however, for an x86 executable this information is not available until after VSA has been run.

ASI exploits the information made available by VSA (such as the values that a-locs can hold, sizes of arrays, and iteration counts for loops), which generally leads to a much more accurate set of a-locs than the initial set of a-locs discovered by IDAPro. For instance, consider a simple loop, implemented in source code as

```
int a[10], i;
for (i = 0; i < 10; i++)
    a[i] = i;
```

From the executable, IDAPro will determine that there are two variables, one of size 4 bytes and one of size 40 bytes, but will provide no information about the substructure of the 40-byte variable. In contrast, in addition to the 4-byte variable, ASI will correctly identify that the 40 bytes are an array of ten 4-byte quantities.

The Connector uses a refinement loop that performs repeated phases of VSA and ASI (see Fig. 3.2). The ASI results are used to refine the previous set of a-locs, and the refined set of a-locs is then used to analyze the program during the next round of VSA. The number of iterations is controlled by a command-line parameter.

ASI also provides information that greatly increases the precision with which VSA can analyze the contents of dynamically allocated objects (i.e., memory locations allocated using `malloc` or `new`). To see why, recall how the initial set of a-locs is identified by IDAPro. The a-loc abstraction exploits the fact that accesses to program variables in a high-level language are either complied into static addresses (for globals, and fields of struct-valued globals) or static stack-frame offsets (for locals and fields of struct-valued locals). However, fields of dynamically allocated objects are accessed in terms of offsets relative to the base address of the object itself, which is something that IDAPro knows nothing about. In contrast, VSA considers each malloc site m to be a "memory region" (consisting of the objects allocated at m), and the memory region for m serves as a representative for the base addresses of those objects.[7] This lets ASI handle the use of an offset from an object's base address similar to the way that it handles a stack-frame offset—with the net result that ASI is able to capture information about the fine-grained structure of dynamically allocated objects. The object fields discovered in this way become a-locs for the next round of VSA, which will then discover an over-approximation of their contents.

ASI is complementary to VSA: ASI addresses only the issue of identifying the structure of aggregates, whereas VSA addresses the issue of (over-approximating) the contents of memory locations. ASI provides an improved method for the "variable-identification" facility of IDAPro, which uses only much cruder techniques (and only takes into account statically known memory addresses and stack offsets). Moreover, ASI requires more information to be on hand than is available in IDAPro (such as the sizes of arrays and iteration counts for loops). Fortunately, this is exactly the information that is available after VSA has been carried out, which means that ASI can be used in conjunction with VSA to obtain improved results: after a first round of VSA, the results of ASI are used to refine the a-loc abstraction, after which VSA is run again—generally producing more precise results.

3.3.2 CodeSurfer/x86

The value sets for the a-locs at each program point are used to determine each point's sets of used, killed, and possibly-killed a-locs; these are emitted in a format that is suitable for input to CodeSurfer.

---

[7] CodeSurfer/x86 actually uses a more refined technique (involving *two* memory regions per malloc site) to overcome some of the imprecision that arises due to the need to perform weak updates—i.e., accumulate information via join—on fields of summary malloc-regions. In particular, this technique, which is described in [4], often allows VSA to establish a definite link between a dynamically-allocated object of a class that uses one or more virtual functions and the appropriate virtual-function table.

CodeSurfer is a tool for code understanding and code inspection that supports both a graphical user interface (GUI) and an API (as well as a scripting language) to provide access to a program's system dependence graph (SDG) [29], as well as other information stored in CodeSurfer's IRs.[8] An SDG consists of a set of program dependence graphs (PDGs), one for each procedure in the program. A vertex in a PDG corresponds to a construct in the program, such as an instruction, a call to a procedure, an actual parameter of a call, or a formal parameter of a procedure. The edges correspond to data and control dependences between the vertices [22]. The PDGs are connected together with interprocedural edges that represent control dependences between procedure calls and entries, data dependences between actual parameters and formal parameters, and data dependences between return values and receivers of return values.

Dependence graphs are invaluable for many applications, because they highlight chains of dependent instructions that may be widely scattered through the program. For example, given an instruction, it is often useful to know its *data-dependence predecessors* (instructions that write to locations read by that instruction) and its *control-dependence predecessors* (control points that may affect whether a given instruction gets executed). Similarly, it may be useful to know for a given instruction its *data-dependence successors* (instructions that read locations written by that instruction) and *control-dependence* successors (instructions whose execution depends on the decision made at a given control point).

CodeSurfer's GUI supports browsing ("surfing") of an SDG, along with a variety of operations for making queries about the SDG—such as slicing [29] and chopping [38].[9] The GUI allows a user to navigate through a program's source code using these dependences in a manner analogous to navigating the World Wide Web.

CodeSurfer's API provides a programmatic interface to these operations, as well as to lower-level information, such as the individual nodes and edges of the program's SDG, call graph, and control-flow graph, and a node's sets of used, killed, and possibly-killed a-locs. By writing programs that traverse CodeSurfer's IRs to implement additional program analyses, the API can be used to extend CodeSurfer's capabilities.

CodeSurfer/x86 provides some unique capabilities for answering an analyst's questions. For instance, given a worm, CodeSurfer/x86's analysis results have been used to obtain information about the worm's target-discovery, propagation, and activation mechanisms by

---

[8] In addition to the SDG, CodeSurfer's IRs include abstract-syntax trees, control-flow graphs (CFGs), a call graph, VSA results, the sets of used, killed, and possibly-killed a-locs at each instruction, and information about the structure and layout of global memory, activation records, and dynamically allocated storage.

[9] A backward slice of a program with respect to a set of program points S is the set of all program points that might affect the computations performed at S; a forward slice with respect to S is the set of all program points that might be affected by the computations performed at members of S [29]. A program chop between a set of source program points S and a set of target program points T shows how S can affect the points in T [38]. Chopping is a key operation in information-flow analysis.

- locating sites of system calls,
- finding the instructions by which arguments are passed, and
- following dependences backwards from those instructions to identify where the values come from.

Because the techniques described in §3.3.1 are able to recover quite rich information about memory-access operations, the answers that CodeSurfer/x86 furnishes to such questions account for the movement of data through memory—not just the movement of data through registers, as in some prior work (e.g., [19, 12]).

3.3.3 Goals, Capabilities, and Assumptions

A few words are in order about the goals, capabilities, and assumptions underlying CodeSurfer/x86.

The constraint that symbol-table and debugging information are off-limits complicated the task of creating CodeSurfer/x86; however, the results of VSA and ASI provide a substitute for such information. This allowed us to create a tool that can be used when symbol-table and debugging information is absent or untrusted.

Given an executable as input, the goal is to check whether the executable conforms to a "standard" compilation model—i.e., a runtime stack is maintained; activation records (ARs) are pushed onto the stack on procedure entry and popped from the stack on procedure exit; each global variable resides at a fixed offset in memory; each local variable of a procedure f resides at a fixed offset in the ARs for f; actual parameters of f are pushed onto the stack by the caller so that the corresponding formal parameters reside at fixed offsets in the ARs for f; the program's instructions occupy a fixed area of memory, are not self-modifying, and are separate from the program's data. If the executable conforms to this model, CodeSurfer/x86 creates an IR for it. If it does not conform to the model, then one or more violations will be discovered, and corresponding error reports are issued.

The goal for CodeSurfer/x86 is to provide (i) a tool for security analysis, and (ii) a general infrastructure for additional analysis of executables. Thus, as a practical measure, when the system produces an error report, a choice is made about how to accommodate the error so that analysis can continue (i.e., the error is optimistically treated as a false positive), and an IR is produced; if the analyst can determine that the error report is indeed a false positive, then the IR is valid.

The analyzer does not care whether the program was compiled from a high-level language, or hand-written in assembly code. In fact, some pieces of the program may be the output from a compiler (or from multiple compilers, for different high-level languages), and others hand-written assembly code. Still, it is easiest to talk about the information that VSA and ASI are capable of recovering in terms of the features that a high-level programming language allows: VSA and ASI are capable of recovering information from programs that use global variables, local variables, pointers, structures, arrays, dynamically allocated storage, pointer arithmetic, indirect jumps, recursive procedures, indirect calls through function pointers, virtual-function calls, and DLLs (but, at present, not run-time code generation or self-modifying code).

Compiler optimizations often make VSA and ASI *less* difficult, because more of the computation's critical data resides in registers, rather than in memory; register operations are more easily deciphered than memory operations.

The major assumption that we make about IDAPro is that it is able to disassemble a program and build an adequate collection of *preliminary* IRs for it. Even though (i) the CFG created by IDAPro may be incomplete due to indirect jumps, and (ii) the call-graph created by IDAPro may be incomplete due to indirect calls, incomplete IRs do *not* trigger error reports. Both the CFG and the call graph are fleshed out according to information recovered during the course of VSA/ASI iteration. In fact, the relationship between VSA/ASI iteration and the preliminary IRs created by IDAPro is similar to the relationship between a points-to-analysis algorithm in a C compiler and the preliminary IRs created by the C compiler's front end. In both cases, the preliminary IRs are fleshed out during the course of analysis.

3.4 Model-Checking Facilities

Model checking [13] involves the use of sophisticated pattern-matching techniques to answer questions about the flow of execution in a program: a model of the program's possible behavior is created and checked for conformance with a model of expected behavior (as specified by a user query). In essence, model-checking algorithms explore the program's state-space and answer questions about whether a bad state can be reached during an execution of the program.

For model checking, the CodeSurfer/x86 IRs are used to build a *weighted pushdown system* (WPDS) [8, 39, 40, 33] that models possible program behaviors. WPDSs generalize a model-checking technology known as *pushdown systems* (PDSs) [7, 23], which have been used for software model checking in the Moped [42, 41] and MOPS [11] systems. Compared to ordinary (unweighted) PDSs, WPDSs are capable of representing more powerful kinds of abstractions of runtime states [40, 33], and hence go beyond the capabilities of PDSs. For instance, the use of WPDSs provides a way to address certain kinds of security-related queries that cannot be answered by MOPS.

WPDS++ [32] is a library that implements the symbolic algorithms from [40, 33] for solving WPDS reachability problems. We follow the standard approach of using a PDS to model the interprocedural CFG (one of CodeSurfer/x86's IRs). The stack symbols correspond to program locations; there is only a single PDS state; and PDS rules encode control flow as follows:

Rule	Control flow modeled
$q\langle u \rangle \hookrightarrow q\langle v \rangle$	Intraprocedural CFG edge $u \to v$
$q\langle c \rangle \hookrightarrow q\langle entry_P\ r \rangle$	Call to P from c that returns to r
$q\langle x \rangle \hookrightarrow q\langle \rangle$	Return from a procedure at exit node x

In a configuration of the PDS, the symbol at the top of the stack corresponds to the current program location, and the rest of the stack holds return-site locations—this allows the PDS to model the behavior of the program's runtime execution stack.

An encoding of the interprocedural CFG as a PDS is sufficient for answering queries about reachable control states (as the Path Inspector does; see below): the reachability algorithms of WPDS++ can determine if an undesirable PDS configuration is reachable. However, WPDS++ also supports *weighted* PDSs, which are PDSs in which each rule is weighted with an element of a (user-defined) semiring. The use of weights allows WPDS++ to perform interprocedural dataflow analysis by using the semiring's *extend* operator to compute weights for sequences of rule firings and using the semiring's *combine* operator to take the join of weights generated by different paths [40, 33]. (When the weights on rules are conservative abstract data transformers, an over-approximation to the set of reachable concrete configurations is obtained, which means that counterexamples reported by WPDS++ may actually be infeasible.)

The advantage of answering reachability queries on WPDSs over conventional dataflow-analysis methods is that the latter merge together the values for all states associated with the same program point, regardless of the states' calling context. With WPDSs, queries can be posed with respect to a regular language of stack configurations [8, 39, 40, 33]. (Conventional merged dataflow information can also be obtained [40].)

CodeSurfer/x86 can also be used in conjunction with GrammaTech's Path Inspector tool. The Path Inspector provides a user interface for automating safety queries that are only concerned with the possible control configurations that an executable can reach. The Path Inspector checks *sequencing properties* of events in a program, which can be used to answer such questions as "Is it possible for the program to bypass the authentication routine?" (which indicates that the program may contain a trapdoor), or "Can this *login* program bypass the code that writes to the log file?" (which indicates that the program may be a Trojan *login* program).

With the Path Inspector, such questions are posed as questions about the existence of problematic event sequences; after checking the query, if a problematic path exists, it is displayed in the Path Inspector tool. This lists all of the program points that may occur along the problematic path. These items are linked to the source code; the analyst can navigate from a point in the path to the corresponding source-code element. In addition, the Path Inspector allows the analyst to step forward and backward through the path, while simultaneously stepping through the source code. (The code-stepping operations are similar to the single-stepping operations in a traditional debugger.)

The Path Inspector uses an automaton-based approach to model checking: the query is specified as a finite automaton that captures forbidden sequences of program locations. This "query automaton" is combined with the program model (a WPDS) using a cross-product construction, and the reachability algorithms of WPDS++ are used to determine if an error configuration is reachable. If an error configuration is reachable, then *witnesses* (see [40]) can be used to produce a program path that drives the query automaton to an error state.

The Path Inspector includes a GUI for instantiating many common reachability queries [20], and for displaying counterexample paths in the disassembly listing. In the current implementation, transitions in the query automaton are triggered by program points that the user specifies either manually, or using result sets from CodeSurfer queries. Future versions of the Path Inspector will support more sophisticated queries in which transitions are triggered by matching an abstract-syntax-tree pattern against a program location, and query states can be instantiated based on pattern bindings.

3.5 Related Work

Previous work on analyzing memory accesses in executables has dealt with memory accesses very conservatively: generally, if a register is assigned a value from memory, it is assumed to take on any value. VSA does a much better job than previous work because it tracks the integer-valued and address-valued quantities that the program's data objects can hold; in particular, VSA tracks the values of data objects other than just the hardware registers, and thus is not forced to give up all precision when a load from memory is encountered.

The basic goal of the algorithm proposed by Debray et al. [19] is similar to that of VSA: for them, it is to find an over-approximation of the set of values that each *register* can hold at each program point; for us, it is to find an over-approximation of the set of values that each (abstract) data object can hold at each program point, where data objects include *memory locations* in addition to registers. In their analysis, a set of addresses is approximated by a set of congruence values: they keep track of only the low-order bits of addresses. However, unlike VSA, their algorithm does not make any effort to track values that are not in registers. Consequently, they lose a great deal of precision whenever there is a load from memory.

Cifuentes and Fraboulet [12] give an algorithm to identify an intraprocedural slice of an executable by following the program's use-def chains. However, their algorithm also makes no attempt to track values that are not in registers, and hence cuts short the slice when a load from memory is encountered.

The two pieces of work that are most closely related to VSA are the algorithm for data-dependence analysis of assembly code of Amme et al. [2] and the algorithm for pointer analysis on a low-level intermediate representation of Guo et al. [25]. The algorithm of Amme et al. performs only an *intra*procedural analysis, and it is not clear whether the algorithm fully accounts for dependences between memory locations. The algorithm of Guo et al. [25] is only partially flow-sensitive: it tracks registers in a flow-sensitive manner, but treats memory locations in a flow-insensitive manner. The algorithm uses partial transfer functions [45] to achieve context-sensitivity. The transfer functions are parameterized by "unknown initial values" (UIVs); however, it is not clear whether the the algorithm accounts for the possibility of called procedures corrupting the memory locations that the UIVs represent.

References

1. . . *.   PREfast with driver-specific rules, Oct. 2004.   WHDC, Microsoft Corp., http://www.microsoft.com/whdc/devtools/tools/PREfast-drv.mspx.

2. W. Amme, P. Braun, E. Zehendner, and F. Thomasset. Data dependence analysis of assembly code. *Int. J. Parallel Proc.*, 2000.
3. G. Balakrishnan and T. Reps. Analyzing memory accesses in x86 executables. In *Comp. Construct.*, pages 5–23, 2004.
4. G. Balakrishnan and T. Reps. Recency-abstraction for heap-allocated storage. In *Static Analysis Symp.*, 2006.
5. G. Balakrishnan, T. Reps, D. Melski, and T. Teitelbaum. WYSINWYX: What You See Is Not What You eXecute. In *IFIP Working Conf. on Verified Software: Theories, Tools, Experiments*, 2005.
6. T. Ball and S. Rajamani. The SLAM toolkit. In *Computer Aided Verif.*, volume 2102 of *Lec. Notes in Comp. Sci.*, pages 260–264, 2001.
7. A. Bouajjani, J. Esparza, and O. Maler. Reachability analysis of pushdown automata: Application to model checking. In *Proc. CONCUR*, volume 1243 of *Lec. Notes in Comp. Sci.*, pages 135–150. Springer-Verlag, 1997.
8. A. Bouajjani, J. Esparza, and T. Touili. A generic approach to the static analysis of concurrent programs with procedures. In *Princ. of Prog. Lang.*, pages 62–73, 2003.
9. W. Bush, J. Pincus, and D. Sielaff. A static analyzer for finding dynamic programming errors. *Software–Practice&Experience*, 30:775–802, 2000.
10. H. Chen, D. Dean, and D. Wagner. Model checking one million lines of C code. In *Network and Dist. Syst. Security*, 2004.
11. H. Chen and D. Wagner. MOPS: An infrastructure for examining security properties of software. In *Conf. on Comp. and Commun. Sec.*, pages 235–244, Nov. 2002.
12. C. Cifuentes and A. Fraboulet. Intraprocedural static slicing of binary executables. In *Int. Conf. on Softw. Maint.*, pages 188–195, 1997.
13. E. Clarke, Jr., O. Grumberg, and D. Peled. *Model Checking*. The M.I.T. Press, 1999.
14. CodeSurfer, GrammaTech, Inc., http://www.grammatech.com/products/codesurfer/.
15. J. Corbett, M. Dwyer, J. Hatcliff, S. Laubach, C. Pasareanu, Robby, and H. Zheng. Bandera: Extracting finite-state models from Java source code. In *Int. Conf. on Softw. Eng.*, pages 439–448, 2000.
16. P. Cousot and R. Cousot. Abstract interpretation: A unified lattice model for static analysis of programs by construction of approximation of fixed points. In *Princ. of Prog. Lang.*, pages 238–252, 1977.
17. D. Coutant, S. Meloy, and M. Ruscetta. DOC: A practical approach to source-level debugging of globally optimized code. In *Prog. Lang. Design and Impl.*, 1988.
18. M. Das, S. Lerner, and M. Seigle. ESP: Path-sensitive program verification in polynomial time. In *Prog. Lang. Design and Impl.*, pages 57–68, New York, NY, 2002. ACM Press.
19. S. Debray, R. Muth, and M. Weippert. Alias analysis of executable code. In *Princ. of Prog. Lang.*, pages 12–24, 1998.
20. M. Dwyer, G. Avrunin, and J. Corbett. Patterns in property specifications for finite-state verification. In *Int. Conf. on Softw. Eng.*, 1999.
21. D. Engler, B. Chelf, A. Chou, and S. Hallem. Checking system rules using system-specific, programmer-written compiler extensions. In *Op. Syst. Design and Impl.*, pages 1–16, 2000.
22. J. Ferrante, K. Ottenstein, and J. Warren. The program dependence graph and its use in optimization. *Trans. on Prog. Lang. and Syst.*, 3(9):319–349, 1987.
23. A. Finkel, B.Willems, and P. Wolper. A direct symbolic approach to model checking pushdown systems. *Elec. Notes in Theor. Comp. Sci.*, 9, 1997.
24. Fast Library Identification and Recognition Technology, DataRescue sa/nv, Liège, Belgium, http://www.datarescue.com/idabase/flirt.htm.

25. B. Guo, M. Bridges, S. Triantafyllis, G. Ottoni, E. Raman, and D. August. Practical and accurate low-level pointer analysis. In *3nd Int. Symp. on Code Gen. and Opt.*, pages 291–302, 2005.
26. K. Havelund and T. Pressburger. Model checking Java programs using Java PathFinder. *Softw. Tools for Tech. Transfer*, 2(4), 2000.
27. J. Hennessy. Symbolic debugging of optimized code. *Trans. on Prog. Lang. and Syst.*, 4(3):323–344, 1982.
28. T. Henzinger, R. Jhala, R. Majumdar, and G. Sutre. Lazy abstraction. In *Princ. of Prog. Lang.*, pages 58–70, 2002.
29. S. Horwitz, T. Reps, and D. Binkley. Interprocedural slicing using dependence graphs. *Trans. on Prog. Lang. and Syst.*, 12(1):26–60, Jan. 1990.
30. M. Howard. Some bad news and some good news. Oct. 2002. MSDN, Microsoft Corp., http://msdn.microsoft.com/library/default.asp?url=/library/en-us/dncode/html/secure10102002.asp.
31. IDAPro disassembler, http://www.datarescue.com/idabase/.
32. N. Kidd, T. Reps, D. Melski, and A. Lal. WPDS++: A C++ library for weighted pushdown systems, 2004. http://www.cs.wisc.edu/wpis/wpds++/.
33. A. Lal, T. Reps, and G. Balakrishnan. Extended weighted pushdown systems. In *Computer Aided Verif.*, 2005.
34. M. Müller-Olm and H. Seidl. Analysis of modular arithmetic. In *European Symp. on Programming*, 2005.
35. G. Ramalingam, J. Field, and F. Tip. Aggregate structure identification and its application to program analysis. In *Princ. of Prog. Lang.*, pages 119–132, 1999.
36. T. Reps, G. Balakrishnan, and J. Lim. Intermediate-representation recovery from low-level code. In *Part. Eval. and Semantics-Based Prog. Manip.*, 2006.
37. T. Reps, G. Balakrishnan, J. Lim, and T. Teitelbaum. A next-generation platform for analyzing executables. In *Asian Symp. on Prog. Lang. and Systems*, 2005.
38. T. Reps and G. Rosay. Precise interprocedural chopping. In *Found. of Softw. Eng.*, 1995.
39. T. Reps, S. Schwoon, and S. Jha. Weighted pushdown systems and their application to interprocedural dataflow analysis. In *Static Analysis Symp.*, 2003.
40. T. Reps, S. Schwoon, S. Jha, and D. Melski. Weighted pushdown systems and their application to interprocedural dataflow analysis. *Sci. of Comp. Prog.*, 58(1–2):206–263, Oct. 2005.
41. S. Schwoon. Moped system. http://www.fmi.uni-stuttgart.de/szs/tools/moped/.
42. S. Schwoon. *Model-Checking Pushdown Systems*. PhD thesis, Technical Univ. of Munich, Munich, Germany, July 2002.
43. D. Wagner, J. Foster, E. Brewer, and A. Aiken. A first step towards automated detection of buffer overrun vulnerabilities. In *Network and Dist. Syst. Security*, Feb. 2000.
44. D. Wall. Systems for late code modification. In R. Giegerich and S. Graham, editors, *Code Generation – Concepts, Tools, Techniques*, pages 275–293. Springer-Verlag, 1992.
45. R. Wilson and M. Lam. Efficient context-sensitive pointer analysis for C programs. In *Prog. Lang. Design and Impl.*, pages 1–12, 1995.
46. P. Zellweger. *Interactive Source-Level Debugging of Optimized Programs*. PhD thesis, Univ. of California, Berkeley, 1984.

4

Behavioral and Structural Properties of Malicious Code

Christopher Kruegel

Secure Systems Lab, Technical University Vienna
chris@seclab.tuwien.ac.at

Summary. Most current systems to detect malicious code rely on syntactic signatures. More precisely, these systems use a set of byte strings that characterize known malware instances. Unfortunately, this approach is not able to identify previously unknown malicious code for which no signature exists. The problem gets exacerbated when the malware is polymorphic or metamorphic. In this case, different instances of the same malicious code have a different syntactic representation.

In this chapter, we introduce techniques to characterize behavioral and structural properties of binary code. These techniques can be used to generate more abstract, semantically-rich descriptions of malware, and to characterize classes of malicious code instead of specific instances. This makes the specification more robust against modifications of the syntactic layout of the code. Also, in some cases, it allows the detection of novel malware instances.

4.1 Introduction

Malicious code (or malware) is defined as software that fulfills the deliberately harmful intent of an attacker when run. Typical examples of malware include viruses, worms, and spyware. The damage caused by malicious code has dramatically increased in the past few years. This is due to both the popularity of the Internet, which leads to a significant increase in the number of available vulnerable machines, and the sophistication of the malicious code itself.

Current systems to detect malicious code (most prominently, virus scanners) are mostly based on syntactic signatures, which specify byte sequences that are characteristic of particular malware instances. This approach has two drawbacks. First, specifying precise, syntactic signatures makes it necessary to update the signature database whenever a previously unknown malware sample is found. As a result, there is always a window of vulnerability between the appearance of a new malicious code instance and the availability of a signature that can detect it. Second, malicious code can be metamorphic. That is, the malware code mutates while reproducing or spreading across the network, thereby rendering detection using signatures completely ineffective.

In this chapter, we will discuss approaches to characterize higher-level properties of malicious code. These properties are captured by abstract models that describe the behavior and structure of malicious code. The key idea is that semantic or structural properties are more difficult to change between different malware variations. Therefore, our approach results in a more general and robust description of malicious code that is not affected by syntactic changes in the binary image. To demonstrate the effectiveness of our approach, we introduce a technique to describe and detect kernel-level rootkits based on their behavior in Section 4.2. In addition, in Section 4.3, we describe a mechanism to capture the structure of executables and its use to identify metamorphic worms.

4.2 Behavioral Identification of Rootkits

A rootkit is a collection of tools often used by an attacker after gaining administrative privileges on a host. This collection includes tools to hide the presence of the attacker (e.g., log editors), utilities to gather information about the system and its environment (e.g., network sniffers), tools to ensure that the attacker can regain access at a later time (e.g., backdoored servers), and means of attacking other systems. Even though the idea of a rootkit is to provide all the tools that may be needed after a system has been compromised, rootkits focus in particular on backdoored programs and tools to hide the attacker from the system administrator. Originally, rootkits mainly included modified versions of system auditing programs (e.g., ps or netstat for Unix systems) [10]. These modified programs (also called *Trojan horses*) do not return any information to the administrator about specific files and processes used by the intruder, making the intruder "invisible" to the administrator's eyes. Such tools, however, are easily detected using file integrity checkers such as Tripwire [3].

Recently, a new type of rootkit has emerged. These rootkits are implemented as loadable kernel modules (LKMs). A loadable kernel module is an extension to the operating system (e.g., a device driver) that can be loaded into and unloaded from the kernel at runtime. This runtime kernel extension is supported by many Unix-style operating systems, most notably Solaris and Linux. When loaded, a kernel module has access to the symbols exported by the kernel and can modify any data structure or function pointer that is accessible. Typically, these kernel rootkits "hijack" entries in the system call table and provide modified implementations of the corresponding system call functions [11, 17]. These modified system calls often perform checks on the data passed back to a user process and can thus efficiently hide information about files and processes. An interesting variation is implemented by the adore-ng rootkit [18, 19]. In this case, the rootkit does not modify the system call table, but, instead, hijacks the routines used by the Virtual File System (VFS), and, therefore, it is able to intercept (and tamper with) calls that access files in both the /proc file system and the root file system. In any case, once the kernel is infected, it is very hard to determine if a system has been compromised without the help of hardware extensions, such as the TCPA chip [13].

4.2.1 Rootkit Detection

In the following, we introduce a technique for the detection of kernel rootkits in the Linux operating system. The technique is based on the general specification of the behavior of a rootkit. Using static analysis (more precisely, symbolic execution), an unknown kernel module is checked for code that exhibits the malicious behavior. If such code is found, the module is classified as rootkit. The advantage of our method compared to byte string signatures is the fact that our specification describes a general property of a *class* of kernel rootkits. As a result, our technique has the capability to identify previously unknown instances. Also, it is robust to obfuscation techniques that change the syntactic layout of the code but retain its semantics.

The idea for our detection approach is based on the observation that the runtime behavior of regular kernel modules (e.g., device drivers) differs significantly from the behavior of kernel rootkits. We note that regular modules have different goals than rootkits, and thus implement different functionality. Our analysis is performed in two steps. First, we have to specify undesirable behavior. Second, each kernel module binary is statically analyzed for the presence of instructions sequences that implement these specifications.

Currently, our specifications are given informally, and the analysis step has to be adjusted appropriately to deal with new specifications. Although it might be possible to introduce a formal mechanism to model behavioral specifications, it is not necessary for our detection prototype. The reason is that a few general specifications are sufficient to accurately capture the malicious behavior of all current LKM-based rootkits. Nevertheless, the analysis technique is powerful enough that it can be easily extended. This may become necessary when rootkit authors actively attempt to evade detection by changing the code such that it does not adhere to any of our specifications.

4.2.2 Specification of Behavior

A specification of malicious behavior has to model a sequence of instructions that is characteristic for rootkits but that does not appear in regular modules (at least, with a high probability). That is, we have to analyze the behavior of rootkits to derive appropriate specifications that can be used during the analysis step.

In general, kernel modules (e.g., device drivers) initialize their internal data structures during startup and then interact with the kernel via function calls, using both system calls or functions internal to the kernel. In particular, it is not often necessary that a module directly writes to kernel memory. Some exceptions include device drivers that read from and write to memory areas that are associated with a managed device and that are mapped into the kernel address space to provide more efficient access or modules that overwrite function pointers to register themselves for event callbacks.

Kernel rootkits, on the other hand, usually write directly to kernel memory to alter important system management data structures. The purpose is to intercept the regular control flow of the kernel when system services are requested by a user process. This is done in order to monitor or change the results that are returned by these services to the user process. Because system calls are the most obvious entry point for requesting kernel services, the earliest kernel rootkits modified the system call table accordingly. For example, one of the first actions of the knark [11] rootkit is to exchange entries in the system call table with customized functions to hide files and processes.

In newer kernel releases, the system call table is no longer exported by the kernel, and thus it cannot be directly accessed by kernel modules. Therefore, alternative approaches to influence the results of operating system services have been investigated. One such solution is to monitor accesses to the /proc file system. This is accomplished by changing the function addresses in the /proc file system root node that point to the corresponding read and write functions. Because the /proc file system is used by many auditing applications to gather information about the system (e.g., about running processes, or open network connections), a rootkit can easily hide important information by filtering the output that is passed back to the application. An example of this approach is the adore-ng rootkit [19] that replaces functions of the virtual file system (VFS) node of the /proc file system.

As a general observation, we note that rootkits perform writes to a number of locations in the kernel address space that are usually not touched by regular modules. These writes are necessary either to obtain control over system services (e.g., by changing the system call table, file system functions, or the list of active processes) or to hide the presence of the kernel rootkit itself (e.g., modifying the list of installed modules). Because write operations to operating system management structures are required to implement the needed functionality, and because these writes are unique to kernel rootkits, they present a salient opportunity to specify malicious behavior.

To be more precise, we identify a loadable kernel module as a rootkit based on the following two behavioral specifications:

1. The module contains a data transfer instruction that performs a write operation to an illegal memory area, or
2. the module contains an instruction sequence that i) uses a *forbidden* kernel symbol reference to calculate an address in the kernel's address space and ii) performs a write operation using this address.

Whenever the destination address of a data transfer can be determined statically during the analysis step, it is possible to check whether this address is within a legitimate area. The notion of legitimate areas is defined by a white-list that specifies the kernel addressed that can be safely written to. For our current system, these areas include function pointers used as event callback hooks (e.g., br_ioctl_hook()) or exported arrays (e.g., blk_dev).

One drawback of the first specification is the fact that the destination address must be derivable during the static analysis process. Therefore, a complementary specification is introduced that checks for writes to any memory address that is calculated using a forbidden kernel symbol.

A kernel symbol refers to a kernel variable with its corresponding address that is exported by the kernel (e.g., via /proc/ksysm). These symbols are needed by the module loader, which loads and inserts modules into the kernel address space.

When a kernel module is loaded, all references to external variables that are declared in this module but defined in the kernel (or in other modules) have to be *patched* appropriately. This patching process is performed by substituting the place holder addresses of the declared variables in the module with the actual addresses of the corresponding symbols in the kernel.

The notion of forbidden kernel symbols can be based on black-lists or white-lists. A black-list approach enumerates all forbidden symbols that are likely to be misused by rootkits, for example, the system call table, the root of the /proc file system, the list of modules, or the task structure list. A white-list, on the other hand, explicitly defines acceptable kernel symbols that can legitimately be accessed by modules. As usual, a white-list approach is more restrictive, but may lead to false positives when a module references a legitimate but infrequently used kernel symbol that has not been allowed previously. However, following the principle of fail-safe defaults, a white-list also provides greater assurance that the detection process cannot be circumvented.

Note that it is not necessarily malicious when a forbidden kernel symbol is declared by a module. When such a symbol is not used for a *write* access, it is not problematic. Therefore, we cannot reject a module as a rootkit by checking the declared symbols only.

Also, it is not sufficient to check for writes that target a forbidden symbol directly. Often, kernel rootkits use such symbols as a starting point for more complex address calculations. For example, to access an entry in the system call table, the system call table symbol is used as a base address that is increased by a fixed offset. Another example is the module list pointer, which is used to traverse a linked list of module elements to obtain a handle for a specific module. Therefore, a more extensive analysis has to be performed to also track indirect uses of forbidden kernel symbols for write accesses.

Naturally, there is an arms-race between rootkits that use more sophisticated methods to obtain kernel addresses, and our detection system that relies on specifications of malicious behavior. For current rootkits, our basic specifications allow for reliable detection with no false positives (see Section 4.2.4 for details). However, it might be possible to circumvent these specifications. In that case, it is necessary to provide more elaborate descriptions of malicious behavior.

Note that our behavioral specifications have the advantage that they provide a general model of undesirable behavior. That is, these specifications characterize an entire class of malicious actions. This is different from fine-grained specifications that need to be tailored to individual kernel modules.

4.2.3 Symbolic Execution

Based on the specifications introduced in the previous section, the task of the analysis step is to statically check the module binary for instructions that correspond to these specifications. When such instructions are found, the module is labeled as a rootkit.

We perform analysis on binaries using symbolic execution. Symbolic execution is a static analysis technique in which program execution is simulated using symbols, such as variable names, rather than actual values for input data. The program state and outputs are then expressed as mathematical (or logical) expressions involving these symbols. When performing symbolic execution, the program is basically executed with all possible input values simultaneously, thus allowing one to make statements about the program behavior.

In order to simulate the execution of a program, or, in our case, the execution of a loadable kernel module, it is necessary to perform two preprocessing steps.

First, the code sections of the binary have to be disassembled. In this step, the machine instructions have to be extracted and converted into a format that is suitable for symbolic execution. That is, it is not sufficient to simply print out the syntax of instructions, as done by programs such as `objdump`. Instead, the type of the operation and its operands have to be parsed into an internal representation. The disassembly step is complicated by the complexity of the Intel x86 instruction set, which uses a large number of variable-length instructions and many different addressing modes for backward-compatibility reasons.

In the second preprocessing step, it is necessary to adjust address operands in all code sections present. The reason is that a Linux loadable kernel module is merely a standard ELF relocatable object file. Therefore, many memory address operands have not been assigned their final values yet. These memory address operands include targets of jump and call instructions but also source and destination locations of load, store, and move instructions.

For a regular relocatable object file, the addresses are adjusted by the linker. To enable the necessary link operations, a relocatable object also contains, besides regular code and data sections, a set of relocation entries. Note, however, that kernel modules are not linked to the kernel code by a regular linker. Instead, the necessary adjustment (i.e., patching) of addresses takes place during module load time by a special module loader. For Linux kernels up to version 2.4, most of the module loader ran in user-space; for kernels from version 2.5 and up, much of this functionality was moved into the kernel. To be able to simulate execution, we perform a process similar to linking and substitute place holders in instruction operands and data locations with the real addresses. This has the convenient side-effect that we can mark operands that represent forbidden kernel symbols so that the symbolic execution step can later trace their use in write operations.

When the loadable kernel module has been disassembled and the necessary address modifications have occurred, the symbolic execution process can commence. To be precise, the analysis starts with the kernel module's initialization routine, called `init_module()`. More details about a possible realization of the binary symbolic execution process can be found in [4]. During the analysis, for each data transfer instruction, it is checked whether data is written to kernel memory areas that are not explicitly permitted by the white-list, or whether data is written to addresses that are tainted because of the use of forbidden symbols. When an instruction is found that violates the specification of permitted behavior, the module is flagged as a kernel rootkit.

4.2.4 Evaluation

The proposed rootkit detection algorithm was implemented as a user-space prototype that simulated the object parsing and symbol resolution performed by the existing kernel module loader before disassembling the module and analyzing the code for the presence of malicious writes to kernel memory.

To evaluate the detection capabilities of our system, three sets of kernel modules were created. The first set comprised the knark and adore-ng rootkits, both of which were used during development of the prototype. As mentioned previously, both rootkits implement different methods of subverting the control flow of the kernel: knark overwrites entries in the system call table to redirect various system calls to its own handlers, while adore-ng patches itself into the VFS layer of the kernel to intercept accesses to the /proc file system. Since each rootkit was extensively analyzed during the prototype development phase, it was expected that all malicious kernel accesses would be discovered by the prototype.

Table 4.1. Evaluation rootkits.

Rootkit	Technique	Description
adore	syscalls	File, directory, process, and socket hiding
		Rootshell backdoor
all-root	syscalls	Gives all processes UID 0
kbdv3	syscalls	Gives special user UID 0
kkeylogger	syscalls	Logs keystrokes from local and network logins
rkit	syscalls	Gives special user UID 0
shtroj2	syscalls	Execute arbitrary programs as UID 0
synapsys	syscalls	File, directory, process, socket, and module hiding
		Gives special user UID 0

The second set consisted of a set of seven additional popular rootkits downloaded from the Internet, described in Table 4.1. Since these rootkits were not analyzed during the prototype development phase, the detection rate for this group can be considered a measure of the generality of the detection technique as applied against previously unknown rootkits that utilize similar means to subvert the kernel as knark and adore-ng.

The final set consisted of a control group of legitimate kernel modules, namely the entire default set of kernel modules for the Fedora Core 1 Linux x86 distribution. This set includes 985 modules implementing various components of the Linux kernel, including networking protocols (e.g., IPv6), bus protocols (e.g., USB), file systems (e.g., EXT3), and device drivers (e.g., network interfaces, video cards). It was assumed that no modules incorporating rootkit functionality were present in this set.

Table 4.2 presents the results of the detection evaluation for each of the three sets of modules. As expected, all malicious writes to kernel memory by both knark and adore-ng were detected, resulting in a false negative rate of 0% for both rootkits.

Table 4.2. Detection results.

Module Set	Modules Analyzed	Detections	Misclassification Rate
Development rootkits	2	2	0 (0%)
Evaluation rootkits	6	6	0 (0%)
Fedora Core 1 modules	985	0	0 (0%)

All malicious writes by each evaluation rootkit were detected as well, resulting in a false negative rate of 0% for this set. We interpret this result as an indication that the detection technique generalizes well to previously unseen rootkits. Finally, no malicious writes were reported by the prototype for the control group, resulting in a false positive rate of 0%. We thus conclude that the detection algorithm is completely successful in distinguishing rootkits exhibiting specified malicious behavior from legitimate kernel modules, as no misclassifications occurred during the entire detection evaluation.

```
kmodscan: initializing scan for rootkits/all-root.o
kmodscan: loading kernel symbol table from boot/System.map
kmodscan: kernel memory configured [c0100000-c041eaf8]
kmodscan: resolving external symbols in section .text
kmodscan: disassembling section .text
kmodscan: performing scan from [.text+40]
kmodscan: WRITE TO KERNEL MEMORY [c0347df0] at [.text+50]
kmodscan: 1 malicious write detected, denying module load
```

Fig. 4.1. all-root rootkit analysis.

To verify that the detection algorithm performed correctly on the evaluation rootkits, traces of the analysis performed by the prototype on each rootkit were examined with respect to the corresponding module code. As a simple example, consider the case of the all-root rootkit, whose analysis trace is shown in Figure 4.1. From the trace, we can see that one malicious kernel memory write was detected at .text+50 (i.e., at an offset of 50 bytes into the .text section). By examining the disassembly of the all-root module, the relevant portion of which is shown in Figure 4.2, we can see that the overwrite occurs in the module's initialization function, init_module()[1]. Specifically, the movl instruction at .text+50 is flagged as a malicious write to kernel memory. Correlating the disassembly with the corresponding rootkit source code, shown in Figure 4.3, we can see that this instruction corresponds to the write to the sys_call_table array to replace the getuid() system call handler with the module's malicious version at line 4. Thus, we conclude that the rootkit's attempt to redirect a system call was properly detected.

---

[1] Note that this disassembly was generated prior to kernel symbol resolution, thus the displayed read and write accesses are performed on place holder addresses. At runtime and for the symbolic execution, the proper memory address would be patched into the code.

```
00000040 <init_module>:
   40:    a1 60 00 00 00         mov     0x60,%eax
   45:    55                     push    %ebp
   46:    89 e5                  mov     %esp,%ebp
   48:    a3 00 00 00 00         mov     %eax,0x0
   4d:    5d                     pop     %ebp
   4e:    31 c0                  xor     %eax,%eax
   50:    c7 05 60 00 00 00 00   movl    $0x0,0x60
   57:    00 00 00
   5a:    c3                     ret
```

Fig. 4.2. all-root module disassembly.

```
1 int init_module(void)
2 {
3    orig_getuid = sys_call_table[__NR_getuid];
4    sys_call_table[__NR_getuid] = give_root;
5
6    return 0;
7 }
```

Fig. 4.3. all-root initialization function.

4.3 Structural Identification of Worms

As mentioned previously, polymorphic code can change its binary representation as part of the replication process. This can be achieved by using self-encryption mechanisms or semantics-preserving code manipulation techniques. As a consequence, copies of polymorphic malware often no longer share a common invariant substring that can be used as a detection signature.

In this section, we present a technique that uses the structural properties of an executable to identify different mutations of the same malware. This technique is resilient to code modifications that make existing detection approaches based on syntactic signatures ineffective. Our approach is based on a novel fingerprinting technique based on control flow information that allows us to detect structural similarities between variations of one malware instance or between members of the same malicious code family. The following properties are desirable for the fingerprinting technique:

- **Uniqueness.** Different executable regions should map to different fingerprints. If *identical* fingerprints are derived for *unrelated* executables, the system cannot distinguish between code that should be correlated and those that should not. If the uniqueness property is not fulfilled, the system is prone to producing false positives.
- **Robustness to insertion and deletion.** When code is added to an executable region, either by prepending it, appending it, or interleaving it with the original ex-

ecutable (i.e., *insertion*), the fingerprints for the original executable region should not change. Furthermore, when parts of a region are removed (i.e., *deletion*), the remaining fragment should still be identified as part of the original executable. Robustness against insertion and deletion is necessary to counter straightforward evasion attempts in which an attacker inserts code before or after the actual malicious code fragment.

- **Robustness to modification.** The fingerprinting mechanism has to be robust against certain code modifications. That is, even when a code sequence is modified by operations such as junk insertion, register renaming, code transposition, or instruction substitution, the resulting fingerprint should remain the same. This property is necessary to identify different variations of a single polymorphic malware program.

Our key observation is that the internal structure of an executable is more characteristic than its representation as a stream of bytes. That is, a representation that takes into account control flow decision points and the sequence in which particular parts of the code are invoked can better capture the nature of an executable and its functionality. Thus, it is more difficult for an attacker to automatically generate variations of an executable that differ in their structure than variations that map to different sequences of bytes.

For our purpose, the structure of an executable is described by its control flow graph (CFG). The nodes of the control flow graph are basic blocks. An edge from a block u to a block v represents a possible flow of control from u to v. A basic block describes a sequence of instructions without any jumps or jump targets in the middle.[2] Note that a control flow graph is not necessarily a single connected graph. It is possible (and also very likely) that it consists of a number of disjoint components.

Given two regions of executable code that belong to two different malware programs, we use their CFGs to determine if these two regions represent two polymorphic instances of the same code. This analysis, however, cannot be based on simply comparing the entire CFG of the regions because an attacker could trivially evade this technique, e.g., by adding some random code to the end of the actual malware instance. Therefore, we have developed a technique that is capable of *identifying common substructures* of two control flow graphs. We identify common substructures in control flow graphs by checking for isomorphic *connected subgraphs of size k (called k-subgraphs)* contained in all CFGs. Two subgraphs, which contain the same number of vertices k, are said to be isomorphic if they are connected in the same way. When checking whether two subgraphs are isomorphic, we only look at the edges between the nodes under analysis. Thus, incoming and outgoing edges to other nodes are ignored.

---

[2] More formally, a basic block is defined as a sequence of instructions where the instruction in each position dominates, or always executes before, all those in later positions, and no other instruction executes between two instructions in the sequence. Directed edges between blocks represent jumps in the control flow, which are caused by control transfer instructions (CTIs) such as calls, conditional and unconditional jumps, or return instructions.

Two code regions are *related* if they share common k-subgraphs. Consider the example of the two control flow graphs in Figure 4.4. While these two graphs appear different at a first glance, closer examination reveals that they share a number of common 4-subgraphs. For example, nodes A to D form connected subgraphs that are isomorphic. Note that the number of the incoming edges is different for the A nodes in both graphs. However, only edges from and to nodes that are part of the subgraph are considered for the isomorphism test.

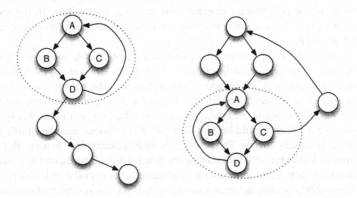

Fig. 4.4. Two control flow graphs with an example of a common 4-subgraph.

Different subgraphs have to map to different fingerprints to satisfy the uniqueness property. The approach is robust to insertion and deletion because two CFGs are related as long as they share sufficiently large, isomorphic subgraphs. In addition, while it is quite trivial for an attacker to modify the string representation of an executable to generate many variations automatically, the situation is different for the CFG representation. Register renaming and instruction substitution (assuming that the instruction is not a control flow instruction) have no influence on the CFG. Also, the reordering of instructions within a basic block and the reordering of the layout of basic blocks in the executable result in the same control flow graph. This makes the CFG representation more robust to code modifications in comparison to syntax-based techniques.

To refine the specification of the control flow graph, we also take into account information derived from each basic block, or, to be more precise, from the instructions in each block. This allows us distinguish between blocks that contain significantly different instructions. For example, the system should handle a block that contains a system call invocation differently from one that does not. To represent information about basic blocks, a *color* is assigned to each node in the control flow graph. This color is derived from the instructions in each block. The block coloring technique is used when identifying common substructures, that is, two subgraphs (with k nodes) are isomorphic only if the vertices are connected in the same way *and* the color of each vertex pair matches. Using graph coloring, the characterization of an executable region can be significantly improved. This reduces the amount of graphs that are incorrectly considered related and lowers the false positive rate.

4.3.1 Control Flow Graph Extraction

The initial task of our system is to construct a control flow graph from the program(s) that should be analyzed. This requires two steps. In the first step, we perform a linear disassembly of the byte stream to extract the machine instructions. In the second step, based on this sequence of instructions, we use standard techniques to create a control flow graph.

Constructing a control flow graph is easy when the executable program is directly available (e.g., as an email attachment or as a file in the file system). However, the situation is very different in the case of network flows. The reason is that it is not known *a priori* where executable code regions are located within a network stream or whether the stream contains executable code at all. Thus, it is not immediately clear which parts of a stream should be disassembled. Nevertheless, network traffic must be analyzed to identify worms. The problem of finding executables in network traffic is exacerbated by the fact that for many instruction set architectures, and in particular for the Intel x86 instruction set, most bit combinations map to valid instructions. As a result, it is highly probable that even a stream of random bytes could be disassembled into a valid instruction sequence. This makes it very difficult to reliably distinguish between valid code areas and random bytes (or ASCII text) by checking only for the presence or absence of valid instructions.

We address this problem by disassembling the entire byte stream first and deferring the identification of "meaningful" code regions after the construction of the CFG. This approach is motivated by the observation that the structure (i.e., the CFG) of actual code differs significantly from the structure of random instruction sequences. The CFG of actual code contains large clusters of closely connected basic blocks, while the CFG of a random sequence usually contains mostly single, isolated blocks or small clusters. The reason is that the disassembly of non-code byte streams results in a number of invalid basic blocks that can be removed from the CFG, causing it to break into many small fragments. A basic block is considered invalid **(i)** if it contains one or more invalid instructions, **(ii)** if it is on a path to an invalid block, or **(iii)** if it ends in a control transfer instruction that jumps into the middle of another instruction.

As mentioned previously, we analyze connected components with at least k nodes (i.e., k-subgraphs) to identify common subgraphs. Because random instruction sequences usually produce subgraphs that have less than k nodes, the vast majority of non-code regions are automatically excluded from further analysis. Thus, we do not require an explicit and *a priori* division of the network stream into different regions nor an oracle that can determine if a stream contains a worm or not. Experimental results (presented in [5]) support our claim that code and non-code regions can be differentiated based on the shape of the control flows.

Another problem that arises when disassembling a network stream is that there are many different processor types that use completely different formats to encode instructions. In our current system, we focus on executable code for Intel x86 only. This is motivated by the fact that the vast majority of vulnerable machines on the Internet (which are the potential targets for malware) are equipped with Intel x86 compatible processors.

As we perform linear disassembly from the start (i.e., the first byte) of a stream, it is possible that the start of the first valid instruction in that stream is "missed". As we mentioned before, it is probable that non-code regions can be disassembled. If the last invalid instruction in the non-code region overlaps with the first valid instruction, the sequence of actual, valid instructions in the stream and the output of the disassembler will be different (i.e., de-synchronized). An example of a missed first instruction is presented in Figure 4.5. In this example, an invalid instruction with a length of three bytes starts one byte before the first valid instruction, which is missed by two bytes.

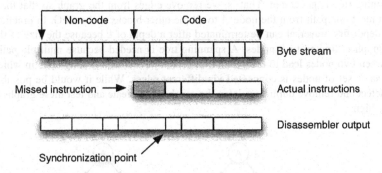

Fig. 4.5. Linear disassembler misses the start of the first valid instruction.

We cannot expect that network flows contain code that corresponds to a valid executable (e.g., in the ELF or Windows PE format), and, in general, it is not possible, to identify the first valid instruction in a stream. Fortunately, two Intel x86 instruction sequences that start at slightly different addresses (i.e., shifted by a few bytes) synchronize quickly, usually after a few (between one and three) instructions. This phenomenon, called *self-synchronizing disassembly*, is caused by the fact that Intel x86 instructions have a variable length and are usually very short. Therefore, when the linear disassembler starts at an address that does not correspond to a valid instruction, it can be expected to re-synchronize with the sequence of valid instructions very quickly [6]. In the example shown in Figure 4.5, the synchronization occurs after the first missed instruction (shown in gray). After the synchronization point, both the disassembler output and the actual instruction stream are identical.

4.3.2 K-Subgraphs and Graph Coloring

Given a control flow graph extracted from a binary program or directly from a network stream, the next task is to generate connected subgraphs of this CFG that have exactly k nodes (k-subgraphs).

The generation of k-subgraphs from the CFG is one of the main contributors to the run-time cost of the analysis. Thus, we are interested in a very efficient algorithm even if this implies that not all subgraphs are constructed. The rationale is that we assume that the number of subgraphs that are shared by two malware samples is sufficiently large that at least one is generated by the analysis. The validity of this thesis is confirmed by our experimental detection results, which are presented in Section 4.3.5.

To produce k-subgraphs, our subgraph generation algorithm is invoked for each basic block, one after another. The algorithm starts from the selected basic block A and performs a depth-first traversal of the graph. Using this depth-first traversal, a spanning tree is generated. That is, we remove edges from the graph so that there is at most one path from the node A to all the other blocks in the CFG. In practice, the depth-first traversal can be terminated after a depth of k because the size of the subgraph is limited to k nodes. A spanning tree is needed because multiple paths between two nodes lead to the generation of many redundant k-subgraphs in which the same set of nodes is connected via different edges. While it would be possible to detect and remove duplicates later, the overhead to create and test these graphs is very high.

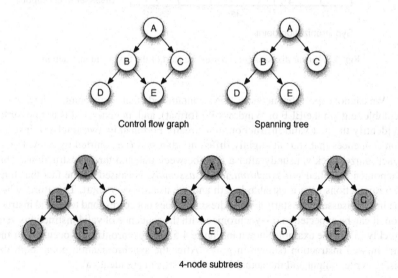

Control flow graph   Spanning tree

4-node subtrees

Fig. 4.6. Example for the operation of the subgraph generation process.

Once the spanning tree is built, we generate all possible k-node subtrees with the selected basic block A as the root node. Note that all identified subgraphs are used in their entirety, also including non-spanning-tree links. Consider the graph shown in Figure 4.6. In this example, k is 4 and node A is the root node. In the first step, the spanning tree is generated. Then, the subtrees $\{A, B, D, E\}$, $\{A, B, C, D\}$, and $\{A, B, C, E\}$ are identified. The removal of the edge from C to E causes the omission of the redundant subgraph $\{A, B, C, E\}$.

4.3.3 Graph fingerprinting

In order to quickly determine which k-subgraphs are shared between different programs or appear in different network streams, it is useful to be able to map each subgraph to a number (a fingerprint) so that two fingerprints are equal only if the corresponding subgraphs are isomorphic. This problem is known as *canonical graph labeling* [1]. The solution to this problem requires that a graph is first transformed into its canonical representation. Then, the graph is associated with a number that uniquely identifies the graph. Since isomorphic graphs are transformed into an identical canonical representation, they will also be assigned the same number.

The problem of finding the canonical form of a graph is as difficult as the graph isomorphism problem. There is no known polynomial algorithm for graph isomorphism testing; nevertheless, the problem has also not been shown to be NP-complete [15]. For many practical cases, however, the graph isomorphism test can be performed efficiently and there exist polynomial solutions. In particular, this is true for small graphs such as the ones that we have to process. We use the Nauty library [8, 9], which is generally considered to provide the fastest isomorphism testing routines, to generate the canonical representation of our k-subgraphs. Nauty can handle vertex-colored directed graphs and is well-suited to our needs.

When the graph is in its canonical form, we use its adjacency matrix to assign a unique number to it. The adjacency matrix of a graph is a matrix with rows and columns labeled by graph vertices, with a 1 or 0 in position (v_i, v_j) according to whether there is an edge from v_i to v_j or not. As our subgraphs contain a fixed number of vertices k, the size of the adjacency matrix is fixed as well (consisting of k^2 bits). To derive a fingerprint from the adjacency matrix, we simply concatenate its rows and read the result as a single k^2-bit value. This value is unique for each distinct graph since each bit of the fingerprint represents exactly one possible edge. Consider the example in Figure 4.7 that shows a graph and its adjacency matrix. By concatenating the rows of the matrix, a single 16-bit fingerprint can be derived.

Of course, when k^2 becomes too large to be practical as a fingerprint, it is also possible to hash the rows of the adjacency matrix instead of concatenating them. In this case, however, fingerprints are no longer unique and a good hash function (for example, one proposed by Jenkins [2]) has to be used to prevent frequent collisions.

4.3.4 Graph coloring

One limitation of a technique that only uses structural information to identify similarities between executables is that the machine instructions that are contained in

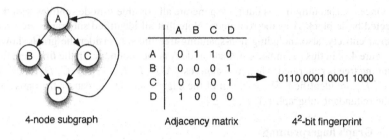

Fig. 4.7. Deriving a fingerprint from a subgraph with 4 nodes.

basic blocks are completely ignored. The idea of graph coloring addresses this shortcoming.

We devised a graph coloring technique that uses the instructions in a basic block to select a color for the corresponding node in the control flow graph. When using colored nodes, the notion of common substructures has to be extended to take into account color. That is, two subgraphs are considered isomorphic only if the vertices in both graphs are connected in the same way *and* have the same color. Including colors into the fingerprinting process requires that the canonical labeling procedure accounts for nodes of different colors. Fortunately, the Nauty routines directly provide the necessary functionality for this task. In addition, the calculation of fingerprints must be extended to account for colors. This is done by first appending the (numerical representation of the) color of a node to its corresponding row in the adjacency matrix. Then, as before, all matrix rows are concatenated to obtain the fingerprint. No further modifications are required to support colored graphs.

It is important that colors provide only a rough indication of the instructions in a basic block, that is, they must not be too closely associated with specific instructions. Otherwise, an attacker can easily evade detection by producing structurally similar executables with instructions that result in different colorings. For example, if the color of a basic block changes when an add instruction is replaced by a semantically equivalent sub (subtraction) instruction, the system could be evaded by malicious code that uses simple instruction substitution.

In our current system, we use 14-bit color values. Each bit corresponds to a certain class of instructions. When one or more instructions of a certain class appear in a basic block, the corresponding bit of the basic block's color value is set to 1. If no instruction of a certain class is present, the corresponding bit is 0.

Table 4.3 lists the 14 color classes that are used in our system. Note that it is no longer possible to substitute an add with a sub instruction, as both are part of the data transfer instruction class. However, in some cases, it might be possible to replace one instruction by an instruction in another class. For example, the value of register %eax can be set to 0 both by a mov 0, %eax instruction (which is in the data transfer class) or by a xor %eax, %eax instruction (which is a logic instruction). While instruction substitution attacks cannot be completely prevented when

Table 4.3. Color classes.

Class	Description	Class	Description
Data Transfer	mov instructions	String	x86 string operations
Arithmetic	incl. shift and rotate	Flags	access of x86 flag register
Logic	incl. bit/byte operations	LEA	load effective address
Test	test and compare	Float	floating point operations
Stack	push and pop	Syscall	interrupt and system call
Branch	conditional control flow	Jump	unconditional control flow
Call	function invocation	Halt	stop instruction execution

using color classes, they are made much more difficult for an attacker. The reason is that there are less possibilities for finding semantically equivalent instructions from different classes. Furthermore, the possible variations in color that can be generated with instructions from different classes is much less than the possible variations on the instruction level. In certain cases, it is even impossible to replace an instruction with a semantically equivalent one (e.g., when invoking a software interrupt).

4.3.5 Worm Detection

In this section, we show how the previously introduced structural properties of executables can be used to detect polymorphic worms in network traffic. To do so, we have to assume that at least some parts of a worm contain executable machine code. While it is possible that certain regions of the code are encrypted, others have to be directly executable by the processor of the victim machine (e.g., there will be a decryption routine to decrypt the rest of the worm). Our assumption is justified by the fact that most contemporary worms contain executable regions. For example, in the 2004 "Top 10" list of worms published by anti-virus vendors [16], all entries contain executable code. Note, however, that worms that do not use executable code (e.g., worms written in non-compiled scripting languages) will not be detected by our system. Based on our assumption, we analyze network flows for the presence of executable code. If a network flow contains no executable code, we discard it immediately. Otherwise, we derive a set of fingerprints for the executable regions.

Our algorithm to detect worms is very similar to the Earlybird approach presented in [14]. In the Earlybird system, the content of each network flow is processed, and all substrings of a certain length are extracted. Each substring is used as an index into a table, called *prevalence table*, that keeps track of how often that particular string has been seen in the past. In addition, for each string entry in the prevalence table, a list of unique source-destination IP address pairs is maintained. This list is searched and updated whenever a new substring is entered. The basic idea is that sorting this table with respect to the substring count and the size of the address lists will produce the set of likely worm traffic samples. That is, frequently occurring substrings that appear in network traffic between many hosts are an indication of worm-related activity. Moreover, these substrings can be used directly as worm signatures.

The key difference between our system and previous work is the mechanism used to index the prevalence table [12]. While Earlybird uses simple substrings, we use the fingerprints that are extracted from control flow graphs. That is, we identify worms by checking for frequently occurring executable regions that have the same structure (i.e., the same fingerprint).

This is accomplished by maintaining a set of network streams S_i for each given fingerprint f_i. Every set S_i contains the distinct source-destination IP address pairs for streams that contained f_i. A fingerprint is identified as corresponding to worm code when the following conditions on S_i are satisfied:

1. m, the number of distinct source-destination pairs contained in S_i, meets or exceeds a predefined threshold M.
2. The number of distinct internal hosts appearing in S_i is at least 2.
3. The number of distinct external hosts appearing in S_i is at least 2.

The last two conditions are required to prevent false positives that would otherwise occur when several clients inside the network download a certain executable file from an external server, or when external clients download a binary from an internal server. In both cases, the traffic patterns are different from the ones generated by a worm, for which one would expect connections between multiple hosts from both the inside and outside networks.

In a first experiment, we analyzed the capabilities of our system to detect polymorphic worms. To this end, we analyzed malicious code that was disguised by ADMmutate [7], a well-known polymorphic engine. ADMmutate operates by first encrypting the malicious payload, and then prepending a metamorphic decryption routine. To evaluate our system, we used ADMmutate to generate 100 encrypted instances of a worm, which produced a different decryption routine for each run. Then, we used our system to identify common substructures between these instances.

Our system could not identify a single fingerprint that was common to all 100 instances. However, there were 66 instances that shared one fingerprint, and 31 instances that shared another fingerprint. Only 3 instances did not share a single common fingerprint at all. A closer analysis of the generated encryption routines revealed that the structure was identical between all instances. However, ADMmutate heavily relies on instruction substitution to change the appearance of the decryption routine. In some cases, data transfer instructions were present in a basic block, but not in the corresponding block of other instances. These differences resulted in a different coloring of the nodes of the control flow graphs, leading to the generation of different fingerprints. This experiment brings to attention the possible negative impact of colored nodes on the detection. However, it also demonstrates that the worm would have been detected quickly since a vast majority of worm instances (97 out of 100) contain one of only two different fingerprints.

In order to evaluate the degree to which the system is prone to generating false detections, we evaluated it on a dataset consisting of 35.7 Gigabyte of network traffic collected over 9 days on the local network of the Distributed Systems Group at the Technical University of Vienna. This evaluation set contained 661,528 total network streams and was verified to be free of known attacks. The data consists to a large extent of HTTP (about 45%) and SMTP (about 35%) traffic. The rest is made up of a wide variety of application traffic including SSH, IMAP, DNS, NTP, FTP, and SMB traffic.

We were particularly interested in exploring the degree to which false positives can be mitigated by appropriately selecting the detection parameter M. Recall that M determines the number of unique source-destination pairs that a network stream set S_i must contain before the corresponding fingerprint f_i is considered to belong to a worm. Also recall that we require that a certain fingerprint must occur in network streams between two or more internal and external hosts, respectively, before being considered as a worm candidate. False positives occur when legitimate network usage is identified as worm activity by the system. For example, if a particular fingerprint appears in too many (benign) network flows between multiple sources and destinations, the system will identify the aggregate behavior as a worm attack. While intuitively it can be seen that larger values of M reduce the number false positives, they simultaneously delay the detection of a real worm outbreak.

Table 4.4. Incorrectly labeled fingerprints as a function of M. 1,400,174 total fingerprints were encountered in the evaluation set.

M	3	4	5	6	7	8	9	10	11
Fingerprints	12,661	7,841	7,215	3,647	3,441	3,019	2,515	1,219	1,174
M	12	13	14	15	16	17	18	19	20
Fingerprints	1,134	944	623	150	44	43	43	24	23
M	21	22	23	24	25				
Fingerprints	22	22	22	22	22				

Table 4.4 gives the number of fingerprints identified by the system as suspicious for various values of M. For comparison, 1,400,174 total fingerprints were observed in the evaluation set. This experiment indicates that increasing M beyond 20 achieves diminishing returns in the reduction of false positives (for this traffic trace). The remainder of this section discusses the root causes of the false detections for the 23 erroneously labeled fingerprint values for $M = 20$.

The 23 stream sets associated with the false positive fingerprints contained a total of 8,452 HTTP network flows. Closer inspection of these showed that the bulk of the false alarms were the result of binary resources on the site that were (a) frequently accessed by outside users and (b) replicated between two internal web servers. These accounted for 8,325 flows (98.5% of the total) and consisted of:

- 5544 flows (65.6%): An image appearing on most of the pages of a Java programming language tutorial.
- 2148 flows (25.4%): The image of a research group logo, which appears on many local pages.
- 490 flows (5.8%): A single Microsoft PowerPoint presentation.

- 227 flows (2.7%): Multiple PowerPoint presentations that were found to contain common embedded images.

The remaining 43 flows accounted for 0.5% of the total and consisted of external binary files that were accessed by local users and had fingerprints that, by random chance, collided with the 23 flagged fingerprints.

The problem of false positives caused by heavily accessed, locally hosted files could be addressed by creating a *white list* of fingerprints, gathered manually or through the use of an automated web crawler. For example, if we had prepared a white list for the 23 fingerprints that occurred in the small number of image files and the single PowerPoint presentation, we would not have reported a single false positive during the test period of 9 days.

4.4 Conclusions

In this chapter, we have introduced behavioral and structural properties of malicious code. These properties allow a more abstract specification of malware, mitigating shortcomings of syntactic signatures.

Behavioral properties are captured by analyzing the effect of a piece of code on the environment. More precisely, the behavior is specified by checking for the destination addresses of data transfer instructions. In the case of kernel modules, malicious behavior is defined as writes to forbidden regions in the kernel address space. Using symbolic execution, each kernel module is statically analyzed before it is loaded into the kernel. Whenever an illegal write is detected, this module is classified as kernel rootkit and loading is aborted.

The structure of an executable is captured by the subgraphs of the executable's control flow graph. Based on the results of graph isomorphism tests, identical structures that appear in different executables can be identified. The precision of the structural description is further refined by taking into account the classes of instructions (not their exact type) that appear in certain nodes of the control flow graph. Using structural properties of executables, the spread of polymorphic worms can be identified. To this end, our system searches for recurring structures in network flows. When the same structure is identified in connections from multiple source hosts to multiple destinations, this structure is considered to belong to a (possibly polymorphic) worm.

References

1. L. B. annd E. Luks. Canonical Labeling of Graphs. In *15th ACM Symposium on Theory of Computing*, 1983.
2. R. Jenkins. Hash Functions and Block Ciphers. http://burtleburtle.net/bob/hash/.
3. G. Kim and E. Spafford. The Design and Implementation of Tripwire: A File System Integrity Checker. Technical report, Purdue University, Nov. 1993.

4. C. Kruegel, E. Kirda, D. Mutz, W. Robertson, and G. Vigna. Automating Mimicry Attacks Using Static Binary Analysis. In *14th Usenix Security Symposium*, 2005.
5. C. Kruegel, E. Kirda, D. Mutz, W. Robertson, and G. Vigna. Polymorphic Worm Detection Using Structural Information of Executables. In *8th International Symposium on Recent Advances in Intrusion Detection (RAID)*, 2005.
6. C. Linn and S. Debray. Obfuscation of Executable Code to Improve Resistance to Static Disassembly. In *ACM Conference on Computer and Communications Security (CCS)*, 2003.
7. S. Macaulay. ADMmutate: Polymorphic Shellcode Engine. http://www.ktwo.ca/security.html.
8. B. McKay. Nauty: No AUTomorphisms, Yes? http://cs.anu.edu.au/~bdm/nauty/.
9. B. McKay. Practical graph isomorphism. *Congressus Numerantium*, 30, 1981.
10. T. Miller. T0rn rootkit analysis. http://www.ossec.net/rootkits/studies/t0rn.txt.
11. T. Miller. Analysis of the KNARK Rootkit. http://www.ossec.net/rootkits/studies/knark.txt, 2004.
12. M. Rabin. Fingerprinting by Random Polynomials. Technical report, Center for Research in Computing Techonology, Harvard University, 1981.
13. D. Safford. The Need for TCPA. IBM White Paper, October 2002.
14. S. Singh, C. Estan, G. Varghese, and S. Savage. Automated Worm Fingerprinting. In *6th Symposium on Operating System Design and Implementation (OSDI)*, 2004.
15. S. Skiena. *Implementing Discrete Mathematics: Combinatorics and Graph Theory*, chapter Graph Isomorphism. Addison-Wesley, 1990.
16. Sophos. War of the Worms: Top 10 list of worst virus outbreaks in 2004. http://www.sophos.com/pressoffice/pressrel/uk/20041208yeartopten.html.
17. Stealth. adore. http://spider.scorpions.net/~stealth, 2001.
18. Stealth. Kernel Rootkit Experiences and the Future. *Phrack Magazine*, 11(61), August 2003.
19. Stealth. adore-ng. http://stealth.7350.org/rootkits/, 2004.

5

Detection and Prevention of SQL Injection Attacks

William G.J. Halfond and Alessandro Orso

Georgia Institute of Technology
{whalfond, orso}@cc.gatech.edu

Summary. We depend on database-driven web applications for an ever increasing amount of activities, such as banking and shopping. When performing such activities, we entrust our personal information to these web applications and their underlying databases. The confidentiality and integrity of this information is far from guaranteed; web applications are often vulnerable to attacks, which can give an attacker complete access to the application's underlying database. SQL injection is a type of code-injection attack in which an attacker uses specially crafted inputs to trick the database into executing attacker-specified database commands. In this chapter, we provide an overview of the various types of SQL injection attacks and present AMNESIA, a technique for automatically detecting and preventing SQL injection attacks. AMNESIA uses static analysis to build a model of the legitimate queries an application can generate and then, at runtime, checks that all queries generated by the application comply with this model. We also present an extensive empirical evaluation of AMNESIA. The results of our evaluation indicate that AMNESIA is, at least for the cases considered, highly effective and efficient in detecting and preventing SQL injection attacks.

5.1 Introduction

SQL Injection Attacks (*SQLIAs*) have emerged as one of the most serious threats to the security of database-driven applications. In fact, the Open Web Application Security Project (OWASP), an international organization of web developers, has placed SQLIAs among the top ten vulnerabilities that a web application can have [7]. Similarly, software companies such as Microsoft [3] and SPI Dynamics have cited SQLIAs as one of the most critical vulnerabilities that software developers must address. SQL injection vulnerabilities can be particularly harmful because they allow an attacker to access the database that underlies an application. Using SQLIAs, an attacker may be able to read, modify, or even delete database information. In many cases, this information is confidential or sensitive and its loss can lead to problems such as identity theft and fraud. The list of high-profile victims of SQLIAs includes Travelocity, FTD.com, Creditcards.com, Tower Records, Guess Inc., and the Recording Industry Association of America (RIAA).

The errors that lead to SQLIAs are well understood. As with most code-injection attacks, SQLIAs are caused by insufficient validation of user input. The vulnerability occurs when input from the user is used to directly build a query to the database. If the input is not properly encoded and validated by the application, the attacker can inject malicious input that is treated as additional commands by the database. Depending on the severity of the vulnerability, the attacker can issue a wide range of SQL commands to the database. Many interactive database-driven applications, such as web applications that use user input to query their underlying databases, can be vulnerable to SQLIA. In fact, informal surveys of database-driven web applications have shown that almost 97% are potentially vulnerable to SQLIA.

Like most security vulnerabilities, SQLIAs can be prevented by using defensive coding. In practice however, this solution is very difficult to implement and enforce. As developers put new checks in place, attackers continue to innovate and find new ways to circumvent these checks. Since the state of the art in defensive coding is a moving target, it is difficult to keep developers up to date on the latest and best defensive coding practices. Furthermore, retroactively fixing vulnerable legacy applications using defensive coding practices is complicated, labor-intensive, and error-prone. These problems motivate the need for an automated and generalized solution to the SQL injection problem.

In this chapter we present AMNESIA (Analysis and Monitoring for NEutralizing SQL Injection Attacks), a fully automated technique and tool for the detection and prevention of SQLIAs.[1] AMNESIA was developed based on two key insights: (1) the information needed to predict the possible structure of all legitimate queries generated by a web application is contained within the application's code, and (2) an SQLIA, by injecting additional SQL statements into a query, would violate that structure. Based on these two insights we developed a technique against SQL injection that combines static analysis and runtime monitoring. In the static analysis phase, AMNESIA extracts from the web-application code a model that expresses all of the legitimate queries the application can generate. In the runtime monitoring phase, AMNESIA checks that all of the queries generated by the application comply with the model. Queries that violate the model are stopped and reported.

We also present an extensive empirical evaluation of AMNESIA. We evaluated AMNESIA on seven web applications, including commercial ones, and on thousands of both legitimate and illegitimate accesses to such applications. We modeled the illegitimate accesses after real attacks that are in use by hackers and penetration testing teams. In the evaluation, AMNESIA did not generate any false positives or negatives and had a very low runtime overhead. These results indicate AMNESIA is an effective and viable technique for detecting and preventing SQLIAs.

The rest of the chapter is organized as follows. Section 5.2 discusses SQLIAs and their various types. Section 5.3 illustrates our technique against SQLIAs. Section 5.4 presents an empirical evaluation of our technique. Section 5.5 compares our approach to related work. Section 5.6 concludes and discusses future directions for the work.

---

[1] An early version of this work was presented in [9].

5.2 SQL Injection Attacks Explained

The presence of an SQL injection vulnerability allows an attacker to issue commands directly to a web application's underlying database and to subvert the intended functionality of the application. Once an attacker has identified an SQLIA vulnerability, the vulnerable application becomes a conduit for the attacker to execute commands on the database and possibly the host system itself.

SQLIAs are a class of code injection attacks that take advantage of a lack of validation of user input. The vulnerabilities occur when developers combine hard-coded strings with user-input to create dynamic queries. If the user input is not properly validated, it is possible for attackers to shape their input in such a way that, when it is included in the final query string, parts of the input are evaluated as SQL keywords or operators by the database.

5.2.1 Example of an SQLIA

To illustrate how an SQLIA can occur, we introduce an example web application that is vulnerable to a type of SQLIA that we call a tautology-based attack. The architecture of this web application is shown in Figure 5.1. In this example, the user interacts with a web form that takes a login name and pin as input and submits them to the web server. The web server passes the user supplied credentials to a servlet (show.jsp, in the example), which resides on the application server. The servlet queries the database to check whether the credentials are valid and, based on the result of the query, generates a response for the user in the form of a web page. The servlet, whose partial implementation is shown in Figure 5.2, uses the user-supplied credentials to dynamically build a database query. Method getUserInfo is called with the login and pin provided by the user. If both login and pin are empty, the method submits the following query to the database:

```
SELECT info FROM users WHERE login='guest'
```

Conversely, if login and pin are specified by the user, the method embeds the submitted credentials in the query. Therefore, if a user submits login and pin as "doe" and "123," the servlet dynamically builds the query:

```
SELECT info FROM users WHERE login='doe' AND pin=123
```

A web site that uses this servlet would be vulnerable to SQLIAs. For example, if a user enters "' OR 1=1 --" and "", instead of "doe" and "123", the resulting query is:

```
SELECT info FROM users WHERE login='' OR 1=1 --' AND pin=
```

The database interprets everything after the WHERE token as a conditional statement and the inclusion of the "OR 1=1" clause turns this conditional into a tautology. (The characters "--" mark the beginning of a comment, so everything after them is ignored.) As a result, the database would return information for all user entries.

It is important to note that tautology-based attacks represent only a small subset of the different types of SQLIAs that attackers have developed. We present this type

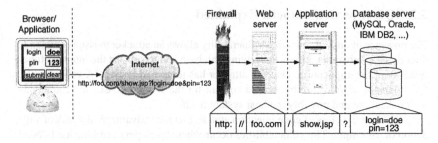

Fig. 5.1. Example of interaction between a user and a typical web application.

```
public class Show extends HttpServlet {
    ...
1.  public ResultSet getUserInfo(String login,
                                  String pin) {
2.     Connection conn = DriverManager.getConnection("MyDB");
3.     Statement stmt = conn.createStatement();
4.     String queryString = "";

5.     queryString = "SELECT info FROM users WHERE ";
6.     if ((! login.equals("")) && (! pin.equals(""))) {
7.        queryString += "login='" + login +
                         "' AND pin=" + pin;
       }
8.     else {
9.        queryString+="login='guest'";
       }
10.    ResultSet tempSet = stmt.execute(queryString);
11.    return tempSet;
    }
    ...
}
```

Fig. 5.2. Example servlet.

of attack as an example because it is fairly straightforward and intuitive. For this same reason, tautology-based attacks have been widely cited in literature and are often mistakenly viewed as the only type of SQLIAs. However, current attack techniques are not limited to only injecting tautologies. In the rest of this section, we first provide a general definition of SQLIAs and then present an overview of the currently known types of SQLIAs.

5.2.2 General Definition of SQLIA

An *SQL injection attack* occurs when an attacker changes the intended logic, semantics, or syntax of a SQL query by inserting new SQL keywords or operators. This definition includes all of the variants of SQLIAs discussed in the following subsections.

5.2.3 Variants of SQLIA

Over the past several years, attackers have developed a wide array of sophisticated attack techniques that can be used to exploit SQL injection vulnerabilities. These techniques go beyond the commonly used tautology-based SQLIA examples and take advantage of esoteric and advanced SQL constructs. Ignoring the existence of these kinds of attacks leads to the development of solutions that address the SQLIA problem only partially.

For example, SQLIA can be introduced into a program using several different types of input sources. Developers and researchers often assume that SQLIAs are only introduced via user input that is submitted as part of a web form or as a response to a prompt for input. This assumption misses the fact that any external string or input that is used to build a query string can be under the control of an attacker and represents a possible input channel for SQLIAs. It is common to see other external sources of input such as fields from an HTTP cookie or server variables being used to build a query. Since cookie values are under the control of the user's browser and server variables are often set via values from HTTP headers, these values represent external strings that can be manipulated by an attacker. In addition, *second-order injections* use advanced knowledge of a vulnerable application to introduce an attack using otherwise properly secured input sources [1]. A developer may properly escape, type-check, and filter input that comes from the user and assume it is safe. Later on, when that data is used in a different context or to build a different type of query, the previously safe input becomes an injection attack. Because there are many input sources that could lead to a SQLIA, techniques that focus on simply checking user input or explicitly enumerating all untrusted input sources are often incomplete and still leave ways for malicious input to affect the generated query strings.

Once attackers have identified an input source that can be used to exploit an SQLIA vulnerability, there are many different types of attack techniques that they can employ. Depending on the type and extent of the vulnerability, the results of these attacks can include crashing the database, gathering information about the tables in the database schema, establishing covert channels, and open-ended injection of virtually any SQL command. We briefly summarize the main techniques for performing SQLIAs using the example code from Figure 5.2. Interested readers can refer to [10] for additional information and examples of how these techniques work.

Tautologies.

The general goal of a tautology-based attack is to inject SQL tokens that cause the query's conditional statement to always evaluate to true. Although the results of this type of attack are application specific, the most common uses are to bypass authentication pages and extract data. In this type of injection, an attacker exploits a vulnerable input field that is used in the query's WHERE conditional. This conditional logic is evaluated as the database scans each row in the table. If the conditional represents a tautology, the database matches and returns all the rows in the table as opposed to matching only one row, as it would normally do in the absence of injection. We showed an example of this type of attack in Section 5.2.1.

Malformed Queries.

This attack technique takes advantage of overly descriptive error messages that are returned by the database when a query is rejected. Database error messages often contain useful debugging information that also allows an attacker to accurately identify which parameters are vulnerable in an application and the complete schema of the underlying database. Attackers exploit this situation by injecting SQL tokens or garbage input that causes the query to contain syntax errors, type mismatches, or logical errors. Consider our example, an attacker could try to cause a type mismatch error by injecting the following text into the *pin* input field: " `convert(int, (select top 1 name from sysobjects where xtype='u'))` ".

The resulting query generated by the web application would be:

```
SELECT info FROM users WHERE login='' AND pin=
convert (int,(select top 1 name from sysobjects where xtype='u'))
```

In the attack string, the injected select query extracts the name of the first user table (`xtype='u'`) from the database's metadata table, `sysobjects`, which contains information on the structure of the database. It then converts this table name to an integer. Because the name of the table is a string, the conversion is illegal, and the database returns an error. For example, an SQL Server may return the following error: *"Microsoft OLE DB Provider for SQL Server (0x80040E07) Error converting nvarchar value 'CreditCards' to a column of data type int."*
There are two useful pieces of information in this message that aid an attacker. First, the attacker can see that the database is an SQL Server database, as the error message explicitly states this. Second, the error message reveals the string that caused the type conversion to occur (in this case, the name of the first user-defined table in the database, "CreditCards"). A similar strategy can be used to systematically extract the name and type of each column in the given table. Using this information about the schema of the database, an attacker can create more precise attacks that specifically target certain types of information. Attacks based on malformed queries are typically used as a preliminary information-gathering step for other attacks.

Union Query.

The Union Query technique refers to injection attacks in which an attacker causes the application to return data from a table that is different from the one that was intended. To this end, attackers inject a statement of the form "`UNION <injected query>`". By suitably defining `<injected query>`, attackers can retrieve information from a specified table. The outcome of this attack is that the database returns a dataset that is the union of the results of the original query with the results of the injected query. In our example, an attacker could perform a Union Query injection by injecting the text "`' UNION SELECT cardNo from CreditCards` where acctNo=10032--" into the login field. The application would then produce the following query:

```
SELECT info FROM users WHERE login='' UNION
SELECT cardNo from CreditCards where acctNo=10032 -- AND pin=
```

Assuming that there is no login equal to "" (the empty string), the original query returns the null set, and the injected query returns data from the "CreditCards" table. In this case, the database returns field "cardNo" for account "10032." The database takes the results of these two queries, unions them together, and returns them to the application. In many applications, the effect of this attack would be that the value for "cardNo" is displayed with the account information.

Piggy-backed Queries.

In the Piggy-backed Query technique, an attacker tries to append additional queries to the original query string. If the attack is successful, the database receives and executes a query string that contains multiple distinct queries. The first query is generally the original, legal query, whereas subsequent queries are the injected, malicious queries. This type of attack can be especially harmful; attackers can use it to inject virtually any type of SQL command. In our example application, an attacker could inject the text "0; drop table users" into the *pin* input field. The application would then generate the query:

```
SELECT info FROM users WHERE login='doe' AND pin=0; drop table users
```

The database treats this query string as two queries separated by the query delimiter, ";", and executes both. The second, malicious query causes the database to drop the users table in the database, which would have the catastrophic consequence of deleting all of the database users. Other types of queries can be executed using this technique, such as insertion of new users into the database or execution of stored procedures. It is worth noting that many databases do not require a special character to separate distinct queries, so simply scanning for a special character is not an effective way to prevent this attack technique.

Stored Procedures.

In this technique, attackers focus on the stored procedures that are present on the database system. Stored procedures are code that is stored in the database and run directly by the database engine. Stored procedures enable a programmer to code database or business logic directly into the database and provide extra layer of abstraction. It is a common misconception that the use of stored procedures protects an application from SQLIAs. Stored procedures are just code and can be just as vulnerable as the application's code. Depending on the specific stored procedures that are available on a database, an attacker has different ways of exploiting a system.

The following example demonstrates how a parameterized stored procedure can be exploited via an SQLIA. In this scenario, we assume that the query string constructed at lines 5, 7, and 9 of our example has been replaced by a call to the stored procedure defined in Figure 5.3. The stored procedure returns a boolean value to indicate whether the user's credentials were authenticated by the database. To perform an SQLIA that exploits this stored procedure, the attacker can simply inject the text "

```
CREATE PROCEDURE DBO.isAuthenticated
    @userName varchar2, @pin int
AS
    EXEC("SELECT info FROM users
    WHERE login='" +@userName+ "' and pin=" +@pin);
GO
```

Fig. 5.3. Stored procedure for checking credentials.

' ; SHUTDOWN; --" into the userName field. This injection causes the stored procedure to generate the following query:

```
SELECT info FROM users WHERE login=' '; SHUTDOWN; -- AND pin=
```

This attack works like a piggy-back attack. When the second query is executed, the database is shut down.

Inference.

Inference-based attacks create queries that cause an application or database to behave differently based on the results of the query. In this way, even if an application does not directly provide the results of the query to the attacker, it is possible to observe side effects caused by the query and deduce the results. These attacks allow an attacker to extract data from a database and detect vulnerable parameters. Researchers have reported that, using these techniques, they have been able to achieve a data extraction rate of one byte per second [2]. There are two well-known attack techniques that are based on inference: blind-injection and timing attacks.

Blind Injection: In this variation, an attacker performs queries that have a boolean result. The queries cause the application to behave correctly if they evaluate to true, whereas they cause an error if the result is false. Because error messages are easily distinguishable from normal results, this approach provides a way for an attacker to get an indirect response from the database. One possible use of blind-injection is to determine which parameters of an application are vulnerable to SQLIA. Consider again the example code in Figure 5.2. Two possible injections into the *login* field are "legalUser' and 1=0 --" and "legalUser' and 1=1 --". These injections result in the following two queries:

```
SELECT info FROM users WHERE login='legalUser' and 1=0 -- ' AND pin=
```

```
SELECT info FROM users WHERE login='legalUser' and 1=1 -- ' AND pin=
```

Now, let us consider two scenarios. In the first scenario, we have a secure application, and the input for *login* is validated correctly. In this case, both injections would return login error messages from the application, and the attacker would know that the *login* parameter is not vulnerable to this kind of attack. In the second scenario, we have a non-secure application in which the *login* parameter is vulnerable to injection. In this case, the first injection would evaluate to false, and the application would return a login-error message. Without additional information, attackers would not know whether the error occurred because the application validated the input correctly and blocked the attack attempt or because the attack itself caused the login error. However, when the attackers observe that the second query does not result in an error message, they know that the attack was successful and that the *login* parameter is vulnerable to injection.

Timing Attacks: A timing attack lets an attacker gather information from a database by observing timing delays in the database's responses. This attack is similar to blind injection, but uses a different type of observable side effect. To perform a timing attack, attackers structure their injected query in the form of an if-then statement whose branch condition corresponds to a question about the contents of the database. The attacker then uses the WAITFOR keyword along one of the branches, which causes the database to delay its response by a specified time. By measuring the increase or decrease in the database response time, attackers can infer which branch was taken and the answer to the injected question.

Using our example, we illustrate how to use a timing-based inference attack to extract a table name from the database. In this attack, the following text is injected into the *login* parameter:

```
legalUser' and ASCII(SUBSTRING((select top 1 name from sysobjects),1,1)) >
X WAITFOR 5 --
```

This injection produces the following query:

```
SELECT info FROM users WHERE login='legalUser' and ASCII(SUBSTRING((select top
1 name from sysobjects),1,1)) > X WAITFOR 5 -- ' AND pin=
```

In this attack, the SUBSTRING function is used to extract the first character of the first table's name. The attacker can then ask a series of questions about this character. In this example, the attacker is asking if the ASCII value of the character is greater-than or less-than-or-equal-to the value of *X*. If the value is greater, the attacker will be able to observe an additional five-second delay in the database response. The attacker can continue in this way and use a binary-search strategy to identify the value of the first character, then the second character, and so on.

Alternate Encodings. Using alternate encoding techniques, attackers modify their injection strings in a way that avoids typical signature- and filter-based checks that developers put in their applications. Alternate encodings, such as hexadecimal, ASCII, and Unicode can be used in conjunction with other techniques to allow an attack to escape straightforward detection approaches that simply scan for certain known "bad characters." Even if developers account for alternative encodings, this technique can still be successful because alternate encodings can target different layers in the application. For example, a developer may scan for a Unicode or hexadecimal encoding of a single quote and not realize that the attacker can leverage a database function (e.g., char(44)) to encode the same character. An effective code-based defense against alternate encodings requires developers to be aware of all of the possible encodings that could affect a given query string as it passes through the different application layers. Because developing such a complete protection is very difficult in practice, attackers have been very successful in using alternate encodings to conceal attack strings. The following example attack (from [11]) shows the level of obfuscation that can be achieved using alter-

nate encodings. In the attack, the *pin* field is injected with the following string: "0;
exec(0x73687574646f776e)," and the resulting query is:

```
SELECT info FROM users WHERE login='' AND pin=0; exec(char(0x73687574646f776e))
```

This example makes use of the char() function and ASCII hexadecimal encoding.
The char() function takes as a parameter an integer or hexadecimal encoding of
one or more characters and replaces the function call with the actual character(s).
The stream of numbers in the second part of the injection is the ASCII hexadecimal
encoding of the attack string. This encoded string is inserted into a query using some
other type of attack profile and, when it is executed by the database, translates into
the shutdown command.

5.3 Detection and Prevention of SQL Injection Attacks

AMNESIA, (Analysis for Monitoring and NEutralizing SQL Injection Attacks) is
a fully-automated and general technique for detecting and preventing all types of
SQLIAs. The approach works by combining static analysis and runtime monitoring.
Our two key insights behind the approach are that (1) the information needed to predict the possible structure of all legitimate queries generated by a web application is
contained within the application's code, and (2) an SQLIA, by injecting additional
SQL statements into a query, would violate that structure. In its static part, our technique uses program analysis to automatically build a model of the legitimate queries
that could be generated by the application. In its dynamic part, our technique monitors the dynamically generated queries at runtime and checks them for compliance
with the statically-generated model. Queries that violate the model represent potential SQLIAs and are reported and prevented from executing on the database.

The technique consists of four main steps. We first summarize the steps and then
describe them in more detail in subsequent sections.

5.3.1 The AMNESIA Approach

Identify hotspots: Scan the application code to identify *hotspots*—points in the application code that issue SQL queries to the underlying database.

Build SQL-query models: For each hotspot, build a model that represents all the
possible SQL queries that may be generated at that hotspot. A *SQL-query model*
is a non-deterministic finite-state automaton in which the transition labels consist
of SQL tokens (SQL keywords and operators), delimiters, and placeholders for
string values.

Instrument Application: At each hotspot in the application, add calls to the runtime
monitor.

Runtime monitoring: At runtime, check the dynamically-generated queries against
the SQL-query model and reject and report queries that violate the model.

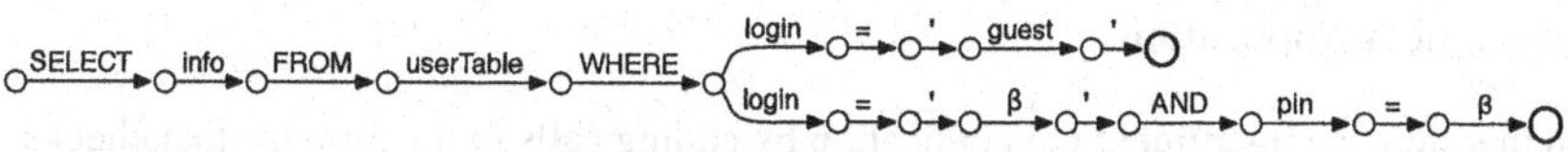

Fig. 5.4. SQL-query model for the servlet in Figure 5.2.

Identify Hotspots

In this step, AMNESIA performs a simple scan of the application code to identify hotspots. In the Java language, all interactions with the database are performed through a predefined API, so identifying all the hotspots is a trivial step. In the case of the example servlet in Figure 5.2, the set of hotspots contains a single element: the call to stmt.execute on line 10.

Build SQL-Query Models

In this step, we build the SQL-query model for each hotspot. We perform this step in two parts. *In the first part*, we use the Java String Analysis (JSA) developed by Christensen, Møller, and Schwartzbach [5] to compute all of the possible values for each hotspot's query string. JSA computes a flow graph that abstracts away the control flow of the program and only represents string-manipulation operations performed on string variables. For each string of interest, the library analyzes the flow graph and simulates the string-manipulation operations that are performed on the string. The result is a Non-Deterministic Finite Automaton (NDFA) that expresses, at the character level, all possible values that the considered string variable can assume. Because JSA is conservative, the NDFA for a given string variable is an overestimate of all of its possible values.

In the second part, we transform the NDFA computed by JSA into an SQL-query model. More precisely, we perform an analysis of the NDFA that produces another NDFA in which all of the transitions are labeled with SQL keywords, operators, or literal values. We create this model by performing a depth first traversal of the character-level NDFA and grouping characters that correspond to SQL keywords, operators, or literal values. For example, a sequence of transitions labeled 'S', 'E', 'L', 'E', 'C', and 'T' would be recognized as the SQL keyword SELECT and grouped into a single transition labeled "SELECT". This step is configurable to recognize different dialects of SQL. In the SQL-query model, we represent *variable strings* (i.e., strings that correspond to a variable related to some user input) using the symbol β. For instance, in our example, the value of the variable login is represented as β. This process is analogous to the one used by Gould, Su, and Devanbu [8], except that we perform it on NDFAs instead of DFAs.

Figure 5.4 shows the SQL-query model for the single hotspot in our example. The model reflects the two different query strings that can be generated by the code depending on the branch followed after the if statement at line 6 in Figure 5.2.

Instrument Application

In this step, we instrument the application by adding calls to the monitor that checks the queries at runtime. For each hotspot, the technique inserts a call to the monitor before the call to the database. The monitor is invoked with two parameters: the query string that is about to be submitted to the database and a unique identifier for the hotspot. Using the unique identifier, the runtime monitor is able to correlate the hotspot with the specific SQL-query model that was statically generated for that point and check the query against the correct model.

Figure 5.5 shows how the example application would be instrumented by our technique. The hotspot, originally at line 10 in Figure 5.2, is now guarded by a call to the monitor at line 10a.

```
...
10a.  if (monitor.accepts (<hotspot ID>, queryString))
      {
10b.      ResultSet tempSet = stmt.execute(queryString);
11.       return tempSet;
      }
...
```

Fig. 5.5. Example hotspot after instrumentation.

Runtime Monitoring

At runtime, the application executes normally until it reaches a hotspot. At this point, the query string is sent to the runtime monitor, which parses it into a sequence of tokens according to the specific SQL syntax considered. In our parsing of the query string, the parser identifies empty string and empty numeric literals by their syntactic position, and we denote them in the parsed query string using ε. Figure 5.6 shows how the last two queries discussed in Section 5.2.1 would be parsed during runtime monitoring.

It is important to point out that our technique parses the query string in the same way that the database would and according to the specific SQL grammar considered. In other words, our technique does not perform a simple keyword matching over the query string, which would cause false positives and problems with user input that happened to match SQL keywords. For example, a user-submitted string that contains SQL keywords but is syntactically a text field, would be correctly recognized as a text field. However, if the user were to inject special characters, as in our example, to force part of the text to be evaluated as a keyword, the parser would correctly interpret this input as a keyword. Using the same parser as the database is essential because it guarantees that we are interpreting the query in the same way that the database will.

(a) SELECT info FROM users WHERE login='doe' AND pin=123

SELECT → info → FROM → users → WHERE → login → = → ' → doe → ' → AND → pin → = → 123

(b) SELECT info FROM users WHERE login='' OR 1=1 -- ' AND pin=

SELECT → info → FROM → users → WHERE → login → = → ' → ε → ' → OR → 1 → = → 1 → -- → ' → AND → pin → = → ε

Fig. 5.6. Example of parsed runtime queries.

After the query has been parsed, the runtime monitor checks it by assessing whether the query violates the SQL-query model associated with the current hotspot. An SQL-query model is an NDFA whose alphabet consists of SQL keywords, operators, literal values, and delimiters, plus the special symbol β. Therefore, to check whether a query is compliant with the model, the runtime monitor can simply check whether the model accepts the the sequence of tokens derived from the query string. A string or numeric literal (including the empty string, ε) in the parsed query string can match either β or an identical literal value in the SQL-query model.

If the model accepts the query, the monitor lets the execution of the query continue. Otherwise, the monitor identifies the query as an SQLIA. In this case, the monitor prevents the query from executing on the database and reports the attack.

To illustrate, consider again the queries shown in Figure 5.6 and recall that the first query is legitimate, whereas the second one corresponds to an SQLIA. When checking query (a), the analysis would start matching from token SELECT and from the initial state of the SQL-query model in Figure 5.4. Because the token matches the label of the only transition from the initial state, the automaton reaches the second state. Again, token info matches the only transition from the current state, so the automaton reaches the third state. The automaton continues to reach new states until it reaches the state whose two outgoing transitions are labeled "=". At this point, the automaton would proceed along both transitions. On the upper branch, the query is not accepted because the automaton does not reach an accept state. Conversely, on the lower branch, all the tokens in the query are matched with labels on transitions, and the automaton reaches the accept state after consuming the last token in the query ("'"). The monitor can therefore conclude that this query is legitimate.

The checking of query (b) proceeds in an analogous way until token OR in the query is reached. Because the token does not match the label of the only outgoing transition from the current state (AND), the query is not accepted by the automaton, and the monitor identifies the query as a SQLIA.

Efficiency and limitations

For the technique to be practical, the runtime overhead of the monitoring must not affect the usability of the web application. We analyze the cost of AMNESIA's runtime monitoring in terms of both space and time. The *space complexity* of the monitoring is dominated by the size of the generated SQL-query models. In the worst case, the size of the query models is quadratic in the size of the application. This case corresponds to the unlikely situation of a program that branches and modifies the query string at each program statement. In typical programs, the generated automata are linear in the program size. In fact, our experience is that most automata are actually quite small with respect to the size of the corresponding application (see Table 5.1). The *time complexity* of the approach depends on the cost of the runtime matching of the query tokens against the models. Because we are checking a set of tokens against an NDFA, the worst case complexity of the matching is exponential in the number of tokens in the query (in the worst case, for each token all states are visited). In practice, however, the SQL-query models typically reduce to trees, and the cost of the matching is almost linear in the size of the query. Our experience shows that the cost of the runtime phase of the approach is negligible (see Section 5.4).

As far as limitations are concerned, our technique can generate false positives and false negatives. Although the string analysis that we use is conservative, false positives can be created in situations where the string analysis is not precise enough. For example, if the analysis cannot determine that a hard-coded string in the application is a keyword, it could assume that it is an input-related value and erroneously represent it as a β in the SQL-query model. At runtime, the original keyword would not match the placeholder for the variable, and AMNESIA would flag the corresponding query as an SQLIA. False negatives can occur when the constructed SQL query model contains spurious queries, and the attacker is able to generate an injection attack that matches one of the spurious queries. For example, if a developer adds conditions to a query from within a loop, an attacker who inserts an additional condition of the same type would generate a query that does not violate the SQL-query model. We expect these cases to be rare in practice because of the peculiar structure of SQLIAs. The attacker would have to produce an attack that directly matches either an imprecision of the analysis or a specific pattern. Moreover, in both cases, the type of attacks that could be exploited would be limited by the constraints imposed by the rest of the model that was used to match the query. It is worth noting that, in our empirical evaluation, neither false positives nor false negatives were generated (see Section 5.4).

5.3.2 Implementation

AMNESIA is the prototype tool that implements our technique for Java-based web applications. The technique is fully automated, requiring only the web application as input, and requires no extra runtime environment support beyond deploying the application with the AMNESIA library. We developed the tool in Java and its implementation consists of three modules:

Analysis module. This module implements Steps 1 and 2 of our technique. It inputs a Java web application and outputs a list of hotspots and a SQL-query model for each hotspot. For the implementation of this module, we leveraged the implementation of the Java String Analysis library by Christensen, Møller, and Schwartzbach [5]. The analysis module is able to analyze Java Servlets and JSP pages.

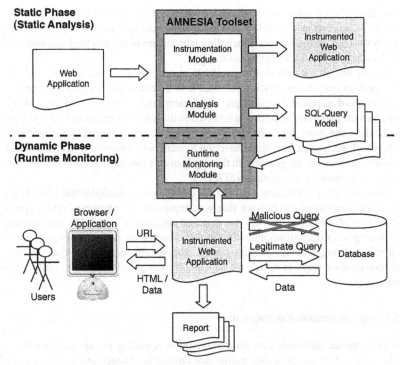

Fig. 5.7. High-level overview of AMNESIA.

Instrumentation module. This module implements Step 3 of our technique. It inputs
a Java web application and a list of hotspots and instruments each hotspot with
a call to the runtime monitor. We implemented this module using INSECTJ, a
generic instrumentation and monitoring framework for Java developed at Georgia Tech [23].

Runtime-monitoring module. This module implements Step 4 of our technique. The
module takes as input a query string and the ID of the hotspot that generated
the query, retrieves the SQL-query model for that hotspot, and checks the query
against the model.

Figure 5.7 shows a high-level overview of AMNESIA. In the static phase, the
Instrumentation Module and the Analysis Module take as input a web application and
produce (1) an instrumented version of the application, and (2) an SQL-query model
for each hotspot in the application. In the dynamic phase, the Runtime-Monitoring
Module checks the dynamic queries while users interact with the web application. If
a query is identified as an attack, it is blocked and reported.

Once an SQLIA has been detected, AMNESIA stops the query before it is executed on the database and reports relevant information about the attack in a way that
can be leveraged by developers. In our implementation of the technique for Java, we

throw an exception when the attack is detected and encode information about the attack in the exception. If developers want to access the information at runtime, they can simply leverage the exception-handling mechanism of the language and integrate their handling code into the application.

Having this attack information available at runtime is useful because it allows developers to react to an attack right after it is detected and develop an appropriate customized response. For example, developers may decide to avoid any risk and shut-down the part of the application involved in the attack. Alternatively, a developer could handle the attack by converting the information into a format that is usable by another tool, such as an Intrusion Detection System, and reporting it to that tool. Because this mechanism integrates with the application's language, it allows developers flexibility in choosing a response to SQLIAs.

Currently, the information reported by our technique includes the time of the attack, the location of the hotspot that was exploited, the attempted-attack query, and the part of the query that was not matched against the model. We are currently considering additional information that could be useful for the developer (e.g., information correlating program execution paths with specific parts of the query model) and investigating ways in which we can modify the static analysis to collect this information.

5.3.3 Implementation Assumptions

Our implementation makes one main assumption regarding the applications that it analyzes. The tool assumes that queries are created by manipulating strings in the application, that is, the developer creates queries by combining hard-coded strings and variables using operations such as concatenation, appending, and insertion. Although this assumption precludes the use of AMNESIA on some applications (e.g., applications that externalize all query-related strings in files), it is not overly restrictive and, most importantly, can be eliminated with suitable engineering.

5.4 Empirical Evaluation

The goal of our empirical evaluation is to assess the effectiveness and efficiency of the technique presented in this chapter when applied to various web applications. We used our prototype tool, AMNESIA, to perform an empirical study on a set of subjects. The study investigates three research questions:

RQ1: What percentage of attacks can AMNESIA detect and prevent that would otherwise go undetected and reach the database?

RQ2: How much overhead does AMNESIA impose on web applications at runtime?

RQ3: What percentage of legitimate accesses does AMNESIA identify as attacks?

The following sections illustrate the setup for the evaluation, and discuss the two studies that we performed to address the research questions.

Table 5.1. Subject programs for the empirical study.

Subject (Description)	LOC	Servlets	Injectable Params	State Params	Hotspots	Automata Size (#nodes)
Checkers (Online checkers game)	5,421	18 (61)	44	0	5	289 (2–772)
Office Talk (Purchase-order management)	4,543	7 (64)	13	1	40	40 (8–167)
Employee Directory (Online employee directory)	5,658	7 (10)	25	9	23	107 (2–952)
Bookstore (Online bookstore)	16,959	8 (28)	36	6	71	159 (2–5,269)
Events (Event tracking system)	7,242	7 (13)	36	10	31	77 (2–550)
Classifieds (Management system for classifieds)	10,949	6 (14)	18	8	34	91 (2–799)
Portal (Portal for a club)	16,453	3 (28)	39	7	67	117 (2–1,187)

5.4.1 Experiment Setup

To investigate our research questions, we leveraged a previously developed testbed for SQLIAs, which was presented in [9]. This testbed provides a set of web applications and a large set of both legitimate and malicious inputs for the applications. In the next two sections we briefly review the testbed, describe the applications it contains, and explain how the inputs were generated. Readers can refer to [9] for additional details.

Subjects

The testbed contains seven subjects. All of the subjects are typical web applications that accept user input via web forms and use that input to build queries to an underlying database. Five of the applications are commercial applications that we obtained from GotoCode (http://www.gotocode.com): Employee Directory, Bookstore, Events, Classifieds, and Portal. The last two applications, Checkers and OfficeTalk, were student-developed applications created for a class project. We consider them because they have been used in previous related studies [8].

In Table 5.1 we provide information about the subject applications. For each subject, the table shows: its name (*Subject*); a concise description (*Description*); its size in terms of lines of code (*LOC*); the number of accessible servlets (*Servlets*), with the total number of servlets in the application in parenthesis; the number of injectable parameters (*Injectable Params*); the number of state parameters (*State Params*); the number of hotspots (*Hotspots*); and the average size of the SQL automata generated by AMNESIA (*Automata Size*), with the minimum–maximum range in parentheses.

The table distinguishes between injectable parameters and state parameters for each application. This distinction is necessary because each type of parameter plays a different role in the application. An *injectable parameter* is an input parameter whose value is used to build part of a query that is then sent to the database. A *state parameter* is a parameter that may affect the control flow within the web application but never becomes part of a query. Because, by definition, state parameters cannot result in SQL injection, we only focus on injectable parameters for our attacks. We also distinguish between total and accessible servlets in the applications. An *accessible servlet* is a servlet that, to be accessed, only requires the user to be logged-in or does not require sessions at all. Some servlets, conversely, must have specific session data (i.e., cookies) to function properly, which considerably complicates the automation of the evaluation. Because we were able to generate enough attacks considering accessible servlets only, we did not consider the remaining servlets.

Input Generation

The sets of inputs provided by the testbed framework represent normal and malicious usages of the applications. In this section we briefly review how these sets were generated and the types of inputs they contain.

In a preliminary step, we identified all of the servlets in each web application and the corresponding parameters that could be submitted to the servlet. Each parameter was identified as either an injectable or state parameter. State parameters must be handled specially because they often determine the behavior of the application. Without a correct and meaningful value assigned to them, the application fails and no attack can be successful. Lastly, we identified the expected type of each injectable parameter. This information helps us in identifying potential attacks that can be used on the parameter and in generating legitimate inputs.

The set of *attack strings* was generated independently using commercial penetration testing techniques. For this task, we leveraged the services of a Masters-level student at Georgia Tech who worked for a local software-security company. The student is an experienced programmer who has developed commercial-level penetration tools for detecting SQL-injection vulnerabilities. In addition, the student was not familiar with our technique, which reduced the risk of developing a set of attacks biased by the knowledge of the approach and its capabilities.

To define the initial set of attack strings, the student used a combination of sources, including (1) exploits developed by commercial penetrating teams to take advantage of SQL-injection vulnerabilities, (2) online sources of vulnerability reports, such as US-CERT (http://www.us-cert.gov/) and CERT/CC Advisories (http://www.cert.org/advisories/), and (3) information extracted from several security-related mailing lists. The resulting set of attack strings contained thirty unique types of attacks. All types of attacks reported in literature (e.g., [1]) were represented in this set with the exception of attacks that take advantage of overly-descriptive database error messages and second-order injections. We excluded these kinds of attacks because they are multi-phase attacks that require intensive human intervention to interpret the attacks' partial results.

The student generated two sets of inputs for each application. The first set contained normal or legitimate inputs for the application. We call this set *LEGIT*. The second set contained malicious inputs, that is, strings that would result in an SQLIA. We call this set *ATTACK*. To populate the LEGIT set, the student generated, for each servlet, different combinations of legitimate values for each injectable parameter. State parameters were assigned a meaningful and correct value. To populate the AT-TACK set, a similar process was used. For each accessible servlet in the application the student generated the Cartesian product of its injectable parameters using values from the initial attack strings and legitimate values. This approach generated a large set of potentially malicious inputs, which we used as the ATTACK set.

5.4.2 Study 1: Effectiveness

In the first study, we investigated **RQ1**, the effectiveness of our technique in detecting and preventing SQLIAs. We analyzed and instrumented each application using AM-NESIA and ran all of the inputs in each of the applications' ATTACK sets. For each application, we measured the percentage of attacks detected and reported by AM-NESIA. (As previously discussed, when AMNESIA detects an attack, it throws an exception, which is in turn returned by the web application. Therefore, it is easy to accurately detect when an attack has been caught.)

The results for this study are shown in Table 5.2. The table shows, for each subject, the number of unsuccessful attacks (*Unsuccessful*),[2] the number of successful attacks (*Successful*), and the number of attacks detected and reported by AMNESIA (*Detected*) in absolute terms and as a percentage over the total number of successful attacks, in parentheses. As the table shows, AMNESIA achieved a perfect score. For all subjects, it was able to correctly identify all attacks as SQLIAs, that is, it generated no false negatives.

Table 5.2. Results of Study 1.

Subject	Unsuccessful	Successful	Detected
Checkers	1195	248	248 (100%)
Office Talk	598	160	160 (100%)
Employee Directory	413	280	280 (100%)
Bookstore	1028	182	182 (100%)
Events	875	260	260 (100%)
Classifieds	823	200	200 (100%)
Portal	880	140	140 (100%)

---

[2] Because the applications performed input validation, they were able to block a portion of the attacks without the attack reaching AMNESIA's monitor.

5.4.3 Study 2: Efficiency and Precision

In the second study, we investigated **RQ2** and **RQ3**. To investigate **RQ2**, the efficiency of our technique, we ran all of the inputs in the LEGIT sets on the uninstrumented web applications and measured the response time of the applications for each web request. We then ran the same inputs on the versions of the web applications instrumented by AMNESIA and again measured the response time. The difference in the two response times corresponds to the overhead imposed by our technique.

We found that the overhead imposed by our technique is negligible and, in fact, barely measurable, averaging about 1 millisecond. Note that this time should be considered an upper bound on the overhead, as our implementation was not optimized. These results confirm our expectations. Intuitively, the time for the network access and the database transaction completely dominates the time required for the runtime checking. As the results show, our technique is efficient and can be used without significantly affecting the response time of a web application.

To investigate **RQ3**, the rate of false positives generated by our technique, we simply assessed whether AMNESIA identified any legitimate query as an attack. The results of the assessment were that AMNESIA correctly identified all such queries as legitimate queries and reported no false positives.

5.4.4 Discussion

The results of our study are very encouraging. For all subjects, our technique was able to correctly identify all attacks as SQLIAs, while allowing all legitimate queries to be performed. In other words, for the cases considered, our technique generated no false positives and no false negatives. The lack of false positives and false negatives is promising and provides evidence of the viability of the technique.

In our study, we did not compare our results with alternative approaches against SQLIAs because most of the existing automated approaches address only a subset of the possible SQLIAs. (For example, the approach in [8] is focused on type safety, and the one in [25] focuses only on tautologies.) Therefore, we can conclude analytically that such approaches would not be able to identify many of the attacks in our test bed.

As for all empirical studies, there are some threats to the validity of our evaluation, mostly with respect to external validity. The results of our study may be related to the specific subjects considered and may not generalize to other web applications. To minimize this risk, we used a set of real web applications (except for the two applications developed by students teams) and an extensive set of realistic attacks. Although more experimentation is needed before drawing definitive conclusions on the effectiveness of the technique, the results we obtained so far are promising.

5.5 Related Approaches

There has been a wide range of techniques proposed to counter SQLIAs. However, when compared to AMNESIA, these solutions have several limitations and short-comings. In this section we review and discuss the main approaches against SQLIAs.

Defensive Programming.

Developers have proposed a range of code-based development practices to counter SQLIAs. These techniques generally focus on proper input filtering, such as escaping potentially harmful characters and rigorous type-checking of inputs. Many of these approaches are summarized in Reference [11]. In general, a rigorous and systematic application of these techniques is an effective solution to the problem. However, in practice, the application of such techniques is human-based and is therefore less than ideal. For example, many SQLIA vulnerabilities that have been discovered in various applications correspond to cases where the applications contained input-validation operations, but the validation was inadequate. The situation is further complicated because attackers continue to find new attack strings or subtle variation on old attacks that are able to avoid the checks programmers put in place. Lastly, retroactively fixing vulnerable legacy applications using defensive coding practices is complicated, labor-intensive, and error-prone.

Two widely suggested "SQLIA remedies" merit specific mention. Both of them initially appear to offer viable solutions to the SQLIA problem, but do not correctly address it. The first remedy consists of simply checking user input for malicious keywords. This approach would clearly result in a high rate of false positives because an input field could legally contain words that match SQL keywords (i.e. "FROM","OR", or "AND"). The second remedy is to use stored procedures for database access. The ability of stored procedures to prevent SQLIAs is dependent on their implementation. The mere fact of using stored procedures does not protect against SQLIA. Interested readers may refer to Section 5.2 and to References [1, 15, 18, 19] for examples of how SQLIAs can be performed in the presence of stored procedures.

Two approaches, SQL DOM [17] and Safe Query Objects [6], use encapsulation of database queries to provide a safe and reliable way to access databases. These techniques offer an effective way to avoid the SQLIA problem by changing the query-building process from one that uses string concatenation to a systematic one that uses a type-checked API. (In this sense, SQL DOM and Safe Query Objects can be considered instances of defensive coding.) Although these techniques are as effective as AMNESIA, they have the drawback that they require developers to learn and use a new programming paradigm or query-development process.

In general, defensive coding has not been successful in completely preventing SQLIA. While improved coding practices can help mitigate the problem, they are limited by the developer's ability to generate appropriate input validation code and recognize all situations in which it is needed. AMNESIA, being fully automated, can provide stronger guarantees about the completeness and accuracy of the protections put in place.

General Techniques Against SQLIAs.

Security Gateway [22] uses a proxy filter to enforce input validation rules on the data that reaches a web application. Using a descriptor language, developers create filters that specify constraints and transformations to be applied to application parameters as they flow from the web page to the application server. By creating appropriate filters, developers can block or transform potentially malicious user input. The effectiveness of this approach is limited by the developer's ability to (1) identify all the input streams that can affect the query string and (2) determine what type of filtering rules should be placed on the proxy.

WAVES [12] is a penetration testing tool that attempts to discover SQLIA vulnerabilities in web applications. This technique improves over normal penetration-testing techniques by using machine learning to guide its testing. However, like all penetration testing techniques, it can not provide guarantees of completeness.

Valeur and colleagues [24] propose the use of an Intrusion Detection System (IDS) to detect SQLIAs. Their IDS is based on a machine learning technique that is trained using a set of typical application queries. The technique builds models of normal queries and then monitors the application at runtime to identify queries that do not match the model. The fundamental limitation of learning based techniques is that they can not provide guarantees about their detection abilities because their success is dependent on the use of an optimal training set. Without such a set, this technique could generate a large number of false positives and negatives.

Boyd and Keromytis propose SQLrand, an approach that uses key-based randomization of SQL instructions [4]. In this approach, SQL code injected by an attacker would result in a syntactically incorrect query because it was not specified using the randomized instruction set. While this technique can be very effective, there are several practical drawbacks to this approach. First, the security of the key may be compromised by looking at the error logs or messages. Furthermore, the approach imposes a significant infrastructure overhead because it requires the integration of an encryption proxy for the database.

Static Detection Techniques.

JDBC-Checker is a technique for statically checking the type correctness of dynamically generated SQL queries [8]. Although this technique was not originally intended to address SQLIA, it can detect one of the root causes of SQL-injection vulnerabilities—improper type checking of input. In this sense, JDBC-Checker is able to detect and help developers eliminate some of the code that allows attackers to exploit type mismatches. However, JDBC-Checker cannot prevent other types of SQLIAs that produce syntactically and type correct queries.

Wassermann and Su propose an approach that uses static analysis combined with automated reasoning to verify that the SQL queries generated in the application layer cannot contain a tautology [25]. The scope of this technique is limited, in that it can only address one type of SQLIAs, namely tautology-based attacks, whereas AMNESIA is designed to address all types of SQLIAs.

Taint-based Approaches.

Two similar approaches have been proposed by Nguyen-Tuong *et al.* [20] and Pietraszek and Berghe [21]. These approaches modify a PHP interpreter to track precise taint information about user input and use a context sensitive analysis to detect and reject queries if untrusted input has been used to create certain types of SQL tokens. In general, these taint-based techniques have shown much promise in their ability to detect and prevent SQLIAs. The main drawback of these approaches concerns their practicality. First, identifying all sources of tainted user input in highly-modular web applications introduces problem of completeness. Second, accurately propagating taint information may result in high runtime overhead for the web applications. Finally, the approach relies on the use of a customized version of the runtime system, which affects portability.

Huang and colleagues define WebSSARI, a white-box approach for detecting input-validation-related errors, that is based on information-flow analysis [13]. This approach uses static analysis to check information flows against preconditions for sensitive functions. The analysis detects where preconditions are not satisfied and suggests filters and sanitization functions that can be automatically added to the application to satisfy the preconditions. The primary drawbacks of this technique are the assumptions that (1) preconditions for sensitive functions can be adequately and accurately expressed using their type system and (2) forcing input to pass through certain types of filters is sufficient to consider it trusted. For many types of functions and applications, these assumptions do not hold.

Livshits and Lam [14] use a static taint analysis approach to detect code that is vulnerable to SQLIA. This approach checks whether user input can reach a hotspot and flags this code for developer intervention. A further extension to this work, Securifly [16], detects vulnerable code and automatically adds calls to a sanitization function. This automated defensive coding practice, while effective in some cases, would not prevent all types of SQLIAs. In particular, it would not prevent SQLIAs that inject malicious text into numeric non-quoted fields.

5.6 Conclusion

SQLIAs have become one of the more serious and harmful attacks on database-driven web applications. They can allow an attacker to have unmitigated access to the database underlying an application and, thus, the power to access or modify its contents. In this article, we have discussed the various types of SQLIAs known to date and presented AMNESIA, a fully automated technique and tool for detecting and preventing SQLIAs. AMNESIA uses static analysis to build a model of the legitimate queries that an application can generate and runtime monitoring to check the dynamically generated queries against this model. Our empirical evaluation, performed on commercial applications using a large number of realistic attacks, shows that AMNESIA is a highly effective technique for detecting and preventing SQLIAs. Compared to other approaches, AMNESIA offers the benefit of being fully automated and is general enough to address all known types of SQLIAs.

Acknowledgments

This material is based upon work supported by NSF award CCR-0209322 to Georgia Tech and by the Department of Homeland Security and United States Air Force under Contract No. FA8750-05-2-0214. Any opinions, findings and conclusions or recommendations expressed in this material are those of the authors and do not necessarily reflect the views of the United States Air Force. Jeremy Viegas developed our test bed infrastructure.

References

1. C. Anley. Advanced SQL Injection In SQL Server Applications. White paper, Next Generation Security Software Ltd., 2002.
2. C. Anley. (more) Advanced SQL Injection. White paper, Next Generation Security Software Ltd., 2002.
3. D. Aucsmith. Creating and maintaining software that resists malicious attack. http://www.gtisc.gatech.edu/aucsmith_bio.htm, September 2004. Distinguished Lecture Series.
4. S. W. Boyd and A. D. Keromytis. SQLrand: Preventing SQL injection attacks. In *Proceedings of the 2nd Applied Cryptography and Network Security (ACNS) Conference*, pages 292–302, June 2004.
5. A. S. Christensen, A. Møller, and M. I. Schwartzbach. Precise analysis of string expressions. In *Proc. 10th International Static Analysis Symposium, SAS '03*, volume 2694 of *LNCS*, pages 1–18. Springer-Verlag, June 2003. Available from http://www.brics.dk/JSA/.
6. W. R. Cook and S. Rai. Safe Query Objects: Statically Typed Objects as Remotely Executable Queries. In *Proceedings of the 27th International Conference on Software Engineering (ICSE 2005)*, 2005.
7. T. O. Foundation. Top ten most critical web application vulnerabilities, 2005. http://www.owasp.org/documentation/topten.html.
8. C. Gould, Z. Su, and P. Devanbu. Static Checking of Dynamically Generated Queries in Database Applications. In *Proceedings of the 26th International Conference on Software Engineering (ICSE 04)*, pages 645–654, 2004.
9. W. G. Halfond and A. Orso. AMNESIA: Analysis and Monitoring for NEutralizing SQL-Injection Attacks. In *Proceedings of the IEEE and ACM International Conference on Automated Software Engineering (ASE 2005)*, Long Beach, CA, USA, Nov 2005.
10. W. G. Halfond, J. Viegas, and A. Orso. A Classification of SQL-Injection Attacks and Counter Techniques. Technical report, Georgia Institute of Technology, August 2005.
11. M. Howard and D. LeBlanc. *Writing Secure Code*. Microsoft Press, Redmond, Washington, second edition, 2003.
12. Y. Huang, S. Huang, T. Lin, and C. Tsai. Web Application Security Assessment by Fault Injection and Behavior Monitoring. In *Proceedings of the 11th International World Wide Web Conference (WWW 03)*, May 2003.
13. Y. Huang, F. Yu, C. Hang, C. H. Tsai, D. T. Lee, and S. Y. Kuo. Securing Web Application Code by Static Analysis and Runtime Protection. In *Proceedings of the 12th International World Wide Web Conference (WWW 04)*, May 2004.

14. V. B. Livshits and M. S. Lam. Finding Security Vulnerabilities in Java Applications with Static Analysis. In *Usenix Security Symposium*, August 2005.
15. O. Maor and A. Shulman. SQL Injection Signatures Evasion. White paper, Imperva, April 2004. `http://www.imperva.com/application_defense_center/white_papers/sql_injection_signatures_evasion.html`.
16. M. Martin, V. B. Livshits, and M. S. Lam. Finding Application Errors and Security Flaws Using PQL: a Program Query Language. In *Proceedings of the ACM Conference on Object-Oriented Programming, Systems, Languages, and Applications (OOPSLA)*, October 2005.
17. R. McClure and I. Krüger. SQL DOM: Compile Time Checking of Dynamic SQL Statements. In *Proceedings of the 27th International Conference on Software Engineering (ICSE 05)*, pages 88–96, 2005.
18. S. McDonald. SQL Injection: Modes of attack, defense, and why it matters. White paper, GovernmentSecurity.org, April 2002. `http://www.governmentsecurity.org/articles/SQLInjectionModesofAttackDefenceandWhyItMatters.php`.
19. S. McDonald. SQL Injection Walkthrough. White paper, SecuriTeam, May 2002. `http://www.securiteam.com/securityreviews/5DP0N1P76E.html`.
20. A. Nguyen-Tuong, S. Guarnieri, D. Greene, J. Shirley, and D. Evans. Automatically Hardening Web Applications Using Precise Tainting Information. In *Twentieth IFIP International Information Security Conference (SEC 2005)*, May 2005.
21. T. Pietraszek and C. V. Berghe. Defending Against Injection Attacks through Context-Sensitive String Evaluation. In *Proceedings of Recent Advances in Intrusion Detection (RAID2005)*, 2005.
22. D. Scott and R. Sharp. Abstracting Application-level Web Security. In *Proceedings of the 11th International Conference on the World Wide Web (WWW 2002)*, pages 396–407, 2002.
23. A. Seesing and A. Orso. InsECTJ: A Generic Instrumentation Framework for Collecting Dynamic Information within Eclipse. In *Proceedings of the eclipse Technology eXchange (eTX) Workshop at OOPSLA 2005*, pages 49–53, San Diego, USA, October 2005.
24. F. Valeur, D. Mutz, and G. Vigna. A Learning-Based Approach to the Detection of SQL Attacks. In *Proceedings of the Conference on Detection of Intrusions and Malware and Vulnerability Assessment (DIMVA)*, Vienna, Austria, July 2005.
25. G. Wassermann and Z. Su. An Analysis Framework for Security in Web Applications. In *Proceedings of the FSE Workshop on Specification and Verification of Component-Based Systems (SAVCBS 2004)*, pages 70–78, 2004.

Distributed Threat Detection and Defense

Distributed Threat Detection and Defense

6

Very Fast Containment of Scanning Worms, Revisited*

Nicholas Weaver[1], Stuart Staniford[2], and Vern Paxson[3]

[1] International Computer Science Institute
nweaver@icsi.berkeley.edu
[2] Nevis Networks
stuart@nevisnetworks.com
[3] International Computer Science Institute and Lawrence Berkeley National Laboratory
vern@icir.org

Summary. Computer worms — malicious, self-propagating programs — represent a significant threat to large networks. One possible defense, *containment*, seeks to limit a worm's spread by isolating it in a small subsection of the network. In this work we develop containment algorithms suitable for deployment in high-speed, low-cost network hardware. We show that these techniques can stop a scanning host after fewer than 10 scans with a very low false-positive rate. We also augment this approach by devising mechanisms for *cooperation* that enable multiple containment devices to more effectively detect and respond to an emerging infection. In addition, we discuss ways that a worm can attempt to bypass containment techniques in general, and ours in particular.

We then report on experiences subsequently implementing our algorithm in Click [13] and deploying it both on our own network and in the DETER testbed [6]. Doing so uncovered additional considerations, including the need to passively map the monitored LAN due to Ethernet switch behavior, and the problem of detecting ARP scanning as well as IP scanning. We finish with discussion of some deployment issues, including broadcast/multicast traffic and the use of NAT to realize sparser address spaces.

6.1 Introduction

Computer worms — malicious, self propagating programs — represent a substantial threat to large networks. Since these threats can propagate more rapidly than human response [30, 15], automated defenses are critical for detecting and responding to infections [16]. One of the key defenses against scanning worms which spread throughout an enterprise is *containment* [36, 29, 27, 9, 17]. Worm containment, also known as virus throttling, works by detecting that a worm is operating in the network and then blocking the infected machines from contacting further hosts. Currently, such containment mechanisms only work against *scanning* worms [33] because they

---

* An earlier version of this chapter appears in *Proceedings of the USENIX Security Symposium*, 2004.

leverage the anomaly of a local host attempting to connect to multiple other hosts as the means of detecting an infectee.

Within an enterprise, containment operates by breaking the network into many small pieces, or *cells*. Within each cell (which might encompass just a single machine), a worm can spread unimpeded. But between cells, containment attempts to limit further infections by blocking outgoing connections from infected cells.

A key problem in containment of scanning worms is efficiently detecting and suppressing the scanning. Since containment *blocks* suspicious machines, it is critical that the false positive rate be very low. Additionally, since a successful infection could potentially subvert any software protections put on the host machine, containment is best effected inside the network rather than on the end-hosts.

We have developed a scan detection and suppression algorithm based on a simplification of the Threshold Random Walk (TRW) scan detector [11]. The simplifications make our algorithm suitable for both hardware and software implementation. We use caches to (imperfectly) track the activity of both addresses and individual connections, and reduce the random walk calculation of TRW to a simple comparison. Our algorithm's approximations generally only cost us a somewhat increased false negative rate; we find that false positives do not increase.

Evaluating the algorithm on traces from a large (6,000 host) enterprise, we find that with a total memory usage of 5 MB we obtain good detection precision while staying within a processing budget of at most 4 memory accesses (to two independent banks) per packet. In addition, our algorithm can detect scanning which occurs at a threshold of one scan per minute, much lower than that used by the throttling scheme in [36], and thus significantly harder for an attacker to evade.

Our trace-based analysis shows that the algorithms are both highly effective and sensitive when monitoring scanning on an Internet access link, able to detect low-rate TCP and UDP scanners which probe our enterprise. One deficiency of our work, however, is that we were unable to obtain internal enterprise traces. These can be very difficult to acquire, but we are currently pursuing doing so. Until we can, the efficacy of our algorithm when deployed internal to an enterprise can only be partly inferred from its robust access-link performance.

We have also investigated how to enhance containment through *cooperation* between containment devices. Worm containment systems have an *epidemic threshold*: if the number of vulnerable machines is few enough relative to a particular containment deployment, then containment will almost completely stop the worm [27]. However, if there are more vulnerable machines, then the worm will still spread exponentially (though less than in the absence of containment). We show that by adding a simple inter-cell communication scheme, the spread of the worm can be dramatically mitigated in the case where the system is above its epidemic threshold.

We next discuss inadvertent and malicious attacks on worm containment systems: what is necessary for an attacker to create either false negatives (a worm which evades detection) or false positives (triggering a response when a worm did not exist), assessing this for general worm containment, cooperative containment, and our particular proposed system. We specifically designed our system to resist some of these attacks.

Subsequent to the publication of the above elements of the paper, we implemented our algorithm in Click [13] and deployed it both on our own network and in the DETER testbed [6]. Doing so uncovered additional considerations, including the need to passively map the monitored LAN due to Ethernet switch behavior, and the problem of detecting ARP scanning as well as IP scanning. In the final section of this chapter, we revisit the algorithm in this light, and also discuss some deployment issues, including broadcast/multicast traffic and the use of NAT to realize sparser address spaces.

6.2 Worm Containment

Worm containment is designed to halt the spread of a worm in an enterprise by detecting infected machines and preventing them from contacting further systems. Current approaches to containment [36, 27, 25] are based on detecting the scanning activity associated with scanning worms, as is our new algorithm.

Scanning worms operate by picking "random" addresses and attempting to infect them. The actual selection technique can vary considerably, from linear scanning of an address space (Blaster [31]), fully random (Code Red [7]), a bias toward local addresses (Code Red II [4] and Nimda [3]), or even more enhanced techniques (Permutation Scanning [30]). While future worms could alter their style of scanning to try to avoid detection, all scanning worms share two common properties: most scanning attempts result in failure, and infected machines will institute many connection attempts.[4] Because containment looks for a class of behavior rather than specific worm signatures, such systems can stop *new* (scanning) worms.

Robust worm defense requires an approach like containment because we know from experience that worms can find (by brute force) small holes in firewalls [4], VPN tunnels from other institutions, infected notebook computers [31], web browser vulnerabilities [3], and email-borne attacks [3] to establish a foothold in a target institution. Many institutions with solid firewalls have still succumbed to worms that entered through such means. Without containment, even a single breach can lead to a complete internal infection.

Along with the epidemic threshold (Section 6.2.1) and sustained sub-threshold scanning (Section 6.2.2), a significant issue with containment is the need for complete deployment within an enterprise. Otherwise, any uncontained-but-infected machines will be able to scan through the enterprise and infect other systems. (A single machine, scanning at only 10 IP addresses per second, can scan through an entire /16 in under 2 hours.)

Thus, we strongly believe that worm-suppression needs to be built into the network fabric. When a worm compromises a machine, the worm can defeat host software designed to limit the infection; indeed, it is already common practice for viruses

---

[4] There are classes of worms—topological, meta-server, flash (during their spreading phase, once the hit-list has been constructed), and contagion [33]—that do *not* exhibit such scanning behavior. Containment for such worms remains an important, open research problem.

and mail-worms to disable antivirus software, so we must assume that future worms will disable worm-suppression software.

Additionally, since containment works best when the cells are small, this strongly suggests that worm containment needs to be integrated into the network's outer switches or similar hardware elements, as proximate to the end hosts as economically feasible. This becomes even more important for cooperative containment (Section 6.6), as this mechanism is based on some cells becoming compromised as a means of better detecting the spread of a worm and calibrating the response necessary to stop it.

6.2.1 Epidemic Threshold

A worm-suppression device must necessarily allow some scanning before it triggers a response. During this time, the worm may find one or more potential victims. Staniford [27] discusses the importance of this "epidemic threshold" to the worm containment problem. If on average an infected computer can find more than a single victim before a containment device halts the worm instance, the worm will still grow exponentially within the institution (until the average replication rate falls below 1.0).

The epidemic threshold depends on

- the sensitivity of the containment response devices
- the density of vulnerable machines on the network
- the degree to which the worm is able to target its efforts into the correct network, and even into the current cell

Aside from cooperation between devices, the other options to raise the epidemic threshold are to increase the sensitivity of the scan detector/suppressor, reduce the density of vulnerable machines by distributing potential targets in a larger address space, or increase the number of cells in the containment deployment.

One easy way to distribute targets across a larger address space arises if the enterprise's systems use NAT and DHCP. If so, then when systems acquire an address through DHCP, the DHCP server can select a random address from within a private /8 subnet (e.g., 10.0.0.0/8). Thus, an institution with 2^{16} workstations could have an internal vulnerability density of $2^{16}/2^{24} = 1/256$, giving plenty of headroom for relatively insensitive worm-suppression techniques to successfully operate.

Alternatively, we can work to make the worm detection algorithm more accurate. The epidemic threshold is directly proportional to the scan threshold T: the faster we can detect and block a scan, the more vulnerabilities there can be on the network without a worm being able to get loose. Thus, we desire highly sensitive scan-detection algorithms for use in worm containment.

6.2.2 Sustained Scanning Threshold

In addition to the epidemic threshold, many (but not all) worm containment techniques also have a *sustained scanning threshold*: if a worm scans slower than this rate, the detector will not trigger. Although there have been systems proposed to detect very stealthy scanning [28], these systems are currently too resource-intensive for use in this application.

Even a fairly low sustained scanning threshold can enable a worm to spread if the attacker engineers the worm to avoid detection. For example, consider the spread of a worm in an enterprise with 256 (2^8) vulnerable machines distributed uniformly in a contiguous /16 address space. If the worm picks random addresses from the entire Internet address space, then we expect only 1 in 2^{24} scans to find another victim in the enterprise. Thus, even with a very permissive sustained scanning threshold, the worm will not effectively spread within the enterprise.

But if the worm biases its scanning such that 1/2 the effort is used to scan the local /16, then on average it will locate another target within the enterprise after 2^9 scans. If the threshold is one scan per second (the default for Williamson's technique [36]), then the initial population's doubling time will be approximately 2^9 seconds, or once every 8.5 minutes. This doubling time is sufficient for a fast-moving worm, as the entire enterprise will be infected in less than two hours. If the worm concentrates its entire scanning within the enterprise's /16, the doubling time will be about four minutes.

Thus, it is vital to achieve as low a sustained scanning threshold as possible. For our concrete design, we target a threshold of 1 scan per minute. This would change the doubling times for our example above to 8.5 and 4 hours respectively — slow enough that humans can notice the problem developing and take additional action. Achieving such a threshold is a much stricter requirement than that proposed by Williamson, and forces us to develop a different scan-detection algorithm.

6.3 Scan Suppression

The key component for today's containment techniques is *scan suppression*: responding to detected *portscans* by blocking future scanning attempts. Portscans— probe attempts to determine if a service is operating at a target IP address—are used by both human attackers and worms to discover new victims. Portscans have two basic types: *horizontal* scans, which search for an identical service on a large number of machines, and *vertical* scans, which examine an individual machine to discover all running services. (Clearly, an attacker can also combine these and scan many services on many machines. For ease of exposition, though, we will consider the two types separately.)

The goal of scan suppression is often expressed in terms of preventing scans coming from "outside" inbound to the "inside." If "outside" is defined as the external Internet, scan suppression can thwart naive attackers. But it can't prevent infection from external worms because during the early portion of a worm outbreak an inbound-scan detector may only observe a few (perhaps only single) scans from any individual source. Thus, unless the suppression device halts all new activity on the target port (potentially disastrous in terms of collateral damage), it will be unable to decide, based on a single request from a previously unseen source, whether that request is benign or an infection attempt.

For worm *containment*, however, we turn the scan suppressor around: "inside" becomes the enterprise's larger internal network, to be protected from the "outside" local area network. Now any scanning worm will be quickly detected and stopped, because (nearly) *all* of the infectee's traffic will be seen by the detector.

We derived our scan detection algorithm from TRW (Threshold Random Walk) scan detection [11]. In abstract terms, the algorithm operates by using an oracle to determine if a connection will fail or succeed. A successfully completed connection drives a random walk upwards, a failure to connect drives it downwards. By modeling the benign traffic as having a different (higher) probability of success than attack traffic, TRW can then make a decision regarding the likelihood that a particular series of connection attempts from a given host reflect benign or attack activity, based on how far the random walk deviates above or below the origin. By casting the problem in a Bayesian random walk framework, TRW can provide deviation thresholds that correspond to specific false positive and false negative rates, if we can parameterize it with good *a priori* probabilities for the rate of benign and attacker connection successes.

To implement TRW, we obviously can't rely on having a connection oracle handy, but must instead track connection establishment. Furthermore, we must do so using data structures amenable to high-speed hardware implementation, which constrains us considerably. Finally, TRW has one added degree of complexity not mentioned above. It only considers the success or failure of connection attempts to *new* addresses. If a source repeatedly contacts the same host, TRW does its random walk accounting and decision-making only for the first attempt. This approach inevitably requires a very large amount of state to keep track of which pairs of addresses have already tried to connect, too costly for our goal of a line-rate hardware implementation. As developed in Section 6.5, our technique uses a number of approximations of TRW's exact bookkeeping, yet still achieves quite good results.

There are two significant alternate scan detection mechanisms proposed for worm containment. The first is the new-destination metric proposed by Williamson [36]. This measures the number of new destinations a host can visit in a given period of time, usually set to 1 per second. The second is dark-address detection, used by both Forescout [9] and Mirage Networks [17]. In these detectors, the device routes or knows some otherwise unoccupied address spaces within the internal network and detects when systems attempt to contact these unused addresses.

6.4 Hardware Implementations

When targeting hardware, memory access speed, memory size, and the number of distinct memory banks become critical design constraints, and, as mentioned above, these requirements drive us to use data structures that sometimes only approximate the network's state rather than exactly tracking it. In this section we discuss these constraints and some of our design choices to accommodate them. The next section then develops a scan detection algorithm based on using these approximations.

Memory access speed is a surprisingly significant constraint. During transmission of a minimum-sized gigabit Ethernet packet, we only have time to access a DRAM at 8 different locations. If we aim to monitor both directions of the link (gigabit Ethernet is full duplex), our budget drops to 4 accesses. The situation is accordingly even worse for 10-gigabit networks: DRAM is no longer an option at all, and we must use much more expensive SRAM. If an implementation wishes to monitor several links in parallel, this further increases the demand on the memory as the number of packets increases.

One partial solution for dealing with the tight DRAM access budget is the use of independent memory banks allowing us to access two distinct tables simultaneously. Each bank, however, adds to the overall cost of the system. Accordingly, we formulated a design goal of no more than 4 memory accesses per packet to 2 separate tables, with each table only requiring two accesses: a read and a write to the same location.

Memory size can also be a limiting factor. For the near future, SRAMs will only be able to hold a few tens of megabytes, compared with the gigabits we can store in DRAMs. Thus, our ideal memory footprint is to stay under 16 MB. This leaves open the option of implementing using only SRAM, and thus potentially running at 10 gigabit speeds.

Additionally, software implementations can also benefit from using the approximations we develop rather than exact algorithms. Since our final algorithm indeed meets our design goals—less than 16 MB of total memory (it is highly effective with just 5 MB) and 2 uncached memory accesses per packet—it could be included as a scan detector within a conventional network IDS such as Bro [20] or Snort [26], replacing or augmenting their current detection facilities.

6.4.1 Approximate Caches

When designing hardware, we often must store information in a fixed volume of memory. Since the information we'd *like* to store may exceed this volume, one approach is to use an *approximate cache*: a cache for which collisions cause imperfections. (From this perspective, a Bloom filter is a type of approximation cache [2].) This is quite different from the more conventional notion of a cache for which, if we find an entry in the cache, we know exactly what it means, but a failed lookup requires accessing a large secondary data-store, or of a hash table, for which we will always find what we put in it earlier, but it may grow beyond bound. Along with keeping the memory bounded, approximate caches allow for very simple lookups, a significant advantage when designing hardware.

However, we then must deal with the fact that collisions in approximate caches can have complicated semantics. Whenever two elements map to the same location in the cache, we must decide how to react. One option is to combine distinct entries into a single element. Another is to discard either the old entry or the new entry. Accordingly, collisions, or *aliasing*, create two additional security complications:

false positives or negatives due to the policy when entries are combined or evicted, and the possibility of an attacker manipulating the cache to exploit these aliasing-related false outcomes.

Since the goal of our scan-suppression algorithm is to generate automatic responses, we consider false positives more severe than false negatives, since they will cause an instance of useful traffic to be completely impaired, degrading overall network reliability. A false negative, on the other hand, often only means that it takes us longer to detect a scanner (unless the false negative is systemic). In addition, if we can structure the system such that several positives or negatives must occur before we make a response decision, then the effect will be mitigated if they are not fully correlated.

Thus, we decided to structure our cache-based approximations to avoid creating additional false positives. We can accomplish this by ensuring that, when removing entries or combining information, the resulting combination could only create a false negative, as discussed below.

Attackers can exploit false negatives or positives by either using them to create worms that evade detection, or by triggering responses to impair legitimate traffic. Attacker can do so through two mechanisms: predicting the hashing algorithm, or simply overwhelming the cache.

The first attack, equivalent to the algorithm complexity attacks described by Crosby and Wallach [5], relies on the attacker using knowledge of the cache's hash function to generate collisions. For Crosby's attack, the result was to increase the length of hash chains, but for an approximation cache, the analogous result is a spate of evicted or combined entries, resulting in excess false positives or negatives. A defense against it is to use a keyed hash function whose output the attacker cannot predict without knowing the key.

The second attack involves flooding the cache in order to hide a true attack by overwhelming the system's ability to track enough network activity. This could be accomplished by generating a massive amount of "normal" activity to cloak malicious behavior. Unlike the first attack, overwhelming the cache may require substantial resources.

While such attacks are a definite concern (see also Section 6.7), approximate caching is vital for a high-performance hardware implementation. Fortunately, as shown below, we are able to still obtain good detection results even given the approximations.

6.4.2 Efficient Small Block Ciphers

Another component in our design is the use of small (32 bit) block ciphers. An N-bit block cipher is equivalent to an N-bit keyed permutation: there exists a one-to-one mapping between every input word and every output word, and changing the key changes the permutation.

In general, large caches are either direct-mapped, where any value can only map to one possible location, or N-way associative. Looking up an element in a direct-mapped cache requires computing the index for the element and checking if it resides at that index. In an associative cache, there are N possible locations for any particular entry, arranged in a contiguous block (cache line). Each entry in an associative cache includes a tag value. To find an element, we compute the index and then in parallel check all possible locations based on the tag value to determine if the element is present.

Block ciphers give us a way to implement efficiently tagged caches that resist attackers predicting their collision patterns. They work by, rather than using the initial N-bit value to generate the cache index and tag values, first permuting the N-bit value, after which we separate the resulting N-bit value into an index and a tag. If we use k bits for the index, we only need $N - k$ bits for the tag, which can result in substantial memory savings for larger caches. If the block-cipher is well constructed and the key is kept secret from the attacker, this will generate cache indices that attackers cannot predict. This approach is often superior to using a hash function, as although a good hash function will also provide an attacker-unpredictable index, the entire N-bit initial value will be needed as a tag.

Ciphers that work well in software are often inefficient in hardware, and vice versa. For our design, we used a simple 32 bit cipher based on the Serpent S-boxes [1], particularly well-suited for FPGA or ASIC implementation as it requires only 8 levels of logic to compute.

6.5 Approximate Scan Suppression

Our scan detection and suppression algorithm approximates the TRW algorithm in a number of ways. First, we track connections and addresses using approximate caches. Second, to save state, rather than only incorporating the success or failure of connection attempts to new addresses, we do so for attempts to new addresses, new ports at old addresses, and old ports at old addresses if the corresponding entry in our state table has timed out. Third, we do not ever make a decision that an address is benign; we track addresses indefinitely as long as we do not have to evict their state from our caches.

We also extend TRW's principles to allow us to detect vertical as well as horizontal TCP scans, and also horizontal UDP scans, while TRW only detects horizontal TCP scans. Finally, we need to implement a "hygiene filter" to thwart some stealthy scanning techniques without causing undue restrictions on normal machines.

Figure 6.1 gives the overall structure of the data structures. We track connections using a fixed-sized table indexed by hashing the "inside" IP address, the "outside" IP address, and, for TCP, the inside port number. Each record consists of a 6 bit age counter and a bit for each direction (inside to outside and outside to inside), recording whether we have seen a packet in that direction. This table combines entries in the case of aliasing, which means we may consider communication to have been bidirectional when in fact it was unidirectional, turning a failed connection attempt into a success (and, thus, biasing towards false negatives rather than false positives).

We track external ("outside") addresses using an associative approximation cache. To find an entry, we encrypt the external IP address using a 32 bit block cipher

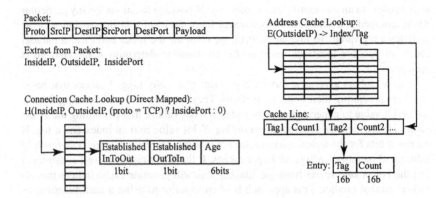

Packet:

| Proto | SrcIP | DestIP | SrcPort | DestPort | Payload |

Extract from Packet:
InsideIP, OutsideIP, InsidePort

Connection Cache Lookup (Direct Mapped):
H(InsideIP, OutsideIP, (proto = TCP) ? InsidePort : 0)

| Established InToOut | Established OutToIn | Age |
| 1bit | 1bit | 6bits |

Address Cache Lookup:
E(OutsideIP) -> Index/Tag

Cache Line:

| Tag1 | Count1 | Tag2 | Count2 | ... |

Entry:

| Tag | Count |
| 16b | 16b |

Fig. 6.1. The structure of the connection cache and the address cache. The connection cache tracks whether a connection has been established in either direction. The age value is reset to 0 every time we see a packet for that connection. Every minute, a background process increases the age of all entries in the connection cache, removing any idle entry more than D_{conn} minutes old. The address cache keeps track of all detected addresses, and records in "count" the difference between the number of failed and successful connections. Every D_{miss} seconds, each positive count in the address cache is reduced by one.

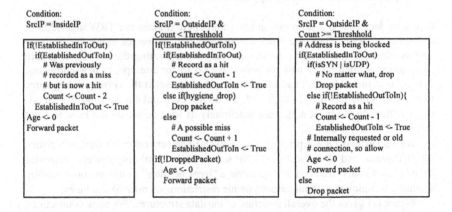

Condition:
SrcIP = InsideIP

```
If(!EstablishedInToOut)
   if(EstablishedOutToIn)
      # Was previously
      # recorded as a miss
      # but is now a hit
      Count <- Count - 2
   EstablishedInToOut <- True
Age <- 0
Forward packet
```

Condition:
SrcIP = OutsideIP &
Count < Threshhold

```
If(!EstablishedOutToIn)
   if(EstablishedInToOut)
      # Record as a hit
      Count <- Count - 1
      EstablishedOutToIn <- True
   else if(hygiene_drop)
      Drop packet
   else
      # A possible miss
      Count <- Count + 1
      EstablishedOutToIn <- True
if(!DroppedPacket)
   Age <- 0
   Forward packet
```

Condition:
SrcIP = OutsideIP &
Count >= Threshhold

```
# Address is being blocked
if(EstablishedInToOut)
   if(isSYN | isUDP)
      # No matter what, drop
      Drop packet
   else if(!EstablishedOutToIn){
      # Record as a hit
      Count <- Count - 1
      EstablishedOutToIn <- True
   # Internally requested or old
   # connection, so allow
   Age <- 0
   Forward packet
else
   Drop packet
```

Fig. 6.2. The high level structure of the detection and response algorithm. We count every successful connection (in either direction) as a "hit", with all failed or possibly-failed connections as "misses". If the difference between the number of hits and misses is greater than a threshold, we block further communication attempts from that address.

as discussed in Section 6.4.2, separating the resulting 32 bit number into an index and a tag, and using the index to find the group (or line) of entries. In our design, we use a 4-way associative cache, and thus each line can contain up to four entries, with each entry consisting of the tag and a counter. The counter tracks the difference between misses and hits (i.e., successful and unsuccessful connection attempts), forming the basis of our detection algorithm.

Whenever the device receives a packet, it looks up the corresponding connection in the connection table and the corresponding external address in the address table. Per Figure 6.2, the status of these two tables, and the direction of the packet, determines the action to take, as follows:

For a non-blocked external address (one we have not already decided to suppress), if a corresponding connection has already been established in the packet's direction, we reduce the connection table's age to 0 and forward the packet. Otherwise, if the packet is from the outside and we have seen a corresponding connection request from the inside, we forward the packet and decrement the address's count in the address table by 1, as we now credit the outside address with a successful connection. Otherwise, we forward the packet but increment the external address's count by 1, as now that address has one more outstanding, so-far-unacknowledged connection request.

Likewise, for packets from internal addresses, if there is a connection establishment from the other direction, the count is reduced, in this case by 2, since we are changing our bookkeeping of it from a failure to a success (we previously incremented the failure-success count by 1 because we initially treat a connection attempt as a failure).

Thus, the count gives us an on-going estimate of the difference between the number of misses (failed connections) and the number of successful connections. Given the assumption that legitimate traffic succeeds in its connection attempts with a probability greater than 50%, while scanning traffic succeeds with a probability less than 50%, by monitoring this difference we can determine when it is highly probable that a machine is scanning.

6.5.1 Blocking and Special Cases

If an address's count exceeds a predefined threshold T, the device blocks it. When we receive subsequent packet from that address, our action depends on the packet's type and whether it matches an existing, successfully-established connection, which we can tell from the connection status bits stored in the connection table. If the packet does not match an existing connection, we drop it. If it does, then we still drop it if it is a UDP packet or a TCP initial SYN. Otherwise, we allow it through. By blocking in this manner, we prevent the blocked machine from establishing subsequent TCP or UDP sessions, while still allowing it to *accept* TCP connection requests and continue with existing connections. Doing so lessens the collateral damage caused by false positives.

We treat TCP RST, RST+ACK, SYN+ACK, FIN, and FIN+ACK packets specially. If they do not correspond to a connection established in the other direction, the hygiene filter simply drops these packets, as they could reflect stealthy scanning attempts, backscatter from spoofed-source flooding attacks, or the closing of very-long-idle connections. Since they might be scans, we need to drop them to limit an attacker's information. But since they might instead be benign activity, we don't use them to trigger blocks.

Likewise, if a connection has been established in the other direction, but not in the current direction, then we forward TCP RST, RST+ACK, FIN, and FIN+ACK packets, but do not change the external address's counter, to avoid counting failed connections as successful. (A FIN+ACK could reflect a successful connection *if* we have seen the connection already established in the current direction, but the actions here are those we take if we have not seen this.)

6.5.2 Errors and Aliasing

Because connection table combines entries when aliasing occurs, it can create a false negative at a rate that depends on the fullness of the table. If the table is 20% full, then we will fail to detect roughly 20% of individual scanning attempts. Likewise, 20% of the successful connection attempts will not serve to reduce an address's failure/success count either, because the evidence of the successful connection establishment aliases with a connection table entry that already indicates a successful establishment.

To prevent the connection table from being overwhelmed by old entries, we remove any connection idle for more than an amount of time D_{conn}, which to make our design concrete we set to $D_{conn} = 10$ minutes. We can't reclaim table space by just looking for termination (FIN exchanges) because aliasing may mean we need to still keep the table entry after one of the aliased connections terminates, and because UDP protocols don't have a clear "terminate connection" message.

While the connection table combines entries, the address table, since it is responsible for blocking connections and contains tagged data, needs to evict entries rather than combining information. Yet evicting important data can cause false negatives, requiring a balancing act in the eviction policy. We observe that standard cache replacement policies such as least recently used (LRU), round robin, and random, can evict addresses of high interest. Instead, when we need to evict an entry, we want to select the entry with the most negative value for the (miss–hit) count, as this constitutes the entry least likely to reflect a scanner; although we thus tend to evict highly active addresses from the table, they represent highly active *normal* machines.

In principle, this policy could occasionally create a transient false positive, if subsequent connections from the targeted address occur in a very short term burst, with several connection attempts made before the first requests can be acknowledged. We did not, however, observe this phenomenon in our testing.

6.5.3 Parameters and Tuning

There are several key parameters to tune with our system, including the response threshold T (miss–hit difference that we take to mean a scan detection), minimum and maximum counts, and decay rates for the connection cache and for the counts. We also need to size the caches.

For T, our observations below in Section 6.5.5 indicate that for the traces we assessed a threshold of 5 suffices for blocking inbound scanning, while a threshold of 10 is a suitable starting point for worm containment.

The second parameters, C_{min} and C_{max}, are the minimum and maximum values the count is allowed to achieve. C_{min} is needed to prevent a previously good address that is subsequently infected from being allowed too many connections before it is blocked, while C_{max} limits how long it takes before a highly-offending blocked machine is allowed to communicate again. For testing purposes, we set C_{min} to -20, and C_{max} to ∞ as we were interested in the maximum count which each address could reach in practice.

The third parameter, D_{miss}, is the decay rate for misses. Every D_{miss} seconds, all addresses with positive counts have their count reduced by one. Doing so allows a low rate of benign misses to be forgiven, without seriously enabling sub-threshold scanning. We set D_{miss} equal to 60 seconds, or one minute, meeting our sub-threshold scanning goal of 1 scan per minute. In the future, we wish to experiment with a much lower decay rate for misses.

We use a related decay rate, D_{conn}, to remove idle connections, since we can't rely on a "connection-closed" message to determine when to remove entries. As mentioned earlier, we set D_{conn} to 10 minutes.

The final parameters specify the size and associativity of the caches. A software implementation can tune these parameters, but a hardware system will need to fix these based on available resources. For evaluation purposes, we assumed a 1 million entry connection cache (which would require 1 MB), and a 1 million entry, 4-way associative address cache (4 MB). Both cache sizes worked well with our traces, although increasing the connection cache to 4 MB would provide increased sensitivity by diminishing aliasing.

6.5.4 Policy Options

Several policy options and variations arise when using our system operationally: the threshold of response, whether to disallow all communication from blocked addresses, whether to treat all ports as the same or to allow some level of benign scanning on less-important ports, and whether to detect horizontal and vertical, or just horizontal, TCP scans.

The desired initial response threshold T may vary from site to site. Since all machines above a threshold of 6 in our traces represent some sort of scanner (some benign, most malicious, per Section 6.5.5), this indicates a threshold of 10 on outbound connections would be conservative for deployment within our environment, while a threshold of 5 appears sufficient for incoming connections.

A second policy decision is whether to block all communication from a blocked machine, or to only limit new connections it initiates. The first option offers a greater degree of protection, while the second is less disruptive for false positives.

Table 6.1. All outbound connections over a threshold of 5 flagged by our algorithm

Anonymized IP	Maximum Count	Cause
221.147.96.4	16	Benign DNS Scanner?
		Dynamic DNS host error?
147.95.58.73	12	AFS-Related Control Traffic?
147.95.35.149	12	NetBIOS "Scanning" and activity
147.95.238.71	8	AFS-Related Control Traffic?
144.240.17.50	6	Benign SNMP (UDP) "Scanning"
144.240.96.234	6	NetBIOS "scanning" of a few hosts

A third decision is how to configure C_{min} and C_{max}, the floor and ceiling on the counter value. We discussed the tradeoffs for these in the previous section.

A fourth policy option would be to treat some ports differently than others. Some applications, such as Gnutella [22], use scanning to find other servers. Likewise, at some sites particular tools may probe numerous machines to discover network topology. One way to give different ports different weights would be to changing the counter from an integer to a fixed-point value. For example, we could assign SNMP a cost of .25 rather than 1, to allow a greater degree of unidirectional SNMP attempts before triggering an alarm. We can also weight misses and hits differently, to alter the proportion of traffic we expect to be successful for benign vs. malicious sources.

Finally, changing the system to only detect horizontal TCP scans requires changing the inputs to the connection cache's hash function. By excluding the internal port number from the hash function, we will include all internal ports in the same bucket. Although this prevents the algorithm from detecting vertical scans, it also eliminates an evasion technique discussed in Section 6.7.6.

6.5.5 Evaluation

We used hour-long traces of packet header collected at the access link at the Lawrence Berkeley National Laboratory. This gigabit/sec link connects the Laboratory's 6,000 hosts to the Internet. The link sustains an average of about 50–100 Mbps and 8–15K packets/sec over the course of a day, which includes roughly 20M externally-initiated connection attempts (most reflecting ambient scanning from worms and other automated malware) and roughly 2M internally-initiated connections. The main trace we analyzed was 72 minutes long, beginning at 1:56PM on a Friday afternoon. It totaled 44M packets and included traffic from 48,052 external addresses (and all 131K internal addresses, due to some energetic scans covering the entire internal address space). We captured the trace using tcpdump, which reported 2,200 packets dropped by the measurement process.

We do not have access to the ideal traces for assessing our system, which would be all internal and external traffic for a major enterprise. However, the access-link traces at least give us a chance to evaluate the detection algorithm's behavior over high-diverse, high-volume traffic.

We processed the traces using a custom Java application so we could include a significant degree of instrumentation, including cache-miss behavior, recording evicted machines, maintaining maximum and minimum counts, and other options not necessary for a production system. Additionally, since we developed the experimental framework for off-line analysis, high performance was not a requirement. Our goal was to extract the necessary information to determine how our conceptual hardware design will perform in terms of false positives and negatives and quickness of response.

For our algorithm, we just recorded the maximum count rather than simulating a specific blocking threshold, so we can explore the tradeoffs different thresholds would yield. We emulated a 1 million entry connection cache, and a 1 million entry, 4-way associative address cache. The connection cache reached 20% full during the primary trace. The eviction rate in the address cache was very low, with no evictions when tested with the Internet as "outside," and only 2 evictions when the enterprise was "outside." Thus, the 5 MB of storage for the two tables was quite adequate.

We first ran our algorithm with the enterprise as outside, to determine which of its hosts would be blocked by worm containment and why. We manually checked all alerts that would be generated for a threshold of 5, shown in Table 6.1. Of these, all represented benign scanning or unidirectional control traffic. The greatest offender, at a count of 16, appears to be a misconfigured client which resulted in benign DNS scanning. The other sources appears to generate AFS-related control traffic on UDP ports 7000–7003; scanning from a component of Microsoft NetBIOS file sharing; and benign SNMP (UDP-based) scanning, apparently for remotely monitoring printer queues.

With the Internet as "outside," over 470 external addresses reached a threshold of 5 or higher. While this seems incredibly high, it in fact represents the endemic scanning which occurs continually on the Internet [11]. We manually examined the top 5 offenders, whose counts ranged from 26,000 to 49,000, and verified that these were all blatant scanners. Of these, one was scanning for the FTP control port (21/tcp), two were apparently scanning for a newly discovered vulnerability in Dameware Remote Administrator (6129/tcp), and two were apparently scanning for a Windows RPC vulnerability (135/tcp; probably from hosts infected with Blaster [31]).

Additionally, we examined the offenders with the lowest counts above the threshold. 10 addresses had a maximum count between 20 and 32. Of these, 8 were scans on a NetBIOS UDP port 137, targeted at a short (20–40 address) sequential range, with a single packet sent to each machine. Of the remaining two offenders, one probed randomly selected machines in a /16 for a response on TCP port 80 using 3 SYN packets per attempt, while the other probed randomly selected machines on port 445/tcp with 2 SYN packets per attempt. All of these offenders represented true scanners: none is a false positive.

We observed 19 addresses with a count between 5 and 19, where we would particularly expect to see false positives showing up. Of these, 15 were NetBIOS UDP scanners. Of the remaining 4, one was scanning 1484/udp, one was scanning 80/tcp, and one was scanning 445/tcp. The final entry was scanning both 138/udp and gener-

Table 6.2. Additional alerts on the outbound traffic generated when the sensitivity was increased.

Anonymized IP	Maximum Count	Cause
147.95.61.87	11	NNTP, sustained low rate of failures
147.95.35.154	11	High port UDP, 10 scans in a row
221.147.96.220	9	TCP port 13 ("daytime"), detected due to reduced sub-threshold
144.240.96.234	9	NetBIOS and failed HTTP, detected due to reduced sub-threshold
144.240.28.138	7	High port UDP, due to reduced sub-threshold
147.95.3.27	6	TCP Port 25, due to reduced sub-threshold
147.95.36.165	5	High port UDP, due to reduced sub-threshold
144.240.43.227	5	High port UDP, due to reduced sub-threshold

ating successful communications on 139/tcp and port 80/tcp. The final entry, which reached a maximum count of 6, represents a NetBIOS-related false positive.

Finally, we also examined ten randomly selected external addresses flagged by our algorithm. Eight were UDP scanners targeting port 137, while two were TCP scanners targeting port 445. All represent true positives.

During this test, the connection cache size of 1 million entries reached about 20% full. Thus, each new scan attempt has a 20% chance of not being recorded because it aliases with an already-established connection. If the connection cache was increased to 4 million entries (4 MB instead of 1 MB), the false negative rate would drop to slightly over 5%.

We conducted a second test to determine the effects of setting the parameters for maximum sensitivity. We increased the connection cache to 4 million entries, reducing the number of false negatives due to aliasing. We also tightened the C_{min} threshold to -5, which increases the sensitivity to possible misbehavior of previously "good" machines, and increased D_{miss} to infinity, meaning that we never decayed misses. Setting the threshold of response to 5 would then trigger an alert for an otherwise idle machine once it made a series of 5 failed connections; while a series of 10 failed connections would trigger an alert regardless of an address's past behavior.

We manually examined all outbound alerts (i.e., alerts generated when considering the enterprise "outside") that would have triggered when using this threshold, looking for additional false positives. Table 6.2 summarizes these additional alerts.

We would expect that, by increasing the sensitivity in this manner, we would observe some non-scanning false positives. Of the additional alerts, only one new alert was generated because of the changed C_{min}. This machine sent out unidirectional UDP to 15 destinations in a row, which was countered by normal behavior when C_{min} was set to -20 instead of -5. The rest of the alerts were triggered because of the reduced decay of misses. In all these cases, the traffic consisted of unidirectional communication to multiple machines. The TCP-based activity (NNTP, daytime, and SMTP) showed definite failed connections, but these may be benign failures.

In summary, even with the aggressive thresholds, there are few false positives, and they appear to reflect quite peculiar traffic.

6.5.6 Williamson Implementation

For comparison purposes, we also included in our trace analysis program an implementation of Williamson's technique [36], which we evaluated against the site's outbound traffic in order to assess its performance in terms of worm containment. Williamson's algorithm uses a small cache of previously-allowed destinations. For all SYNs and any UDP packets, if we find the destination in the allowed-destination cache, we forward it regularly. If not, but if the source has not sent to a new destination (i.e., we haven't added anything to its allowed-destination cache) during the past second, then we put an entry in the cache to note that we are allowing communication between the source and the given destination, and again forward the packet.

Table 6.3. All outbound connections with a delay queue of size 15 or greater for Williamson's algorithm

Anonymized IP	Delay Queue Size	Cause
144.240.84.131	11,395	DNS Server
147.95.15.21	8,772	DNS Server
144.240.84.130	3,416	DNS Server
147.95.3.37	23	SMTP Server
144.240.25.76	19	Bursty DNS Client
147.95.52.12	18	Active HTTP Client
147.95.208.255	17	Active HTTP Client
147.95.208.18	15	Active HTTP Client

Otherwise, we add the packet to a delay queue. We process this queue at the rate of one destination per second. Each second, for each source we determine the next destination it attempted to send to but so far has not due to our delay queue. We then forward the source's packets for that destination residing in the delay queue and add the destination to the allowed-destination cache. The effect of this mechanism is to limit sources to contacting a single new destination each second. One metric of interest with this algorithm then is the maximum size the delay queue reaches.

A possible negative consequence of the Williamson algorithm is that the cache of previously established destinations introduces false positives rather than false negatives. Due to its limited size, previously established destinations may be evicted prematurely. For testing purposes, we selected cache sizes of 8 previously-allowed destinations per source (3 greater than the cache size used in [36]). We manually examined all internal sources where the delay queue reached 15 seconds or larger, enough to produce a significant disturbance for a user (Table 6.3).

In practice, we observed that the Williamson algorithm has a very low false positive rate, with only a few minor exceptions. First, the DNS servers in the trace greatly overflow the delay queue due to their high fanout when resolving recursive queries, and thus would need to be special-cased. Likewise, a major SMTP server also triggered a response due to its high connection fanout, and would also require white-listing. However, of potential note is that three HTTP clients reached a threshold greater than 15, which would produce a user-noticeable delay but not trigger a permanent alarm, based on Williamson's threshold of blocking machines when their delay queue reaches a depth of 100 [32].

6.6 Cooperation

Staniford analyzed the efficacy of worm containment in an enterprise context, finding that such systems exhibit a phase structure with an epidemic threshold [27]. For sufficiently low vulnerability densities and/or T thresholds, the system can almost completely contain a worm. However, if these parameters are too large, a worm can escape and infect a sizeable fraction of the vulnerable hosts despite the presence of the containment system. The epidemic threshold occurs when on average a worm instance is able to infect exactly one child before being contained. Less than this, and the worm will peter out. More, and the worm will spread exponentially. Thus we desire to set the response threshold T as low as possible, but if we set it too low, we may incur unacceptably many false positives. This tends to place a limit on the maximum vulnerability density that a worm containment system can handle.

In this section, we present a preliminary analysis of performance improvements that come from incorporating communication between cells. The improvement arises by using a second form of a-worm-is-spreading detector: the alerts generated by other containment devices. The idea is that every containment device knows how many blocks the other containment devices currently have in effect. Each devise uses this information to dynamically adjust its response threshold: as more systems are being blocked throughout the enterprise, the individual containment devices become more sensitive. This positive feedback allows the system to adaptively respond to a spreading worm.

The rules for doing so are relatively simple. All cells communicate, and when one cell blocks an address, it communicates this status to the other cells. Consequently, at any given time each cell can compute that X other blocks are in place, and thereby reduces T by $(1 - \theta)^X$, where θ is a parameter that controls how aggressively to reduce the threshold as a worm spreads. For our algorithm, the cell also needs to increase C_{min} by a similar amount, to limit the scanning allowed by a previously normal machine.

In our simulations, very small values of θ make a significant difference in performance. This is good, since reducing the threshold also tends to increase false positive rates.[5]

---

[5] Large values of θ risk introducing catastrophic failure modes in which some initial false positive drives thresholds low enough to create more false positives, which drive thresholds still lower. This could lead to a complete blockage of traffic due to a runaway positive

However, we can have the threshold return to its normal (initial) value using an exponentially weighted time delay to ensure that this effect is short lived.

A related policy question is whether this function should allow a complete shutdown of the network (no new connections tolerated), or should have a minimum threshold below which the containment devices simply will not go, potentially allowing a worm to still operate at a slower spreading rate, depending on its epidemic threshold. The basic tradeoff is ensuring a degree of continued operation, vs. a stronger assure that we will limit possible damage from the worm.

6.6.1 Testing Cooperation

To evaluate the effects of cooperation, we started with the simulation program used in the previous evaluation of containment [27]. We modified the simulator so that each response would reduce the threshold by θ. We then reran some of the simulations examined in [27] to assess the effect on the epidemic threshold for various values of θ.

The particular set of parameters we experimented with involved an enterprise network of size 2^{17} addresses. We assumed a worm that had a 50% probability of scanning inside the network, with the rest falling outside the enterprise. We also assumed an initial threshold of $T = 10$, that the network was divided into 512 cells of 256 addresses each, and that the worm had no special preference to scan within its cell. We considered a uniform vulnerability density. These choices correspond to Figure 2 in [27], and, as shown there, the epidemic threshold is then at a vulnerability density of $v = 0.2$ (that is, it occurs when 20% of the addresses are vulnerable to the worm).

We varied the vulnerability density across this epidemic threshold for different values of θ, and studied the resulting average infection density (the proportion of vulnerable machines which actually got infected). This is shown in Figure 6.3, where each point represents the average of 5,000 simulated worm runs. The top curve shows the behavior when communication does not modify the threshold (i.e., $\theta = 0$), and successively lower curves have $\theta = 0.00003$, $\theta = 0.0001$, and $\theta = 0.0003$. It is to be emphasized that these are tiny values of θ (less than 3/100 of 1%). One would not expect there to be any significant problem of increased false positives with such small changes; but that they are larger than zero suffices to introduce significant positive feedback in the presence of a propagating worm (i.e., the overall rate of blocked scans within the network rises over time).

The basic structure of the results is clear. Changing θ does not significantly change the epidemic threshold, but we can greatly reduce the infection density that

---

feedback loop. This is unlikely with the small values of θ in this study, and moreover could be addressed by introducing a separate threshold for communication that was *not* adaptively modified. The two thresholds would begin at the same value, but the blocking threshold would lower as the worm spread, while the communication threshold — i.e., the degree of scanning required before a device *tells* other devices that it has blocked the corresponding address — would stay fixed. This would sharply limit the positive feedback of more false positives triggering ever more changes to the threshold.

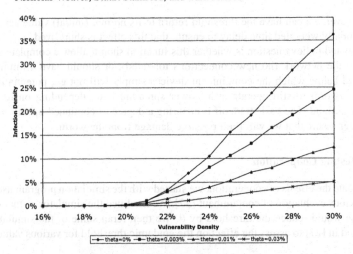

Fig. 6.3. Plot of worm infection density against vulnerability density v for varying values of the threshold modification value θ. See the text for more details.

the worm can achieve above the epidemic threshold. It makes sense that the epidemic threshold is not changed, since below the epidemic threshold, the worm cannot gain much traction and so the algorithm that modifies T has no chance to engage and alter the situation. However, above the epidemic threshold, adaptively changing T can greatly reduce the infection density a worm can achieve. Clearly, inter-cell communication mechanisms hold great promise at improving the performance of containment systems.[6]

We must however discuss a simplification we made in our simulation. We effectively assumed that communication amongst cells occurs instantaneously compared to the worm propagation. Clearly, this an idealization. A careless design of the communication mechanism could result in speeds that cause the threshold modification to always substantially lag behind the propagation of the worm, greatly limiting its usefulness. (See [18] for a discussion of the competing dynamics of a response to a worm and the worm itself).

For example, it can be shown that a design in which we send a separate packet to each cell that needs notification allows worm instances to scan (on average) a number of addresses equal to half the number of cells before any threshold modification occurs (assuming that the worm can scan at the same speed as the communication mechanism can send notifications). This isn't very satisfactory.

One simple approach to achieve very fast inter-cell communication is to use broadcast across the entire network. However, this is likely to pose practical risks

---

[6] Particularly in parts of the parameter space where the epidemic threshold vulnerability density is much lower than 20% — e.g., if the worm has the ability to differentially target its own cell.

to network performance in the case where there are significant numbers of false positives.

A potentially better approach is for the containment devices to cache recently contacted addresses. Then when a source IP crosses the threshold for scan detection, the cells it recently communicated with can be contacted first (in order). These cells will be the ones most in need of the information. In most cases, this will result in threshold modification occurring before the threshold is reached on any cells that got infected as a result (rather than the message arriving too late and the old unmodified threshold being used).

6.7 Attacking Worm Containment

Security devices do not exist in a vacuum, but represent both targets and obstacles for possible attackers. By creating a false positive, an attacker can trigger responses which wouldn't otherwise occur. Since worm containment *must* restrict network traffic, false positives create an attractive DOS target. Likewise, false negatives allow a worm or attacker to slip by the defenses.

General containment can incur inadvertent false positives both from detection artifacts and from "benign" scanning. Additionally, attackers can generate false positives if they can forge packets, or attempt to evade containment if they detect it in operation. When we also use cooperation, an attacker who controls machines in several cells can cause significant network disruption through cooperative collapse: using the network of compromised machines to trigger an institution-wide response by driving down the thresholds used by the containment devices through the institute (if θ is large enough to allow this). Our scan detection algorithm also has an algorithm-specific, two-sided evasion, though we can counter these evasions with some policy changes, which we discuss below. Although we endeavor in this section to examine the full range of possible attacks, undoubtedly there are more attacks we haven't considered.

6.7.1 Inadvertent False Positives

There are two classes of inadvertent false positives: false positives resulting from artifacts of the detection routines, and false positives arising from "benign" scanning. The first are potentially the more severe, as these can severely limit the use of containment devices, while the second is often amenable to white-listing and other policy-based techniques.

In our primary testing trace, we observed only one instance of an artifact-induced false positive, due to unidirectional AFS control traffic. Thus, this does not appear to be a significant problem for our algorithm. Our implementation of Williamson's mechanism showed artifact-induced false positives involving 3 HTTP clients that would have only created a minor disruption. Also, Williamson's algorithm is specifically not designed to apply to traffic generated by servers, requiring these machines to be white-listed.

Alerting on benign scanning is less severe. Indeed, such scans should trigger all good scan-detection devices. More generally, "benign" is fundamentally a policy distinction: is this particular instance of scanning a legitimate activity, or something to prohibit?

We have observed benign scanning behavior from Windows File Sharing (Net-BIOS) and applications such as Gnutella which work through a list of previously-connected peers to find access into a peer-to-peer overlay. We note that if these protocols were modified to use a rendezvous point or a meta-server then we could eliminate their scanning behavior. The other alternative is to whitelist these services. By whitelisting, their scanning behavior won't trigger a response, but the containment devices can no longer halt a worm targeting these services.

6.7.2 Detecting Worm Containment

If a worm is propagating within an enterprise that has a containment system operating, then the worm could slow to a sub-threshold scanning rate to avoid being suppressed. But in the absence of a containment system, the worm should instead scan quickly. Thus, attackers will want to devise ways for a worm to detect the presence of a containment system.

Assuming that the worm instance knows the address of the host that infected it, and was told by it of a few other active copies of the worm in the enterprise, then the worm instance can attempt to establish a normal communication channel with the other copies. If each instance sets up these channels, together they can form a large distributed network, allowing the worm to learn of all other active instances.

Having established the network, the worm instance then begins sending out probes at a low rate, using its worm peers as a testing ground: if it can't establish communication with already-infected hosts, then it is likely the enterprise has a containment system operating. This information can be discovered even when the block halts all direct communication: the infection can send a message into the worm's overlay network, informing the destination worm that it will attempt to probe it. If the ensuing direct probe is blocked, the *receiving* copy now knows that the sender is blocked, as it was informed about the experimental attempt.

This information can then be spread via the still-functional connections among the worm peers in order to inform future infections in the enterprise. Likewise, if the containment system's blocks are only transient, the worm can learn this fact, and its instances can remain silent, waiting for blocks to lift, before resuming sub-threshold scanning.

Thus we must assume that a sophisticated worm can determine that a network employs containment, and probably deduce both the algorithm and parameters used in the deployment.

6.7.3 Malicious False Negatives

Malicious false negatives occur when a worm is able to scan in spite of active scan-containment. The easiest evasion is for the worm to simply not scan, but propagate via a different means: topological, meta-server, passive, and target-list (hit-list) worms all use non-scanning techniques [33]. Containing such worms is outside the scope of our work. We note, however, that scanning worms represent the largest class of worms seen to date and, more generally, a broad class of attack. Thus, eliminating scanning worms from a network clearly has a great deal of utility even if it does not address the entire problem space.

In addition, scanning worms that operate below the sustained-scanning threshold can avoid detection. Doing so requires more sophisticated scanning strategies, as the worms must bias their "random" target selection to effectively exploit the internal network in order to take advantage of the low rate of allowed scanning. The best countermeasure for this evasion technique is simply a far more sensitive threshold. We argue that a threshold of 1 scan per second (as in Williamson [36]), although effective for stopping current worms, is too permissive when a worm is attempting to evade containment. Thus we targeted a threshold of 1 scan per minute in our work.

Additionally, if scanning of some particular ports has been white-listed (such as Gnutella, discussed above), a worm could use that port to scan for liveness—i.e., whether a particular address has a host running on it, even though the host rejects the attempted connection—and then use followup scans to determine if the machine is actually vulnerable to the target service. While imperfect—failed connection attempts will still occur—the worm can at least drive the failure rate lower because the attempts will fail less often.

Another substantial evasion technique can occur if a corrupted system can obtain multiple network addresses. If a machine can gain k distinct addresses, then it can issue k times as many scans before being detected and blocked. This has the effect of reducing the epidemic threshold by a factor of k, a huge enhancement on a worm's ability to evade containment.

6.7.4 Malicious False Positives

If attackers can forge packets, they can frame other hosts in the same cell as scanners. We can engineer a local area network to resist such attacks by using the MAC address and switch features that prevent spoofing and changing of MAC addresses. This is not an option, though, for purported scans inbound to the enterprise coming from the external Internet. While the attacker can use this attack to deny service to external addresses, preventing them from initiating new connections to the enterprise, at least they can't block new connections initiated by internal hosts.

There is an external mechanism which could cause this internal DOS: a malicious web page or HTML-formatted email message could direct an internal client to attempt a slew of requests to nonexistent servers. Since this represents an attacker gaining a limited degree of control over the target machine (i.e., making it execute actions on the attacker's behalf), we look to block the attack using other types of techniques, such as imposing HTTP proxies and mail filtering to detect and block the malicious content.

6.7.5 Attacking Cooperation

Although cooperation helps defenders, an attacker can still attempt to outrace containment if the initial threshold is highly permissive. However, this is unlikely to occur simply because the amount of communication is very low, so it is limited by network latency rather than bandwidth. Additionally, broadcast packets could allow quick, efficient communication between all of the devices. Nevertheless, this suggests that the communication path should be optimized.

The attacker could also attempt to flood the containment coordination channels before beginning its spread. Thus, containment-devices should have reserved communication bandwidth, such as a dedicated LAN or prioritized VLAN channels, to prevent an attacker from disrupting the inter-cell communication.

Of greater concern is *cooperative collapse*. If the rate of false positives is high enough, the containment devices respond by lowering their thresholds, which can generate a cascade of false positives, which further reduces the threshold. Thus, it is possible that a few initial false positives, combined with a highly-sensitive response function, could trigger a maximal network-wide response, with major collateral damage.

An attacker that controls enough of the cells could attempt to trigger or amplify this effect by generating scanning in those cells. From the viewpoint of the worm containment, this appears to reflect a rapidly spreading worm, forcing a system-wide response. Thus, although cooperation appears highly desirable due to the degree to which it allows us to begin the system with a high tolerance setting (minimizing false positives), we need to develop models of containment cooperation that enable us to understand any potential exposure an enterprise has to the risk of maliciously induced cooperative collapse.

6.7.6 Attacking Our Algorithm

Our approximation algorithm adds two other risks: attackers exploiting the approximation caches' hash and permutation functions, and vulnerability to a two-sided evasion technique. We discussed attacking the hash functions earlier, which we address by using a block-cipher based hash. In the event of a delayed response due to a false negative, the attacker will have difficulty determining which possible entry resulted in a collision.

Another evasion is for the attacker to embed their scanning within a large storm of spoofed packets which cause thrashing in the address cache and which pollute the connection cache with a large number of half-open connections. Given the level of resources required to construct such an attack (hundreds of thousands or millions of forged packets), however, the attacker could probably spread just as well simply using a slow, distributed scan. Determining the tradeoffs between cache size and where it becomes more profitable to perform distributed scanning is an area for future work.

A more severe false negative is a two-sided evasion: two machines, one on each side of the containment device, generate normal traffic establishing connections on a multitude of ports. A worm could use this evasion technique to balance out the worm's scanning, making up for each failed scanning attempt by creating another successful connection between the two cooperating machines. Since our algorithm treats connections to distinct TCP ports as distinct attempts, two machines can generate enough successes to mask any amount of TCP scanning.

There is a counter-countermeasure available, however. Rather than attempting to detect both vertical and horizontal TCP scanning, we can modify the algorithm to detect only horizontal scans by excluding port information from the connection-cache tuple. This change prevents the algorithm from detecting vertical scans, but greatly limits the evasion potential, as now any pair of attacker-controlled machines can only create a single success.

More generally, however, for an Internet-wide worm infection, the huge number of external infections could allow the worm to generate a large amount of successful traffic even when we restrict the detector to only look for horizontal scans. We can counter this technique, though, by splitting the detector's per-address count into one count associated with scanning within the internal network and a second count to detect scanning on the Internet. By keeping these counts separate, an attacker could use this evasion technique to allow Internet scanning, but they could not exploit it to scan the internal network. Since our goal is to protect enterprise and not the Internet in the large, this is acceptable.

A final option is to use two containment implementations, operating simultaneously, one targeting scans across the Internet and the other only horizontal scans within the enterprise. This requires twice the resources, although any hardware can be parallelized, and allows detection of both general scanning and scanning behavior designed to evade containment.

6.8 Related Work

In addition to the TRW algorithm used as a starting point for our work [11], a number of other algorithms to detect scanning have appeared in the literature.

Both the Network Security Monitor [10] and Snort [26] attempt to detect scanning by monitoring for systems which exceed a count of unique destination addresses contacted during a given interval. Both systems can exhibit false positives due to active, normal behavior, and may also have a significant scanning sub-threshold which an attacker can exploit.

Bro [20] records failed connections on ports of interest and triggers after a user-configurable number of failures. Robinson *et al.* [23] used a similar method.

Leckie *et al* [14] use a probabilistic model based on attempting to learn the probabilistic structure of normal network behavior. The model assumes that access to addresses made by scanners follows a uniform distribution rather than the non-homogeneous distribution learned for normal traffic, and attempts to classify possible scanning sources based on the degree to which one distribution or the other better fits their activity.

Finally, Staniford *et al*'s work on SPICE [28] detects very stealthy scans by correlating anomalous events. Although effective, it requires too much computation to use it for line-rate detection on high-speed networks.

In addition to Williamson's [36, 32] and Staniford's [27, 29] work on worm containment, Jung et al [12] have developed a similar containment technique based on TRW. Rather than using an online algorithm which assumes that all connections fail until proven successful, it uses the slightly delayed (until response seen or timeout) TRW combined with a mechanism to limit new connections similar to Williamson's algorithm.

Zou *et al.* [38] model some requirements for dynamic-quarantine defenses. They also demonstrate that, with a fixed threshold of detection and response, there are epidemic thresholds. Additionally, Moore *et al.* have studied abstract requirements for containment of worms on the Internet [16], and Nojiri *et al* have studied the competing spread of a worm and a not-specifically-modeled response to it [18].

There have been two other systems attempting to commercialize scan containment: Mirage networks [17] and Forescout [9]. Rather than directly detecting scanning, these systems intercept communication to unallocated (dark) addresses and respond by blocking the infected systems.

6.9 Future Work

We have plans for future work in several areas: implementing the system in hardware and deploying it; integrating the algorithm into a software-based IDS; attempting to improve the algorithm further by reducing the sub-threshold scanning available to an attacker; exploring optimal communication strategies; and developing techniques to obtain a complete enterprise-trace for further testing.

The hardware implementation will target the ML300 demonstration platform by Xilinx [37]. This board contains 4 gigabit Ethernet connections, a small FPGA, and a single bank of DDR-DRAM. The DRAM bank is sufficiently large to meet our design goals, while the DRAM's internal banking should enable the address and connection tables to be both implemented in the single memory.

We will integrate our software implementation into the Bro IDS, with the necessary hooks to pass IP blocking information to routers (which Bro already does for its current, less effective scan-detection algorithm). Doing so will require selecting a different 32-bit block cipher, as our current cipher is very inefficient in software. For both hardware and software, we aim to operationally deploy these systems.

Finally, we are investigating ways to capture a full-enterprise trace: record every packet in an large enterprise network of many thousands of users. We believe this is necessary to test worm detection and suppression devices using realistic traffic, while reflecting the diversity of use which occurs in real, large intranets. Currently, we are unaware of any such traces of contemporary network traffic.

6.10 Conclusions

We have demonstrated a highly sensitive approximate scan-detection and suppression algorithm suitable for worm containment. It offers substantially higher sensitivity over previously published algorithms for worm containment, while easily operating within an 8 MB memory footprint and requiring only 2 uncached memory accesses per packet. This algorithm is suitable for both hardware and software implementations.

The scan detector used by our system can limit worm infectees to sustained scanning rates of 1 per minute or less. We can configure it to be highly sensitive, detecting scanning from an idle machine after fewer than 10 attempts in short succession, and from an otherwise normal machine in less than 30 attempts.

We developed how to augment the containment system with using *cooperation* between the containment devices that monitor different cells. By introducing communication between these devices, they can dynamically adjust their thresholds to the level of infection. We showed that introducing a very modest degree of bias that grows with the number of infected cells makes a dramatic difference in the efficacy of containment above the epidemic threshold. Thus, the combination of containment coupled with cooperation holds great promise for protecting enterprise networks against worms that spread by address-scanning.

6.11 Revisited

Since we target our algorithm for use in a local network, we needed to construct a LAN implementation to evaluate it. Although we were confident in the basic correctness of our algorithm (now called Approximate-Cache TRW, or AC-TRW), we appreciated a need to determine if any difficulties might arise when operating it in a full LAN environment.

We implemented AC-TRW in Click[13], a software framework for building router forwarding planes. Our implementation is designed to run transparently in Ethernet networks: unless blocking packets, it behaves like a wire, completely preserving Ethernet packets (including not changing the MAC addresses). The only significant change we made to our algorithm was to use a truncated RC5 variant (RC5 with a 32-bit wordsize and 6 rounds) as our permutation function. We discuss it further below.

We tested this implementation both in our own LAN and using sythentic traffic generated in the DETER [6] testbed (an Emulab[34] environment). During our testing in both the testbed and the LAN, we discovered unanticipated interactions between end-system ARP caches, Ethernet switches, and our algorithm, which led to false positives. Additionally, we came to realize that IP scanning might not occur at all, as the standard system calls will not generate IP packets to the LAN unless a previous ARP is successful.

As a result, we needed to modify our system to passively map the local network. This map is used to determine whether a packet crossing through our device is a spurious broadcast packet (such as from the use of a hub on one side of the network, or an uninitialized MAC cache). If we determine the packet to be a spurious broadcast, we ignore it (but pass it unchanged). We also use this map to determine if an ARP ought to cross our viewpoint. If so, we incorporate ARP requests and responses into our TRW implementation, with a modification. Failed or unacknowledged ARPs count as +1, the same as for initial IP traffic; but acknowledged ARPs count as 0 rather than -1, as an ARP is invariably a prelude to further IP communication. We also need to whitelist the gateway system, as this system generates ARPs based on incoming communication.

Although this mechanism differs from the one described by Whyte et al[35], the goal is the same: to detect ARPs used during scans of the local environment in addition to IP scans of machines as they are discovered. We also use the map we construct to recognize and ignore packets that are initially broadcast onto the network, but would not normally cross the device if the Ethernet switch's MAC cache was complete. Without the map, we would erroneously charge these as the equivalent of a failed connection attempt.

6.11.1 Containment on Ethernet Networks

We implemented our Click-based algorithm as a software Ethernet bridge: it reads packets from one Ethernet and, unless it blocks a packet, forwards the packet unchanged (including the original Ethernet MAC addresses) to the other Ethernet on the system, with any non-IP/non-ARP packets simply passed without examination. This allows us to deploy our devices anywhere in the network, rather than only at IP gateways, without affecting the spanning tree protocol or other non-IP network mechanisms. Additionally, since other containment algorithms have been integrated commercially into Ethernet switches such as the HP ProCurve 5300xl [19][7], it is important to understand the issues in integrating IP-derived containment devices into Ethernet-based networks.

Our device does not just monitor but also actively blocks, to give us a direct imperative (i.e., displeased end users) to uncover and remove any lingering bugs. We were particularly interested whether a liberal threshold (block at +18, max +20, min -20) would incur false positives from normal Windows background chatter. However, we found that such a liberal threshold did not prove a problem: except for the false-positive due to packets not always being switched (discussed below, and subsequently addressed through our passive network mapping), and an expected false-positive when as a test we ran the Limewire installer (an unstructured P2P program), we had no false positives over several weeks of normal operation, including a Windows system, several Linux systems, and an occasional Macintosh connecting through the device.

Initially we made an assumption that because the network is fully switched, only packets that were supposed to cross through the spliced link would pass through

---

[7] The HP technology, however, ignores many of the issues we've encountered because it only performs containment between distinct subnets on distinct VLANs, using the switch's IP routing facility.

our device. As we discuss below, however, this assumption is not correct: switched networks occasionally broadcast IP packets, which can create false positives.

6.11.2 ARPs and the ARP/MAC-cache interaction

The normal means for one system to find another on an Ethernet network is ARP[21]. When IP host A wants to contact IP host B on the same subnet, it broadcasts an ARP request to the Ethernet broadcast ($FF{:}FF{:}FF{:}FF{:}FF{:}FF$) address. B then replies directly to A with an ARP response, sending B's Ethernet MAC address to A. In the future (until host A's ARP cache expires), any request for A to talk to B will just use the entry in the ARP cache.

At the same time as the ARP reply is sent, any Ethernet switch along the path between B and A will initialize its MAC cache with B's MAC address. Thus any subsequent packets destined for B's MAC will not be broadcast on the network, but will be directly routed along the path to B's port. Our initial implementation passed ARPs without modification; thus, if our monitor is not on the path between A and B, we assumed that it would not see the initial TCP SYN or any subsequent packets. Or, if it did see the TCP SYN (because a broadcast hub rather than a switch was used), it would also see the subsequent packets in the connection.

These caches do not expire at an equal rate, however. If a system's ARP cache is still valid, but the switch's MAC cache has expired, when A initiates a new connection to B, the SYN from A to B will be broadcast throughout the network. The response (and all subsequent packets) will reinitialize the MAC cache, causing all further packets to be switched. Thus, if our device is not on the path between A and B, it will see the initial SYN, counting it as a scan attempt, but not see the subsequent dialog.

We have observed this in practice, both in testbed experiments and on our live network. In our LAN, there is a system outside our containment device that regularly performs a global update to all clients on the LAN. Our device once detected and blocked this system as a scanner during its nightly update; the connections to off-path systems were treated as scan attempts, as the system's ARP cache remained valid, but the switch's MAC cache entries had timed out.

Additionally, AC-TRW needs to examine the ARPs themselves. In most cases, a connection attempt to the local network is proceeded by an ARP. If the receiving host is live, the initiating host will see an ARP response, which it then uses to follow up with the IP-level connection request. But if the receiving host is down, the subsequent IP packets will never be sent. Thus, we need to count unacknowledged ARPs as scan attempts.

A problem arises, however, in that although the ARP request is a broadcast packet, the ARP reply is not. Thus, if our device is not on the path between the two hosts in question, it will see the ARP request but not the ARP reply, so we must not blindly count ARPs as scan attempts. We now turn to addressing this problem.

6.11.3 The LAN Map

Our solution to both the ARP/MAC cache interactions and detecting ARP scanning is to passively gather and maintain a map of all active addresses in the subnet. For each host on the subnet, we track when it was last seen and on which side of the network. We also track on which side of the network the gateway system resides. If these locations ever change (such as a system moving from one side to the other), we simply note the change without taking action.

AC-TRW then uses this map to determine if a packet is a spurious broadcast. If the destination (if on the same subnet) or gateway (if to a non-local address) is on the same side of the network as the originating packet, AC-TRW assumes that this packet is a spurious broadcast packet and simply ignores it during its analysis. If AC-TRW does not know which side the destination should be on, it always analyzes the packet, assuming the packet was supposed to cross through the link.

We also use this approach to determine whether to consider an ARP request as a connection attempt. If the destination might be on the other side of the network, we increment the source's count by $+1$, a provisional scan attempt. Then the subsequent reply, which we will observe, results in the count being reduced by -1, rather than by -2 as we would for an IP-level response. By doing so, we count an unacknowledged ARP as $+1$, but a successful ARP as 0 (compared with $+1$ for failed IP connections and -1 for successful connections). This is because although an unacknowledged ARP needs to be considered a scan attempt, an acknowledged ARP is not a successful contact: the ARP will be followed by an IP-based connection attempt.

This passive mapping can introduce a rare false-positive: If system A and B are on the same side of the network, and B has *never* sent a packet across our monitored link (including broadcast ARP requests), or if B has moved from the other side to the same side without ever sending a packet across our monitored link, an ARP from A to B will be considered falsely as a scan attempt. Since it takes several scan attempts before a system is actually blocked, and because most systems are not *completely* silent, we do not believe this false positive will be a problem in practice.

6.11.4 Software Performance

Although we only designed our Click implementation for prototyping, it's pure-software performance is actually respectable, suggesting that many networks can use a software-only implementation. On a 2.8 GHz, dual processor system with 2 Gigabit Ethernet cards in the DETER testbed, we were able to stream 450 Mbps of TCP data (in two streams) through our AC-TRW implementation. This represents the best-case performance for our implementation: there are no cache misses, and all the packets are maximum size.

However, we did not optimize our implementation. We used user-level Click, which means every packet crosses through the kernel twice. We also did not optimize our implementation beyond correctly implementing the AC-TRW algorithm. Thus, it should be possible to significantly increase performance through a combination of profiling to determine locations to recode and compiling our module into kernel-space Click.

Another useful property of our implementation is that after startup, it performs no dynamic memory allocation; we have run our algorithm on our own network for weeks without memory leaks.

6.11.5 Open Problem: Broadcast Packets

One item which we have yet to address is a proper policy for broadcast and multi-cast packets. A broadcast packet, especially a broadcast ping, can instantly reveal all live systems on the local LAN. A natural proposal would be to block *all* broadcast packets, but this could prove untenable in some environments. Of particular concern are the broadcast and multicast packets used by both Windows and Macs to discover other systems in the network.

Currently, we falsely count broadcast and multicast packets as scan attempts. But since these are UDP, each broadcast or multicast address contacted by a host only counts as a single failure, which quickly gets forgiven. Determining a proper policy for such packets remains an open question. Any solution will need to carefully consider the requirements of the target network.

6.11.6 Reverse TRW

Concurrent with our work, Jung et al developed a TRW variant called "Reverse TRW" [24]. It analyzes connection events looking backward through time rather than forward, in order to more quickly detect that a system has transitioned from a benign to a scanning state. We have not implemented reverse TRW, but our use of a floor on the count accomplishes a similar task, albeit with some loss of promptness of detection for systems that transition from benign to scanning.

6.11.7 Network Construction

All these scan containment algorithms suffer from the epidemic threshold problem [27]: if they are not suitably sensitive, a worm can still spread exponentially. We believe that network construction, rather than attempting to make the algorithms more sensitive (and therefore risking more false positives), likely provides the best solution to the epidemic threshhold problem.

A promising architecture for doing so is to restructure networks which deploy scan-containment technology using NAT [8] to make the address space sparser, and thus increase the likelihood that blind scanning generates numerous connection failures. For example, rather than providing end hosts with routable IP addresses, al-locate their addresses allocated from the 10.0.0.0/8 private address space in a uni-formly random fashion. By creating far less dense networks, where only 1 in 100 or 1 in 1000 internal addresses are actually live, even a very insensitive algorithm can successfully contain a scanning worm.

One issue with this approach, however, is that broadcast or multicast packets can still discover hosts in the current subnet. Thus, there needs to be a mechanism for suitably addressing and restricting broadcast packets.

6.12 Acknowledgments

Funding has been provided in part by the National Science Foundation under grants ITR/ANI-0205519, NSF-0433702, and STI-0334088, and by NSF/DHS under grant NRT-0335290. Special thanks to those at ICSI who agreed to have their systems serve as guinea pigs by having all their packets routed through experimental software, and the system administration staff who have reconfigured networks to enable these experiments.

References

1. R. Anderson, E. Biham, and L. Knudsen. Serpent: A Proposal for the Advanced Encryption Standard.
2. B. Bloom. Space/Time Trade-Offs in Hash Coding with Allowable Errors. *CACM*, July 1970.
3. CERT. CERT Advisory CA-2001-26 Nimda Worm, http://www.cert.org/advisories/ca-2001-26.html.
4. CERT. Code Red II: Another Worm Exploiting Buffer Overflow in IIS Indexing Service DLL, http://www.cert.org/incident_notes/in-2001-09.html.
5. S. Crosby and D. Wallach. Denial of Service via Algorithmic Complexity Attacks. In *Proceedings of the 12th USENIX Security Symposium*. USENIX, August 2003.
6. Deter: A laboratory for security research, http://www.isi.edu/deter/.
7. eEye Digital Security. .ida "Code Red" Worm, http://www.eeye.com/html/Research/Advisories/AL20010717.html.
8. K. Egevang and P. Francis. Rfc 1631 - the ip network address translator (nat).
9. Forescout. Wormscout, http://www.forescout.com/wormscout.html.
10. L. T. Heberlein, G. Dias, K. Levitt, B. Mukerjee, J. Wood, and D. Wolber. A Network Security Monitor. In *Proceedings of the IEEE Symopisum on Research in Security and Privacy*, 1990.
11. J. Jung, V. Paxson, A. W. Berger, and H. Balakrishnan. Fast Portscan Detection Using Sequential Hypothesis Testing. In *2004 IEEE Symposium on Security and Privacy, to appear*, 2004.
12. J. Jung, S. Schechter, and A. Berger. Fast Detection of Scanning Worm Infections, in submission.
13. E. Kohler, R. Morris, B. Chen, J. Jannotti, and M. F. Kaashoek. The click modular router. *ACM Transactions on Computer Systems*, 18(3):264–297, August 2000.
14. C. Leckie and R. Kotagiri. A Probabilistic Approach to Detecting Network Scans. In *Proceedings of the Eighth IEEE Network Operations and Management Symposium (NOMS 2002)*, 2002.
15. D. Moore, V. Paxson, S. Savage, C. Shannon, S. Staniford, and N. Weaver. Inside the Slammer Worm. *IEEE Magazine of Security and Privacy*, pages 33–39, July/August 2003 2003.

16. D. Moore, C. Shannon, G. M. Voelker, and S. Savage. Internet Quarantine: Requirements for Containing Self-Propagating Code, 2003.
17. M. Networks. http://www.miragenetworks.com/.
18. D. Nojiri, J. Rowe, and K. Levitt. Cooperative Response Strategies for Large Scale Attack Mitigation. In *Proc. DARPA DISCEX III Conference*, 2003.
19. H. Packard. Connection-rate filtering based on virus-trottling tecnology, http://www.hp.com/rnd/pdf_html/virus-throttling_tech_brief.htm.
20. V. Paxson. Bro: a System for Detecting Network iltruders in Real-Time. *Computer Networks*, 31(23–24):2435–2463, 1999.
21. D. Plummer. Rfc 826 - ethernet address resolution protocol.
22. G. Project. Gnutella, A Protocol for Revolution, http://rfc-gnutella.sourceforge.net/.
23. S. Robertson, E. V. Siegel, M. Miller, and S. J. Stolfo. Surveillance Detection in High Bandwidth Environments. In *Proc. DARPA DISCEX III Conference*, 2003.
24. S. E. Schechter, J. Jung, and A. W. Berger. Fast Detection of Scanning Worm Infections. In *Proceedings of the Seventh International Symposium on Recent Advances in Intrusion Detection (RAID 2004)*, Sept. 15–17, 2004.
25. Silicon Defense. Countermalice Worm Containment, http://www.silicondefense.com/products/countermalice/.
26. Snort.org. Snort, the Open Source Network Intrusion Detection System, http://www.snort.org/.
27. S. Staniford. Containment of Scanning Worms in Enterprise Networks. *Journal of Computer Security, to appear*, 2004.
28. S. Staniford, J. Hoagland, and J. McAlerney. Practical Automated Detection of Stealthy Portscans. *Journal of Computer Security*, 10:105–136, 2002.
29. S. Staniford and C. Kahn. Worm Containment in the Internal Network. Technical report, Silicon Defense, 2003.
30. S. Staniford, V. Paxson, and N. Weaver. How to Own the Internet in Your Spare Time. In *Proceedings of the 11th USENIX Security Symposium*. USENIX, August 2002.
31. Symantec. W32.blaster.worm, http://securityresponse.symantec.com/avcenter/venc/data/w32.blaster.worm.html.
32. J. Twycross and M. M. Williamson. Implementing and Testing a Virus Throttle. In *Proceedings of the 12th USENIX Security Symposium*. USENIX, August 2003.
33. N. Weaver, V. Paxson, S. Staniford, and R. Cunningham. A Taxonomy of Computer Worms. In *The First ACM Workshop on Rapid Malcode (WORM)*, 2003.
34. B. White, J. Lepreau, L. Stoller, R. Ricci, S. Guruprasad, M. Newbold, M. Hibler, C. Barb, and A. Joglekar. An integrated experimental environment for distributed systems and networks. In *Proc. of the Fifth Symposium on Operating Systems Design and Implementation*, pages 255–270, Boston, MA, Dec. 2002. USENIX Association.
35. D. Whyte, P. vas Oorschot, and E. Kranakis. Arp-based detection of scanning worms within an enterprise network. In *In proceedings of Annual Computer Security Applications Conference (ACSAC 2005)*, Tucson, AZ, December 2005.
36. M. M. Williamson. Throttling Viruses: Restricting Propagation to Defeat Mobile Malicious Code. In *ACSAC*, 2002.
37. Xilinx Inc. Xilinx ML300 Development Platform, http://www.xilinx.com/products/boards/ml300/.
38. C. C. Zou, W. Gong, and D. Towsley. Worm Propagation Modeling and Analysis under Dynamic Quarantine Defense. In *The First ACM Workshop on Rapid Malcode (WORM)*, 2003.

7

Sting: An End-to-End Self-Healing System for Defending against Internet Worms

David Brumley, James Newsome, and Dawn Song

Carnegie Mellon University, Pittsburgh, PA, USA
dbrumley@cs.cmu.edu, jnewsome@ece.cmu.edu, dawnsong@cmu.edu

7.1 Introduction

We increasingly rely on highly available systems in all areas of society, from the economy, to military, to the government. Unfortunately, much software, including critical applications, contains vulnerabilities unknown at the time of deployment, with memory-overwrite vulnerabilities (such as buffer overflow and format string vulnerabilities) accounting for more than 60% of total vulnerabilities [10]. These vulnerabilities, when exploited, can cause devastating effects, such as self-propagating worm attacks which can compromise millions of vulnerable hosts within a matter of minutes or even seconds [32, 61], and cause millions of dollars of damage [30]. Therefore, we need to develop effective mechanisms to protect vulnerable hosts from being compromised and allow them to continue providing critical services, even under aggressively spreading attacks on previously unknown vulnerabilities.

We need *automatic* defense techniques because manual response to new vulnerabilities is slow and error prone. A worm exploiting a previously unknown vulnerability and advanced techniques such as hit-lists can infect the vulnerable population on a time scale orders of magnitude faster than a human mediated response [7, 61, 60]. Automatic techniques have the potential to be more accurate than manual efforts because vulnerabilities exploited by worms tend to be complex and require intricate knowledge of details such as realizable program paths and corner conditions. Understanding the complexities of a vulnerability has consistently proven very difficult and time consuming for humans at even the source code level [9], let alone COTS software at the assembly level.

Overview and Contributions. By carefully uniting a suite of new techniques, we create a new end-to-end self-healing architecture, called *Sting*, as a first step towards automatically defending against fast Internet-scale worm attacks.

At a high level, the Sting self-healing architecture enables programs to efficiently and automatically (1) self-monitor their own execution behavior to detect a large class of errors and exploit attacks, (2) self-diagnose the root cause of an error or exploit attack, (3) self-harden to be resilient against further attacks, and (4) quickly self-recover to a safe state after a state corruption. Furthermore, once a Sting host detects and diagnoses an error or attack, it can generate a verifiable *antibody*, which is then distributed to other vulnerable hosts, who verify the correctness of the anti-bodyand use it to self-harden against attacks on that vulnerability. We provide a more detailed overview below.

First, we propose dynamic taint analysis to detect new attacks, and to provide information about discovered attacks which can be used to automatically generate antibodies that protect against further attacks on the corresponding vulnerability. Dynamic taint analysis monitors software execution at the instruction level to track what data was derived from untrusted sources, and detect when untrusted data is used in ways that signify that an attack has taken place. This technique reliably detects a large class of exploit attacks, and does not require access to source code, allowing it to be used on commodity software. This work is described in detail in [43, 44].

Once a new attack is detected, there are several types of antibodies that can be generated, and several methods to generate them. We have investigated automatic methods of generating input-filters by finding common byte-patterns in collected worm samples, even for polymorphic worms. This work is described in detail in [41]. However, we have found that a worm author can severely cripple such methods by including spurious features in samples of the worm [42].

In [8], we propose *vulnerability*-based signatures, in which signatures are created based upon the vulnerability itself. Vulnerability signatures are input signatures which provably have zero-false positives (or false negatives, if desired). Therefore, vulnerability signatures are appropriate even in an adversarial environment where malicious parties may try to mislead the signature creation algorithm.

In some circumstances input-based filters may not be practical. For example, performance requirements may only allow for token-based signatures, but token-based signatures may be too imprecise to be useful. Therefore, we propose an alternative of automatically generating *execution* filters, which are specifications of where the vulnerability lies in the vulnerable program. These are used to automatically insert a small piece of instrumentation into the vulnerable program, which in turn allows the vulnerable program to efficiently and reliably detect when that vulnerability is exploited. This work is described in [39].

Once a new attack has been found, and an antibodygenerated for that attack, we disseminate that antibodyto other vulnerable hosts. These vulnerable hosts can verify both that an attack exists and that the antibodysuccessfully stops it by *replaying* the attack against the antibody-protected software in a confined environment.

Finally, we integrate the above techniques to form Sting, an end-to-end self-healing system capable of defending commodity software against even zero-day hit-list worm attacks. In this system, users use light-weight detectors (such as address randomization [45, 5, 6, 11, 20, 22, 68]) and random sampling to initially detect new attacks with little performance cost. When a potential attack is detected, we then use dynamic taint analysis to perform automatic self-diagnosis, which verifies whether it is truly an attack, and automatically generates an execution filter. That execution filter is used to harden the vulnerable binary, and is distributed to others running the vulnerable software to allow them to also harden their own vulnerable binaries.

When an exploit is detected, the system performs diagnosis-directed self-recovery using process checkpointing and recovery [59, 46]. To the best of our knowledge, we are the first to demonstrate that we can defend against even hit-list worms under realistic deployment scenarios.

Organization. In Section 7.2, we briefly describe the design space for worm defense systems. Our analysis indicates that the best designs incorporate both a proactive protection component and a reactive antibodycomponent. This analysis motivates our Sting architecture. We then describe TaintCheck in Section 7.3, which is one of the primary mechanism we use to detect new exploits and vulnerabilities. In Section 7.4, we discuss automatic input-based signature creation. We show many proposed algorithms are fragile and can be mislead by an adversary into creating incorrect signatures. We then describe a new class of signatures called vulnerability signatures which are provably correct, even in an adversarial environment. In Section 7.5, we describe an alternative to input-based filters called vulnerability-based execution filters (VSEF). Section 7.6 describes the complete Sting architecture and our experiences creating it. We then present related work, and conclude.

7.2 Worm Defense Design Space

The design space for worm defense systems is vast. For example, should a worm defense system try to contain infected machines from further propagation of the worm, blacklist known infected hosts, or filter infection attempts? In [7], we propose a taxonomy for worm defense strategies and perform theoretical and experimental evaluation to compare different strategies in the design space. Our analysis shows a hybrid scheme using proactive protection and a reactive antibodydefense is the most promising approach. Thus, we adopt this strategy in the Sting architecture.

7.2.1 Defense Strategy Taxonomy

We analyze a taxonomy of possible solutions in the worm defense design space in [7]. The taxonomy is depicted in Figure 7.1. At a high level, the four defense strategies are:

Reactive Defense. This approach reactively generates an *antibody*, which is a protective measure that prevents further infections. The scheme is reactive because the antibodyis created based upon a known worm sample. Many input-based filtering schemes such as in Section 7.4 and [27, 29, 41] are examples of a reactive antibodydefense since the input filters are created from known worm samples. Vulnerability-specific execution filters (Section 7.5) are another example.

Proactive Protection. A proactive protection scheme is always in place and prevents at least some worm infection attempts from succeeding. Running Taint-Check on all programs, all the time is an example of a proactive protection scheme. However, running TaintCheck all the time is unrealistic due to the potentially high overhead. An example of a *probabilistic* proactive protection is

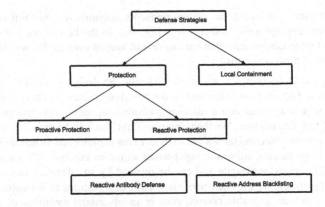

Fig. 7.1. Worm Defense Strategy Taxonomy

address space randomization [45, 5, 6, 11, 20, 22, 68], in which each infection attempt succeeds with some probability p.

Reactive Address Blacklisting. Blacklisting generates a worm defense based upon the address of an attacking host. For example, filtering any subsequent connections from a known infected host [34].

Local Containment. Local containment is a "good neighbor" strategy in which a site filters outgoing infection attempts to other sites. Scan rate throttling schemes such [64, 67] are an example of this strategy.

7.2.2 The Sting Architecture

We show in [7] that the most effective strategy in a realistic setting is combining proactive protection with a reactive antibodydefense. The intuition is that proactive protection will slow down the initial worm outbreak, which allows time to develop and deploy a permanent antibody.

Sting is designed around the hybrid proactive protection with reactive antibodydefense. Sting utilizes TaintCheck, address space randomization, and random sampling as proactive protection mechanisms. The combination of these mechanisms provides efficient probabilistic protection. Sting develops verifiable antibodies which can be distributed and installed. The antibodies provide efficient protection against subsequent infections.

7.3 Dynamic Taint Analysis for Automatic Detection of New Exploits

Many approaches have been proposed to detect new attacks. These approaches roughly fall into two categories: *coarse-grained detectors*, that detect anomalous behavior, such as scanning or unusual activity at a certain port; and *fine-grained detectors*, that detect attacks on a program's vulnerabilities. While coarse-grained detectors are relatively inexpensive, they can have frequent false positives, and do not provide detailed information about the vulnerability and how it is exploited. Thus, it is desirable to develop fine-grained detectors that produce fewer false positives, and provide detailed information about the vulnerability and exploit.

Several approaches for fine-grained detectors have been proposed that detect when a program is exploited. Most of these previous mechanisms require source code or special recompilation of the program, such as StackGuard [16], PointGuard [15], full-bounds check [25, 51], LibsafePlus [3], FormatGuard [14], and CCured [36]. Some of them also require recompiling the libraries [25, 51], or modifying the original source code, or are not compatible with some programs [36, 15]. These constraints hinder the deployment and applicability of these methods, especially for commodity software, because source code or specially recompiled binaries are often unavailable, and the additional work required (such as recompiling the libraries and modifying the original source code) makes it inconvenient to apply these methods to a broad range of applications. Note that most of the large-scale worm attacks to date are attacks on commodity software.

Thus, it is important to design fine-grained detectors that work on commodity software, *i.e.*, work on arbitrary binaries without requiring source code or specially recompiled binaries. This goal is difficult to achieve because important information, such as data types, is not generally available in binaries. As a result, existing exploit detection mechanisms that do not use source code or specially compiled binary programs, such as LibSafe [4], LibFormat [50], Program Shepherding [28], and the Nethercote-Fitzhardinge bounds check [37], are typically tailored for narrow types of attacks and fail to detect many important types of common attacks.

We propose a new approach, *dynamic taint analysis*, for the automatic detection of exploits on commodity software. In dynamic taint analysis, we label data originating from or arithmetically derived from untrusted sources such as the network as *tainted*. We keep track of the propagation of tainted data as the program executes (*i.e.*, what data in memory is tainted), and detect when tainted data is used in dangerous ways that could indicate an attack. This approach allows us to detect *overwrite attacks*, attacks that cause a sensitive value (such as return addresses, function pointers, format strings, *etc.*) to be overwritten with the attacker's data. Most commonly occurring exploits fall into this class of attacks. We have developed an automatic tool, *TaintCheck*, to demonstrate our dynamic taint analysis approach.

7.3.1 Dynamic Taint Analysis

Our technique is based on the observation that in order for an attacker to change the execution of a program illegitimately, he must cause a value that is normally derived from a trusted source to instead be derived from his own input. For example, values such as return addresses, function pointers, and format strings should usually be supplied by the code itself, not from external untrusted inputs. In an *overwrite attack,* an attacker exploits a program by overwriting sensitive values such as these with his own data, allowing him to arbitrarily change the execution of the program.

We refer to data that originates or is derived arithmetically from an untrusted input as being *tainted.* In our dynamic taint analysis, we first mark input data from untrusted sources tainted, then monitor program execution to track how the tainted attribute propagates (*i.e.*, what other data becomes tainted) and to check when tainted data is used in dangerous ways. For example, use of tainted data as a function pointer or a format string indicates an exploit of a vulnerability such as a buffer overrun or format string vulnerability [1], respectively.

Note that our approach detects attacks at the time of *use, i.e.,* when tainted data is used in dangerous ways. This significantly differs from many previous approaches which attempt to detect when a certain part of memory is illegitimately overwritten by an attacker at the time of the *write.* Without source code, it is not always possible at the time of a write to detect whether an illegitimate overwrite is taking place, because it cannot always be statically determined what kind of data is being overwritten, *e.g.* whether the boundary of a buffer has been exceeded. Hence, techniques that detect attacks at the time of write without source code are only applicable to certain type of attacks and/or suffer from limited accuracy. However, at the time that data is *used* in a sensitive way, such as as a function pointer, we know that if that data is tainted, then a previous write was an illegitimate overwrite, and an attack has taken place. By detecting attacks at the time of use instead of the time of write, we reliably detect a broad range of overwrite attacks.

7.3.2 Design and Implementation Overview

We have designed and implemented TaintCheck, a new tool for performing dynamic taint analysis. TaintCheck performs dynamic taint analysis on a program by running the program in its own emulation environment. This allows TaintCheck to monitor and control the program's execution at a fine-grained level. We have two implementations of TaintCheck: we implemented TaintCheck using Valgrind [38]. Valgrind is an open source x86 emulator that supports extensions, called *skins,* which can instrument a program as it is run.[2] We also have a Windows implementation of TaintCheck that uses DynamoRIO [21], another dynamic binary instrumentation tool. For sim-

---

[1] Note that the use of tainted data as a format string often indicates a format string *vulnerability,* whether or not there is an actual exploit. That is, the program unsafely uses untrusted data as a format string (`printf(user_input)` instead of `printf(''%s'', user_input)`), though the data provided by a particular user input may be innocuous.

[2] Note that while Memcheck, a commonly used Valgrind extension, is able to assist in debugging memory errors, it is not designed to detect attacks. It can detect some conditions relevant to vulnerabilities and attacks, such as when unallocated memory is used, when memory is freed twice, and when a memory write passes the boundary of a `malloc`-allocated block. However, it does not detect other attacks, such as overflows within an area allocated by one `malloc` call (such as a buffer field of a struct), format string attacks, or stack-allocated buffer overruns.

plicity of explanation, for the remainder of this section, we refer to the Valgrind implementation unless otherwise specified.

Whenever program control reaches a new basic block, Valgrind first translates the block of x86 instructions into its own RISC-like instruction set, called *UCode*. It then passes the UCode block to TaintCheck, which instruments the UCode block to incorporate its taint analysis code. TaintCheck then passes the rewritten UCode block back to Valgrind, which translates the block back to x86 code so that it may be executed. Once a block has been instrumented, it is kept in Valgrind's cache so that it does not need to be re-instrumented every time it is executed.

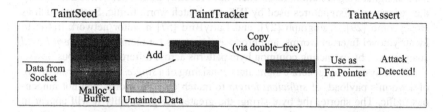

Fig. 7.2. TaintCheck detection of an attack. (Exploit Analyzer not shown).

To use dynamic taint analysis for attack detection, we need to answer three questions: (1) What inputs should be tainted? (2) How should the taint attribute propagate? (3) What usage of tainted data should raise an alarm as an attack? To make TaintCheck flexible and extensible, we have designed three components: *TaintSeed, TaintTracker,* and *TaintAssert* to address each of these three questions in turn. Figure 7.2 shows how these three components work together to track the flow of tainted data and detect an attack. Each component has a default policy and can easily incorporate user-defined policies as well. In addition, each component can be configured to log information about taint propagation, which can be used by the fourth component we have designed, the *Exploit Analyzer*. When an attack is detected, the Exploit Analyzer performs post-analysis to provide information about the attack, including identifying the input that led to the attack, and semantic information about the attack payload. This information can be used to automatically generate antibodies against the attack, including input-based filters (Section 7.4) and execution filters (Section 7.5).

7.4 Automatic Generation of Input-based Filters

We first describe previous attempts at automatically generating signatures by syntax pattern-extraction techniques. These techniques find and create signatures based on syntactic differences between exploits and benign inputs. Our experience shows these methods are fragile, and thus not suitable in an adversarial environment where

an adversary may try to mislead the signature generation algorithm. We then introduce *vulnerability signatures*, which produce signatures with zero false positives
(even in an adversarial setting). In addition, vulnerability signatures are generally of
a higher quality (i.e., more accurate and less fragile) than signatures generated by
syntax pattern-extraction techniques.

7.4.1 Limitations of Pattern-Extraction based techniques

First generation worms: identical byte strings. Motivated by the slow pace of
manual signature generation, researchers have recently given attention to *automating*
the generation of signatures used by IDSes to match worm traffic. Systems such as
Honeycomb [29], Autograph [27], and EarlyBird [57] monitor network traffic to
identify novel Internet worms, and produce signatures for them using *pattern-based*
analysis, *i.e.*, by extracting common byte patterns across different suspicious flows.

These systems all generate signatures consisting of a *single, contiguous substring*
of a worm's payload, of *sufficient length* to match only the worm, and not innocuous traffic. The shorter the byte string, the greater the probability it will appear in
some flow's payload, regardless of whether the flow is a worm or innocuous. These
syntax pattern-extraction signature generation systems all make the same underlying
assumption: that there exists a single payload substring that will remain *invariant*
across worm connections, and will be sufficiently unique to the worm such that it
can be used as a signature without causing false positives.

Second generation worms: polymorphism. Regrettably, the above payload in-
variance assumption is naïve, and gives rise to a critical weakness in these previously proposed signature generation systems. A worm author may craft a worm that
substantially changes its payload on every successive connection, and thus evades
matching by any single substring signature that does not also occur in innocuous
traffic. *Polymorphism* techniques[3], through which a program may encode and re-
encode itself into successive, different byte strings, enable production of changing
worm payloads. It is pure serendipity that worm authors thus far have not chosen
to render worms polymorphic; virus authors do so routinely [35, 63]. The effort required to do so is trivial, given that libraries to render code polymorphic are readily
available [1, 18].

In Polygraph [41], we showed that for many vulnerabilities, there are several
invariant byte strings that must be present to exploit that vulnerability. While using a single one of these strings would not be specific enough to generate an accurate signature, they can be combined to create an accurate *conjunction* signature,
subsequence signature, or *Bayes signature*. We proposed algorithms that automatically generate accurate signatures of these types, for *maximally varying* polymorphic
worms. That is, we assumed the worm minimized commonality between each instance, such that only the invariant byte strings necessary to trigger the vulnerability
were present.

---

[3] We refer to both polymorphism and metamorphism as polymorphism, in the interest of
brevity.

Third generation worms: Attacks on learning. The maximal variation model of a polymorphic worm's content bears further scrutiny. If one seeks to understand whether a worm can vary its content so widely that a particular signature type, *e.g.,* one comprised of multiple disjoint substrings, cannot sufficiently discriminate worm instances from innocuous traffic, this model is appropriate, as it represents a worst case, in which as many of a worm's bytes vary randomly as possible. But the maximally varying model is one of many choices a worm author may adopt. Once a worm author knows the signature generation algorithm in use, he may adopt payload variation strategies chosen specifically in an attempt to defeat that algorithm or class of algorithm. Thus, maximal variation is a distraction when assessing the robustness of a signature generation algorithm in an adversarial environment; some other strategy may be far more effective in causing poor signatures (*i.e.,* those that cause many false negatives and/or false positives) to be generated .

In *Paragraph* [42], we demonstrated several attacks that make the problem of automatic signature generation via pattern-extraction significantly more difficult. The approach taken by pattern-extraction based signature generation systems such as Polygraph is to find common byte patterns in samples of a worm, and then apply some type of *learning* algorithm to generate a classifier, or signature. Most research in machine learning algorithms is in the context in which the content of samples is determined randomly, or even by a *helpful teacher,* who constructs examples in an effort to assist learning.

However, learning algorithms, when applied to polymorphic worm signature generation, attempt to function with examples provided by a *malicious teacher*. That is, a clever worm author may manipulate the particular features found in the worm samples, innocuous samples, or both—not to produce maximal variation in payload, but to *thwart learning itself.*

We demonstrate this concept in Paragraph [42] by constructing attacks against the signature generation algorithms in Polygraph [41]. We have shown that these attacks are practical to perform, and that they prevent an accurate signature from being generated quickly enough to prevent wide-spread infection. From our analysis, we conclude that generating worm signatures purely by syntax pattern-extraction techniques seems limited in robustness against a determined adversary.

7.4.2 Automatic Vulnerability Signature Generation

A realistic signature generation mechanism should succeed in an adversarial environment without requiring assumptions about the amount of polymorphism an unknown vulnerability may have. Thus, to be effective, the signature should be constructed based on the property of the vulnerability, instead of an exploit (this observation has been made by others as well [66]).

We show that signatures with zero false positives, even in an adversarial setting, can be created by analyzing the vulnerability itself. We call these signatures *vulnerability signatures* [8]. Vulnerability signatures are provably correct with respect to the goal of the administrator: they are constructed with zero false positives or zero false negatives *regardless of how the attacker may try and deceive the generation algorithm.*

Requirements for Vulnerability Signature Generation

We motivate our work and approach to vulnerability signatures in the following setting: a new exploit is just released for an unknown vulnerability. A site has detected the exploit through some means such as dynamic taint analysis (Section 7.3), and wishes to create a signature that recognizes any further exploits. The site can furnish our analysis with the tuple $\{\mathcal{P}, T, x, c\}$ where $\mathcal{P}$ is the program, x is the exploit string, c is a vulnerability condition, and T is the execution trace of $\mathcal{P}$ on x. Since our experiments are at the assembly level, we assume $\mathcal{P}$ is a binary program and T is an instruction trace, though our techniques also work at the source-code level. Our goal is to create a vulnerability signature which will *match* future malicious inputs x' by examining them without running $\mathcal{P}$.

Vulnerability Signature Definition

A *vulnerability* is 2-tuple $(\mathcal{P}, c)$, where $\mathcal{P}$ is a program (which is a sequence of instructions $\langle i_1, \cdots, i_k \rangle$), and c is a vulnerability condition (defined formally below). The execution trace obtained by executing a program $\mathcal{P}$ on input x is denoted by $T(\mathcal{P}, x)$. An execution trace is simply a sequence of actual instructions that are executed. A vulnerability condition c is evaluated on an execution trace T. If T satisfies the vulnerability condition c, we denote it by $T \models c$. The *language* of a vulnerability $L_{\mathcal{P},c}$ consists of the set of all inputs x to a program $\mathcal{P}$ such that the resulting execution trace satisfies c. Let Σ^* be the domain of inputs to $\mathcal{P}$. Formally, $L_{\mathcal{P},c}$ is the language defined by:

$$L_{\mathcal{P},c} = \{x \in \Sigma^* \mid T(\mathcal{P}, x) \models c\}$$

An *exploit* for a vulnerability $(\mathcal{P}, c)$ is simply an input $x \in L_{\mathcal{P},c}$, i.e., executing $\mathcal{P}$ on input x results in a trace that satisfies the vulnerability condition c. A *vulnerability signature* is a matching function MATCH which for an input x returns either EXPLOIT or BENIGN without running $\mathcal{P}$. A *perfect* vulnerability signature satisfies the following property:

$$\text{MATCH}(x) = \begin{cases} \text{EXPLOIT when } x \in L_{\mathcal{P},c} \\ \text{BENIGN when } x \notin L_{\mathcal{P},c} \end{cases}$$

As we show in Section 7.4.2, the language $L_{\mathcal{P},c}$ can be represented in many different ways ranging from Turing machines which are precise, i.e., accept exactly $L_{\mathcal{P},c}$, to regular expressions which may not be precise, i.e., have an error rate.

Soundness and completeness for signatures.. We define completeness for a vulnerability signature MATCH to be $\forall x : x \in L_{\mathcal{P},c} \Rightarrow \text{MATCH}(x) = \text{EXPLOIT}$, i.e., MATCH accepts everything $L_{\mathcal{P},c}$ does. Incomplete solutions will have false negatives. We define soundness as $\forall x : x \notin L_{\mathcal{P},c} \Rightarrow \text{MATCH}(x) = \text{BENIGN}$, i.e., MATCH does not accept anything extra not in $L_{\mathcal{P},c}$. [4] Unsound solutions will have false positives. A consequence of Rice's theorem [23] is that no signature representation other than a Turing machine can be both sound and complete, and therefore for other representations we must pick one or the other. In our setting, we focus on soundness, i.e., we tolerate false negatives but not false positives. Vulnerability signature creation algorithms can easily be adapted to generate complete by unsound signatures [8].

Vulnerability Signature Representation Classes

We explore the space of different language classes that can be used to represent $L_{\mathcal{P},c}$ as a vulnerability signature. Which signature representation we pick determines the precision and matching efficiency. We investigate three concrete signature representations which reflect the intrinsic trade-offs between accuracy and matching efficiency: *Turing machine* signatures, *symbolic constraint* signatures, and *regular expression* signatures. A Turing machine signature can be precise, i.e., no false positives or negatives. However, matching a Turing machine signature may take an unbounded amount of time because of loops and thus is not applicable in all scenarios. Symbolic constraint signatures guarantee that matching will terminate because they have no loops, but must approximate certain constructs in the program such as looping and memory aliasing, which may lead to imprecision in the signature. Regular expression signatures are the other extreme point in the design space because matching is efficient but many elementary constructions such as counting must be approximated, and thus the least accurate of the three representations.

Turing machine signatures. A Turing machine (TM) signature is a program T consisting of those instructions which lead to the vulnerability point with the vulnerability condition algorithm in-lined. Paths that do not lead to the vulnerability point will return BENIGN, while paths that lead to the vulnerability point and satisfy the vulnerability condition return EXPLOIT. [5] TM signatures can be precise, e.g., a trivial TM signature with no error rate is emulating the full program.

Symbolic constraint signatures. A symbolic constraint signature is a set of boolean formulas which approximate a Turing machine signature. Unlike Turing machine signatures which have loops, matching (evaluating) a symbolic constraint signature on an input x will always terminate because there are no loops. Symbolic constraint signatures only approximate constructs such as loops and memory updates statically. As a result, symbolic constraint signatures may not be as precise as the Turing machine signature.

Regular expression signatures. Regular expressions are the least powerful signature representation of the three, and may have a considerable false positive rate in some circumstances. For example, a well-known limitation is regular expressions cannot count [23], and therefore cannot succinctly express conditions such as checking a

---

[4] Normally soundness is $\forall x : x \in S \Rightarrow x \in L_{\mathcal{P},c}$. Here we are stating the equivalent contra-positive.

[5] A path in a program is a path in the program's control flow graph.

message has a proper checksum or even simple inequalities such as $x[i] < x[j]$. However, regular expression signatures are widely used in practice.

Vulnerability Signature Generation

At a high level, our algorithm for computing a vulnerability signature for program $\mathcal{P}$, vulnerability condition c, a sample exploit x, and the corresponding instruction trace T is depicted in Figure 7.3. Our algorithm for computing vulnerability signatures is:

1. Pre-process the program before any exploit is received by:
   a) Disassembling the program $\mathcal{P}$. Disassemblers are available for all modern architectures and OS's.
   b) Converting the assembly into an intermediate representation (IR). The IR disambiguates any machine-level instructions. For example, an assembly statement add a, b may perform $a + b$ but also set a hardware overflow flag. The IR captures both operations.
2. Compute a chop with respect to the execution trace T of a sample exploit. The chop includes all paths to the vulnerability point including that taken by the sample exploit [24, 48]. Intuitively, the chop contains all and only those program paths any exploit of the vulnerability may take.
3. Compute the signature:
   a) Compute the Turing machine signature. Stop if this is the final representation.
   b) Compute the symbolic constraint signature from the TM signature. Stop if this is the final representation.
   c) Solve the regular expression signature from the symbolic constraint signature.

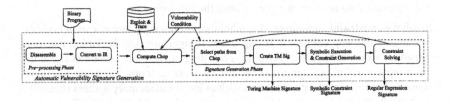

Fig. 7.3. A high level view of the steps to compute a vulnerability signature.

At a high level, the resulting signature is provably correct since only input strings that can be proved to exploit the vulnerability are included, i.e., a TM signature by construction accepts an input iff the input would exploit the original program; the symbolic constraints are satisfiable iff the TM signature would accept the input; and the regular expression contains only those strings that satisfy the symbolic constraints.

Vulnerability Signature Results

We show in [8] that our automatically generated vulnerability signatures are of much higher quality than those generated with syntax pattern-extraction techniques. The higher quality is because given only a single exploit sample, our vulnerability signature creation algorithm will deduce properties of other unseen exploits. For example, in the atphttpd webserver vulnerability the get HTTP request method is case-insensitive [47], and in the DNS TSIG vulnerability that there must be multiple DNS "questions" (which is a field in DNS protocol messages) present for any exploit to work [65].

7.5 Automatic Generation of Vulnerability-Specific Execution Filters

In some situations input-based filters are not an appropriate solution. For some vulnerabilities, it is not possible to generate an input-based filter that is accurate, efficient, and of reasonable size. In addition, while one of the desirable properties of input-based filters is that they can be evaluated off the host (*e.g.*, by a network intrusion detection system), this advantage is largely negated in cases where it is impossible to perform accurate filtering without knowledge of state that is on the vulnerable host, such as what encryption key is being used for a particular connection. On the other hand, various host-based approaches have been proposed which are more accurate, but have other drawbacks. For example, previous approaches have focused on: (1) *Patching*: patching a new vulnerability can be a time-consuming task—generating high quality patches often require source code, manual effort, and extensive testing. Applying patches to an existing system also often requires extensive testing to ensure that the new patches do not lead to any undesirable side effects on the whole system. Patching is far too slow to respond effectively to a rapidly spreading worm. (2) *Binary-based full execution monitoring*: many approaches have been proposed to add protection to a binary program. However, these previous approaches are either inaccurate and only defend against a small classes of attacks [4, 50, 28, 37] or require hardware modification or incur high performance overhead when used to protect the entire program execution [17, 43, 62, 13].

We propose a new approach for automatic defense: *vulnerability-specific execution-based filtering* (VSEF) [39]. At a high-level, VSEF filters out exploits based on the program's execution, as opposed to filtering based solely upon the input string. However, instead of instrumenting and monitoring the full execution, VSEF only monitors and instruments the part of program execution which is relevant to the specific vulnerability. VSEF therefore takes the best of both input-based filtering and full execution monitoring: it is much more accurate than input-based filtering and much more efficient than full execution monitoring.

We also develop the first system for automatically creating a VSEF filter for a known vulnerability *given only a program binary*, and a sample input that exploits that vulnerability. Our VSEF Filter Generator automatically generates a VSEF filter which encodes the information needed to detect future attacks against the vulnerability. Using the VSEF filter, the vulnerable host can use our VSEF Binary Instrumentation Engine to automatically add instrumentation to the vulnerable binary program to obtain a hardened binary program. The hardened program introduces very little overhead and for normal requests performs just as the original program. On the other hand, the hardened program detects and filters out attacks against the same vulnerability. Thus, VSEF protects vulnerable hosts from attacks and allow the vulnerable hosts to continue providing critical services.

Using the execution trace of an exploit of a vulnerability, our VSEF automatically generates a hardened program which can defend against further (polymorphic) exploits of the same vulnerability. VSEF achieves the following desirable properties:

- Our VSEF is an extremely fast defense. In general, it takes a few milliseconds for our VSEF to generate the hardened program from an exploit execution trace.
- Our VSEF filtering techniques provide a way of detecting exploits of a vulnerability more accurately than input-based filters and more efficiently than full execution monitoring.
- Our techniques do not require access to source code, and are thus applicable in realistic environments.
- Our experiments show that the performance overhead of the hardened program is usually only a few percent.
- Our approach is general, and could potentially be applied to other faults such as integer overflow, divide-by-zero, *etc.*

These properties make VSEF an attractive approach toward building an automatic worm defense system that can react to extremely fast worms.

7.6 Sting Self-healing Architecture and Experience

We integrate the aforementioned new techniques with each-other and with existing techniques to form a new end-to-end self-healing architecture, called *Sting* [40], as a first step towards automatically defending against fast Internet-scale worm attacks.

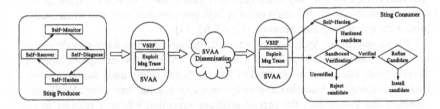

Fig. 7.4. Sting distributed architecture

Figure 7.4 illustrates Sting's distributed architecture. At a high level, the Sting self-healing architecture enables programs to efficiently and automatically (1) self-monitor their own execution behavior to detect a large class of errors and exploit attacks, (2) self-diagnose the root cause of an error or exploit attack, (3) self-harden to be resilient against further attacks, and (4) quickly self-recover to a safe state after a state corruption. Further, once a Sting host detects and diagnoses an error or attack, it generates a Self-Verifiable antibodyAlert (SVAA), to be distributed to other vulnerable hosts, who verify the correctness of the antibodyand use it to self-harden against attacks against that vulnerability.

Our Sting self-healing architecture achieves the following properties: Our techniques are accurate, apply to a large class of vulnerabilities and attacks, and enable critical applications and services to continue providing high-quality services even under new attacks on previously unknown vulnerabilities. Moreover, our techniques work on black-box applications and commodity software since we do not require access to source code. Furthermore, such a system integration allows us to achieve a set of salient new features that were not possible in previous systems: (1) By integrating checkpointing and system call logging with diagnosis-directed replay, we can quickly recover a compromised program to a safe and consistent state for a large class of applications. In fact, our self-recovery procedure does not require program restart for a large class of applications, and our experiments demonstrate that our self-recovery can be orders of magnitude faster than program restart. (2) By integrating faithful and zero side-effect system replay with in-depth diagnosis, we can seamlessly combine light-weight detectors and heavy-weight diagnosis to obtain the benefit of both: the system is efficient due to the low overhead of the light-weight detectors; and the system is able to faithfully replay the attack with no side effect for in-depth diagnosis once the light-weight detectors have detected an attack, which are important properties lacking in previous work [12, 2]. Such seamless integration is also particularly important for *retro-active random sampling*, where randomly selected requests can be later examined by in-depth diagnosis without the attacker being able to tell which request has been sampled. This is a property that previous approaches such as [2] do not guarantee.

Moreover, our self-healing approach not only allows a computer program to self-heal, but also allows a community of nodes that run the same program to share automatically generated antibodies quickly and effectively. In particular, once a node self-heals, it generates an Self-Verifiable Antibody Alerts containing an antibodythat other nodes can use to self-harden before being attacked. The antibodyis a response generated in reaction to a new exploit and can be used to prevent future exploits of the underlying vulnerability. Moreover, the disseminated alerts containing the antibodyare *self-verifiable*, so recipients of alerts need not trust each other. We call this type of defense *reactive anti-body defense*, similar to Vigilante [12].

Our evaluation demonstrates that our system has an extremely fast response time to an attack: it takes under one second to diagnose, recover from, and harden against a new attack. And it takes about one second to generate and verify a Self-Verifiable Antibody Alerts. Furthermore, our evaluation demonstrates that with reasonably low deployment ratio of nodes creating antibodies (Sting producers), our approach will protect most of the vulnerable nodes which can receive and deploy antibodies (Sting consumers) from very fast worm attacks such as the Slammer worm attack.

Finally, despite earlier work showing that proactive protection mechanisms such as address randomization are not effective as defense mechanisms [52], we show that reactive anti-body defense alone (as proposed in [12]) is insufficient to defend against extremely fast worms such as hit-list worms. By combining proactive protection and reactive anti-body defense, we demonstrate for the first time that it is possible to defend against even hit-list worms. We demonstrate that if the Sting consumers also deploy address space randomization techniques, then our system will also be able to protect most of the Sting consumers from extremely fast worm attacks such as hit-list worms. To the best of our knowledge, we are the first to demonstrate a practical end-to-end approach which can defend against hit-list worms.

By developing and carefully uniting a suite of new techniques, we design and build the first end-to-end system that has reasonable performance overhead, yet can respond to worm attacks quickly and accurately, and enable safe self-recovery faster than program restart. The system also achieves properties not possible in previous work as described above. Furthermore, by proposing a hybrid defense strategy, a combination of reactive anti-body defense and proactive protection, we show for the first time that it is possible to defend against hit-list worms.

7.7 Evaluation

7.7.1 Reactive Anti-body Defense Evaluation

In this section, we evaluate the effectiveness of our reactive anti-body defense against fast worm outbreaks, using the Slammer Worm and a hit-list worm as concrete examples. In particular, given a worm's contact rate β (the number of vulnerable hosts an infected host contacts within a unit of time), the effectiveness of our reactive anti-body defense depends on two factors: the deployment ratio of Sting producers α (the fraction of the vulnerable hosts which are Sting producers) and the response time r (the time it takes from a producer receiving an infection attempt to all the vulnerable hosts receiving the SVAA generated by the producer). We illustrate below the total infection ratio (the fraction of vulnerable hosts infected throughout the worm break) under our collaborative community defense vs. α given different β and r.

Defense against Slammer worm. Figure 5(a) shows the overall infection ratio vs. the producer deployment ratio α for a Slammer worm outbreak (where $\beta = 0.1$ [33]) with different response time r. For example, the figure indicates that given $\alpha = 0.0001$ and $r = 5$ seconds, the overall infection ratio is only 15%; and for $\alpha = 0.001$ and $r = 20$ seconds, the overall infection ratio is only about 5%. This analysis shows that our reactive anti-body defense can be very effective against fast worms such as Slammer. Next we investigate the effectiveness of this defense against hit-list worms.

Defense against Hit-list worm. Figure 6(c) shows the result of a hit-list worm for $\beta = 1000$ and $\beta = 4000$, and $n = 100,000$[6]. From the figure we see that (ignoring

---

[6] This is basically the same parameters as the Slammer worm, except that instead of a random scanning worm, the worm is a hit-list.

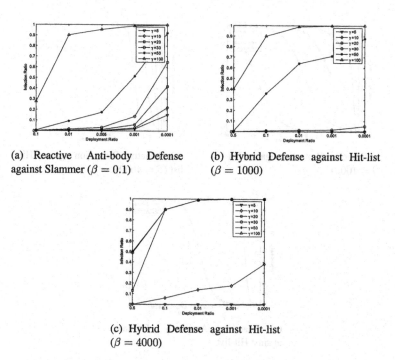

(a) Reactive Anti-body Defense against Slammer ($\beta = 0.1$)

(b) Hybrid Defense against Hit-list ($\beta = 1000$)

(c) Hybrid Defense against Hit-list ($\beta = 4000$)

Fig. 7.5. Effectiveness of Community Defense

network delay) a hit-list worm can infect the entire vulnerable population (Sting consumers) in a fraction of a second. This is similar to earlier estimates [32, 61] which shows that a hit-list worm can propagate through the entire Internet within a fraction of a second. Thus, our reactive anti-body defense alone will be insufficient to defend against such fast worms because the anti-bodies will not be generated and disseminated fast enough to protect the Sting consumers.

7.7.2 Proactive Protection against Hit-list Worm

Another defense strategy is a proactive one instead reactive. For example, for a large class of attacks, address space randomization can provide proactive protection, albeit a probabilistic one. The attack, with high probability, will crash the program instead of successfully compromise it. This probabilistic protection is an instant defense, which does not need to wait for the anti-body to be generated and distributed. However, because the protection is only probabilistic, repeated or brute-force attacks may succeed. Figure 6(a) and 6(b) show the effectiveness of such proactive protection against hit-list worms when a certain fraction α of the total vulnerable hosts deploy the proactive protection mechanism, where $p = 1/2^{12}$ (the probability of an

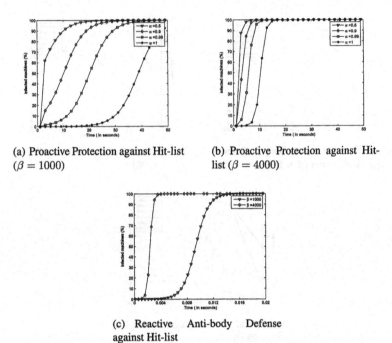

(a) Proactive Protection against Hit-list ($\beta = 1000$)

(b) Proactive Protection against Hit-list ($\beta = 4000$)

(c) Reactive Anti-body Defense against Hit-list

Fig. 7.6. Defense Effectiveness Evaluation

attack trial succeeding), and $\beta = 1000$ and $\beta = 4000$ respectively. As shown in the figure, for $\beta = 1000$, when $\alpha = 0.5$ 50% of the vulnerable hosts deploy the proactive protection defense, it will take about 10 seconds for the worm to infect 90% of the vulnerable population; whereas if 100% of the vulnerable hosts deploy the proactive protection defense, it only slows down the worm to about 45 seconds to infect 90% of the vulnerable population. When $\beta = 4000$, the worm propagates even faster as shown in Figure 6(b).

Thus, proactive protection alone can slow down the worm propagation to a certain extent, but is clearly not a completely effective defense.

7.7.3 Hybrid Defense against Hit-list Worm: Combining Proactive Protection and Reactive Anti-body Defense

As explained above, our reactive anti-body defense alone is not fast enough to defend against hit-list worms. Thus, we propose a hybrid defense mechanism where the Sting consumers deploy proactive protection mechanisms such as address space randomization in addition to receiving SVAA using the reactive anti-body defense. In both cases, we assume the probability that an infection attempt succeeds against the proactive protection mechanism (e.g., guessing the correct program internal state with address space randomization) is again 2^{-12}.

Figure 5(b) and Figure 5(c) show the effectiveness of this hybrid defense approach, i.e., the overall infection ratio vs. the producer deployment ratio α, with different response time r, under two different Hit-list worm outbreaks (where $\beta = 1000$ and $\beta = 4000$ respectively). For example, the figures indicate that given $\alpha = 0.0001$ and $r = 10$ seconds, the overall infection ratio is only 5%; for $\beta = 1000$ and 40% for $\beta = 4000$; and for $\alpha = 0.0001$ and $r = 5$ seconds, the overall infection ratio is negligible (less than 1%) for both cases.

Our simulations show a total end-to-end time (self-detection, self-diagnosis, dissemination, and self-hardening) of about 5 seconds will stop a hit-list worm. Note that our experiments show that self-detection and self-hardening are almost instantaneous, and the total time it takes for a producer to self-diagnose to create a SVAA and for a consumer to verify a SVAA is under 2 seconds. Vigilante shows that the dissemination of an alert could take less than 3 seconds [12]. Thus our system achieves an $r = 2 + 3 = 5$, demonstrating that our system is the first to effectively defend against even hit-list worms.

7.8 Related Work

Antibody Generation Systems. Vigilante has independently proposed a distributed architecture, where dynamic taint analysis is used to detect new attacks and automatically generate verifiable antibodies [12]. It was a very nice piece of work. There are several important technical differences between Vigilante and Sting. Unlike Sting, Vigilante does not provide self-recovery, and also does not allow the seamless combination of light-weight detectors and heavy-weight detectors. Vigilante automatically generates a specific type of input-based filters, where Sting automatically produces a suite of different antibodies including a wider range of input-based filters and execution-based filters which could provide higher accuracy.

Sidiroglou et al. have proposed a method for automatically generating patches when source code is available [53, 54]. They have also proposed *application communities* [55], in which entities running the same software share the burden of monitoring for flaws and attacks, and notify the rest of the community when such are detected.

Anagnostakis et al. propose shadow honeypots to enable a suspicious request to be examined by a more expensive detector [2]. However, their approach requires source code access and manual identification of beginning and end of transactions and thus does not work on commodity software. In addition, because they only reverse memory states but do not perform system call logging and replay, their approach can cause side effects. Moreover, because the suspicious request is handled directly by the more expensive detector instead of the background analysis as in our approach, the attacker could potentially detect when its attack request is being monitored by a more expensive detector and thus end the attack prematurely and retry later, whereas our retro-active random sampling addresses this issue.

Liang and Sekar [31] and Xu et. al. [69] independently propose different approaches to use address space randomization as a protection mechanism and automatically generate a signature by analyzing the corrupted memory state after a crash.

Recovery. Our diagnosis-directed self-recovery provides a different point in the design space compared to previous work. For example, Rinard et. al. has proposed an interesting line of research, failure-oblivious computing in which invalid memory operations are discarded and manufactured values are returned [49]. Instead of rolling back execution to a known safe point, Sidiroglou et al have explored aborting the active function when an error is detected [56]. While interesting, these approaches do not provide semantic correctness, and is thus unsuitable for automatic deployment on critical services. DIRA is another approach that modifies the source code so that overwrites of control data structures can be rolled back and undone [58]. All of these approaches require source code access, and thus cannot be used on commodity software.

There is a considerable body of research on rollback schemes: see [46] for a more detailed discussion. We choose to use FlashBack [59], a kernel-level approach for transactional rollback that does not require access to source code and deterministically replays execution. Another approach is to use virtual machines (VM) for rollback [19, 26]. This approach is more heavy-weight but has advantages such as it is secure against kernel attacks. We plan to explore this direction in the future.

Rx proposes an interesting new approach of using environmental changes to defend against failures, using execution rollback and environment perturbation [46]. However, their approach does not support detailed self-diagnosis and self-hardening, and simply retries execution with different environmental changes until the failure is successfully avoided.

Dynamic Taint Analysis. We use TaintCheck [43, 44] to perform dynamic taint analysis on the binary for self-diagnosis. Others have implemented similar tools [12] which can also be used. Hardware-assisted taint analysis has also been proposed [62, 17]. Unfortunately, such hardware does not yet exist, though we can take advantage of any developments in this area.

7.9 Conclusion

We presented a self-healing architecture for software systems where programs (1) self-monitor and detect exploits, (2) self-diagnose the root cause of the vulnerability, (3) self-harden against future attacks, and (4) self-recover from attacks. We develop the first architecture, called Sting, that realizes this four step self-healing architecture for commodity software. Moreover, our approach allows a community to share antibodies through Self-Verifiable Antibody Alerts, which eliminate the need for trust among nodes. We validate our design through (1) experiments which shows our system can react quickly and efficiently and (2) deployment models which show Sting can defend against hit-list worms. To the best of our knowledge, we are the first to design and develop a complete architecture capable of defending against hit-list worms.

We are one of the first to realize a self-healing architecture that protects software with light-weight techniques, and enables more sophisticated techniques to perform accurate post-analysis. We are also the first to provide semantically correct recovery of a process after an attack without access to its source code, and our experiments demonstrate that our self-recovery can be orders of magnitude faster than program restart which significantly reduces the down time of critical services under continuous attacks.

References

1. K2, admmutate. http://www.ktwo.ca/c/ADMmutate-0.8.4.tar.gz.
2. K. Anagnostakis, S. Sidiroglou, P. Akritidis, K. Xinidis, E. Markatos, and A. Keromytis. Detecting targeted attacks using shadow honeypots. In *Proceedings in USENIX Security Symposium*, 2005.
3. K. Avijit, P. Gupta, and D. Gupta. Tied, libsafeplus: Tools for runtime buffer overflow protection. In *USENIX Security Symposium*, August 2004.
4. A. Baratloo, N. Singh, and T. Tsai. Transparent run-time defense against stack smashing attacks. In *USENIX Annual Technical Conference 2000*, 2000.
5. S. Bhatkar, D. C. DuVarney, and R. Sekar. Address obfuscation: An efficient approach to combat a broad range of memory error exploits. In *Proceedings of 12th USENIX Security Symposium*, 2003.
6. S. Bhatkar, R. Sekar, and D. C. DuVarney. Efficient techniques for comprehensive protection from memory error exploits. In *Proceedings of the 14th USENIX Security Symposium*, 2005.
7. D. Brumley, L.-H. Liu, P. Poosank, and D. Song. Design space and analysis of worm defense systems. In *Proc of the 2006 ACM Symposium on Information, Computer, and Communication Security (ASIACCS)*, 2006. Full version in CMU TR CMU-CS-05-156.
8. D. Brumley, J. Newsome, D. Song, H. Wang, and S. Jha. Towards automatic generation of vulnerability-based signatures. In *Proceedings of the IEEE Symposium on Security and Privacy*, 2006.
9. C. Cerrudo. Story of a dumb patch. http://argeniss.com/research/MSBugPaper.pdf, 2005.
10. CERT/CC. CERT/CC statistics 1988-2005. http://www.cert.org/stats/cert_stats.html.
11. M. Chew and D. Song. Mitigating buffer overflows by operating system randomization. Technical report, Carnegie Mellon University, 2002.
12. M. Cost, J. Crowcroft, M. Castro, A. Rowstron, L. Zhou, L. Zhang, and P. Barham. Vigilante: End-to-end containment of internet worms. In 20th *ACM Symposium on Operating System Principles (SOSP 2005)*, 2005.
13. M. Costa, J. Crowcroft, M. Castro, A. Rowstron, L. Zhou, L. Zhang, and P. Barham. Vigilante: End-to-end containment of internet worms. In *Proceedings of the twentieth ACM symposium on Operating systems principles (SOSP)*, Oct. 2005.
14. C. Cowan, M. Barringer, S. Beattie, and G. Kroah-Hartman. FormatGuard: automatic protection from printf format string vulnerabilities. In *Proceedings of the 10th USENIX Security Symposium*, August 2001.
15. C. Cowan, S. Beattie, J. Johansen, and P. Wagle. PointGuard: Protecting pointers from buffer overflow vulnerabilities. In *12th USENIX Security Symposium*, 2003.

16. C. Cowan, C. Pu, D. Maier, J. Walpole, P. Bakke, S. Beattie, A. Grier, P. Wagle, Q. Zhang, and H. Hinton. StackGuard: automatic adaptive detection and prevention of buffer-overflow attacks. In *Proceedings of the 7th USENIX Security Symposium*, January 1998.

17. J. R. Crandall and F. Chong. Minos: Architectural support for software security through control data integrity. In *International Symposium on Microarchitecture*, December 2004.

18. T. Detristan, T. Ulenspiegel, Y. Malcom, and M. V. Underduk. Polymorphic shellcode engine using spectrum analysis. http://www.phrack.org/show.php?p=61&a=9.

19. G. Dunlap, S. King, S. Cinar, M. Basrai, and P. Chen. Revirt: Enabling intrusion analysis through virtual-machine logging and replay. In *Proceedings of the 2002 Symposium on Operating System Design and Implementation (OSDI)*, 2002.

20. D. C. DuVarney, R. Sekar, and Y.-J. Lin. Benign software mutations: A novel approach to protect against large-scale network attacks. Center for Cybersecurity White Paper, October 2002.

21. Dynamorio. http://www.cag.lcs.mit.edu/dynamorio/.

22. S. Forrest, A. Somayaji, and D. H. Ackley. Building diverse computer systems. In *Proceedings of 6th workshop on Hot Topics in Operating Systems*, 1997.

23. J. Hopcroft, R. Motwani, and J. Ullman. *Introduction to automata theory, langauges, and computation*. Addison-Wesley, 2001.

24. D. Jackson and E. Rollins. Chopping: A generalization of slicing. In *Proc. of the Second ACM SIGSOFT Symposium on the Foundations of Software Engineering*, 1994.

25. R. Jones and P. Kelly. Backwards-compatible bounds checking for arrays and pointers in C programs. In *Proceedings of the Third International Workshop on Automated Debugging*, 1995.

26. A. Joshi, S. T. King, G. W. Dunlap, and P. M. Chen. Detecting past and present intrusions through vulnerability-specific predicates. In *Proceedings of the 2005 Symposium on Operating Systems Principles (SOSP)*, 2005.

27. H.-A. Kim and B. Karp. Autograph: toward automated, distributed worm signature detection. In *Proceedings of the 13th USENIX Security Symposium*, August 2004.

28. V. Kiriansky, D. Bruening, and S. Amarasinghe. Secure execution via program shepherding. In *Proceedings of the 11th USENIX Security Symposium*, August 2002.

29. C. Kreibich and J. Crowcroft. Honeycomb - creating intrusion detection signatures using honeypots. In *Proceedings of the Second Workshop on Hot Topics in Networks (HotNets-II)*, November 2003.

30. R. Lemos. Counting the cost of the slammer worm. http://news.com.com/2100-1001-982955.html, 2003.

31. Z. Liang and R. Sekar. Fast and automated generation of attack signatures: A basis for building self-protecting servers. In *Proc. of the 12th ACM Conference on Computer and Communications Security (CCS)*, 2005.

32. D. Moore, V. Paxson, S. Savage, C. Shannon, S. Staniford, and N. Weaver. Inside the slammer worm. In *IEEE Security and Privacy*, volume 1, 2003.

33. D. Moore, V. Paxson, S. Savage, C. Shannon, S. Staniford, and N. Weaver. Inside the slammer worm. In *IEEE Security and Privacy*, volume 1, 2003.

34. D. Moore, C. Shannon, G. Voelker, and S. Savage. Internet quarantine: Requirements for containing self-propagating code. In *2003 IEEE Infocom Conference*, 2003.

35. C. Nachanberg. Computer virus-antivirus coevolution. *Communications of The ACM*, 1997.

36. G. C. Necula, S. McPeak, and W. Weimer. CCured: type-safe retrofitting of legacy code. In *Proceedings of the Symposium on Principles of Programming Languages*, 2002.

37. N. Nethercote and J. Fitzhardinge. Bounds-checking entire programs without recompiling. In *Proceedings of the Second Workshop on Semantics, Program Analysis, and Computing Environments for Memory Management (SPACE 2004)*, Venice, Italy, Jan. 2004. (Proceedings not formally published.).

38. N. Nethercote and J. Seward. Valgrind: A program supervision framework. In *Proceedings of the Third Workshop on Runtime Verification (RV'03)*, Boulder, Colorado, USA, July 2003.

39. J. Newsome, D. Brumley, and D. Song. Vulnerability-specific execution filtering for exploit prevention on commodity software. In *Proceedings of the 13th Annual Network and Distributed System Security Symposium (NDSS)*, 2006.

40. J. Newsome, D. Brumley, D. Song, and M. R. Pariente. Sting: An end-to-end self-healing system for defending against zero-day worm attacks on commodity software. Technical Report CMU-CS-05-191, Carnegie Mellon University, February 2006.

41. J. Newsome, B. Karp, and D. Song. Polygraph: Automatically generating signatures for polymorphic worms. In *Proceedings of the IEEE Symposium on Security and Privacy*, May 2005.

42. J. Newsome, B. Karp, and D. Song. Paragraph: Thwarting signature learning by training maliciously. In *Proceedings of the International Symposium on Recent Advances in Intrusion Detection*, Sept. 2006.

43. J. Newsome and D. Song. Dynamic taint analysis for automatic detection, analysis, and signature generation of exploits on commodity software. In *Proceedings of the 12th Annual Network and Distributed System Security Symposium (NDSS)*, February 2005.

44. J. Newsome and D. Song. Dynamic taint analysis for automatic detection, analysis, and signature generation of exploits on commodity software. Technical Report CMU-CS-04-140, Carnegie Mellon University, May 2005.

45. PaX. http://pax.grsecurity.net/.

46. F. Qin, J. Tucek, J. Sundaresan, and Y. Zhou. Rx: Treating bugs as allergies—a safe method to survive software failures. In *20th ACM Symposium on Operating System Principles (SOSP)*, 2005.

47. r code. ATPhttpd exploit. http://www.cotse.com/mailing-lists/todays/att-0003/01-atphttp0x06.c.

48. T. Reps and G. Rosay. Precise interprocedural chopping. In *Proc. of the Third ACM SIGSOFT Symposium on the Foundations of Software Engineering*, 1995.

49. M. Rinard, C. Cadar, D. Dumitran, D. Roy, T. Leu, and W. B. Jr. Enhancing server availability and security through failure-oblivious computing. In *Operating System Design & Implementation (OSDI)*, 2004.

50. T. J. Robbins. libformat. http://www.securityfocus.com/tools/1818, 2001.

51. O. Ruwase and M. Lam. A practical dynamic buffer overflow detector. In *Proceedings of the 11th Annual Network and Distributed System Security Symposium*, February 2004.

52. H. Shacham, M. Page, B. Pfaff, E.-J. Goh, N. Modadugu, and D. Boneh. On the effectiveness of address-space randomization. In *Proceedings of the 11th ACM Conference on Computer and Communications Security*, October 2004.

53. S. Sidiroglou and A. D. Keromytis. A network worm vaccine architecture. In *Proceedings of the IEEE International Workshops on Enabling Technologies: Infrastructure for Collaborative Enterprises (WETICE)*, *Workshop on Enterprise Security*, pages 220–225, June 2003.

54. S. Sidiroglou and A. D. Keromytis. Countering network worms through automatic patch generation. *IEEE Security and Privacy*, 2005.

55. S. Sidiroglou, M. Locasto, and A. Keromytis. Software self-healing using collaborative application communities. In *Proceedings of the 13th Annual Network and Distributed System Security Symposium (NDSS)*, 2006.

56. S. Sidiroglou, M. E. Locasto, S. W. Boyd, and A. D. Keromytis. Building a reactive immune system for software services. In *USENIX Annual Technical Conference*, 2005.

57. S. Singh, C. Estan, G. Varghese, and S. Savage. Automated worm fingerprinting. In *Proceedings of the 6th ACM/USENIX Symposium on Operating System Design and Implementation (OSDI)*, Dec. 2004.

58. A. Smirnov and T. cker Chiueh. DIRA: Automatic detection, identification, and repair of control-hijacking attacks. In *Proceedings of the 12th annual Network and Distributed System Security Symposium (NDSS)*, 2005.

59. S. M. Srinivasan, S. Kandula, C. R. Andrews, and Y. Zhou. Flashback: A lightweight extension for rollback and deterministic replay for software debugging. In *Proceedings of the 2004 USENIX Technical Conference*, 2004.

60. S. Staniford, D. Moore, V. Paxson, and N. Weaver. The top speed of flash worms. In *ACM CCS WORM*, Oct. 2004.

61. S. Staniford, V. Paxson, and N. Weaver. How to Own the Internet in your spare time. In *11th USENIX Security Symposium*, 2002.

62. G. E. Suh, J. Lee, and S. Devadas. Secure program execution via dynamic information flow tracking. In *Proceedings of ASPLOS*, 2004.

63. P. Szor. Hunting for metamorphic. In *Proceedings of the Virus Bulletin Conference*, 2001.

64. J. Twycross and M. M. Williamson. Implementing and testing a virus throttle. In *Proceedings of 12th USENIX Security Symposium*, August 2003.

65. US-CERT. Vulnerability note vu#196945 - isc bind 8 contains buffer overflow in transaction signature (tsig) handling code. http://www.kb.cert.org/vuls/id/196945.

66. H. J. Wang, C. Guo, D. Simon, and A. Zugenmaier. Shield: Vulnerability-driven network filters for preventing known vulnerability exploits. In *ACM SIGCOMM*, August 2004.

67. M. M. Williamson. Throttling viruses: Restricting propagation to defeat malicious mobile code. In *Proceedings of the 18th Annual Computer Security Applications Conference*, 2002.

68. J. Xu, Z. Kalbarczyk, and R. K. Iyer. Transparent runtime randomization for security. Technical report, Center for Reliable and Higher Performance Computing, University of Illinois at Urbana-Champaign, May 2003.

69. J. Xu, P. Ning, C. Kil, Y. Zhai, and C. Bookholt. Automatic diagnosis and response to memory corruption vulnerabilities. In *Proceedings of the 12th Annual ACM Conference on Computer and Communication Security (CCS)*, 2005.

An Inside Look at Botnets

Paul Barford and Vinod Yegneswaran

Computer Sciences Department, University of Wisconsin, Madison
{pb,vinod}@cs.wisc.edu

Summary. The continued growth and diversification of the Internet has been accompanied by an increasing prevalence of attacks and intrusions [40]. It can be argued, however, that a significant change in motivation for malicious activity has taken place over the past several years: from vandalism and recognition in the hacker community, to attacks and intrusions for financial gain. This shift has been marked by a growing sophistication in the tools and methods used to conduct attacks, thereby escalating the network security arms race.

Our thesis is that the *reactive* methods for network security that are predominant today are ultimately insufficient and that more *proactive* methods are required. One such approach is to develop a foundational understanding of the mechanisms employed by malicious software (malware) which is often readily available in source form on the Internet. While it is well known that large IT security companies maintain detailed databases of this information, these are not openly available and we are not aware of any such open repository. In this chapter we begin the process of codifying the capabilities of malware by dissecting four widely-used Internet Relay Chat (IRC) botnet codebases. Each codebase is classified along seven key dimensions including botnet control mechanisms, host control mechanisms, propagation mechanisms, exploits, delivery mechanisms, obfuscation and deception mechanisms. Our study reveals the complexity of botnet software, and we discusses implications for defense strategies based on our analysis.

8.1 Introduction

Software for malicious attacks and intrusions (malware) has evolved a great deal over the past several years. This evolution is driven primarily by the desire of the authors (black hats) to elude improvements in network defense systems and to expand and enhance malware capabilities. The evolution of malcode can be seen both in terms of variants of existing tools (*e.g.*, there are over 580 variants of the Agobot malware since it's first release in 2002 [33]) and in the relatively frequent emergence of completely new codebases (*e.g.*, there were six major Internet worm families introduced in 2004: Netsky, Bagle, MyDoom, Sassser, Korgo and Witty as well as the Cabir virus - the first for cell phones [11]).

While worm outbreaks and DoS attacks have been widely reported in the popular press and evaluated extensively by the network and security research communities (*e.g.*, [25, 23, 24, 9]), perhaps the most serious threat to the Internet today are collections of compromised systems that can be controlled by a single person. These *botnets* have actually been in existence for quite some time and trace their roots to the Eggdrop bot created by Jeff Fisher for benign network management in 1993. High level overviews of malicious botnet history and their basic functionality can be found in [29, 4]. Over the years botnet capability has increased substantially to the point of blurring the lines between traditional categories of malware. There have been numerous reports of botnets of over one hundred thousand systems (although the average size appears to be dropping) and the total number of estimated systems used in botnets today is in the millions [13, 19, 10].

A plausible reason for the rise of malicious botnets is that the basic motivations for malicious activity are shifting. In the past, the primary motivations for attacks appear to have been simple (but potent) "script kiddie" vandalism and demonstrations of programming prowess in the black hat community. However, there are an increasing number of reports of for-profit malicious activity including identity theft and extortion that may be backed by organized crime (*e.g.*, [28, 35, 37]). This trend toward an economic motivation is likely to catalyze development of new capabilities in botnet code making the task of securing networks against this threat much more difficult.

The thesis for our work is that effective network security in the future will be based on detailed understanding of the mechanisms used by malware. While this high level statement does not represent a significant departure from what has been the modus operandi of the IT security industry for some time, unfortunately, data sharing between industry and research to date has not been common. We argue that greater openness and more detailed evaluations of the mechanisms of malware are required across the network security research community. In some respects this broadens the Internet Center for Disease Control vision outlined by Staniford *et al.* in [34]. We advocate analysis that includes both static inspection of malware source code when it is available and dynamic profiling of malware executables in a controlled environment. An argument for the basic feasibility of this approach is that a good deal of malware is, in fact, available on line (*e.g.*, [22]) and there are emerging laboratory environments such as WAIL [3] and DETER [8] that enable safe evaluation of executables. It is important to emphasize that these analyses are meant to *complement* the ongoing empirical measurement-based studies (*e.g.*, [36, 26, 2]) which provide important insight on how malware behaves in the wild, and are critical in identifying new instances of outbreaks and attacks.

This chapter presents a first step in the process of codification of malware mechanisms. In particular, we present an initial breakdown of four of the major botnet source codebases including Agobot, SDBot, SpyBot and GT Bot. We conduct this analysis by creating a taxonomy of seven key mechanisms and then describe the associated capabilities for specific instances of each bot family. Our taxonomy emphasizes botnet architecture, control mechanisms, and methods for propagation and attack. Our objectives are to highlight the richness and diversity of each codebase, to identify commonalities between codebases and to consider how knowledge of these mechanisms can lead to development of more effective defense mechanisms.

A summary of our findings and their implications are as follows:

- **Finding:** The overall architecture and implementation of botnets is complex, and is evolving toward the use of common software engineering techniques such as modularity. **Implication:** The regularization of botnet architecture provides insight on potential extensibility and could help to facilitate systematic evaluation of botnet code in the future.

- **Finding:** The predominant remote control mechanism for botnets remains Internet Relay Chat (IRC) and in general includes a rich set of commands enabling a wide range of use. **Implication:** Monitors of botnet activity on IRC channels and disruption of specific channels on IRC servers should continue to be an effective defensive strategy for the time being.

- **Finding:** The host control mechanisms used for harvesting sensitive information from host systems are ingenious and enable data from passwords to mailing lists to credit card numbers to be gathered. **Implication:** This is one of the most serious results of our study and suggests design objectives for future operating systems and applications that deal with sensitive data.

- **Finding:** There is a wide diversity of exploits for infecting target systems written into botnet codebases including many of those used by worms that target well known Microsoft vulnerabilities. **Implication:** This is yet additional evidence that keeping OS patches up to date is essential and also informs requirements for network intrusion detection and prevention systems.

- **Finding:** All botnets include denial of service (DoS) attack capability. **Implication:** The specific DoS mechanisms in botnets can inform designs for future DoS defense architectures.

- **Finding:** Shell encoding and packing mechanisms that can enable attacks to circumvent defensive systems are common. However, Agobot is the only botnet codebase that includes support for (limited) polymorphism. **Implication:** A significant focus on methods for detecting polymorphic attacks may not be warranted at this time but encodings will continue to present a challenge for defensive systems.

- **Finding:** All botnets include a variety of sophisticated mechanisms for avoiding detection (*e.g.*, by anti-virus software) once installed on a host system. **Implication:** Development of methods for detecting and disinfecting compromised systems will need to keep pace.

- **Finding:** There are at present only a limited set of propagation mechanisms available in botnets with Agobot showing the widest variety. Simple horizontal and vertical scanning are the most common mechanism. **Implication:** The specific propagation methods used in these botnets can form the basis for modeling and simulating botnet propagation in research studies.

The remainder of this chapter is structured as follows. While there have been relatively few studies of botnets in the research literature to date, we discuss other related work in Section 8.2. In Section 8.3 we present our taxonomy of botnet code and the results of evaluating four instances of botnet source code. In Section 8.4 we summarize our work and comment on our next steps.

8.2 Related Work

Empirical studies have been one of the most important sources of information on malicious activity for some time. Moore *et al.* characterized the Code Red I/II worm outbreaks in [25] and the Sapphire/Slammer worm outbreak [23] providing key details on propagation methods and infection rates. Recently, Kumar *et al.* show how a broad range of details of the Witty worm outbreak can be inferred using information about that malware's random number generator [20]. In [40], firewall and intrusion detection system logs collected from sites distributed throughout the Internet are used to characterize global attack activity. Several recent studies have demonstrated the utility of unused address space monitors (honeynets) [15] that include active response capability as a means for gathering details on network attacks [2, 39, 26]. Honeynet measurement studies have also provided valuable information on botnet activity [39, 12]. Cooke *et al.* discuss the potential of correlating data from multiple sources as a means for detecting the botnet command and control traffic in [5]. Finally, the virtual honeyfarm capabilities described in [38] could prove to be very useful for botnet tracking in the future.

As we advocated in the prior section, another way to study malware is to gather and then decompose instances of both source code (many instances of malware source code can be found by searching the Web and Usenet news groups) and executable code (executables can be gathered by enhancing honeynet environments). There are standard tools available for reverse engineering executables including disassemblers, debuggers and system monitors such as [17, 30, 27]. Despite the capabilities of these tools, the complexity and deception techniques of certain instances of malware executables often complicate this analysis [16]. Likewise, there are many tools available for static analysis of source code such as [7, 6]. While these tools are often focused on the problems of identifying run time errors and security vulnerabilities, the general information they provide such as parse trees, symbol tables and call graphs could be valuable in our malware analysis. While we present a simple taxonomy of malware mechanisms in this chapter, we look forward to using both static and dynamic analysis tools for in depth study in the future.

8.3 Evaluation

Our process of codification of malware begins with a comparison of four botnet families: Agobot, SDBot, SpyBot and GT Bot. These were selected based on the age of their first known instances, the diversity in their design and capabilities, and reports in the popular press, commercial and research communities identifying these as the most commonly used bot families. While each of these families have many versions and variants, for this study we evaluate one version of source code from each: Agotbot (4.0 pre-release), SDBot (05b) and SpyBot (1.4). GT Bot variants are commonly listed with extensions after the word "Bot" *e.g.*, "GT Bot Foo" – we evaluated the "GT Bot with DCOM" version of this code.

The attributes we consider in our analysis include: (*i*) architecture, (*ii*) botnet control mechanisms, (*iii*) host control mechanisms, (*iv*) propagation mechanisms, (*v*) target exploits and attack mechanisms, (*vi*) malware delivery mechanisms, (*v*) obfuscation methods, and (*vii*) deception strategies. This taxonomy was developed based on our goal of improving both host and network-based defensive systems by exploiting knowledge of basic features of botnet systems.

8.3.1 Architecture

Architecture refers to the design and implementation characteristics of bot code. Architecture is readily analyzed from source code and includes assessment of the overall organization, data design, interface design and component design of the system. An important additional objective in this analysis is to assess the potential long term viability of each bot family by considering how each codebase might be extended to include new functionality.

- **Agobot:** The earliest references to Agobot that we could find were in the October, 2002 time frame [31]. There are now many hundreds of variants of this code which is also commonly referred to as Phatbot. It is arguably the most sophisticated and best-written source code among the four families we evaluated. A typical source bundle is around 20,000 lines of C/C++. The bot consists of several high level components including, (*i*) an IRC-based command and control mechanism, (*ii*) a large collection of target exploits, (*iii*) the ability to launch different kinds of DoS attacks, (*iv*) modules that support shell encodings and limited polymorphic obfuscations, (*v*) the ability to harvest the local host for Paypal passwords, AOL keys and other sensitive information either through traffic sniffing, key logging or searching registry entries, (*vi*) mechanisms to defend and fortify compromised systems either through closing back doors, patching vulnerabilities or disabling access to anti-virus sites, and (*vii*) mechanisms to frustrate disassembly by well known tools such as SoftIce, Ollydbg and others. Agobot has a monolithic architecture, demonstrates creativity in design, and adheres to structured design and software engineering principles through its modularity, standard data structures and code documentation.
- **SDBot:** The earliest references to SDBot that we could find were in the October, 2002 time frame [32]. There are now hundreds of variants of this code that provide a wide range of capabilities. In contrast with Agobot, SDBot is a fairly simple, more compact instance of bot code written in slightly over 2,000 lines of C. The main source tree does not include any overtly malicious code modules such as target exploits or DoS capabilities, and is published under GPL. SDBot primarily provides a utilitarian IRC-based command and control system. However, the code is obviously easy to extend, and a large number of patches are readily available that provide more sophisticated malicious capabilities such as scanning, DoS attacks, sniffers, information harvesting routines and encryption routines. This organization facilitates generation of custom botnets with specialized capabilities that suit a specific botmaster. We speculate that an important

motivation for this patch-style dissemination strategy is diffusion of accountability. We easily found around 80 patches for SDBot [1] on the Web, not all of which were malicious.

- **SpyBot:** The earliest references to SpyBot that we could find were in the April, 2003 time frame [21]. Like Agobot and SDBot there are now hundreds of variants of SpyBot. The codebase is relatively compact, written in under 3,000 lines of C. Much of SpyBot's command and control engine appears to be shared with SDBot, and it is likely, in fact, that it evolved from SDBot. However, unlike SDBot, there is no explicit attempt to diffuse accountability or to hide the malicious intent of this codebase. The version of SpyBot that we evaluated includes NetBIOS/Kuang/Netdevil/KaZaa exploits, scanning capability, and modules for launching flooding attacks. Overall, the codebase for Spybot is efficient, but does not exhibit the modularity or breadth of capabilities of Agobot.

- **GT Bot:** The earliest references to GT Bot that we could find were in the April, 1998 time frame [1]. At present there are well over a hundred variants of GT (Global Threat) Bot which is also referred to as Aristotles. GT Bot's design is quite simple, providing a limited set of functions based on the scripting capabilities of mIRC which is a widely used shareware IRC client for Windows. mIRC provides functionality for writing event handlers that responds to commands received by remote nodes. GT Bot also includes the HideWindow program which keeps the bot hidden on the local system. While this bot has proved easy to modify, there is nothing that suggests it was designed with extensibility in mind. GT Bot capabilities including port scanning, DoS attacks, and exploits for RPC and NetBIOS services. GT Bot scripts are commonly stored in a file called *mirc.ini* on compromised local hosts. However GT Bot is often packaged with its own version of the *mIRC.exe* that has been hex-edited to include other configuration files. Other useful pieces of software that are often packaged with GT Bot include BNC (pronounced "bounce") which is a proxy system that allows users to bounce through shells to a IRC server providing anonymity and DoS protection, and *psexec.exe* (SysInternals) which is a utility that facilitates remote process execution. Based on the limited capabilities in GT Bot, it appears that different versions have been generated for specific malicious intent, instead of general enhancement of the code to provide a broad set of capabilities. As the name suggests, the "with DCOM" version of GT Bot that we evaluated includes DCOM exploit capabilities.

Implications: While bot codebases vary in size, structure, complexity, and implementation approach, there appears to be a convergence in the set of functions that are available (this will be further highlighted in subsequent sections of this report). This suggests the possibility that defensive systems may be eventually be effective across bot families. Further, as demonstrated by the fact that there are so many variants in each codebase, all of the bot families are at least somewhat extensible. However, we project that over the next several years, due to economic motivations, capabilities

---

[1] These are not UNIX-style patches, rather they are simply well-commented source code fragments that can be copied and inserted before recompilation.

and open availability, the Agobot codebase is likely to become dominant. It's modular design makes it easy to extend, and we anticipate future enhancements such as improved command and control systems (*e.g..*, peer-to-peer) and additional target exploits. While an open-source-like approach to Agobot's development is somewhat daunting, it's open availability means that it can be examined for elements which can be exploited by defensive systems.

8.3.2 Botnet Control Mechanisms

Botnet control refers to the command language and control protocols used to operate botnets remotely after target systems have been compromised. The command and control mechanisms for the bots that we evaluated are all based on IRC. Thus, an understanding of that system (*e.g.*, see IETF RFC #1459 which defines IRC) will help to make sense out of the botnet commands detailed in this section. In general, there is a broad range of commands that are available. These include directing botnets to deny service, send spam, phish, forward sensitive information about hosts, and look for new systems to add to the botnet.

The most important reason for understanding the details of the communication mechanisms is that their disruption can render a botnet useless. For example, by sniffing for specific commands in IRC traffic, network operators can identify compromised systems, and IRC server operators can shutdown channels that are used by botnets (this is commonly done today). Additionally, knowledge of these mechanisms can be used in development of large botnet monitors (*e.g.*, via active honeynet systems), and it also facilitates the process of detecting new variants. While control mechanisms occasionally change between versions, there is strong commonality within each family we analyzed. This bodes well for continued focus on these mechanisms when designing network defenses against botnets.

- **Agobot:** The command and control system implemented in Agobot is a derivative of IRC. The protocol used by compromised systems to establish connections to control channels is standard IRC. The command language consists of both standard IRC commands and specific commands developed for this bot. Details of the command language are summarized in Table 8.1. The bot command set includes directives that request the bot to perform a specific function *e.g.*, **bot.open** which opens a specific file on the host. The control variables are used in conjunction with the **cvar.set** command to turn on/off features or otherwise manipulate fields that affect modes of operation *e.g.* **ddos_max_threads** which directs the bot to SYN flood a specified host using a maximum number of threads.
- **SDBot:** The command language implemented in SDBot is essentially a lightweight version of IRC. Figure 8.1 illustrates the state transition sequence of a compromised host interacting with an IRC server. The bot begins by establishing a connection to the IRC server through the following steps: (*i*) send NICK (name) and USER (name) to login to the server, (*ii*) if a PING is received, respond with a PONG, (*iii*) when connected to the server (*i.e.*, return code 001 or 005), send

Table 8.1. Partial listing of the Agobot command and control language. The "variables" are passed as parameters to the `cvar.set` set command.

Variable	Description
bot_ftrans_port	Set bot - file transfer port
bot_ftrans_port_ftp	Set bot - file transfer port for FTP
si_chanpass	IRC server information - channel password
si_mainchan	IRC server information - main channel
si_nickprefix	IRC server information - nickname prefix
si_port	IRC server information - server port
si_server	IRC server information - server address
si_servpass	IRC server information - server password
si_usessl	IRC server information - use SSL ?
si_nick	IRC server information - nickname
bot_version	Bot - version
bot_filename	Bot - runtime filename
bot_id	Bot - current ID
bot_prefix	Bot - command prefix
bot_timeo	Bot - timeout for receiving (in milliseconds)
bot_seclogin	Bot - enable login only by channel messages
bot_compnick	Bot - use the computer name as a nickname
bot_randnick	Bot - random nicknames of letters and numbers
bot_meltserver	Bot - melt the original server file
bot_topiccmd	Bot - execute topic commands
do_speedtest	Bot - do speed test on startup
do_avkill	Bot - enable anti-virus kill
do_stealth	Bot - enable stealth operation
as_valname	Autostart - value name
as_enabled	Autostart - enabled
as_service	Autostart - start as service
as_service_name	Autostart - short service name
scan_maxthreads	Scanner - maximum number of threads
scan_maxsockets	Scanner - Maximum number of sockets
ddos_maxthreads	DDoS - maximum number of threads
redir_maxthreads	Redirect - maximum number of threads
identd_enabled	IdentD - enable the server
cdkey_windows	Return windows product keys on cdkey.get
scaninfo_chan	Scanner - output channel
scaninfo_level	Info level 1 (less) - (3) more
spam_aol_channel	AOL spam - channel name
spam_aol_enabled	AOL spam - enabled ?
sniffer_enabled	Sniffer - enabled ?
sniffer_channel	Sniffer - output channel
vuln_channel	Vulnerability daemon sniffer channel
inst_polymorph	Installer - polymorphoic on install ?

Command	Description
bot.about	Displays information (e.g., version) about the bot code
bot.die	Terminates the bot
bot.dns	Resolves IP/hostname via DNS
bot.execute	Makes the bot execute a specific .exe
bot.id	Displays the ID of the current bot code
bot.nick	Changes the nickname of the bot
bot.open	Opens a specified file
bot.remove	Removes the bot from the host
bot.removeallbut	Removes the bot if ID does not match
bot.rndnick	Makes the bot generate a new random nickname
bot.status	Echo bot status information
bot.sysinfo	Echo the bot's system information
bot.longuptime	If uptime > 7 days then bot will respond
bot.highspeed	If speed > 5000 then bot will respond
bot.quit	Quits the bot
bot.flushdns	Flushes the bot's DNS cache
bot.secure	Delete specified shares and disable DCOM
bot.unsecure	Enable specified shares and enables DCOM
bot.command	Executes a specified command with system()

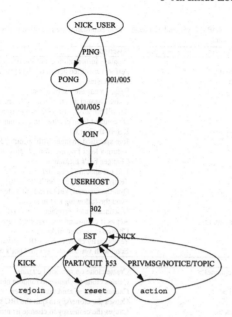

Fig. 8.1. Typical interaction between an SDBot and IRC server.

a JOIN message followed by a USERHOST request to obtain the hostname, (iv) wait for a 302 response that indicates a connection is established, (v) listen and react to commands sent by the master which can include the following:

1. KICK: the bot rejoins the channel if it is kicked off. Otherwise the bot resets the master if the master is kicked.
2. NICK: if master's nickname is replaced, then it is updated on the bot.
3. PART (or QUIT): resets the master if the master parts or quits.
4. 353: return code that indicates that the bot has successfully joined the IRC channel.

The bot then expects all other commands will be sent as part of the PRIVMSG, NOTICE or TOPIC IRC messages. The commands available in SDBot are listed in Table 8.2. Additional features supported by SDBot but absent from Agobot include IRC cloning and spying. Cloning is when a bot connects to an IRC channel multiple times. This can be used to deny service on a particular IRC server. Spying is simply the act of logging activity on a specified IRC channel.

- **SpyBot:** The command language implemented in SpyBot is quite simple and essentially represents a subset of the SDBot command language. The commands available in SpyBot are listed in Table 8.3. The IRC connection set up protocol for SpyBot is the same as SDBot, and the mechanisms to pass and execute commands on bots are also identical.

Table 8.2. Partial listing of the SDBot command language. These commands are passed to bots via the PRIVMSG, NOTICE or TOPIC IRC commands.

Command	Description
about	Displays information about the bot code
action <channel/user>, <text>	Perform specified action on the channel
addalias <alias, command>	Add an alias
aliases	Return a current list of aliases
cycle<N> <channel>	Leave channel and return after N seconds
die	Kill all threads, close IRC connection and stop running
disconnect	Disconnect from channel and reconnect in 30 minutes
id	Return the bot ID
join <channel> <key>	Join specified channel with specified key
log	Return a log of connections, logins and time stamps
nick <newnick>	Changes bot's nickname
part	Part the specified channel
prefix	Temporary change to bot's IP prefix
quit	Quit the channel, kill threads and close the bot
raw <text>	Send the following text to server
reconnect	Disconnect and reconnect to receive new nickname and ID
repeat <numtimes> <command>	Act as if command was received numtimes
rndnick	Change to random nickname
server <servername>	Temporarily changes bot's IRC server
status	Echo with version number and bot's uptime
Clones and Spies	
clone <server> <port> <channel>	Create clone on specified channel
c_rndnick <threadnum>	Causes clone to change to random nickname
c_raw <threadnum> <text>	Causes clone to send text to server
c_quit <threadnum>	Causes the clone/spy to quit the IRC server
c_nick <threadnum> <nick>	Causes the clone/spy to change its nickname
c_privmsg <threadnum> <user> <text>	Causes clone/spy to send message channel with text
c_part <threadnum> <channel>	Causes clone/spy to part channel
c_mode <threadnum> <channel> <mode> <user>	Causes clone to set a channel or user mode
c_join <threadnum> <channel>	Causes clone/spy to join channel
c_action <threadnum> <channel> <text>	Causes clone/spy to perform an action to the given channel.
spy <nick> <server> <port> <channel>	Creates spy with specified nickname on server,port,channel

Table 8.3. Partial listing of the SpyBot command language. These commands are passed to bots via the PRIVMSG, NOTICE or TOPIC IRC commands.

Command	Description
login < password >	Login to the bot
info	Provides information about host system
passwords	Lists the RAS passwords in MS Windows 9x versions
disconnect < secs >	Disconnect bot for t seconds (default is 30 minutes)
reconnect	Disconnect and then reconnect
server < new server addr >	Temporarily changes the bot's IRC server
quit	Quit the channel, kill threads and close bot
uninstall	Uninstalls the bot
redirect <in port> <host> <out port>	Redirect traffic from host to output port
raw <command>	Echo command to server
download <url> <filename>	Copy contents of url to filename
list <path+filter>	List c:\ *.*
spy	Redirects all traffic from the IRC server to the DCC chat
stopspy	Stops the spy
redirectspy	Redirects all traffic from the port redirect to the DCC chat
stopredirectspy	Stops redirect spy
loadclones <server> <port> <numclones>	Load numclones clones on server
killclones	Kills all the clones
rawclones <command>	Execute raw command on all clones

- **GT Bot:** Like the other families, GT Bot uses IRC as its control infrastructure. The command language implemented in GT Bot is the simplest of all of those that we evaluated, but it varies quite a bit across versions within this family. This is likely due to the architecture of GT Bot which facilitates creation of versions with specific intent instead of developing a broad range of capabilities within a single line of the codebase. We provide a list of the commands supported by the GTBot-with-dcom source code used in our analysis in Table 8.4.

Table 8.4. Partial listing of the GT Bot command language. These commands are passed to bots via the PRIVMSG, NOTICE or TOPIC IRC commands.

Command	Description
!ver	Returns the version of the botnet
!info	Returns local host information e.g., OS, uptime, etc.
!scan <ip.*> <port>	Scan specified address prefix on specified port
!portscan <IP> <sport> <eport>	Scan specified address across specified ports
!stopscan	Stops all scans
!packet <IP> <number>	Start denial of service attack (ping.exe) of IP
!bnc	Execute commands specific to the bounce proxy system
!clone.*	Directs all IRC clone behavior (attacks, etc.)
!update<url>	Update version of bot code from a specified Web page
!-	Executes command on local host

Implications: Understanding command and control systems has direct and immediate implications for creation of methods and systems to disrupt botnets. The continued reliance on IRC as the foundation for botnet command and control means that IRC server operators can play a central role in blocking botnet traffic (anecdotally, they already do). However, monitoring and shutting down botnet channels by hand is arduous, and automated mechanisms for identifying botnet traffic are required. The botnet command languages outlined in this section can be used in the development of such systems and we project this will be a fruitful short term focus area. However, we anticipate that future botnet development will include the use of encrypted communication, eventually a movement away from IRC and adopt peer-to-peer style communication (some versions of Phatbot are already reported to have rudimentary P2P capability). While this will certainly make defending against botnets more difficult, botnet traffic may still be able to be identified via statistical finger printing methods.

8.3.3 Host Control Mechanisms

Host control refers to the mechanisms used by the bot to manipulate a victim host once it has been compromised. The general intent of host control is to fortify the local system against other malicious attacks, to disable anti-virus software, and to harvest sensitive information.

- **Agobot:** The set of host control capabilities provided in Agobot is quite comprehensive. These include, (*i*) commands to secure the system *e.g.,* close NetBIOS shares, RPC-DCOM, etc. (*ii*) a broad set of commands to harvest sensitive information (*iii*) `pctrl` commands to list the processes running on the host and kill specific processes (*iv*) `inst` commands to add or delete autostart entries. A summary of Agobot host control commands is provided in Table 8.5.

Table 8.5. Agobot host control commands.

Command	Description
harvest.cdkeys	Return a list of CD keys
harvest.emails	Return a list of emails
harvest.emailshttp	Return a list of emails via HTTP
harvest.aol	Return a list of AOL specific information
harvest.registry	Return registry information for specific registry path
harvest.windowskeys	Return Windows registry information
pctrl.list	Return list of all processes
pctrl.kill	Kill specified process set from service file
pctrl.listsvc	Return list of all services that are running
pctrl.killsvc	Delete/stop a specified service
pctrl.killpid	Kill specified process
inst.asadd	Add an autostart entry
inst.asdel	Delete an autostart entry
inst.svcadd	Adds a service to SCM
inst.svcdel	Delete a service from SCM

- **SDBot:** The host control capabilities provided in the base distribution of SDBot are somewhat limited. They include some basic remote execution commands and some capability to gather local information. The lack of host control capabilities in the basic distribution is likely due to SDBot's benign intent as described above. However, these capabilities can be easily enhanced through auxiliary patches and a large number of these are readily available. A summary of SDBot host control commands is provided in Table 8.6.

Table 8.6. SDBot host control commands.

Command	Description
download <url> <dest> <action>	Downloaded specified file and execute if action is 1
killthread <thread#>	Kill specified thread
update <url> <id>	If bot ID is different than current, download "sdbot executable" and update
sysinfo	List host system information (CPU/RAM/OS and uptime)
execute <visibility> <file> parameters	Run a specified program (visibility is 0/1)
cdkey/getcdkey	Return keys of popular games *e.g.*, Halflife, Soldier of Fortune etc.

- **SpyBot:** The host control capabilities included in SpyBot are relatively rich, and similar in most respects to what is provided by Agobot. These include commands for local file manipulation, key logging, process/system manipulation and remote command execution. A summary of the SpyBot host control commands is provided in Table 8.7.
- **GT Bot:** The set of host control commands provided in GT Bot is the most limited of all of the families we evaluated. The base capabilities include only gathering local system information and the ability to run or delete local files.

Table 8.7. SpyBot host control commands.

Command	Description
delete <filename>	Delete a specified file
execute <filename>	Execute a specified file
rename <origfilename> <newfile>	Rename a specified file
makedir <dirname>	Create a specified directory
startkeylogger	Starts the on-line keylogger
stopkeylogger	Stops the keylogger
sendkeys <keys>	Simulates key presses
keyboardlights	Flashes remote keyboard lights 50x
passwords	Lists the RAS passwords in Windows 9x systems
listprocesses	Return a list of all running processes
killprocess <processname>	Kills the specified process
threads	Returns a list of all running threads
killthread < number >	Kills a specified thread
disconnect <number>	Disconnect the bot for number seconds
reboot	Reboot the system
cd-rom <0/1>	Open/close cd-rom. cd-rom 1 = open, cd-rom 0 = close
opencmd	Starts cmd.exe (hidden)
cmd <command>	Sends a command to cmd.exe
get <filename>	Triggers DCC send on bot
update <url>	Updates local copy of the bot code

However, like SDBot, there are many versions of GT Bot that include diverse capabilities for malicious host control.

Implications: The capabilities and diversity of the host control mechanisms in botnets are frightening and have serious implications. First they underscore the need to patch and protect systems from known vulnerabilities. Second, they informs software development and the need for stronger protection boundaries across applications in operating systems. Third, the capabilities of gathering sensitive information such as Paypal passwords and software keys provide clear economic incentives for people to operate botnets and for sponsorship by organized crime.

8.3.4 Propagation Mechanisms

Propagation refers to the mechanisms used by bots to search for new host systems. Traditional propagation mechanisms consist of simple horizontal scans on a single port across a specified address range, or vertical scans on a single IP address across a specified range of ports. However, as botnet capability expands, it is likely that they will adopt more sophisticated propagation methods such as those proposed in [34].

- **Agobot:** The scanning mechanisms included in Agobot are relatively simple and do not extend very far beyond horizontal and vertical scanning. Agobot scanning is based on the notion of network ranges (network prefixes) that are configured on individual bots. When so directed, a bot can scan across a range or randomly select IP addresses within a range. However, the current scanning command set provides no means for efficient distribution of a target address space among a collection of bots. Table 8.8 provides a summary of the scanning commands in Agobot.

Table 8.8. Agobot propagation and scanning commands.

Command	Description
scan.addnetrange <IP range> <priority>	Adds a network range to a bot
scan.delnetrange <IP range>	Deletes a network range from a bot
scan.listnetranges	Returns all network ranges registered with a bot
scan.clearnetranges	Clears all network ranges registered with a bot
scan.resetnetranges	Resets the network ranges to the localhost
scan.enable <module name>	Enables a scanner module e.g., DCOM
scan.disable <module name>	Disables a scanner module
scan.startall	Directs all bots to start scanning their network ranges
scan.stopall	Directs all bots to stop scanning
scan.start	Directs all enabled bots start scanning
scan.stop	Directs all bots to stop scanning
scan.stats	Returns results of scans

- **SDBot:** As discussed in Section 8.3.1, by virtue of its benign intent, SDBot does not have scanning or propagation capability in its base distribution. However, many variants of SDBot include scanning and propagation capability. Among these, the scanning control interface is often quite similar to Agobot providing horizontal and vertical search capabilities. There are also instance where slightly more complex scanning methods are available. For example, the interface for a NetBIOS scanner for SDBot accepts starting and ending IP addresses as parameters and then randomly selects addresses between these two markers.

- **SpyBot:** The command interface for Spybot scanning is quite simple, consisting of horizontal and vertical capability. A typical example is given below:

```
Command:
    scan <start IP address> <port> <delay>
                            <spreaders> <logfilename>
Example:
    scan 127.0.0.1 17300 1 netbios portscan.txt
```

Scanning begins at the start address and opens MAX_PORTSCAN_SOCKETS_-TO_USE sockets. The default value for this parameter is set to 20. Scanning then proceeds sequentially. The only spreader supported by the version of SpyBot that we evaluated is via NetBIOS.

- **GTBot:** As shown in Table 8.4, GT Bot only includes support for simple horizontal and vertical scanning.

Implications: There are several implications for bot propagation mechanisms. First, at present, botnets use relatively simple scanning techniques. This means that it may be possible to develop statistical finger printing methods to identify scans from botnets in distributed monitors. Second, scanning methods inform requirements for building and configuring network defenses based on firewalls and intrusion detection systems that consider scanning frequency. Finally, source code examination reveals detail of scanning mechanisms that can enable development of accurate botnet propagation models for analytic and simulation-based evaluation. We project that future versions of bot codebases will focus on propagation as an area of improvement, including both flash mechanisms and more stealthy mechanisms.

8.3.5 Exploits and Attack Mechanisms

Exploits refer to the specific methods for attacking known vulnerabilities on target systems. Exploits are usually attempted in conjunction with scanning for target hosts. In this section we discuss the specific exploit modules included in each bot, and other capabilities for launching remote attacks against target systems.

- **Agobot:** The most elaborate set of exploit modules among the families that we analyzed is included with Agobot. In contrast with the other bot families, Agobot's evolution has included an ever broadening set of exploits instead of individual versions with their own exploits. This increases Agobot's potential for compromising targeted hosts. The exploits in the version of Agobot that we evaluated include:

  1. Bagle scanner: scans for back doors left by Bagle variants on port 2745.
  2. Dcom scanners (1/2): scans for the well known DCE-RPC buffer overflow.
  3. MyDoom scanner: scans for back doors left by variants of the MyDoom worm on port 3127.
  4. Dameware scanner: scans for vulnerable versions of the Dameware network administration tool.
  5. NetBIOS scanner: brute force password scanning for open NetBIOS shares.
  6. Radmin scanner: scans for the Radmin buffer overflow.
  7. MS-SQL scanner: brute force password scanning for open SQL servers.
  8. Generic DDoS module: enables seven types of denial service attack against a targeted host. A list of the commands used to control these attacks is given in Table 8.9.

Table 8.9. Agobot DDos attack commands.

Command	Description
ddos.udpflood<target> <port><0=rand> <time>(secs) <delay>(ms)	Starts a UDP flood
ddos.synflood<host> <time> <delay> <port>	Starts a SYN flood
ddos.httpflood <url> <number> <referrer> <delay> <recursive>	Starts an HTTP flood
ddos.phatsyn <host> <time> <delay> <port>	Starts a PHAT SYN flood
ddos.phaticmp <host> <time> <delay>	Starts PHAT ICMP flood
ddos.phatwonk <host> <time> <delay>	Starts PHATwonk flood
ddos.targa3 <target> <time>(secs)	Start a targa3 flood
ddos.stop	stops all floods

- **SDBot:** As discussed in Section 8.3.1, by virtue of its benign intent, SDBot does not have any exploits packaged in its standard distribution. There are, however, numerous variants that include specific exploits. SDBot does include modules for sending both UDP and ICMP packets. While not overtly malicious, these can certainly be used for simple flooding attacks. Commands to control these capabilities are listed in Table 8.10. As might be expected, there are also numerous variants of SDBot that include different kinds of DDoS attack modules.
- **Spybot:** The exploits included in the version of Spybot that we evaluated only included attacks on NetBIOS open shares. However, as with SDBot, there are

Table 8.10. SDBot commands which could be used for DDoS attacks.

Command	Description
udp <host> <# pkts> <pkt sz> <delay> <port>	Send a specified number of UDP packets
ping <host> <# pkts> <pkt sz> <timeout>	Send a specified number of ICMP echo packets

many variants that include a wide range of exploits. SpyBot's DDoS interface is also closely related to SDBot and includes the capabilities for launching simple UDP, ICMP and TCP SYN floods.

- **GTBot:** As mentioned earlier, the exploit set for the GT Bot code that we evaluated was developed to include RPC-DCOM exploits. Like SDBot and Spybot, there are many variants of GT Bot that include other well known exploits. Our version of GT Bot only included capability to launch simple ICMP floods. However, there are many variants of GT Bot that have other DDoS capabilities such as UDP and TCP SYN floods.

Implications: The set of exploits packaged with botnets suggest basic requirements for host-based anti-virus systems and network intrusion detection and prevention signature sets. It seems clear that in the future, more bots will include the ability to launch multiple exploits as in Agobot since this increases the opportunity for success. The DDoS tools included in bots, while fairly straightforward, highlight the potential danger of large botnets. They also inform possibilities for DDoS protection strategies such as [18].

8.3.6 Malware Delivery Mechanisms

Packers and shell encoders have long been used in legitimate software distribution to compress and obfuscate code. The same techniques have been adopted in botnet malware for the same reasons. GT/SD/Spy Bots all deliver their exploit and encoded malware packaged in a single script. However, Agobot has adopted a new strategy for malware delivery based on separating exploits and delivery. The idea is to first exploit a vulnerability (*e.g.,* via buffer overflow) and open a shell on the remote host. The encoded malware binary is then uploaded using either HTTP or FTP. This separation enables an encoder to be used across exploits thereby streamlining the codebase and potentially diversifying the resulting bit streams.

In Figure 8.2 we provide an example of the shell-encoder used in Agobot for malware delivery. An important function of a shell-encoder is to remove null bytes (that terminate c-strings) from x86 instruction sequences. As can be seen in the Figure, the code begins with an XOR key value of 0x98 then checks to see if this results in a string without null characters. If the check fails, it simply tries successive values for the XOR key until it finds a value that works. This value is then copied over to the shell code at position ENCODER_OFFSET_XORKEY.

Implications: The malware delivery mechanisms used by botnets have implications for network intrusion detection and prevention signatures. In particular, NIDS/NIPS benefit from knowledge of commonly used shell codes and ability to perform simple decoding. If the separation of exploit and delivery becomes more widely adopted in bot code (as we anticipate it will), it suggests that NIDS could benefit greatly by incorporating rules that can detect follow-up connection attempts.

```
char encoder[]=
        "\xEB\x02\xEB\x05\xE8\xF9\xFF\xFF\xFF\x5B\x31\xC9\x66\xB9\xFF\xFF"
        "\x80\x73\x0E\xFF\x43\xE2\xF9";

    int xorkey=0x98;

    // Create local copies of the shellcode and encoder
    char *szShellCopy=(char*)malloc(iSCSize);
    memset(szShellCopy, 0, iSCSize); memcpy(szShellCopy, szOrigShell, iSCSize);
    char *szEncoderCopy=(char*)malloc(iEncoderSize);
    memset(szEncoderCopy, 0, iEncoderSize);
    memcpy(szEncoderCopy, encoder, iEncoderSize);

    if(pfnSC)
      pfnSC(szShellCopy, iSCSize);

    char *szShellBackup=(char*)malloc(iSCSize);
    memset(szShellBackup, 0, iSCSize);
    memcpy(szShellBackup, szShellCopy, iSCSize);

    // Set the content size in the encoder copy
    char *szShellLength=(char*)&iSCSize;
    szEncoderCopy[ENCODER_OFFSET_SIZE]=(char)szShellLength[0];
    szEncoderCopy[ENCODER_OFFSET_SIZE+1]=(char)szShellLength[1];

    // XOR the shellcode while it contains 0x5C, 0x00, 0x0A or 0x0D
    while(contains(szShellCopy, iSCSize, '\x5C') ||
        contains(szShellCopy, iSCSize, '\x00') || \
        contains(szShellCopy, iSCSize, '\x0A') ||
        contains(szShellCopy, iSCSize, '\x0D'))
    {
        memcpy(szShellCopy, szShellBackup, iSCSize); xorkey++;
        for(int i=0;i<iSCSize;i++) szShellCopy[i]=szShellCopy[i]^xorkey;
        szEncoderCopy[ENCODER_OFFSET_XORKEY]=xorkey;
    }

    free(szShellBackup);
```

Fig. 8.2. Agobot shell-encoding routine for malware delivery.

8.3.7 Obfuscation Mechanisms

Obfuscation refers to mechanisms that are used to hide the details of what is being transmitted through the network and what arrives for execution on end hosts. While none of the bots we evaluated included TCP obfuscations such as those described in [14], the aforementioned encoders provide obfuscation in a limited way. However, if the same key is used in each encoded delivery, then signatures could be generated quickly that would recognize a particular bit sequence. *Polymorphism* has been suggested as a means for evading signatures based on specific bit sequences by generating random encodings.

The only bot that currently supports any kind of polymorphism is Agobot. There are currently four different polymorphic encoding strategies that are supported: POLY_TYPE_XOR, POLY_TYPE_SWAP (swap consecutive bytes), POLY_TYPE_-ROR (rotate right), POLY_TYPE_ROL (rotate left). While this code appears to function as advertised, thorough analysis of its capabilities is left for future work.

Implications: While polymorphic botnet delivery appears to be a reality, it is not yet widely available across bot families. As such, a concentrated focus on polymorphism by the network security community may not be warranted at this time. However, while the polymorphic routine packaged with Agobot is rather simplistic, it is conceivable that future botnets will have significantly support for polymorphism. As a result, anti-virus systems and NIDS will need to eventually develop mechanisms to account for this capability.

8.3.8 Deception Mechanisms

Deception refers to the mechanisms used to evade detection once a bot is installed on a target host. These mechanisms are also referred to as *rootkits*. Of the four bots we analyzed, only Agobot had elaborate deception mechanisms. These include (i) tests for debuggers such as OllyDebug, SoftIce and procdump, (ii) test for VMWare, (iii) killing anti-virus processes, and (iv) altering DNS entries of anti-virus software companies to point to localhost.

Implications: The elaborate deception strategy of Agobot some ways represents a merging of botnets with other forms of malware such as trojans and has several implications. First, honeynet monitors need to be aware of malware that specifically targets virtual machine environments. Second, it suggests the need for better tools for dynamic analysis of this malware since simply executing them in VMware or debuggers will provide false information. Finally, as these mechanisms improve, it is likely to become increasingly difficult to know that a system has been compromised, thereby complicating the task for host-based anti-virus and rootkit detection systems.

8.4 Conclusions

Continued improvements and diversification of malware are making the task of securing networks against attacks and intrusions increasingly difficult. The objective of our work is to expand the knowledge base for security research through systematic evaluation of malicious codebases. We advocate an approach that includes both static analysis of source code and dynamic profiling of executables. In this chapter we take a first step in this process by presenting an evaluation of four instances of botnet source code. We selected botnet code as our initial focus due to its relatively recent emergence as one of the most lethal classes of Internet threats.

Overall, our source code evaluation highlights the sophistication and diverse capabilities of botnets. The details of our findings include descriptions of the primary functional components of botnets organized into seven categories. Some of the most important of findings within these categories include the diverse mechanisms for sensitive information gathering on compromised hosts, the effective mechanisms for remaining invisible once installed on a local host, and the relatively simple command and control systems that are currently used. While the IRC-based command and control systems remain an area that the network security community can potentially exploit for defensive purposes, it is likely that these systems will evolve toward something like a peer-to-peer infrastructure in the near future (if they are not already doing so).

The results in this chapter represent a first step in a much larger process of decomposing and documenting malware of all types. Ultimately, we anticipate that the resulting database will enable *proactive* network security. Our immediate next steps will be to begin the process of dynamic profiling of botnet executables using tools like IDA Pro [17] and by running the executables in our own laboratory environment. Beyond that, we plan to use the lessons learned from this study to begin an IRC monitoring effort at our university border router with the objective of developing new methods for identifying botnet communications. We also plan to expand our on-going honeynet measurement efforts to include botnet monitoring.

Acknowledgements

This work is supported in part by ARO grant DAAD19-02-1-0304 and NSF grant CNS-0347252. The second author was supported in part by a Lawrence H.Landweber NCR Graduate Fellowship. The views and conclusions contained herein are those of the authors and should not be interpreted as necessarily representing the official policies or endorsements, either expressed or implied, of the above government agencies or the U.S. Government.

References

1. C. Associates. GTBot1. http://www3.ca.com/securityadvisor/pest/pest.aspx?id=453073312, 1998.
2. M. Bailey, E. Cooke, F. Jahanian, J. Nazario, and D. Watson. The Internet Motion Sensor: A Distributed Blackhole Monitoring System. In *Proceedings of the Network and Distributed Security Symposium*, San Diego, CA, January 2005.
3. P. Barford. The Wisconsin Advanced Internet Laboratory. http://wail.cs.wisc.edu, 2005.
4. J. Canavan. The evolution of irc bots. In *Proceedings of Virus Bulletin Conference 2005*, October 2005.
5. E. Cooke, F. Jahanian, and D. McPherson. The zombie roundup: Understanding, detecting and disrupting botnets. In *Proceedings of Usenix Workshop on Stepts to Reducing Unwanted Traffic on the Internet (SRUTI '05)*, Cambridge, MA, July 2005.
6. P. Cousot, R. Cousot, J. Feret, L. Mauborgne, A. Mine, D. Monniaux, and X. Rival. The Astree Static Analyzer. http://www.astree.ens.fr, 2005.
7. Coverity. Coverity Prevent. http://www.coverity.com, 2005.
8. DETER. A laboratory for security research. http://www.isi.edu/deter, 2005.
9. D. Dietrich. Distributed Denial of Service (DDoS) Attacks/tools. http://staff.washington.edu/dittrich/misc/ddos/, 2005.

10. J. Evers. Dutch Police Nab Suspected Bot Herders. CNET News.com, October 2005.

11. F-Secure Corporation's Data Security Summary for 2004. http://www.f-secure.com/2004, 2004.

12. German Honeynet Project. Tracking Botnets. http://]www.honeynet.org/papers/bots, 2005.

13. A. Gostev. Malware Evolution: January - March, 2005. http://www.viruslist.com, 2005.

14. M. Handley, C. Kreibich, and V. Paxson. Network Intrusion Detection: Evasion, Traffic Normalization, and End-to-End Protocol Semantics. In *Proceedings of the USENIX Security Symposium*, Washington, DC, August 2001.

15. The Honeynet Project. http://project.honeynet.org, 2003.

16. Honeynet Scan of the Month 32. http://www.honeynet.org/scans/scan32/, 2005.

17. IDA Pro. http://www.datarescue.com, 2005.

18. S. Kandula, D. Katabi, M. Jacob, and A. Berger. Botz-4-Sale: Surviving Organized DDos Attacks That Mimic Flash Crowds . In *Proceedings of the USENIX Symposium on Network Systems Design and Implementation*, Boston, MA, May 2005.

19. D. Kawamoto. Bots Slim Down to get Tough. CNET News.com, November 2005.

20. A. Kumar, V. Paxson, and N. Weaver. Exploiting underlying structure for detailed reconstruction of an internet scale event. In *Proceedings of ACM Internet Measurement Conference*, November 2002.

21. McAfee. W32-Spybot.worm. http//vil.nai.com/vil/content/v_100282.htm, 2003.

22. Metasploit. http://www.metasploit.com, 2005.

23. D. Moore, V. Paxson, S. Savage, C. Shannon, S. Staniford, and N. Weaver. Inside the slammer worm. In *Proceedings of IEEE Security and Privacy*, July 2003.

24. D. Moore and C. Shannon. The Spread of the Witty Worm. $http : // - www.caida.org/analysis/security/witty/$, 2004.

25. D. Moore, C. Shannon, and K. Claffy. Code red: A case study on the spread and victims of an internet worm. In *Proceedings of ACM Internet Measurement Workshop*, November 2002.

26. R. Pang, V. Yegneswaran, P. Barford, V. Paxson, and L. Peterson. Characteristics of internet background radiation. In *Proceedings of ACM Internet Measurement Conference*, Taormina, Italy, October 2004.

27. Regmon. http://www.sysinternals.com, 2005.

28. California Man Charged in Botnet Attacks. Reuters, November 2005.

29. B. Saha and A. Gairola. Botnet: An Overivew. CERT-In White Paper, CIWP-2005-05, June 2005.

30. SoftICE Driver Suite. http://www.compuware.com/products/driverstudio/softice.htm, 2005.

31. Sophos. Troj/Agobot-A. http//www.sophos.com/virusinfo/analyses/trojagobota.html, 2002.

32. Sophos. Troj/SDBot. http//www.sophos.com/virusinfo/analyses/trojsdbot.html, 2002.

33. Sophos virus analyses. http://www.sophos.com/virusinfo/analyses, 2005.

34. S. Staniford, V. Paxson, and N. Weaver. How to Own the Internet in Your Spare Time. In *Proceedings of the 11th USENIX Security Symposium*, 2002.

35. I. Thomson. Hackers Fight to Create Worlds Largest Botnet. http://www.vnunet.com, August 2005.

36. J. Ullrich. Dshield. http://www.dshield.org, 2005.

37. D. Verton. Organized Crime Invades Cyberspace. http://www.computerworld.com, August 2004.

38. M. Vrable, J. Ma, J. Chen, D. Moore, E. Vandekieft, A. Snoeren, G. Voelker, and S. Savage. Scalability, fidelity and containment in the potemkin virtual honeyfarm. In *Proceedings of ACM Symposium on Operating Systems Principles (SOSP)*, Brighton, England, October 2005.

39. V. Yegneswaran, P. Barford, and D. Plonka. On the design and use of Internet sinks for network abuse monitoring. In *Proceedings of Recent Advances on Intrusion Detection*, Sophia, France, September 2004.

40. V. Yegneswaran, P. Barford, and J. Ullrich. Internet intrusions: Global characteristics and prevalence. In *Proceedings of ACM SIGMETRICS*, San Diego, CA, June 2003.

9

Can Cooperative Intrusion Detectors Challenge the Base-Rate Fallacy?

Mihai Christodorescu and Shai Rubin

Department of Computer Sciences, University of Wisconsin, Madison
{mihai,shai}@cs.wisc.edu

9.1 Introduction

In recent years, researchers have focused on the ability of intrusion detection systems to resist evasion: techniques attackers use to bypass intrusion detectors and avoid detection. Researchers have developed successful evasion techniques either for network-based (e.g., [14, 19]) or host-based (e.g., [18, 20]) detectors.

Unlike the problem of evasion, the problem of *false positives* has yet to attract much attention. False positives, cases in which a IDS raises an alert but no intrusion has occurred, are a major problem for IDS users [6, 16]. If the number of false positives is large, the security officer that uses the IDS quickly learns to treat every alert as false, rendering the IDS useless.

In a recent work, Axelsson [2] mathematically showed that even with a reasonably accurate detector, one out of three alerts is likely to be false positive. Axelsson observed that a few IDS mistakes are translated into a large number of false positives because of the volume of benign events dwarfs the volume of intrusions. Axelsson concluded that false positives will always remain a major problem and called this phenomenon, the *base-rate fallacy* of intrusion detection.

We attempt to address the base-rate fallacy. We claim that, even though the fallacy mandates the use of detectors with a low false positive rate, it also suggests that it is feasible to build such a detector.

Our approach is based on two observations. First, we observe that false positives occur not because it is impossible to distinguish between benign and malicious events but only because it is difficult to do so *efficiently*. For example, there is a simple procedure to determine whether an HTTP request triggers a buffer overflow: executing it in a protected environment (sandbox). Sandboxing, however, is too expensive [1]; an IDS that must analyze thousands of HTTP requests per second cannot afford to sandbox all of them.

Second, like Axelsson, we observe that most events are benign. However, we extend the observation further and notice that it is possible to efficiently distinguish between the majority of benign events and malicious events. It is possible to split the set of benign events into subsets based on the effort required to determine whether an event is malicious or benign. For the vast majority of benign events, it is easy to determine that they are benign. We believe that false positives occur not because it is difficult to distinguish between an intrusion and *any* other benign event, but because it is difficult to distinguish between an intrusion and a *small set* of benign events.

We leverage these observations to build a detection system with a low false-positive rate and a low cost. We know that ideal detectors exist, but only with a high cost of detection. We also know that detectors with a low cost exist, but only with a high rate of false positives. The goal is then to design a detector that bridges the gap between these two extremes. To achieve such a detector, we use the concept of *detector combination*. Intuitively, we first use an efficient detector to distinguish between the majority of benign events and *might-be-intrusion* events. Then, as a second step, a less efficient detector can further distinguish between might-be-intrusion events and malicious events. We show that Axelsson's fallacy actually facilitates efficiency. Since the majority of the events are benign, and since it is possible to efficiently distinguish between the majority of benign events and malicious ones, the efficiency of the combined detector is close to the efficiency of the more efficient detector.

In particular, this chapter makes the following contributions:

1. **We formulate the detector-combination problem**: given two detectors D_1 and D_2, find a function, f, that combines the two such that the combined detector, $f(D_1, D_2)$ is (i) more accurate than both detectors and (ii) its operation cost is smaller than some upper bound.
2. **We mathematically analyze solutions to the detector-combination problem**. We investigate three potential solutions to the detector-combination problem. For each solution, we investigate the conditions that must hold for D_1 and D_2, so the function is a valid solution.
3. **We derive recommendations for IDS development**. Base on our analysis, we derive recommendations for IDS developers. Example recommendations are:
   - To achieve a combined detector with a low false positive rate, design two detectors with high false positive rates such that they eliminate the false positive of each other.
   - It is not always more efficient to use the most efficient detector to distinguish between benign and might-be-attack events. The decision depends on the relation between costs of the two detectors and their false positive rates.

9.2 Overview

In this section we present in detail the false-positive problem, initially formulated by Stefan Axelsson as the base-rate fallacy. Then we introduce our proposed solution for reducing false positives with no significant increase in cost and no decrease in intrusion-detection rate. The discussion of our solution makes use of a practical example highlighting the choices a security analyst makes when building an intrusion detection system.

9.2.1 The Base-Rate Fallacy of Intrusion Detection

Axelsson's *Base-Rate Fallacy* [2] is best understood via an example. Consider a network-based IDS that attempts to identify an FTP attack, called *ftp-cwd* (CAN-2002-0126 [13]), which causes a buffer overflow in the Blackmoon FTP server for Windows. The overflow occurs when the attacker supplies an overly long, more than 256 bytes, directory name for the CWD (change directory) command. In an effective *ftp-cwd* attack, this long name must contain shell code that hijacks the control from the FTP server into the hands of an attacker.

Like Axelsson, we assume that effective instances of the *ftp-cwd* attack are rare. For example, assume that out of a million packets observed by a network-based IDS (NIDS), only half a dozen packets are real *ftp-cwd* attacks. Recall that a false positive is a situation in which the NIDS raises an alert *given a non-attack event*. Then, a NIDS that mistakenly generates an alert once every 100,000 non-attack packets (this means the false-positive rate of this NIDS is 10^{-5}), would raise about 10 alerts per a million packets. In total, such a NIDS would raise about 16 alerts: 6 alerts because of the real instances of *ftp-cwd* and 10 alerts that are false.

9.2.2 Our Observations

We embrace Axelsson assumption that the number of intrusions is significantly smaller than the number of benign events. We also understand that false positives would always be a major problem because they are dominated by the number of non-attack events. We understand that the only way to address Axelsson's fallacy is to develop a highly accurate detector. However, we believe that Axelsson's fallacy can be used as a guideline for building such accurate detectors.

We illustrate our observation using the *ftp-cwd* example. Assume that the example IDS monitors both the FTP and HTTP servers of our organization. We first describe two detectors that distinguish between benign events and *might-be-ftp-cwd* attacks. As we argue, the operational cost of these two detectors is moderate.

Detector 1: Identify benign HTTP events.
    HTTP events are clearly not our attack. It is easy to differentiate between HTTP and FTP events just by looking at the port numbers in the TCP header.

Detector 2: Identify possibly malicious CWD commands with long arguments.
    The computational effort requires to identify a Level 3 event is equivalent to the effort to identify a regular expression of the form ('\nCWD')('¬\n'){256,}: a line starts with CWD, followed by at least 256 characters that are not '\n'. This requires matching of a regular expression that can be done in a linear time (with respect to the length of the input stream).

Detectors 1 and 2 above can be combined to differentiate between benign and might-be-ftp-cwd events. It is important to understand that, in our scenario, an FTP CWD command with an argument longer than 256 bytes is an extremely rare event. In other words, Detectors 1 and 2 can be used to determine that more than 99.9% of the events on our site are **not** *ftp-cwd* attacks.

Detector 3: Identify CWD commands with long arguments containing shell code.

Detector 3 requires the highest computational effort. Like Detector 2, it requires regular expression matching. However, it also requires inspection of the FTP payload to determine whether the payload contains valid shell code. One way to determine whether the FTP command contains shell code is sandboxing [1], which simulates the CWD command on a shadow FTP server where a successful buffer overflow cannot cause any damage.

Note that Detector 3 requires significant computational effort, several orders of magnitudes larger than the cost of Detector 2. However, Detector 3 false positive rate is zero (if we assume that a CWD command that does not cause an overflow on the shadow FTP server also does not cause an overflow on the real FTP server). Below, we show that one can combine all three detectors to get the false positive rate of Detector 3 at an operational cost close to the cost of Detector 2.

9.2.3 Combining Detectors

Consider a developer that builds a network-based IDS (NIDS). Assume that according to the developer's measurement, the NIDS has to handle 4,000 TCP packets per second, both FTP and HTTP traffic. For the sake of computation, assume that the developer implements the NIDS on a 3.5 MHz processor. Thus, on average, the NIDS must analyze a single packet using less than 8.75×10^5 cycles per packet:

$$\frac{3.5 \times 10^9}{4 \times 10^3} = 8.75 \times 10^5 \ cycles/packet$$

The developer notices that it is possible to define a Snort signature to match CWD FTP commands with arguments longer than 256 bytes (i.e., Snort could serve as both Detector 1 and Detector 2 above). The developer measures Snort's performance and notices that (i) Snort requires, on average, 20,000 cycles to analyze a single packet, and (ii) Snort generates only one *ftp-cwd* alert per 100,000 packets it analyzes, that is $P(A_{snort}) = 10^{-5}$ (we chose these number based on our experience with Snort).

While Snort meets the cost bound of 8.75×10^5 cycles per packet, its false-alert rate is too high for the given volume of traffic. In this scenario, Snort would generate approximately 58 false alerts per hour for 86 actual intrusions per hour. The developer realizes that the false alert rate is too high; it will cause the NIDS user to ignore all alerts. The developer decides to consider a different detection approach.

The developer implements a shadow FTP honeypot. The developer measures the performance of this shadow FTP server and discovers that it requires half a second to simulate a single FTP command. In other words, it takes 1.75×10^9 cycles to run a single FTP command on the shadowed FTP server.

The developer then implements the following system. All packets, either FTP or HTTP, are fed first fed into Snort. Each packet that matches the signature above is passed to the shadow FTP server. If the FTP command causes an overflow on the shadow server, the system raises an *ftp-cwd* alert.

Let us calculate the average time it takes for the combined system to analyze a single packet. Denote the time it takes for Snort to analyze a packet as T_{snort}, and the time it takes for the shadow server to analyze a packet as T_{shadow}. Then the average time per packet for the combined detector is:

$$T_{average} = T_{snort} + P(A_{snort}) \cdot T_{shadow}$$
$$= 2 \times 10^4 + 10^{-5} \times 1.75 \times 10^9$$
$$= 3.75 \times 10^4 \ cycles$$

That is, the average time per packet is 23 times lower than the upper bound set by the developer (8.75×10^5).

This example construction shows that, while Axelsson's fallacy holds, it is also possible to build a highly accurate detector with a reasonable performance. Snort alone is not accurate and requires 2×10^4 cycles per event. However, the combined detector, which is highly accurate, requires 3.75×10^4 cycles per event, only 87% less efficient than snort. In other words, the high volume of benign events dominates the false positive rate, but it also dominates the average cost of detection.

9.3 The Problem of Detector Combination

Intuitively speaking, the problem of *detector combination* is how to combine two detectors such that the combined detector is both more accurate than each component detector alone and the operational cost of the combined detector is smaller than some fixed upper bound.

A detector is characterized by its true positive rate, false positive rate, and operational cost. To define the detector's operational cost, we use the notion of *universal detection cost*. The universal detection cost for a detector D, denoted *udc*, is a positive integer that represents the effort D invests per event, the higher the cost the higher the effort. By effort, we mean computation time, computation space, energy consumed, or maintenance cost in person-hours.

We use the universal detection cost as a design tool rather than a scientific measurement. Developers considering the detector-combination problem should assign different costs to the detectors they wish to combine according to their analysis or experimental measurement. For example, in Section 9.2.3 we use cycles per packet as our cost function. We derive the costs based on our experience with Snort and our estimate for a shadow FTP server.

Definition 1 (Intrusion Detector) *Let E be a set of events and $I \subseteq E$ a set of intrusions. Let f be a detection function $f : E \rightarrow \{A, \neg A\}$, with the universal detection cost C. An intrusion detector system is a tuple* $\text{ID} \stackrel{def}{=} \langle E, I, f, C \rangle$. *We further define:*

1. *The true-positive rate of* ID, $tp \stackrel{def}{=} P(f(e) = A | e \in I)$.
2. *The false-positive false of* ID, $fp \stackrel{def}{=} P(f(e) = A | e \notin I)$.

Table 9.1. Notation used throughout the chapter.

Formal definition	Notation	Description
$P(f(e) = A\|e \in I)$	$P(A\|I)$	*true positive (tp)* rate.
$P(f(e) = A\|e \notin I)$	$P(A\|\neg I)$	*false positive (fp)* rate.
$P(f(e) = \neg A\|e \in I)$	$P(\neg A\|I) = 1 - P(A\|I)$	*false negative (fn)* rate.
$P(f(e) = \neg A\|e \notin I)$	$P(\neg A\|\neg I) = 1 - P(\neg A\|I)$	*true negative (tn)* rate.

All detectors operate over the same set of events by definition. We chose this abstraction because it facilitates detector combination. It is possible to combine a network-based detector with a host-based detector. Although in practice such detectors operate over a different set of events, these events are signs of the same attack. For example, an attack exploiting a buffer overflow in an FTP server manifests itself both at the network level (the FTP session) and at the host audit log level (the execution of a new shell).

We note that it is enough to use the true-positive and false-positive rates to characterize a detector completely. The other two rates, the true-negative and false-negative rates, are the complement of the first two rates. For clarity we use the notation used by Axelsson as depicted in Table 9.1.

Definition 2 (The Problem of Detector Combination) *Let* $D_1 = \langle E, I, f_1, C_1 \rangle$ *and* $D_2 = \langle E, I, f_2, C_3 \rangle$ *be two detectors. Let* $\mathcal{X} > 0$ *be the cost upperbound. The detector-combination problem is to find a detection function* $f_3(f_1, f_2)$ *such that the following requirements hold for the combined detector* $D_3 = \langle E, I, f_3, C_3 \rangle$:

$$tp_3 \geq \max(tp_1, tp_2) \qquad \text{(True-Positive Requirement)}$$
$$fp_3 \leq \min(fp_1, fp_2) \qquad \text{(False-Positive Requirement)}$$
$$C_3 \leq \mathcal{X} \qquad \text{(Cost Requirement)}$$

Any solution to this problem needs to produce a combined detector D_3 with a true-positive rate that is at least as high as the maximum between the rates of D_1 and D_2, a false-positive rate that is at least as low as the minimum between the rates of D_1 and D_2, and with a universal cost smaller than $\mathcal{X}$.

9.4 Possible Solutions to the Detector-Combination Problem

We discuss specific solutions to the detector-combination problem and determine for which instances of the problem these solutions are valid. A general solution to the detector-combination problem, if one exists, is left for future work.

9.4.1 Trivial Solutions: $f_3 = f_1$ or $f_3 = f_2$

There are instances of the detector-combination problem for which one of the detector is a solution. For example, consider detectors D_1 and D_2 such that $C_1 \leq \mathcal{X}$,

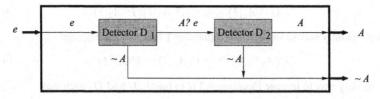

Fig. 9.1. A schematic view of the cascade-on-alert scheme. The notation $A?e$ means that the event e is passed on to the next component if the previous component raised the alert A.

$tp_1 \geq tp_2$, and $fp_1 \leq fp_2$ (an analogous case exists for D_2). D_1 has true-positive and false-positive rates better than D_2 and its detection cost is lower than the upper bound $\mathcal{X}$.

Notice though that there are instances in which $C_1 \leq \mathcal{X}$ and $C_2 \leq \mathcal{X}$ but neither $f_3 = f_1$ nor $f_3 = f_2$ is a feasible solution. For example, consider D_1 and D_2 such that $tp_1 > tp_2$ but $fp_1 > fp_2$, that is, D_1 has better true-positive rate but worse false-positive rate. Below, we discuss functions that solve the detector-combination problem for such cases.

9.4.2 $f_3 =$ Cascade on Alert

We analyze a specific solution to the detector-combination problem called *cascade-on-alert*. As we show, the cascade on alert is not a general solution to the problem. Therefore, we derive the constraints on D_1 and D_2 that must hold for the cascade-on-alert function to be a valid solution.

Definition 3 (Cascade-on-Alert) *For every event, e, perform the following. Analyze e using D_1. If D_1 returns $\neg A$, then return $\neg A$. If D_1 return A, then analyze e using D_2 and return D_2's answer. Formally:*

$$f_3(e) = \begin{cases} A & \text{if } (f_1(e) = A) \wedge (f_2(e) = A) \\ \neg A & \text{if } f_1(e) = \neg A \vee (f_1(e) = A \wedge f_2(e) = \neg A) \end{cases}$$

Cascade-on-alert is not a general solution. For example, consider (a useless) D_2 that returns $\neg A$ for every e. Therefore, the combined detector D_3 returns $\neg A$ for every event and its true positive rate is zero. Such D_3 is not a valid solution in case the true positive rate of D_1 is greater than zero.

Satisfying the True-Positive Requirement.

The true-positive requirement mandates that $tp_3 \geq \max(tp_1, tp_2)$:

$$P(A_3|I) \geq \max(P(A_1|I), P(A_2|I))$$
$$\Updownarrow$$
$$P(A_1 \cap A_2|I) \geq \max(P(A_1|I), P(A_2|I)) \tag{9.1}$$

However, $A_1 \cap A_2 \subseteq A_1$ and $A_1 \cap A_2 \subseteq A_2$ which means that:

$$P(A_1 \cap A_2|I) \leq \min(P(A_1|I), P(A_2|I)) \tag{9.2}$$

Hence, the only way to satisfy both Equations 1 and 9.2 is to impose:

$$P(A_1 \cap A_2|I) = P(A_1|I) = P(A_2|I) \tag{9.3}$$

and the only way to impose Equation 9.3 is to build D_1 and D_2 such that:

$$\{A_1 \cap I\} = \{A_2 \cap I\} \tag{9.4}$$

Satisfying the False-Positive Requirement.

The false-positive requirement mandates that $fp_3 \leq \min(fp_1, fp_2)$. The cascade-on-alert function always satisfies this condition because:

$$fp_3 = P(A_1 \cap A_2|\neg I) \leq \min(P(A_1|\neg I), P(A_2|\neg I)) = \min(fp_1, fp_2) \tag{9.5}$$

Moreover, if we want to reduce the false positive rate to zero the we must impose:

$$(\{A_1 \cap \neg I\}) \cap (\{A_2 \cap \neg I\}) = \emptyset \tag{9.6}$$

Satisfying the Cost Requirement.

We want a detector that its cost of operation is lower than $\mathcal{X}$. That is:

$$C_3 = C_1 + P(A_1) \times C_2 \leq \mathcal{X} \Leftrightarrow P(A_1) \leq \frac{\mathcal{X} - C_1}{C_2} \tag{9.7}$$

Notice that in Equation 9.7 we use the fact that D_1 is the "first" detector and D_2 is the "second" one in the cascade-on-alert sequence (Figure 9.1). However, this does not mean that that the universal cost of D_1 is lower than the cost of D_2. Indeed, in Section 9.5.2 we show there are cases in which it is more efficient to put the more expensive detector in front of the less expensive one.

Summary: Cascade-on-alert is a valid solution to the detector-combination problem only if D_1 and D_2 satisfy Equations 9.4 and 9.7. If we want a cascade-on-alert function with zero false positives, then D_1 and D_2 must satisfy Equation 9.6.

9.4.3 f_3 = Cascade on Non-Alert

The *cascade-on-non-alert* function is analogous to cascade-on-alert. However, instead of invoking D_2 when the output of D_1 is A, the cascade-on-non-alert invokes D_2 when D_1's output is $\neg A$. Below we derive the necessary conditions for cascade-on-non-alert to be a valid solution.

Definition 4 (Cascade-on-Non-Alert) *For every event, e, perform the following. Analyze e using D_1. If D_1 returns A, then return A. If D_1 return $\neg A$, then analyze e using D_2 and return D_2's answer. Formally:*

$$f_3(e) = \begin{cases} A & \text{if } f_1(e) = A \vee (f_1(e) = \neg A \wedge f_2(e) = A) \\ \neg A & \text{if } f_1(e) = \neg A \wedge f_2(e) = \neg A \end{cases}$$

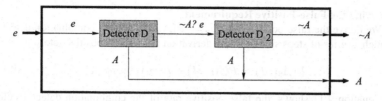

Fig. 9.2. A schematic view of the cascade-on-non-alert scheme. The notation $\neg A?e$ means that the event e is passed on to the next component if the previous component did not raise an alert A.

Analogous to cascade-on-alert, the cascade-on-non-alert is not a general solution. We wish to find the constraints that detectors D_1 and D_2 must satisfy for the cascade-on-non-alert scheme to be a valid solution to the conditions problem.

Satisfying the True-Positive Requirement.

The true positive rate of D_3 can be derived as follows:

$$P(A_3|I) = P(A_1 \cup (\neg A_1 \cap A_2)|I)$$

Note that $P(A_3|I) = P(A_1|I) + P(\neg A_1 \cap A_2|I) - P(A_1 \cap (\neg A_1 \cap A_2)|I)$. Therefore:

$$P(A_3|I) = P(A_1|I) + P(\neg A_1 \cap A_2|I)$$

Given that $0 \leq P(\neg A_1 \cap A_2|I) \leq 1$, the true positive rate of D_3 is at least as good as the true positive rate of D_1. For the cascade-on-no-alert to be a valid solution, we need to find the conditions under which $P(A_3|I)$ is greater than $P(A_2|I)$.

$$P(A_1|I) + P(\neg A_1 \cap A_2|I) \geq P(A_2|I)$$

As $\{\neg A_1 \cap A_2\} = \{A_2\} \setminus \{A_1 \cap A_2\}$, we get:

$$P(A_1|I) + P(A_2|I) - P(A_1 \cap A_2|I) \geq P(A_2|I) \tag{9.8}$$

$$\Updownarrow$$

$$P(A_1|I) \geq P(A_1 \cap A_2|I) \tag{9.9}$$

Because $A_1 \cap A_2 \subseteq A_1$, Equation 9.9 is always true. Thus, the true positive rate of the combined detector is at least as large as the maximum of the true positive rates of the two detectors.

Furthermore, we can see from Equation 9.8 that the true positive rate of the combined detector is maximized when $P(A_1 \cap A_2|I) = 0$. This implies that $\{A_1 \cap A_2 \cap I\} = \emptyset$, or, equivalently:

$$(\{A_1 \cap I\}) \cap (\{A_2 \cap I\}) = \emptyset \tag{9.10}$$

In other words, the cascade-on-non-alert scheme achieves maximum true positive (detection) rate when the two detectors D_1 and D_2 raise true alerts on distinct sets of events.

Satisfying the False-Positive Requirement.

We derive the false positive rate $fp_3 = P(A_3|\neg I)$ for the combination detector through a series of steps similar to the derivation for the true positive rate.

$$P(A_3|\neg I) = P(A_1|\neg I) + P(\neg A_1 \cap A_2|\neg I) \qquad (9.11)$$

As Equation 9.11 shows, the false positive rate of the combination detector could increase beyond the false positive rate of the first detector, D_1. The best we can achieve is to *keep the false positive rate equal to that of detector D_1*. This implies that $P(\neg A_1 \cap A_2|\neg I) = 0$, and the following has to hold:

$$\{\neg A_1\} \cap \{A_2\} \cap \{\neg I\} = \emptyset \qquad (9.12)$$

Satisfying the Cost Requirement.

The average cost (per event) of the cascade-on-non-alert detector is captured by the following formula:

$$
\begin{aligned}
C_3 &= C_1 + P(\neg A_1) \times C_2 \\
&= C_1 + (1 - P(A_1)) \times C_2 \\
&= C_1 + \big(1 - P(A_1|I) \times P(I) - P(A_1|\neg I) \times P(\neg I)\big) \times C_2
\end{aligned}
$$

Then the condition becomes:

$$\frac{\mathcal{X} - C_1}{C_2} \geq 1 - P(A_1|I) \times P(I) - P(A_1|\neg I) \times P(\neg I) \qquad (9.13)$$

Summary: Cascade-on-non-alert is a valid solution to the detector-combination problem only if D_1 and D_2 satisfy Equations 9.12 and 9.13. If we want a cascade-on-non-alert function with maximum true positive rate, then D_1 and D_2 must satisfy Equation 9.10.

9.5 Recommendations to IDS Developers

In Section 9.4 we mathematically analyzed solutions to the detector-combination problem. In this section we interpret our mathematical results into practical guidelines for IDS developers.

In Section 9.4.2, we showed that cascade-on-alert cannot improve the true-positive rate of either D_1 or D_2 (Equation 9.3). Similarly, in Section 9.4.3, we showed that the cascade-on-non-alert cannot improve the false positive rate of the combined detector (Equation 9.11). Since the main motivation of our work is reducing false positives, we focus on the cascade-on-alert scheme.

For cascade-on-alert to be a viable solution, one must build two detectors that satisfy Equations 9.4 and 9.7. We translate these equations into practical considerations.

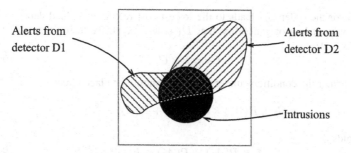

Fig. 9.3. True positives for cascade-on-alert

9.5.1 Satisfying Equation 9.4: The True-Positive Requirement

Equation 9.4 requires that $\{A_1 \cap I\} = \{A_2 \cap I\}$. Practically, this means that both detectors must agree when a real attack occurs. Note that this does not mean that both detectors should detect all real attacks, but only that they should detect the same set of attacks (Figure 9.3). Detectors D_1 and D_2 in Figure 9.3 detect that same set of real attacks (the crosshatched half of the set of real attacks) and miss the same set of real attacks (the bottom half of the set of real attacks). The combined detector detects the same set of real attacks as either component detector, but it cannot do better than that.

To increase the set of detected real attacks of a cascade-on-alert combination, both sets of real attacks detected by the component detectors must increase. The best case is shown in Figure 9.4, where both component detectors D_1 and D_2 detect all of the real attacks. In this case, the cascade-on-alert combination detects all of the real attacks as well.

9.5.2 Satisfying Equation 9.7: The Cost Requirement

Notice that satisfying the false positive and true positive requirement does not impose an order between D_1 and D_2: we can either put D_1 in front of D_2, or vice versa. This is evident from Equation 9.4 which does not reflect the order between the detectors. Thus, we need to look at the cost requirement to determine how to order the detectors.

The cost requirements for the cascade-on-alert scheme when detector D_1 is first and when D_2 is first are, respectively, as follows:

$$C_{1 \to 2} = C_1 + P(A_1) \times C_2 \leq \mathcal{X} \tag{9.14}$$
$$C_{2 \to 1} = C_2 + P(A_2) \times C_1 \leq \mathcal{X} \tag{9.15}$$

If none of these requirements are satisfied, then the cascade-on-alert scheme cannot solve this instance of the detector-combination problem. If only one of these requirements is satisfied, then the solution is to choose the order corresponding to that requirement. If both of these requirements are satisfied, then either order (D_1 followed by D_2 and D_2 followed by D_1) are possible solutions.

We favor the order that leads to the lowest cost for the combined detector. We assume, without loss of generality, that D_1 is less expensive to run than D_2, by a factor of $k > 1$:

$$C_2 = k \times C_1 \qquad (9.16)$$

Let us consider the conditions under which D_1 should be placed first:

$$C_1 + P(A_1) \times C_2 \leq C_2 + P(A_2) \times C_1$$

which holds if:

$$k \times P(A_1) - P(A_2) \leq k - 1 \qquad (9.17)$$

If Equation 9.17 holds, then D_1 should be placed first in the cascade-on-alert scheme. However, if Equation 9.17 does not hold, we reach a surprising result. The expensive detector, D_2, should be placed first. Intuitively, the reason is that even though D_1 is less expensive, it will invoke D_2 too frequently (because $P(A_1) \geq \frac{k-1+P(A_2)}{k}$).

9.5.3 Optimizing Cascade-On-Alert for False Positives

Recall that cascade-on-alert scheme always improves the false-positive rate (Equation 9.5). Furthermore, cascade-on-alert enables us to reduce the false-positive rate to zero when we satisfy Equation 9.6.

There can be four cases that satisfy Equation 9.6:

	Condition	Description
1.	$\{A_1\} \cap \{A_2\} = \emptyset$	Detectors D_1 and D_2 have no alerts in common.
2.	$\{A_1\} \cap \{\neg I\} = \emptyset$	Detector D_1 produces no false alerts.
3.	$\{A_2\} \cap \{\neg I\} = \emptyset$	Detector D_2 produces no false alerts.
4.	$\{A_1\} \cap \{A_2\} \cap \{\neg I\} = \emptyset$	None of the three cases above applies.

When attempting to satisfy Equation 9.6, we also need to remember that we must satisfy Equation 9.4, which ensures that the true-positive rate requirement holds. In Case (1) above, this means that $\{A_1\} \cap \{A_2\} = \emptyset$ and $\{A_1 \cap I\} = \{A_2 \cap I\}$, thus, $\{A_1 \cap I\} = \{A_2 \cap I\} = \emptyset$. This scenario is not useful, because both the component detectors and the combined detector fail to detect any attacks.

Case (2) describe scenarios in which the detector D_1 has no false positives. Given the fact that $\{A_1 \cap I\} = \{A_2 \cap I\}$ (Equation 9.4), it means that D_1 detects all attacks detected by D_2 and does not produce false positives. In this case, we would like to use D_1 alone. The only reason to use D_2 is to reduce the operational cost. This case is similar to the example case presented in Section 9.2.

Case (3) is analogous to case (2).

Case (4) means that the D_1 and D_2 have some false positives, but none of these false positives are common to both detectors. In other words, whatever the false positives from the two component detectors, as long as they are distinct, the cascade-on-alert detector will have no false positives. We can combine this case with the

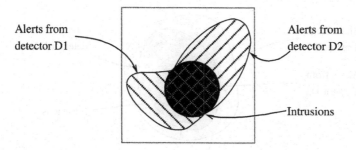

Fig. 9.4. Best case for cascade-on-alert.

best case for the true-positive requirement (described next) to obtain the only ideal detector that cascade-on-alert can build.

The Ideal Cascade-On-Alert Combination.

Based on the analysis for the true-positive requirement, a cascade-on-alert detector can attain 100% true positives only if both component detectors have 100% true positives. Based on the analysis for the false-positive requirement, a cascade-on-alert detector can attain 0% false positives if the two component detectors have no false positives in common. This scenario is illustrated in Figure 9.4. In this scenario, the resulting cascade-on-alert detector is ideal (no false alerts with 100% attacks detected).

If we furthermore assume that both component detectors have low detection costs detectors (since they can have relatively large numbers of false positives), then the resulting cascade-on-alert detector has a relatively low detection cost as well. Thus cascade-on-alert can combine two low-cost detectors with large false positive rates (which further satisfy the true-positive and false-positive requirements) to obtain a *low-cost ideal detector*!

Realistic Cascade-On-Alert Combinations.

The best case for the cascade-on-alert scenario, as discussed above, holds the promise of building ideal detectors from low-cost, high false-positive detectors. Unfortunately, it is unrealistic to expect to find detectors with disjoint false-alert sets. We discuss two cascade-on-alert cases that, although do not yield ideal detectors, have realistic requirements.

The first case was presented in Section 9.2, where multiple detectors of increasing cost and decreasing false positives are chained in a cascade-on-alert setup. This is best illustrated using the diagram in figure 9.5. We show here three detectors (the three outer areas around the black circle) that could correspond to levels 1, 3, and 4 from Section 9.2. Both the true-positive and the false-positive requirements from Section 9.3 hold true:

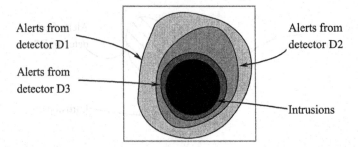

Fig. 9.5. An implementation of the cascade-on-alert scheme that combines three detectors with decreasing false positives, $P(A_1|\neg I) > P(A_2|\neg I) > P(A_3|\neg I)$, and corresponding increasing costs, $udc(D_1) < udc(D_2) < udc(D_3)$.

$$\{A_1 \cap I\} = \{A_2 \cap I\} = \{A_3 \cap I\} \qquad \text{(True-Positive Requirement)}$$
$$\{A_1 \cap A_2 \cap A_3 \cap \neg I\} = \{A_3 \cap \neg I\}$$
$$\subseteq \{A_2 \cap \neg I\} \qquad \text{(False-Positive Requirement)}$$
$$\subseteq \{A_1 \cap \neg I\}$$

This design scenario reflect the intuition expressed in the beginning of the chapter. We can chain multiple detectors using cascade-on-alert to obtain a combined detector with the lowest false positive rate and an averaged detection cost.

The second design scenario for cascade-on-alert combinations is a more realistic version of the ideal cascade-on-alert combination. The difference is that we allow some false positives to occur from the combined detector, while maintaining the focus on getting disjoint sets of false positives. This still allows us to minimize the resulting number of false positives, as shown in Figure 9.6. The key element of this design scenario is the choice of the component detectors. The detectors D_1 and D_2 can have high false positive rates, as long as the rate of false positives they have in common is small. We believe this option provides a lot of latitude to the IDS designer, because many existing detectors have high false positive rates, making them valid candidates for this design process.

9.6 Related Work

We review related work in the areas of the false positives and combining detectors.

The Problem of False Positives.

Researchers [2, 6, 17] and users [16] of intrusion detection systems have acknowledged that false positives are a major problem in adopting and using intrusion detection devices.

In our opinion, Axelsson's fallacy [2] is the best explanation for the large number of false positives. Our work is based on the same observation as Axelsson's: unless a

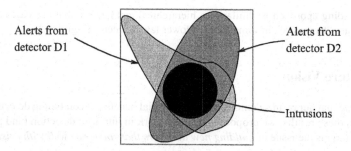

Fig. 9.6. Combining detectors with disjoint false positives in a cascade-on-alert scheme results in a detector with (almost) no false positives. If $\{I\} \subseteq \{A_1\} \cap \{A_2\}$, then the combined detector has few false positives and no false negatives.

detector does not produce any false positives, the large number of benign events leads to a high number of false positives. We extended Axelsson's work by adding the cost of detection into the equation. We observed that the majority of benign events can be efficiently and safely classified as benign. This means that the average classification cost can be close to the cost of classifying benign events.

In the literature, one can find two main methods to fight false positives: alarm clustering and accurate signatures. The goal of alarm clustering [3, 5, 9] is to group together related alerts, so the security administrator can analyze a group of alerts rather than each alert individually. Generally speaking, alarm clustering deals with the symptoms rather the causes. In comparison, the detector-combination approach attempts to reduce the overall number of false alerts.

Using more accurate signatures is an attractive approach for fighting false positives. Unfortunately, accurate signatures usually require a higher computational cost. For example, researchers have suggested to use victim responses [15, 17] as part of signatures or to verify the alert [11], using a monitoring tool like Nessus [7]. Our work is based on the assumption that even inaccurate signatures are enough to distinguish between benign and might-be-malicious events, thus leaving the use of more expensive signatures to distinguish between might-be-malicious and malicious events.

Combining Detectors.

A common way to combine detectors is by using a voting scheme, where the output of the combined detector is the output that the majority vote among all detectors. Giacinto *et al.* [8] found that a voting-based detector is more accurate than detectors that were used in the DARPA evaluation [12]. Our work considers other combination schemes like cascading (Section 9.4.2). Furthermore, we consider the question of operating under cost constraints, which was not addressed by Giacinto *et al.*.

Other researchers consider hierarchical architectures for intrusion detection. In a typical hierarchical architecture (e.g., [21]), the detectors are ordered in layers, and the input for a detector in a lower layer is the output of a detector in a higher layer.

Our cascading approach is similar to a hierarchical architecture, but our cascading architecture "bypasses", in some cases, a lower level detector (Figure 9.1).

9.7 Future Vision

We believe that our results demonstrate the potential benefits of combining detectors. Based on these results, we propose that future work in intrusion detection (and prevention) targets the issue of *building new detectors that cooperate well with existing detectors*.

There are two research problems that require solutions before cooperative IDS development becomes practical. First, for the development of a new detector not to overlap existing detectors, a way to evaluate the event space covered by existing detectors is needed. Note that the goal is not to measure the true-positive and false-positive rates, but to identify the sets of true positives and false positives in the event space. Recent work on language-based techniques for NIDS evaluation could prove useful in developing analytic solutions [15]. Another possible approach is based on the empirical assessment of an IDS. By learning the rules used by network-based and host-based intrusion detection systems, the event space covered by a particular IDS can be characterized precisely [4, 10]. Extending these techniques to answer the problem of event-space coverage for an existing IDS accurately is one direction for future research.

The second research goal in support of cooperative IDS development is to identify additional solutions to the detector-combination problem. In this chapter we presented a set of possible solutions (the cascade-on-alert and the cascade-on-non-alert schemes) that each enable multiple design strategies (Section 9.5). Other ways of combining detectors could provide different tradeoffs between true positives, false positives, and cost. Decision trees, based on the idea of breaking up a complex decision ("Is this event a real attack?") into multiple simpler decisions, can provide the conceptual framework for finding other ways to combine detectors. At each node in the decision tree a intrusion detector is placed, and the output of this detector influences that path taken through the tree. The problem of constructing an optimal decision tree, given a set of intrusion detectors as blackbox decision procedures, is another direction for future research.

References

1. K. G. Anagnostakis, S. Sidiroglon, P. Akritidis, K. Xinidis, E. Markatos, and A. D. Keromytis. Detecting targeted attacks using shadow honeypots. In *USENIX Security Symposium*, Baltimore, MD, August 2005.
2. S. Axelsson. The base-rate fallacy and the difficulty of intrusion detection. *ACM Transactions on Information and System Security*, 3(3):186 – 205, 2000.
3. S. Axelsson. Visualisation for intrusion detection: Hooking the worm. In *European Symposium on Research in Computer Security*, Gjvik, Norway, Sep. 2003.

4. M. Christodorescu and S. Jha. Testing malware detectors. In *Proceedings of the 2004 ACM SIGSOFT International Symposium on Software Testing and Analysis (ISSTA 2004)*, pages 34–44, Boston, MA, USA, July 2004. ACM Press.
5. F. Cuppens and A. Miege. Alert correlation in a cooperative intrusion detection framework. In *IEEE Symposium on Security and Privacy*, Oakland, CA, May 2002.
6. M. Dacier, editor. *Design of an Intrusion-Tolerant Intrusion Detection System*. IBM Zurich Research Laboratory, Aug. 2002. Deliverable D10, Project MAFTIA IST-1999-11583, Available at www.maftia.org.
7. R. Deraison. Nessus, a network security scanner. Available at www.nessus.org.
8. G. Giacinto, F. Roli, and L. Didaci. A modular multiple classifier system for the detection of intrusions in computer networks. In *Multiple Classifier Systems, 4th International Workshop, MCS*, Guilford, UK, June 2003.
9. K. Julisch. Clustering intrusion detection alarms to support root cause analysis. *ACM Transactions on Information and System Security*, 6(4):443 – 471, 2003.
10. C. Kruegel, D. Mutz, W. Robertson, G. Vigna, and R. Kemmerer. Reverse engineering of network signatures. In *Proceedings of the AusCERT Asia Pacific Information Technology Security Conference*, Gold Coast, Australia, May 2005.
11. C. Kruegel and W. Robertson. Alert verification - determining the success of intrusion attempts. In *In Proceedings of the Workshop on Detection of Intrusions and Malware and Vulnerability Assessment (DIMVA)*, Germany, July 2004.
12. R. Lippmann, J. W. Haines, D. J. Fried, J. Korba, and K. Das. Analysis and results of the 1999 DARPA off-line intrusion detection evaluation. In *International Symposium on Recent Advances in Intrusion Detection*, Toulouse, France, Oct. 2000.
13. MITRE Corporation. CVE: Common Vulnerabilities and Exposures. Available at www.cve.mitre.org.
14. S. Rubin, S. Jha, and B. P. Miller. Automatic generation and analysis of NIDS attacks. In *Annual Computer Security Applications Conference*, Tucson, AZ, Dec. 2004.
15. S. Rubin, S. Jha, and B. P. Miller. Language-based generation and evaluation of NIDS signatures. In *IEEE Symposium on Security and Privacy*, Oakland, CA, May 2005.
16. SecurityFocus. Focus on IDS. Mailing list. Available at http://www.securityfocus.com/archive.
17. R. Sommer and V. Paxson. Enhancing byte-level network intrusion detection signatures with context. In *ACM Conference on Computer and Communications Security*, Washington, DC, Oct. 2003.
18. K. M. C. Tan, K. S. Killourhy, and R. A. Maxion. Undermining an anomaly-based intrusion detection system using common exploits. In *International Symposium on Recent Advances in Intrusion Detection*, Zurich, Switzerland, Oct. 2002.
19. G. Vigna, W. Robertson, and D. Balzarotti. Testing network-based intrusion detection signatures using mutant exploits. In *ACM Conference on Computer and Communications Security*, Washington, DC, Oct. 2004.
20. D. Wagner and P. Soto. Mimicry attacks on host-based intrusion detection systems. In *ACM Conference on Computer and Communications Security*, Washington, DC, Nov. 2002.
21. Z. Zhang, J. Li, C. Manikopoulos, J. Jorgenson, and J. Ucles. HIDE: a hierarchical network intrusion detection system using statistical preprocessing and neural network classification. In *Workshop on Information Assurance and Security*, West Point, NY,, June 2001.

Part IV

Stealthy and Targeted Threat Detection and Defense

Stealth and Targeted Threat Detection and Defense

10

Composite Hybrid Techniques For Defending Against Targeted Attacks

Stelios Sidiroglou and Angelos D. Keromytis

Department of Computer Science, Columbia University
{stelios,angelos}@cs.columbia.edu

Summary. We investigate the use of hybrid techniques as a defensive mechanism against targeted attacks and introduce *Shadow Honeypots*, a novel hybrid architecture that combines the best features of honeypots and anomaly detection. At a high level, we use a variety of anomaly detectors to monitor all traffic to a protected network/service. Traffic that is considered anomalous is processed by a "shadow honeypot" to determine the accuracy of the anomaly prediction. The shadow is an instance of the protected software that shares all internal state with a regular ("production") instance of the application, and is instrumented to detect potential attacks. Attacks against the shadow are caught, and any incurred state changes are discarded. Legitimate traffic that was misclassified will be validated by the shadow and will be handled correctly by the system transparently to the end user. The outcome of processing a request by the shadow is used to filter future attack instances and could be used to update the anomaly detector.

Our architecture allows system designers to fine-tune systems for performance, since false positives will be filtered by the shadow. Contrary to regular honeypots, our architecture can be used both for server and client applications. We also explore the notion of using Shadow Honeypots in Application Communities in order to amortize the cost of instrumentation and detection across a number of autonomous hosts.

10.1 Introduction

Due to the increasing level of malicious activity seen on today's Internet, organizations are beginning to deploy mechanisms for detecting and responding to new attacks or suspicious activity, called Intrusion Prevention Systems (IPS). Since current IPS's use rule-based intrusion detection systems (IDS) such as Snort [37] to detect attacks, they are limited to protecting, for the most part, against already known attacks. As a result, new detection mechanisms are being developed for use in more powerful reactive-defense systems. The two primary such mechanisms are honeypots [32, 13, 62, 45, 20, 4] and anomaly detection systems (ADS) [53, 57, 52, 6, 19]. In contrast with IDS's, honeypots and ADS's offer the possibility of detecting (and thus responding to) previously unknown attacks, also referred to as *zero-day attacks*.

Honeypots and anomaly detection systems offer different tradeoffs between accuracy and scope of attacks that can be detected, as shown in Figure 10.1. Honeypots can be heavily instrumented to accurately detect attacks, but depend on an attacker attempting to exploit a vulnerability against them. This makes them good for detecting scanning worms [8, 9, 13], but ineffective against manual directed attacks or topological and hit-list worms [48, 47]. Furthermore, honeypots can typically only be used for server-type applications. Anomaly detection systems can theoretically detect both types of attacks, but are usually much less accurate. Most such systems offer a tradeoff between false positive (FP) and false negative (FN) rates. For example, it is often possible to tune the system to detect more *potential* attacks, at an increased risk of *misclassifying* legitimate traffic (low FN, high FP); alternatively, it is possible to make an anomaly detection system more insensitive to attacks, at the risk of missing some real attacks (high FN, low FP). Because an ADS-based IPS can adversely affect legitimate traffic (*e.g.,* drop a legitimate request), system designers often tune the system for low false positive rates, potentially misclassifying attacks as legitimate traffic.

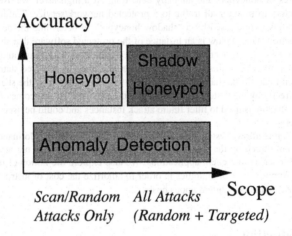

Fig. 10.1. A simple classification of honeypots and anomaly detection systems, based on attack detection accuracy and scope of detected attacks. Targeted attacks may use lists of known (potentially) vulnerable servers, while scan-based attacks will target any system that is believed to run a vulnerable service. AD systems can detect both types of attacks, but with lower accuracy than a specially instrumented system (honeypot). However, honeypots are blind to targeted attacks, and may not see a scanning attack until after it has succeeded against the real server.

We propose a novel hybrid approach that combines the best features of honeypots and anomaly detection, named *Shadow Honeypots*. At a high level, we use a variety of anomaly detectors to monitor all traffic to a protected network. Traffic that is considered anomalous is processed by a shadow honeypot. The shadow version is an instance of the protected application (*e.g.,* a web server or client) that shares all internal state with a "normal" instance of the application, but is instrumented to detect potential attacks. Attacks against the shadow honeypot are caught and any incurred state changes are discarded. Legitimate traffic that was misclassified by the anomaly detector will be validated by the shadow honeypot and will be *transparently* handled correctly by the system (*i.e.,* an HTTP request that was mistakenly flagged as suspicious will be served correctly). Our approach offers several advantages over stand-alone ADS's or honeypots:

- First, it allows system designers to tune the anomaly detection system for low false negative rates, minimizing the risk of misclassifying a real attack as legitimate traffic, since any false positives will be weeded out by the shadow honeypot.
- Second, and in contrast to typical honeypots, our approach can defend against attacks that are *tailored* against a specific site with a particular internal state. Honeypots may be blind to such attacks, since they are not typically mirror images of the protected application.
- Third, shadow honeypots can also be instantiated in a form that is particularly well-suited for protecting against *client-side* attacks, such as those directed against web browsers and P2P file sharing clients.
- Finally, our system architecture facilitates easy integration of additional detection mechanisms.

In addition to the server-side scenario, we also investigate a client-targeting attack-detection scenario, unique to shadow honeypots, where we apply the detection heuristics to content retrieved by protected clients and feed any positives to shadow honeypots for further analysis. Unlike traditional honeypots, which are idle whilst waiting for active attackers to probe them, this scenario enables the detection of passive attacks, where the attacker lures a victim user to download malicious data.

Finally, we explore the combination of Shadow Honeypots with Application Communities to create a distributed collaborative environment where detection and the processing cost incured by the use Shadow Honeypots is shared across a large number of hosts.

Chapter Organization. The remainder of this chapter is organized as follows. Section 10.2 discusses the shadow honeypot architecture in greater detail. Some of the limitations of our approach are briefly discussed in Section 10.3. We give an overview of related work in Section 10.4, and conclude the chapter with a summary of our work and plans for future work in Section 10.5.

10.2 Architecture

The Shadow Honeypot architecture is a systems approach to handling network-based attacks, combining filtering, anomaly detection systems and honeypots in a way that exploits the best features of these mechanisms, while shielding their limitations. We focus on transactional applications, *i.e.*, those that handle a series of discrete requests. Our architecture is *not* limited to server applications, but can be used for client-side applications such as web browsers, P2P clients, *etc.* As illustrated in Figure 10.2, the architecture is composed of three main components: a filtering engine, an array of anomaly detection sensors and the shadow honeypot, which validates the predictions of the anomaly detectors. The processing logic of the system is shown graphically in Figure 10.3.

The filtering component blocks known attacks. Such filtering is done based either on payload content [56, 1] or on the source of the attack, if it can be identified with reasonable confidence (*e.g.*, confirmed traffic bi-directionality). Effectively, the filtering component short-circuits the detection heuristics or shadow testing results by immediately dropping specific types of requests before any further processing is done.

Traffic passing the first stage is processed by one or more anomaly detectors. There are several types of anomaly detectors that may be used in our system, including payload analysis [57, 42, 18, 52] and network behavior [16, 60]. Although we do not impose any particular requirements on the AD component of our system, it is preferable to tune such detectors towards high sensitivity (at the cost of increased false positives). The anomaly detectors, in turn, signal to the protected application whether a request is potentially dangerous.

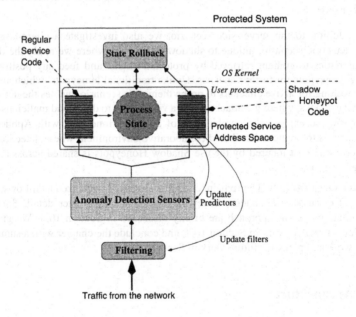

Fig. 10.2. Shadow Honeypot architecture.

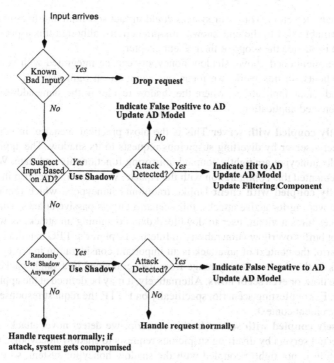

Fig. 10.3. System workflow.

Depending on this prediction by the anomaly detectors, the system invokes either the regular instance of the application or its *shadow*. The shadow is an instrumented instance of the application that can detect specific types of failures and rollback any state changes to a known (or presumed) good state, *e.g.*, before the malicious request was processed. Because the shadow is (or should be) invoked relatively infrequently, we can employ computationally expensive instrumentation to detect attacks. The shadow and the regular application fully share state, to avoid attacks that exploit differences between the two; we assume that an attacker can only interact with the application through the filtering and AD stages, *i.e.*, there are no side-channels. The level of instrumentation used in the shadow depends on the amount of latency we are willing to impose on suspicious traffic (whether truly malicious or misclassified legitimate traffic). In our reference implementation, described in [3], we focus on memory-violation attacks, but any attack that can be determined algorithmically can be detected and recovered from, at the cost of increased complexity and potentially higher latency.

If the shadow detects an actual attack, we notify the filtering component to block further attacks. If no attack is detected, we update the prediction models used by the anomaly detectors. Thus, our system could in fact self-train and fine-tune itself using verifiably bad traffic and known mis-predictions, although this aspect of the approach is outside the scope of the present chapter.

As we mentioned above, shadow honeypots can be integrated with servers as well as clients. In this work, we focus our attention on tight coupling with both server and client applications, where the shadow resides in the same address space as the protected application.

- **Tightly coupled with server** This is the most practical scenario, in which we protect a server by diverting suspicious requests to its shadow. The application and the honeypot are tightly coupled, mirroring functionality and state. We have implemented this configuration with the Apache web server, described in [3].
- **Tightly coupled with client** Unlike traditional honeypots, which remain idle while waiting for active attacks, this scenario targets passive attacks, where the attacker lures a victim user to download data containing an attack, as with the recent buffer overflow vulnerability in Internet Explorer's JPEG handling. In this scenario, the context of an attack is an important consideration in replaying the attack in the shadow. It may range from data contained in a single packet to an entire flow, or even set of flows. Alternatively, it may be defined at the application layer. For our testing scenario, specifically on HTTP, the request/response pair is a convenient context.
- **Loosely coupled with server** In this scenario, we detect novel attacks against protected servers by diverting suspicious requests to shadow honeypots. The application is not tightly coupled with the shadow honeypot system, so multiple versions of the application may have to be maintained, and its exact configuration is not known. The requests are captured using passive monitoring and no attempt is made to prevent the attack. This approach has the benefit of being able to "outsource" the detection of vulnerabilities to third entities, potentially taking advantage of economies of scale.
- **Loosely coupled with client** For this approach, suspicious flows are redirected to loosely coupled (do not share state or configuration) versions of an application. One can envision protected client farms where suspicious traffic is tested against multiple versions of the application one is trying to protect.

Tight coupling assumes that the application can be modified. The advantage of this configuration is that attacks that exploit differences in the state of the shadow *vs.* the application itself become impossible. However, it is also possible to deploy shadow honeypots in a *loosely coupled* configuration, where the shadow resides on a different system and does not share state with the protected application. The advantage of this configuration is that management of the shadows can be "outsourced" to a third entity as a service.

Note that the filtering and anomaly detection components can also be tightly coupled with the protected application, or may be centralized at a natural aggregation point in the network topology (*e.g.*, at the firewall).

Finally, it is worth considering how our system would behave against different types of attacks. For most attacks we have seen thus far, once the AD component

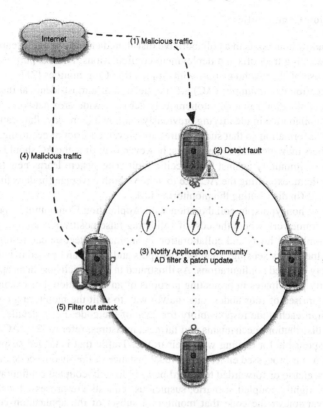

Fig. 10.4. Application Community workflow

has identified an anomaly and the shadow has validated it, the filtering component will block all future instances of it from getting to the application. However, we cannot depend on the filtering component to prevent polymorphic or metamorphic [51] attacks. For low-volume events, the cost of invoking the shadow for each attack may be acceptable. For high-volume events, such as a Slammer-like outbreak, the system will detect a large number of correct AD predictions (verified by the shadow) in a short period of time; should a configurable threshold be exceeded, the system can enable filtering at the second stage, based on the unverified verdict of the anomaly detectors. Although this will cause some legitimate requests to be dropped, this could be acceptable for the duration of the incident. Once the number of (perceived) attacks seen by the ADS drop beyond a threshold, the system can revert to normal operation.

Application Communities

Using shadow honeypots in a collaborative distributed environment presents another set of interesting tradeoffs and deployment configurations. For this purpose, we explore the use of shadow honeypots with Application Communities [21].

Application Communities (AC) are a collection of almost-identical instances of the same application running autonomously across a wide area network. Members of an AC collaborate in identifying previously unknown (zero day) flaws/attacks and exchange information so that such failures are prevented from re-occurring. Individual members may succumb to new flaws; however, over time the AC should converge to a state of immunity against that specific fault. The system learns new faults and adapts to them, exploiting the AC size to achieve both coverage (in detecting faults) and fairness (in distributing the monitoring task).

Shadow honeypots, in collaboration with Application Communities, provides a systemic framework where the cost of validating false positives is amortized across a large number of hosts and collaboration in anomaly detection can result in more robust vulnerability sensing. Shadow honeypots and AC's can be used in both tightly and loosely coupled configurations. As illustrated in 10.4, each host in an application community participates in protecting portions of an application. For example, if an AC is comprised of four nodes, one (naive) way to split the monitoring cost would be to assign each node responsibility for 25% of the code. For a detailed analysis on work distribution mechanisms and fairness measures, refer to [21]. AC hosts are solely responsible for dealing with their traffic. Traffic that is tagged suspicious by the local AD is processed either by the local instance of the shadow code in a tightly coupled scenario or forwarded to a third party in loosely coupled configuration.

In the tightly coupled scenario, suspicious requests are processed locally by a shadow version of the code that monitors a subset of the application code. This translates into a lower per host cost for processing false positives but relies on collaboration and the size of an AC to achieve both coverage and low overhead. If a vulnerability is detected, it is first processed locally and then information pertinent to the attack is propagated to the AC. In more detail, given a fault, the application is modified so that it can both detect and recover from any future manifestations of the specific fault and the anomaly detectors are updated with signatures derived from the attack vector. This information, along with the attack vector, is then dispatched to the rest of the AC, where hosts can independently validate the vulnerability.

Similarly, for the loosely couple configuration, suspicious requests to a host are sent to a remote sensor that is responsible for monitoring one portion of the application. If the remote sensor detects a fault, the vulnerability specific information is reported back to the host that will, in turn, update the anomaly detector filters and update the application with a version that is protected against the specific fault. At that point, information derived from the remote sensor is communicated to the rest of the AC.

10.3 Limitations

There are three limitations of the shadow honeypot design presented in this chapter that we are aware of. First, the effectiveness of the rollback mechanism depends on the detection and recovery capabilities of the vulnerability sensor, and the latency of the detector. The detector used in [3] can instantly detect attempts to overwrite a buffer, and therefore the system cannot be corrupted. Other detectors [41], however, may have higher latency, and the placement of commit calls is critical to recovering from the attack. Depending on the detector latency and how it relates to the cost of implementing rollback, one may have to consider different approaches. The trade-offs involved in designing such mechanisms are thoroughly examined in the fault-tolerance literature (c.f. [15]).

Second, the loosely coupled client shadow honeypot is limited to protecting against relatively static attacks. The honeypot cannot effectively emulate user behavior that may be involved in triggering the attack, for example, through DHTML or Javascript. The loosely coupled version is also weak against attacks that depend on local system state on the user's host that is difficult to replicate. This is not a problem with tightly coupled shadows, because we accurately mirror the state of the real system. In some cases, it may be possible to mirror state on loosely coupled shadows as well, but we have not considered this case in the experiments presented in this chapter.

Finally, we have not explored in depth the use of feedback from the shadow honeypot to tune the anomaly detection components. Although this is likely to lead to substantial performance benefits, we need to be careful so that an attacker cannot launch blinding attacks, e.g., "softening" the anomaly detection component through a barrage of false positives before launching a real attack.

10.4 Related Work

Much of the work in automated attack reaction has focused on the problem of network worms, which has taken truly epidemic dimensions (pun intended). For example, the system described in [60] detects worms by monitoring probes to unassigned IP addresses ("dark space") or inactive ports and computing statistics on scan traffic, such as the number of source/destination addresses and the volume of the captured traffic. By measuring the increase on the number of source addresses seen in a unit of time, it is possible to infer the existence of a new worm when as little as 4% of the vulnerable machines have been infected. A similar approach for isolating infected nodes inside an enterprise network [46] is taken in [16], where it was shown that as little as 4 probes may be sufficient in detecting a new port-scanning worm. [58] describes an approximating algorithm for quickly detecting scanning activity that can be efficiently implemented in hardware. [38] describes a combination of reverse sequential hypothesis testing and credit-based connection throttling to quickly detect and quarantine local infected hosts. These systems are effective only against scanning worms (not topological, or "hit-list" worms), and rely on the assumption that most scans will result in non-connections. As such, they as susceptible to false positives, either accidentally (*e.g.*, when a host is joining a peer-to-peer network such as Gnutella, or during a temporary network outage) or on purpose (*e.g.*, a malicious web page with many links to images in random/not-used IP addresses). Furthermore, it may be possible for several instances of a worm to collaborate in providing the illusion of several successful connections, or to use a list of *known repliers* to blind the anomaly detector. Another algorithm for finding fast-spreading worms using 2-level filtering based on sampling from the set of distinct source-destination pairs is described in [54].

[59] correlates DNS queries/replies with outgoing connections from an enterprise network to detect anomalous behavior. The main intuition is that connections due to random-scanning (and, to a degree, hit-list) worms will not be preceded by DNS transactions. This approach can be used to detect other types of malicious behavior, such as mass-mailing worms and network reconnaissance.

[18] describes an algorithm for correlating packet payloads from different traffic flows, towards deriving a worm signature that can then be filtered [24]. The technique is promising, although further improvements are required to allow it to operate in real time. Earlybird [42] presents a more practical algorithm for doing payload sifting, and correlates these with a range of unique sources generating infections and destinations being targeted. However, polymorphic and metamorphic worms [51] remain a challenge; Spinelis [44] shows that it is an NP-hard problem. Buttercup [28] attempts to detect polymorphic buffer overflow attacks by identifying the ranges of the possible return memory addresses for existing buffer overflow vulnerabilities. Unfortunately, this heuristic cannot be employed against some of the more sophisticated overflow attack techniques [30]. Furthermore, the false positive rate is very high, ranging from 0.01% to 1.13%. Vigna *et al.* [55] discuss a method for testing detection signatures against mutations of known vulnerabilities to determine the quality of the detection model and mechanism. Polygraph [27] attempts to detect polymorphic exploits by identifying common invariants among the various attack instances, such as return addresses, protocol framing and poor obfuscation. Toth and Kruegel [52] propose to detect buffer overflow payloads (including previously unseen ones) by treating inputs received over the network as code fragments. The use restricted symbolic execution to show that legitimate requests will appear to contain relatively short sequences of valid *x86* instruction opcodes, compared to attacks that will contain long sequences. They integrate this mechanism into the Apache web server, resulting in a small performance degradation. STRIDE [2] is a similar system that seeks to detect polymorphic NOP-sleds in buffer overflow exploits. [29] describes a hybrid polymorphic-code detection engine that combines several heuristics, including NOP-sled detector and abstract payload execution.

HoneyStat [13] runs sacrificial services inside a virtual machine, and monitors memory, disk, and network events to detect abnormal behavior. For some classes of attacks (*e.g.*, buffer overflows), this can produce highly accurate alerts with relatively few false positives, and can detect zero-day worms. Although the system only protects against scanning worms, "active honeypot" techniques [62] may be used to make it more difficult for an automated attacker to differentiate between HoneyStats and real servers. FLIPS (Feedback Learning IPS) [22] is a similar hybrid approach that incorporates a supervision framework in the presence of suspicious traffic. Instruction-set randomization is used to isolate attack vectors, which are used to train the anomaly detector. Shadow honeypots [3] combine the best features found in anomaly detectors and honeypots to create what an application-aware network intrusion detection system. The anomaly detectors differentiate between trusted and untrusted traffic; trusted traffic is processed normally whilst untrusted traffic is forwarded to a protected instance of the application, its "shadow." The system provides an elegant way to deal with false positives, since all requests are processed albeit some incur additional latency. The authors of [14] propose to enhance NIDS alerts using host-based IDS information. Nemean [63] is an architecture for generating semantics-aware signatures, which are signatures aware of protocol semantics (as opposed to general byte strings). Shield [56] is a mechanism for pushing to workstations vulnerability-specific, application-aware filters expressed as programs in a simple language. These programs roughly mirror the state of the protected service, allowing for more intelligent application of content filters, as opposed to simplistic payload string matching.

The Internet Motion Sensor [4] is a distributed blackhole monitoring system aimed at measuring, characterizing, and tracking Internet-based threats, including worms. [11] explores the various options in locating honeypots and correlating their findings, and their impact on the speed and accuracy in detecting worms and other attacks. [33] shows that a distributed worm monitor can detect non-uniform scanning worms two to four times as fast as a centralized telescope [25], and that knowledge of the vulnerability density of the population can further improve detection time. However, other recent work has shown that it is relatively straightforward for attackers to detect the placement of certain types of sensors [5, 39]. Shadow Honeypots [3] are one approach to avoiding such mapping by pushing honeypot-like functionality at the end hosts.

The Worm Vaccine system [40] proposes the use of honeypots with instrumented versions of software services to be protected, coupled with an automated patch-generation facility. This allows for quick ($<$ 1 minute) fixing of buffer overflow vulnerabilities, even against zero-day worms, but depends on scanning behavior on the part of worms.

The HACQIT architecture [17, 36, 34, 35] uses various sensors to detect new types of attacks against secure servers, access to which is limited to small numbers of users at a time. Any deviation from expected or known behavior results in the possibly subverted server to be taken off-line. A sandboxed instance of the server is used to conduct "clean room" analysis, comparing the outputs from two different implementations of the service (in their prototype, the Microsoft IIS and Apache web servers were used to provide application diversity). Machine-learning techniques are used to generalize attack features from observed instances of the attack. Content-based filtering is then used, either at the firewall or the end host, to block inputs that may have resulted in attacks, and the infected servers are restarted. Due to the feature-generalization approach, trivial variants of the attack will also be caught by the filter. [53] takes a roughly similar approach, although filtering is done based on port numbers, which can affect service availability. Cisco's Network-Based Application Recognition (NBAR) [1] allows routers to block TCP sessions based on the presence of specific strings in the TCP stream. This feature was used to block CodeRed probes, without affecting regular web-server access. Porras *et al.* [31] argue that hybrid defenses using complementary techniques (in their case, connection throttling at the domain gateway and a peer-based coordination mechanism), can be much more effective against a wide variety of worms.

DOMINO [61] is an overlay system for cooperative intrusion detection. The system is organized in two layers, with a small core of trusted nodes and a larger collection of nodes connected to the core. The experimental analysis demonstrates that a coordinated approach has the potential of providing early warning for large-scale attacks while reducing potential false alarms. A similar approach using a DHT-based overlay network to automatically correlate all relevant information is described in [7]. Reference [64] describes an architecture and models for an early warning system, where the participating nodes/routers propagate alarm reports towards a centralized site for analysis. The question of how to respond to alerts is not addressed, and, similar to DOMINO, the use of a centralized collection and analysis facility is weak against worms attacking the early warning infrastructure.

Suh *et al.* [49], propose a hardware-based solution that can be used to thwart control-transfer attacks and restrict executable instructions by monitoring "tainted" input data. In order to identify "tainted" data, they rely on the operating system. If the processor detects the use of this tainted data as a jump address or an executed instruction, it raises an exception that can be handled by the operating system. The authors do not address the issue of recovering program execution and suggest the immediate termination of the offending process. DIRA [43] is a technique for automatic detection, identification and repair of control-hijaking attacks. This solution is implemented as a GCC compiler extension that transforms a program's source code adding heavy instrumentation so that the resulting program can perform these tasks. The use of checkpoints throughout the program ensures that corruption of state can be detected if control sensitive data structures are overwritten. Unfortunately, the performance implications of the system make it unusable as a front line defense mechanism. Song and Newsome [26] propose dynamic taint analysis for automatic detection of overwrite attacks. Tainted data is monitored throughout the program execution and modified buffers with tainted information will result in protection faults. Once an attack has been identified, signatures are generated using automatic semantic analysis. The technique is implemented as an extension to Valgrind and does not require any modifications to the program's source code but suffers from severe performance degradation. One way of minimizing this penalty is to make the CPU aware of memory tainting [10]. Crandall *et al.* report on using a taint-based system for capturing live attacks in [12].

The Safe Execution Environment (SEE) [50] allows users to deploy and test untrusted software without fear of damaging their system. This is done by creating a virtual environment where the software has read access to the real data; all writes are local to this virtual environment. The user can inspect these changes and decide whether to commit them or not. We envision use of this technique for unrolling the effects of filesystem changes in our system, as part of our future work plans. A similar proposal is presented in [23] for executing untrusted Java applets in a safe "playground" that is isolated from the user's environment.

10.5 Conclusion

We have described a novel approach to dealing with zero-day attacks by combining features found today in honeypots and anomaly detection systems. The main advantage of this architecture is providing system designers the ability to fine tune systems with impunity, since any false positives (legitimate traffic) will be filtered by the underlying components.

We have implemented this approach in an architecture called Shadow Honeypots. In this approach, we employ an array of anomaly detectors to monitor and classify all traffic to a protected network; traffic deemed anomalous is processed by a shadow honeypot, a protected instrumented instance of the application we are trying to protect. Attacks against the shadow honeypot are detected and caught before they infect the state of the protected application. This enables the system to implement policies that trade off between performance and risk, retaining the capability to re-evaluate this trade-off effortlessly. We also explore the use of Shadow Honeypots in Application Communities where, the cost of instrumentation is spread across numerous hosts and anomaly detector models can be updated to reflect the findings of hosts that service a variety of different traffic flows.

Finally, the preliminary performance experiments indicate that despite the considerable cost of processing suspicious traffic on our Shadow Honeypots and overhead imposed by instrumentation, our system is capable of sustaining the overall workload of protecting services such as a Web server farm, as well as vulnerable Web browsers. In the future, we expect that the impact on performance can be minimized by reducing the rate of false positives and tuning the AD heuristics using a feedback loop with the shadow honeypot. Our plans for future work also include evaluating different components and extending the performance evaluation.

References

1. . . *. Using Network-Based Application Recognition and Access Control Lists for Blocking the "Code Red" Worm at Network Ingress Points. Technical report, Cisco Systems, Inc., 2006.
2. P. Akritidis, E. P. Markatos, M. Polychronakis, and K. Anagnostakis. STRIDE: Polymorphic Sled Detection through Instruction Sequence Analysis. In *Proceedings of the 20th IFIP International Information Security Conference (IFIP/SEC)*, June 2005.
3. K. Anagnostakis, S. Sidiroglou, P. Akritidis, K. Xinidis, E. Markatos, and A. D. Keromytis. Detecting Targetted Attacks Using Shadow Honeypots. In *Proceedings of the 14th USENIX Security Symposium*, pages 129–144, August 2005.

4. M. Bailey, E. Cooke, F. Jahanian, J. Nazario, and D. Watson. The Internet Motion Sensor: A Distributed Blackhole Monitoring System. In *Proceedings of the 12th ISOC Symposium on Network and Distributed Systems Security (SNDSS)*, pages 167–179, February 2005.

5. J. Bethencourt, J. Franklin, and M. Vernon. Mapping Internet Sensors With Probe Response Attacks. In *Proceedings of the 14th USENIX Security Symposium*, pages 193–208, August 2005.

6. M. Bhattacharyya, M. G. Schultz, E. Eskin, S. Hershkop, and S. J. Stolfo. MET: An Experimental System for Malicious Email Tracking. In *Proceedings of the New Security Paradigms Workshop (NSPW)*, pages 1–12, September 2002.

7. M. Cai, K. Hwang, Y.-K. Kwok, S. Song, and Y. Chen. Collaborative Internet Worm Containment. *IEEE Security & Privacy Magazine*, 3(3):25–33, May/June 2005.

8. CERT Advisory CA-2001-19: 'Code Red' Worm Exploiting Buffer Overflow in IIS Indexing Service DLL. http://www.cert.org/advisories/CA-2001-19.html, July 2001.

9. Cert Advisory CA-2003-04: MS-SQL Server Worm. http://www.cert.org/advisories/CA-2003-04.html, January 2003.

10. S. Chen, J. Xu, N. Nakka, Z. Kalbarczyk, and C. Verbowski. Defeating Memory Corruption Attacks via Pointer Taintedness Detection. In *Proceedings of the International Conference on Dependable Systems and Networks (DSN)*, pages 378–387, June 2005.

11. E. Cook, M. Bailey, Z. M. Mao, and D. McPherson. Toward Understanding Distributed Blackhole Placement. In *Proceedings of the ACM Workshop on Rapid Malcode (WORM)*, pages 54–64, October 2004.

12. J. R. Crandall, S. F. Wu, and F. T. Chong. Experiences Using Minos as a Tool for Capturing and Analyzing Novel Worms for Unknown Vulnerabilities. In *Proceedings of the Conference on Detection of Intrusions and Malware & Vulnerability Assessment (DIMVA)*, July 2005.

13. D. Dagon, X. Qin, G. Gu, W. Lee, J. Grizzard, J. Levine, and H. Owen. HoneyStat: Local Worm Detection Using Honepots. In *Proceedings of the 7th International Symposium on Recent Advances in Intrusion Detection (RAID)*, pages 39–58, October 2004.

14. H. Dreger, C. Kreibich, V. Paxson, and R. Sommer. Enhancing the Accuracy of Network-based Intrusion Detection with Host-based Context. In *Proceedings of the Conference on Detection of Intrusions and Malware & Vulnerability Assessment (DIMVA)*, July 2005.

15. E. N. Elnozahy, L. Alvisi, Y.-M. Wang, and D. B. Johnson. A survey of rollback-recovery protocols in message-passing systems. *ACM Comput. Surv.*, 34(3):375–408, 2002.

16. J. Jung, V. Paxson, A. W. Berger, and H. Balakrishnan. Fast Portscan Detection Using Sequential Hypothesis Testing. In *Proceedings of the IEEE Symposium on Security and Privacy*, May 2004.

17. J. E. Just, L. A. Clough, M. Danforth, K. N. Levitt, R. Maglich, J. C. Reynolds, and J. Rowe. Learning Unknown Attacks – A Start. In *Proceedings of the 5th International Symposium on Recent Advances in Intrusion Detection (RAID)*, October 2002.

18. H. Kim and B. Karp. Autograph: Toward Automated, Distributed Worm Signature Detection. In *Proceedings of the 13th USENIX Security Symposium*, pages 271–286, August 2004.

19. C. Kruegel and G. Vigna. Anomaly Detection of Web-based Attacks. In *Proceedings of the 10th ACM Conference on Computer and Communications Security (CCS)*, pages 251–261, October 2003.

20. J. G. Levine, J. B. Grizzard, and H. L. Owen. Using Honeynets to Protect Large Enterprise Networks. *IEEE Security & Privacy*, 2(6):73–75, November/December 2004.

21. M. Locasto, S. Sidiroglou, and A. D. Keromytis. Application Communities: Using Monoculture for Dependability. In *Proceedings of the 1st Workshop on Hot Topics in System Dependability (HotDep)*, pages 288–292, June 2005.
22. M. Locasto, K. Wang, A. Keromytis, and S. Stolfo. FLIPS: Hybrid Adaptive Intrusion Prevention. In *Proceedings of the 8th Symposium on Recent Advances in Intrusion Detection (RAID)*, September 2005.
23. D. Malkhi and M. K. Reiter. Secure Execution of Java Applets Using a Remote Playground. *IEEE Trans. Softw. Eng.*, 26(12):1197–1209, 2000.
24. D. Moore, C. Shannon, G. Voelker, and S. Savage. Internet Quarantine: Requirements for Containing Self-Propagating Code. In *Proceedings of the IEEE Infocom Conference*, April 2003.
25. D. Moore, G. Voelker, and S. Savage. Inferring Internet Denial-of-Service Activity. In *Proceedings of the 10th USENIX Security Symposium*, pages 9–22, August 2001.
26. J. Newsome and D. Dong. Dynamic Taint Analysis for Automatic Detection, Analysis, and Signature Generation of Exploits on Commodity Software. In *Proceedings of the 12th ISOC Symposium on Network and Distributed System Security (SNDSS)*, pages 221–237, February 2005.
27. J. Newsome, B. Karp, and D. Song. Polygraph: Automatically Generating Signatures for Polymorphic Worms. In *Proceedings of the IEEE Security & Privacy Symposium*, pages 226–241, May 2005.
28. A. Pasupulati, J. Coit, K. Levitt, S. F. Wu, S. H. Li, J. C. Kuo, and K. P. Fan. Buttercup: On Network-based Detection of Polymorphic Buffer Overflow Vulnerabilities. In *Proceedings of the Network Operations and Management Symposium (NOMS)*, pages 235–248, vol. 1, April 2004.
29. U. Payer, P. Teufl, and M. Lamberger. Hybrid Engine for Polymorphic Shellcode Detection. In *Proceedings of the Conference on Detection of Intrusions and Malware & Vulnerability Assessment (DIMVA)*, July 2005.
30. J. Pincus and B. Baker. Beyond Stack Smashing: Recent Advances in Exploiting Buffer Overflows. *IEEE Security & Privacy*, 2(4):20–27, July/August 2004.
31. P. Porras, L. Briesemeister, K. Levitt, J. Rowe, and Y.-C. A. Ting. A Hybrid Quarantine Defense. In *Proceedings of the ACM Workshop on Rapid Malcode (WORM)*, pages 73–82, October 2004.
32. N. Provos. A Virtual Honeypot Framework. In *Proceedings of the 13th USENIX Security Symposium*, pages 1–14, August 2004.
33. M. A. Rajab, F. Monrose, and A. Terzis. On the Effectiveness of Distributed Worm Monitoring. In *Proceedings of the 14th USENIX Security Symposium*, pages 225–237, August 2005.
34. J. Reynolds, J. Just, E. Lawson, L. Clough, and R. Maglich. On-line Intrusion Protection by Detecting Attacks with Diversity. In *Proceedings of the 16th Annual IFIP 11.3 Working Conference on Data and Application Security Conference*, April 2002.
35. J. C. Reynolds, J. Just, L. Clough, and R. Maglich. On-Line Intrusion Detection and Attack Prevention Using Diversity, Generate-and-Test, and Generalization. In *Proceedings of the 36th Annual Hawaii International Conference on System Sciences (HICSS)*, January 2003.
36. J. C. Reynolds, J. Just, E. Lawson, L. Clough, and R. Maglich. The Design and Implementation of an Intrusion Tolerant System. In *Proceedings of the International Conference on Dependable Systems and Networks (DSN)*, June 2002.
37. M. Roesch. Snort: Lightweight intrusion detection for networks. In *Proceedings of USENIX LISA*, November 1999. (software available from *http://www.snort.org/*).

38. S. E. Schechter, J. Jung, and A. W. Berger. Fast Detection of Scanning Worm Infections. In *Proceedings of the 7th International Symposium on Recent Advances in Intrusion Detection (RAID)*, pages 59–81, October 2004.
39. Y. Shinoda, K. Ikai, and M. Itoh. Vulnerabilities of Passive Internet Threat Monitors. In *Proceedings of the 14th USENIX Security Symposium*, pages 209–224, August 2005.
40. S. Sidiroglou and A. D. Keromytis. A Network Worm Vaccine Architecture. In *Proceedings of the IEEE Workshop on Enterprise Technologies: Infrastructure for Collaborative Enterprises (WETICE), Workshop on Enterprise Security*, pages 220–225, June 2003.
41. S. Sidiroglou, M. E. Locasto, S. W. Boyd, and A. D. K. omytis. Building A Reactive Immune System for Software Services. In *Proceedings of the 11th USENIX Annual Technical Conference*, pages 149–161, April 2005.
42. S. Singh, C. Estan, G. Varghese, and S. Savage. Automated worm fingerprinting. In *Proceedings of the 6th Symposium on Operating Systems Design & Implementation (OSDI)*, December 2004.
43. A. Smirnov and T. Chiueh. DIRA: Automatic Detection, Identification, and Repair of Control-Hijacking Attacks. In *Proceedings of the 12th ISOC Symposium on Network and Distributed System Security (SNDSS)*, February 2005.
44. D. Spinellis. Reliable identification of bounded-length viruses is NP-complete. *IEEE Transactions on Information Theory*, 49(1):280–284, January 2003.
45. L. Spitzner. *Honeypots: Tracking Hackers*. Addison-Wesley, 2003.
46. S. Staniford. Containment of Scanning Worms in Enterprise Networks. *Journal of Computer Security*, 2005. (to appear).
47. S. Staniford, D. Moore, V. Paxson, and N. Weaver. The Top Speed of Flash Worms. In *Proceedings of the ACM Workshop on Rapid Malcode (WORM)*, pages 33–42, October 2004.
48. S. Staniford, V. Paxson, and N. Weaver. How to Own the Internet in Your Spare Time. In *Proceedings of the 11th USENIX Security Symposium*, pages 149–167, August 2002.
49. G. E. Suh, J. W. Lee, D. Zhang, and S. Devadas. Secure program execution via dynamic information flow tracking. *SIGOPS Operating Systems Review*, 38(5):85–96, 2004.
50. W. Sun, Z. Liang, R. Sekar, and V. N. Venkatakrishnan. One-way Isolation: An Effective Approach for Realizing Safe Execution Environments. In *Proceedings of the 12th ISOC Symposium on Network and Distributed Systems Security (SNDSS)*, pages 265–278, February 2005.
51. P. Ször and P. Ferrie. Hunting for Metamorphic. Technical report, Symantec Corporation, June 2003.
52. T. Toth and C. Kruegel. Accurate Buffer Overflow Detection via Abstract Payload Execution. In *Proceedings of the 5th Symposium on Recent Advances in Intrusion Detection (RAID)*, October 2002.
53. T. Toth and C. Kruegel. Connection-history Based Anomaly Detection. In *Proceedings of the IEEE Workshop on Information Assurance and Security*, June 2002.
54. S. Venkataraman, D. Song, P. B. Gibbons, and A. Blum. New Streaming Algorithms for Fast Detection of Superspreaders. In *Proceedings of the 12th ISOC Symposium on Network and Distributed Systems Security (SNDSS)*, pages 149–166, February 2005.
55. G. Vigna, W. Robertson, and D. Balzarotti. Testing Network-based Intrusion Detection Signatures Using Mutant Exploits. In *Proceedings of the 11th ACM Conference on Computer and Communications Security (CCS)*, pages 21–30, October 2004.
56. H. J. Wang, C. Guo, D. R. Simon, and A. Zugenmaier. Shield: Vulnerability-Driven Network Filters for Preventing Known Vulnerability Exploits. In *Proceedings of the ACM SIGCOMM Conference*, pages 193–204, August 2004.

57. K. Wang and S. J. Stolfo. Anomalous Payload-based Network Intrusion Detection. In *Proceedings of the 7th International Symposium on Recent Advanced in Intrusion Detection (RAID)*, pages 201–222, September 2004.
58. N. Weaver, S. Staniford, and V. Paxson. Very Fast Containment of Scanning Worms. In *Proceedings of the 13th USENIX Security Symposium*, pages 29–44, August 2004.
59. D. Whyte, E. Kranakis, and P. van Oorschot. DNS-based Detection of Scanning Worms in an Enterprise Network. In *Proceedings of the 12th ISOC Symposium on Network and Distributed Systems Security (SNDSS)*, pages 181–195, February 2005.
60. J. Wu, S. Vangala, L. Gao, and K. Kwiat. An Effective Architecture and Algorithm for Detecting Worms with Various Scan Techniques. In *Proceedings of the ISOC Symposium on Network and Distributed System Security (SNDSS)*, pages 143–156, February 2004.
61. V. Yegneswaran, P. Barford, and S. Jha. Global Intrusion Detection in the DOMINO Overlay System. In *Proceedings of the ISOC Symposium on Network and Distributed System Security (SNDSS)*, February 2004.
62. V. Yegneswaran, P. Barford, and D. Plonka. On the Design and Use of Internet Sinks for Network Abuse Monitoring. In *Proceedings of the 7th International Symposium on Recent Advances in Intrusion Detection (RAID)*, pages 146–165, October 2004.
63. V. Yegneswaran, J. T. Giffin, P. Barford, and S. Jha. An Architecture for Generating Semantics-Aware Signatures. In *Proceedings of the 14th USENIX Security Symposium*, pages 97–112, August 2005.
64. C. C. Zou, L. Gao, W. Gong, and D. Towsley. Monitoring and Early Warning for Internet Worms. In *Proceedings of the 10th ACM International Conference on Computer and Communications Security (CCS)*, pages 190–199, October 2003.

Towards Stealthy Malware Detection[1]

Salvatore J. Stolfo, Ke Wang, and Wei-Jen Li

Department of Computer Science, Columbia University
{sal,kewang,wei-jen}@cs.columbia.edu

Abstract

Malcode can be easily hidden in document files and go undetected by standard technology. We demonstrate this opportunity of stealthy malcode insertion in several experiments using a standard COTS Anti-Virus (AV) scanner. Furthermore, in the case of *zero-day* malicious exploit code, signature-based AV scanners would fail to detect such malcode even if the scanner knew where to look. We propose the use of statistical binary content analysis of files in order to detect suspicious anomalous file segments that may suggest insertion of malcode. Experiments are performed to determine whether the approach of n-gram analysis may provide useful evidence of a tainted file that would subsequently be subjected to further scrutiny. We further perform tests to determine whether known malcode can be easily distinguished from otherwise "normal" Windows executables, and whether self-encrypted files may be easy to spot. Our goal is to develop an efficient means by static content analysis of detecting suspect infected files. This approach may have value for scanning a large store of collected information, such as a database of shared documents. The preliminary experiments suggest the problem is quite hard requiring new research to detect stealthy malcode.

[1] This work was partially supported by a grant from ARDA under a contract with Batelle, Pacific Northwest Labs.

11.1   Introduction

Attackers have used a variety of ways of embedding malicious code in otherwise normal appearing files to infect systems. Viruses that attach themselves to system files, or normal appearing media files, are nothing new. State-of-the-art COTS products scan and apply signature analysis to detect these known malware. For various performance optimization reasons, however, COTS Anti-Virus (AV) scanners may not perform a deep scan of all files in order to detect known malcode that may have been embedded in an arbitrary file location. Other means of stealth to avoid detection are well known. Various self-encryption or code obfuscation techniques may be used to avoid detection simply making the content of malcode unavailable for inspection by an AV scanner. In the case of new *zero day* malicious exploit code, signature-based AV scanners would fail to detect such malcode even if the scanner had access to the content and knew where to look.

In this chapter we explore the use of statistical content analysis of files in order to detect anomalous file segments that may suggest infection by malcode. Our goal is to develop an efficient means of detecting suspect infected files for application to scanning a large store of collected information, such as a database of content in a file sharing network. The work reported in this chapter is preliminary. Our ongoing studies have uncovered a number of other techniques that are under development and evaluation. Here we present background summary on our work on *Fileprints*, followed by several experiments applying the method to malcode detection.

The threat model needs to be clarified in this work. We do not consider the methods by which stealthy malcode embedded in tainted files may be automatically launched and executed. One may posit that detecting a tainted file may be easy simply by opening the file and detecting whether the application issues a fault. This might be the case if the malcode was embedded in such a way as to damage the expected file format causing the application to fault. As we show in Section 11.2 , one can embed malcode without creating such a fault when opening a tainted file. In this work, we focus specifically on static analysis techniques to determine whether or not we may be able to identify a tainted file. The approach we propose is to use generic statistical feature analysis of binary content irrespective of the type of file used to transport the malcode into a protected environment.

Files typically follow naming conventions that use standard extensions describing its type or the applications used to open and process the file.

However, although a file may be named *Paper.doc*[2], it may not be a legitimate Word document file unless it is successfully opened and displayed by Microsoft Word, or parsed and checked by tools, such as the Unix *file* command, if such tools exist for the file type in question. We proposed a method to analyze the contents of exemplar files using statistical modeling techniques. In particular, we apply n-gram analysis to the binary content of a set of exemplar "training" files and produce normalized n-gram distributions representing all files of a specific type. Our aim is to determine the validity of files claiming to be of a certain type (even though the header may indicate a certain file type, the actual content may not be what is claimed) or to determine the type of an unnamed file object.

The conjecture is that we may model different types of files to produce a model of what all files of that type should look like. Any significant deviation from this model may indicate the file is infected with embedded malcode. Suspect files identified using this technique may then be more deeply analyzed using a variety of techniques under investigation by other researchers (e.g., [9, 16, 18].)

In our prior work [11, 19, 20], we demonstrated an efficient statistical n-gram method to analyze the binary contents of network packets and files. This work followed our earlier work on applying machine learning techniques applied to binary content to detect malicious email attachments [15]. The method trains n-gram models from a collection of input data, and uses these models to test whether other data is similar to the training data, or sufficiently different to be deemed an anomaly. The method allows for each file type to be represented by a compact representation of statistical n-gram models. Using this technique, we can successfully classify files into different types, or validate the declared type of a file, according to their content, instead of using the file extension only or searching for embedded "magic numbers" [11] (that may be spoofed).

We do not presume to replace other detection techniques, but rather to augment approaches with perhaps new and useful evidence to detect suspicious files. Under severe time constraints, such as real-time testing of network file shares, or inspection of large amounts of newly acquired media, the technique may be useful in prioritizing files that are subjected to a deeper analysis for early detection of malcode infection.

In the next section, we describe some simple experiments of inserting malware into normal files and how well a commercial AV scanner performed in detecting these infected files. Amazingly, in several cases the

---

[2] For our purposes here, we refer to .DOC as Microsoft Word documents, although other applications use the .DOC extension such as Adobe Framemaker, Interleaf Document Format, and Palm Pilot format, to name a few.

tainted files were opened without problem by the associated application. Section 11.3 summarizes our work on fileprints using 1-gram distributions for pedagogical reasons. The same principles apply to higher order grams. We present several experiments using these techniques to detected infected files. Our concluding remarks in Section 11.4 identify several areas of new work to extend the preliminary ideas explored in this paper.

11.2   Deceiving anti-virus software

Malware may be easily transmitted among machines as (P2P) network shares. One possible stealthy way to infect a machine is by embedding the malicious payload into files that appear normal and that can be opened without incident. A later penetration by an attacker or an embedded Trojan may search for these files on disk to extract the embedded payload for execution or assembly with other malcode. Or an unsuspecting user may be tricked into launching the embedded malcode in some crafty way. In the latter case, malcode placed at the head of a PDF file can be directly executed to launch the malicious software. Social engineering can be employed to do so. One would presume that an AV scanner can check and detect such infected file shares if they are infected with known malcode for which a signature is available. The question is whether a commercial AV scanner can do so. Will the scanning and pattern-matching techniques capture such embeddings successfully? An intuitive answer would be "yes". We show that is not so in all cases.

We conducted the following experiments. First we collected a set of malware [22], and each of them was tested to verify they can be detected by a COTS anti-virus system[3]. We concatenate each of them to normal PDF files, both at the head and tail of the file. Then we manually test whether the COTS AV can still detect each of them, and whether Acrobat can open the PDF file without error. These tests were performed on a Windows platform. The results are summarized in Table 11.1. The COTS anti-virus system has surprisingly low detection rate on these infected files with embedded malware, especially when malware is attached at the tail. For those that were undetected, quite a few can still be successfully opened by Acrobat appearing exactly as the untouched original file. Thus, the mal-

---

[3] This work does not intend to evaluate nor denigrate any particular COTS product. We chose a widely used AV scanner that was fully updated at the time the tests were performed. We prefer not to reveal which particular COTS AV scanner was used. It is not germane to the research reported in this paper.

code can easily reside inside a PDF file without being noticed at all. An example of the manipulated PDF file is displayed in Figure 11.1. The apparent reason Adobe Acrobat Reader (version 7.0) opens infected files with no trouble is that it scans the head of a file looking for the PDF "magic numbers" signaling the beginning header meta-data necessary to interpret the rest of the binary content. Thus, the portions passed over by the reader while searching for its header data provides a convenient place to hide malcode.

Table 11.1. COTS AV detection rate and Acrobat behavior on embedded malcode.

Total virus/worm	Virus at the head of PDF		Virus at the tail of PDF	
	AV can detect	Acrobat can open	AV can detect	Acrobat can open
223	162 (72.6%)	4 /not detected	43 (19.3%)	17 /not detected

Fig. 11.1. Screenshot of original and malware embedded PDF file

We also performed another experiment by inserting the malware into some random position in the middle of the PDF file. But since PDF has its own encoding and such blind insertion can easily break the encoding, generally this is easily noticed by the Acrobat Reader when opening the file. This was the case and hence malware simply appended to the head/tail is obviously easier without causing any errors by the reader. We repeated this experiment on DOC files using some selected malwares, and got a similar result. The following table provides the detailed results of several malware insertion experiments using well known malware. Only CRII can be reliably detected no matter where it is inserted, while Slammer and Sasser were missed.

Table 11.2. Detailed example of insertion using several well-known malware

Slammer			
	Virus at head	In the middle	At tail
PDF file	Not detect/open fine	Not detect/open error	Not detect/open fine
DOC file	Not detect/open error	Not detect/open error	Not detect/open fine

CodeRed II	
	Can be detected anywhere

Sasser			
	Virus at head	In the middle	At tail
PDF file	Can detect	Not detect/open error	Not detect/open error
DOC file	Can detect	Not detect/open error	Not detect/open fine

Another experiment focused on Windows executables, like WINWORD.EXE. After analyzing the byte value distributions of executables, we noticed that byte value 0 dominated all others. Application executables are stored on disk using a standard block alignment strategy of padding of executables (falling at addresses n*4096) for fast disk loading. These zero'ed portions of application files provide ample opportunity to insert hidden malcode. Instead of concatenating malcode, in this case we insert the malcode in a continuous block of 0's long enough to hold the whole malcode and store the file back on disk. Again, we tested whether a COTS AV scanner would detect these poisoned applications. It did not. We performed this experiment by replacing the padded segments of WINWORD.EXE, from byte positions 2079784 to 2079848. Figure 11.2 shows two versions of the application, the normal executable and the other infected with malcode, and both were able to open DOC files with no trouble.

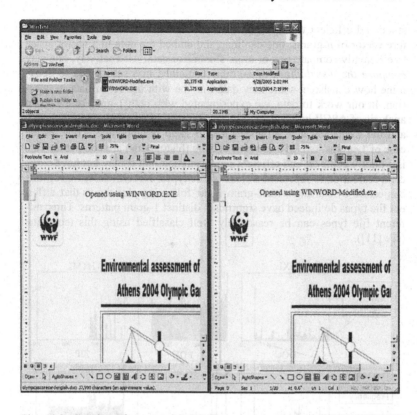

Fig. 11.2. Opening of a normal DOC file using the original WINWORD.EXE (left) and the infected one WINWORD-Modified.EXE (right).

11.3   N-gram experiments on files

Here we introduce the modeling and testing techniques and present the results of applying these techniques to detect tainted malware-embedded files from normal files of the same type.

11.3.1   Fileprints – n-gram distributions of file content

An n-gram [4] is a subsequence of n consecutive tokens in a stream of tokens. N-gram analysis has been applied in many tasks, and is well understood and efficient to implement. By converting a string of data to a feature vector of n-grams, one can map and embed the data in a vector space to efficiently compare two or more streams of data. Alternatively, one may *compare the distributions* of n-grams contained in a set of data to determine how consistent some new data may be with the set of data in question. In our work to date, we experimented with both 1-gram and 2-gram analysis of ASCII byte values. The sequence of binary content is analyzed, and the frequency and variance of each gram is computed. Thus, in the case of 1-grams, two 256-element vectors (histograms) are computed. This is a highly compact and efficient representation, but it may not have sufficient resolution to represent a class of file types. Nevertheless, we test this conjecture by starting with 1-grams. The following plot shows that different file types do indeed have significant distinct 1-gram patterns. Thus, different file types can be reasonably well classified using this technique (see [11]).

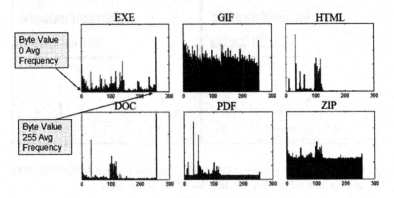

Fig. 11.3. 1-gram distribution for different file types.

Once a set of models are computed from a set of normal files, a test file is measured to determine how closely its content conforms to the normal models. This is accomplished by computing the Mahalanobis distance [20] between the test file in question and the normal (centroid) models previously computed. The score produced is a distance measure; a distance threshold is then used to determine whether to declare the file normal or not.

11.3.2 Truncation and multiple centroids

Truncation simply means we model only a fixed portion of a file when computing a byte distribution. That portion may be a fixed prefix, say the first 1000 bytes, or a fixed portion of the tail of a file, as well as perhaps a middle portion. This has several advantages. First, for most files, it can be assumed that the most relevant part of the file, as far as its particular type is concerned, is located early in the file to allow quick loading of meta-data by the handler program that processes the file type. Second, viruses often have their malicious code at the very beginning of a file. Hence, viruses may be more readily detected from this portion of the file. However, viruses indeed may also be appended to the end of a file, hence truncation may also be applied to the tail of a file to determine whether a file varies substantially from the expected distribution of that file type. The last, truncation dramatically reduces the computing time for model building and file testing.

On the other hand, files with the same extension do not always have a distribution similar enough to be represented by a single model. For example, EXE files might be totally different when created for different purpose, such as system files, games, or media handlers. Thus, an alternative strategy for representing files of a particular type is to compute "multiple models". We do this via a clustering strategy. Rather than computing a single model M_A for files of type A, we compute a set of models M^k_A, $k>1$. The multiple model strategy requires a different test methodology, however. During testing, a test file is measured against all centroids to determine if it matches at least one of the centroids. The set of such centroids is considered a composite fileprint for the entire class. The multiple model technique creates more accurate models, and separates foreign files from the normal files of a particular type in more precise manner. The multiple models are computed by the *K-Means* algorithm under *Manhattan Distance* as the similarity metric. The result is a set of K centroid models, M^k_A which are later used in testing files for various purposes.

11.3.3 Data sets

To test the effectiveness of the n-gram analysis on files, we conducted several experiments to determine whether it can correctly classify files and whether it can detect malcode.

The test files used in the experiments include 140 PDF files. The malicious files used for embedding were collected from emails, internet sources [22] and some target honeypot machines setup for this purpose in our lab. The PDF files were collected from the internet using a general search on *Google*. In this way, they can be considered randomly chosen as an unbiased sample. These tests are preliminary; considerable more effort is needed to compose a proper set of training and test data to ensure the files in question represent a true sample of interest. Here we collected documents from an open source and have no means to accurately characterize whether this sample is truly representative of a collection of interest. Nevertheless, this experiment provides some evidence of whether the proposed techniques show promise or not.

11.3.4 Detecting malware embedded files

First we revisit our malcode embedding experiment. We've seen that the COTS AV system we used can easily miss the malcode hidden inside normal appearing files. Here we apply the 1-gram analysis and see how well it may be able to detect the malicious code sequences. 100 of the 140 PDF files were used to build head and tail 1-gram models. Then we tested the remaining 40 normal PDF files and hundreds of malware-embedded files against the model. Since we know ground truth, we measure the detection rate exactly when the false positive rate is zero, i.e., no normal PDF files been misclassified as malware-infected. The result is displayed in Table 11.3, which is much higher than the COTS anti-virus software detection rate, which for these files is effectively zero. Notice that the total number of malware-embedded files is different for different truncation sizes. That is because the malware used in this study differ in size and we only consider the problem of classifying a pure malcode block fully embedded in a portion of the PDF file. We consider a concatenated PDF file as a test candidate only if the malcode size is equal to or greater than the truncation size used for modeling.

Table 11.3. Detection rate using truncated head and tail modeling

Models head N bytes			
Detect	1000 bytes	500 bytes	200 bytes
	49/56(87.5%)	314/347(90.5%)	477/505(94.5%)
Models tail N bytes			
Detect	1000 bytes	500 bytes	200 bytes
	42/56(75%)	278/347(80.1%)	364/505(72.1%)

It may be the case that it is easier to detect the malcode if it is concatenated at the head or tail of a file, since different file types usually have their own standard header information and ending encoding. Malcode may be significantly different from these standardized encodings. However, we test whether malware can effectively be hidden in some middle portion of a file (presuming that the file would still possibly be opened correctly). A reasonable assumption about such insertion is that the malware is inserted as a continuous whole block. So we apply the n-gram detection method to each block of a file's binary content and test whether the model can distinguish PDF blocks from malware blocks. If so, then we can detect the malcode hidden inside PDF files.

We compute byte distribution models using N consecutive byte blocks from 100 PDF files, then test the blocks of the malware and another 40 PDF files against the model, using Mahalanobis distance. Figure 11.4 shows the distance of the malware blocks and PDF blocks to the normal model, using N=500 byte blocks and N=1000 byte blocks, respectively. In the plot we display the distance of the malcode blocks on the left side of the separating line and the normal PDF on the right. As the plots show, there is a large overlap between malcode and PDF blocks. The poor results indicate that malware blocks cannot be easily distinguished from normal PDF file blocks using 1-gram distributions.

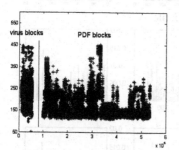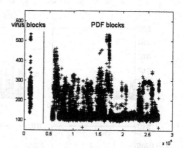

Fig. 11.4. The Mahalanobis distance of the normal PDF and malware blocks to the trained PDF block model. The left is 500-byte block and the right plot is 1000-byte block.

In order to understand why the block-based detection using 1-grams does not work well, we plot the byte distribution of each block of a normal PDF file and the Sasser worm code. The first 9 blocks of the PDF file and the first 6 blocks of Sasser are displayed in the following plots. These plots clearly show that different blocks inside a PDF file differ much in their byte distribution, and we cannot determine an absolute difference of the malcode blocks from PDF blocks. Therefore, it appears that a 1-gram statistical content analysis might not have sufficient resolution for malware block detection. Either higher order grams (perhaps 2-grams or 3-grams) may suffice, or we may need more syntactic information about the file formats to adequately distinguish malcode embedded in PDF files. A search for better statistical features is part of our ongoing research.

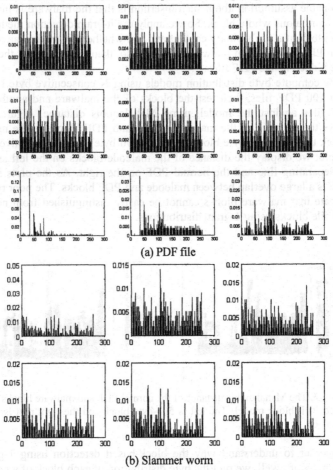

(a) PDF file

(b) Slammer worm

Fig. 11.5. Byte value distributions of blocks of the PDF file and Sasser worm.

11.3.5   Classifying normal executables and viruses

In this experiment, we use a collection of malcode executables gathered from other external sources, and compare the 1-gram and 2-gram distributions of these to the corresponding distributions of "normal" Windows executables to determine whether viruses exhibit any clear separating characteristics. We conjecture that the Windows executables are generated by programming environments and compilers that may create standard "headers" different from those used by virus writers who deliver their viruses via email or file shares.

We apply three modeling methods to these experiments, which are one-centroid, multi-centroids and exemplar files as centroids. The one centroid method trains one single model for each class (or type) of file. We build n models M_1, M_2, ..., M_n, from n different file types. Then, we compute the distance of the test file F to each model, and F is classified to the model with the closest distance.

Alternatively, the multi-centroids method, we build k models M'_1, M'_2, ..., M'_k using k-means algorithm for each file type t as described in Section 11.3.2 . There are $k*T$ models in total, where T is the number of file types. k is set to 10 in this test. The test strategy is the same as in the case of one centroid. The test file F is classified to the model with the closest distance.

A third method is also tested. Here we use a set of exemplar files of each type as centroids. Thus, a set of randomly chosen normal files for each file type are used as centroids. There are N models if there are N chosen exemplar files. We also analyze the accuracy of the method using different truncations – first 10, 50, 100, 200, 400, 600, 1000, 2000, 4000, 6000, and 8000 bytes, and the entire file. In this experiment, we evaluate both 1-gram and 2-gram analysis.

We trained models on 80% of the randomly selected files of each group (normal and malicious) to build a set of models for each class. The remaining 20% of the files are used as test files. Again, we know ground truth and hence can accurately evaluate performance. Note that all of the malicious files extensions are EXE. For each of the test files, we evaluate their distance from both the "normal model" and the "malicious model". 31 normal application executable files, 45 spyware, 331 normal executable under folder System32 and 571 viruses were tested. Three "pairs" of groups of files are tested – Normal executable vs. spyware, normal application vs. spyware and normal executable vs. viruses. We report the average accuracy over 100 trials using cross validation for each of the modeling techniques.

The results are shown in Figure 11.6. Each column represents each modeling method: one-centroid, muli-centroids and exemplar file centroids. The rows indicate the testing "pairs". In each plot, the X and Y-axis are the false positive rate and detection rate, respectively. The asterisk marks are 1-gram tests using different truncation sizezs, and the circle marks represent the results of 2-gram centoids. In these plots, the truncation sizes are not arranged in order. In these two dimensional plots, the optimum performance appears closest to the upper left corner of each plot. That is to say, a false positive rate of 0 and a detection rate of 1 is perfect performance.

The results show relatively good performance in some case of normal executable vs. spyware and normal executable vs. virus. Because viruses and worms usually target the System32 folder, we can reasonable well detect non-standard malicious files in that folder. Moreover, the performance

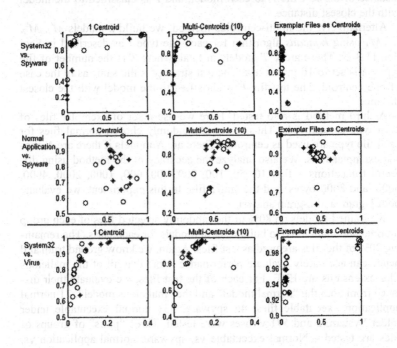

Fig. 11.6. 2-class classification of malware and normal EXE files. X-Axis: false positive, Y-Axis: detection rate. Asterisk marks: 1-gram test, Circle marks: 2-gram test.

results varied under different truncation sizes. Thus, we have considerable additional analysis to perform in our future work to identify appropriate file sizes (and normalization strategies) to improve detection performance. However, the plots clearly indicate that performance varies widely, which suggests the comparison method is too weak to reliably detect malicious code.

Notice that there is a high false positive rate in the case of testing normal applications to the Spyware samples. This is due to two reasons. First, the range of the normal application file size is too large, ranging from 10KB to 10MB. It is hard to normalize the models when the data ranges so widely. Second, the spyware files are somewhat similar to normal application files. They are both MS Windows applications, and they may be used for similar purposes. Hence, other features may be necessary to explore ways of better distinguishing this class of files.

In the experiments performed to date, there is no strong evidence to indicate that 2-gram analysis is better than 1-gram analysis. Even though the 1-gram memory usage is much smaller and the computation speed is much faster, we may need to analyze far more many files to determine whether the heavy price paid in performing 2-gram analysis will perform better ultimately.

11.3.6 Uniform Distributions of 1-gram analysis: encrypted files and spyware

In this experiment we scan Windows files to determine whether any are close to a uniform 1-gram distribution. We thus test whether spyware that is obfuscated by self-encryption technology may be revealed as substantially different from other executable files on a Windows host platform. We conjecture that self-encrypted files, such as stealthy Trojans and spyware, may be detectable easily via 1-gram analysis.

The normal EXE from System32, spyware and virus files used in the experiments reported in the previous section are used here again. Moreover, we randomly select 600 files (DOC, PPT, GIF, JPG, PDF, DLL) from *Google*, 100 for each type. Since the models are normalized, the uniform distribution is an array with uniform value $1/n$, where n is the length of the array and n is 256 in the 1-gram test. For each of the test files, we compute the Manhattan distance against the uniform model and plot the distance in Figure 11.7. The files that are closest to uniform distribution are listed in Table 11.4.

As the plot shows, JPG, GIF and PDF files are self-encoded, so they are more similar to the uniform distribution. System32 files and DLL files are not self-encrypted, and most of the virus and spyware tested are also not self-encrypted. However, some of the normal files are self-encrypted and quite similar to the random distribution. An interesting example is the application *ad-aware.exe*, which is a COTS adware detection application that apparently uses self-encryption, perhaps to attempt to protect its intellectual property.

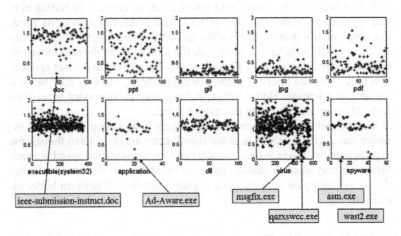

Fig. 11.7. The distance of testing files against the uniform distribution. X-Axis: the test files, Y-Axis: the distance.

Table 11.4. Files whose content is deemed close to a uniform 1-gram distribution (hence likely encrypted).

File name	Description
Ieee-submission-instruct.doc	An ieee submission format instruction Word file. It is unclear why this file follows a normal distribution.
Ad-Aware.exe	Ad-Aware.exe: ad-aware from lavasoft, searches and removes spyware and/or adware programs from your computer.
msgfix.exe	msgfix.exe is the W32.Gaobot.SN Trojan. This Trojan allows attackers to access your computer, stealing passwords and personal data.
Qazxswcc.exe	qazxswcc.exe is as a backdoor Trojan.
Asm.exe	asm.exe is a commercial spyware program by Gator. This program monitors browsing habits and distributes the data back to a Gator server for analysis. This also prompts advertising pop-ups.

wast2.exe	wast2.exe is an adware based Internet Explorer browser helper object that delivers targeted ads based on a user's browsing patterns.

11.4 Concluding Remarks

In this paper, we demonstrate that simple techniques to embed known malcode in normal files can easily bypass signature-based detection. We successfully inserted known malcode in non-executable (PDF and DOC) files without being detected by AV scanners, and several were normally opened and executed. Various code obfuscation techniques can also be used by crafty attackers to avoid inspection by signature-based methods. We propose an alternative approach to augment existing signature-based protection mechanisms with statistical content analysis techniques. Rather than only scanning for signatures, we compute the statistical binary content of files in order to detect anomalous files or portions of files which may indicate a malcode embedding. Although it may be relatively easy to detect tainted files where malcode is embedded in the head (where normal metadata is expected) or at the tail of a file, detecting embeddings within the interior portion of a file poses a significant challenge. The results show that far more work is needed to identify files tainted by stealthy malcode embeddings. On the positive side, self-encrypted files are relatively easy to spot.

The results reported here are preliminary, and have opened up other avenues of future work. For example, adherence to a 1-gram model may not be the right strategy. Higher order grams may reveal more structure in files, and help identify unusual segments worthy of deeper analysis. Furthermore, file formats are defined by, typically, proprietary and unpublished syntactic conventions providing markers delimiting regions of files handled different (eg., embedded objects with specialized methods for their processing) that may be analyzed by alternative methods. Utilizing this information may provide a finer granularity of modeling normal file formats and perhaps produce improved performance.

Finally, we believe another path may be useful, profiling application execution when opening typical/normal files. It may be possible to identify portions of files that harbor malcode by finding possible deviations from normal application behavior. Combining static analysis with dynamic program behavior analysis may be the best option for detecting tainted files with embedded stealthy malcode.

References

1. K. G. Anagnostakis, S. Sidiroglou, P. Akritidis, K.Xinidis, E. Marka-tos, and A. D. Keromytis. "Detecting Targeted Attacks Using Shadow Honeypots", Proceedings of the 14th USENIX Security Symposium, 2005.
2. R. Balzer and N. Goldman, "Mediating Connectors", Proceedings of the 19 IEEE International Conference on Distributed Computing Systems Workshop, 1994.
3. M. Christodorescu and S. Jha, "Static Analysis of Executables to Detect Malicious Patterns", In Proceedings of the 12th USENIX Security Symposium, August 2003
4. M. Damashek. "Gauging similarity with n-grams: language independent categorization of text." Science, 267(5199):843--848, 1995
5. E. Eskin, W. Lee and S. J. Stolfo. ``Modeling System Calls for Intrusion Detection with Dynamic Window Sizes." Proceedings of DISCEX II. June 2001.
6. J. Giffin, S. Jha, and B. Miller. "Detecting Manipulated Remote Call Streams". In the 11th USENIX Security Symposium, 2002
7. C. Ko, M. Ruschitzka, and K. Levitt. "Execution monitoring of security-critical programs in distributed systems: A specification-based approach". In Proceedings of the IEEE Symposium on Security and Privacy, 1997.
8. J. Kolter and M. Maloof. "Learning to Detect Malicious Executables in the Wild." In the Proceedings of ACM SIGKDD, 2004
9. C. Krugel, W. Robertson, F. Valeur, G. Vigna. "Static Disassembly of Obfuscated Binaries". In Proceedings of USENIX Security Symposium, 2004.
10. A. Kurchuk and A. Keromytis. "Recursive Sandboxes: Extending Systrace to Empower Applications". In Proceeding of the 19th IFIP International Information Security Conference (SEC), Aug. 2004
11. W. Li, K. Wang, S. Stolfo and B. Herzog. "Fileprints: identifying file types by n-gram analysis". 6th IEEE Information Assurance Workshop, West Point, NY, June, 2005.
12. M. McDaniel, M. Heydari. "Content Based File Type Detection Algorithms". 36th Annual Hawaii International Conference on System Sciences (HICSS'03).
13. G. Necula, P. Lee. "Proof-Carrying Code" In Proceedings of the 24th ACM SIGPLAN-SIGACT Symposium on Principles of Programming Languages (POPL), 1997

14. F. B. Schneider. "Enforceable security politics". Technical Report 98-1664, Cornell University, 1998
15. M. Schultz, E. Eskin, and S. Stolfo. "Malicious Email Filter - A UNIX Mail Filter that Detects Malicious Windows Executables." In Proceedings of USENIX Annual Technical Conference - FREENIX Track. Boston, MA: June 2001.
16. R. Sekar, A. Gupta, J. Frullo, T. Shanbhag, A. Tiwari, H. Yang and S. Zhou. "Specification-Based Anomaly Detection: a new approach for detecting network intrusions", RAID 2002
17. A. Shamir and N. van Someren. "Playing Hide and Seek with stored keys", Financial Cryptography 1999.
18. D. Wagner and D. Dean. "Intrusion Detection via Static Analysis". In IEEE Symposium in Security and Privacy, Oakland, CA, 2001
19. K. Wang, G. Cretu and S. Stolfo. "Anomalous Payload-based Worm Detection and Signature Generation". To appear in Proceedings of the Eighth International Symposium on Recent Advances in Intrusion Detection, Sept. 2005.
20. K. Wang and S. Stolfo. "Anomalous Payload-based Network Intrusion Detection". In Proceedings of the Seventh International Symposium on Recent Advance in Intrusion Detection (RAID), Sept. 2004.
21. C. Warrender, S. Forrest, and B. Pearlmutter. "Detecting intrusions using System calls: alternative data models, Proc. of 1999 IEEE Symposium on Security and Privacy, 1999.
22. VX Heavens http://vx.netlux.org/
23. Net Alliance http://www.shellcode.com.ar/docz/bof/pe.pdf

Novel Techniques for Constructing Trustworthy Services

Part V

Novel Techniques for Constructing Trustworthy
Services

Pioneer: Verifying Code Integrity and Enforcing Untampered Code Execution on Legacy Systems*

Arvind Seshadri[1], Mark Luk[1], Adrian Perrig[1], Leendert van Doorn[2], and Pradeep Khosla[1]

[1] CyLab, Carnegie Mellon University
arvinds@cs.cmu.edu, mark.luk@gmail.com,
{adrian,pkk}@ece.cmu.edu
[2] IBM Research
leendert@us.ibm.com

Summary. We propose a primitive, called Pioneer, as a first step towards verifiable code execution on untrusted legacy hosts. Pioneer does not require any hardware support such as secure co-processors or CPU-architecture extensions. We implement Pioneer on an Intel Pentium IV Xeon processor. Pioneer can be used as a basic building block to build security systems. We demonstrate this by building a kernel rootkit detector.

12.1 Introduction

Obtaining a guarantee that a given code has executed untampered on an untrusted legacy computing platform has been an open research challenge. We refer to this as the problem of *verifiable code execution*. An untrusted computing platform can tamper with code execution in at least three ways: 1) by modifying the code before invoking it; 2) executing alternate code; or 3) modifying execution state such as memory or registers when the code is running.

In this chapter, we propose a *software-based* primitive called Pioneer[3] as a first step towards addressing the problem of verifiable code execution on legacy computing platform without relying on secure co-processors or CPU architecture extensions such as secure virtualization support. Pioneer is based on a challenge-response protocol between an external trusted entity, called the *dispatcher*, and an untrusted computing platform, called the *untrusted platform*. The dispatcher communicates with

---

* This research was supported in part by CyLab at the Carnegie Mellon University under grant DAAD19-02-1-0389 from the Army Research Office, by NSF under grant CNS-0509004, and by a gift from IBM, Intel and Microsoft. The views and conclusions contained here are those of the authors and should not be interpreted as necessarily representing the official policies or endorsements, either express or implied, of ARO, Carnegie Mellon University, IBM, Intel, Microsoft, NSF, or the U.S. Government or any of its agencies.

[3] We call our primitive Pioneer because it can be used to instantiate a trusted base on an untrusted platform.

the untrusted platform over a communication link, such as a network connection. After a successful invocation of Pioneer, the dispatcher obtains assurance that: 1) an arbitrary piece of code, called the *executable*, on the untrusted platform is unmodified; 2) the unmodified executable is invoked for execution on the untrusted platform; and 3) the executable is executed untampered, despite the presence of malicious software on the untrusted platform.

To provide these properties, we assume that the dispatcher knows the hardware configuration of the untrusted platform, and that the untrusted platform cannot collude with other devices during verification. We also assume that the communication channel between the dispatcher and the untrusted platform provides the property of *message-origin authentication*, i.e., the communication channel is configured so that the dispatcher obtains the guarantee that the Pioneer packets it receives originate from the untrusted platform. Furthermore, to provide the guarantee of untampered code execution, we assume that the executable is self-contained, not needing to invoke any other software on the untrusted platform, and that it can execute at the highest processor privilege level with interrupts turned off.

The dispatcher uses Pioneer to dynamically establish a trusted computing base on the untrusted platform, called the *dynamic root of trust*. All code contained in the dynamic root of trust is guaranteed to be unmodified and is guaranteed to execute in an untampered execution environment. Once established, the dynamic root of trust measures the integrity of the executable and invokes the executable. The executable is guaranteed to execute in the untampered execution environment of the dynamic root of trust. In Pioneer, the dynamic root of trust is instantiated through the *verification function,* a *self-checking* function that computes a checksum over its own instructions. The checksum computation slows down noticeably if the adversary tampers with the computation. Thus, if the dispatcher receives the correct checksum from the untrusted platform within the expected amount of time, it obtains the guarantee that the verification function code on the execution platform is unmodified.

Pioneer can be used as a basic primitive for developing security applications. We illustrate this by designing a kernel rootkit detector. Our rootkit detector uses a software-based kernel integrity monitor. Instead of using rootkit signatures or low level filesystem scans to find files hidden by a rootkit, our kernel integrity monitor computes periodic hashes of the kernel code segment and static data structures to detect unauthorized kernel changes. The trusted computer uses Pioneer to obtain a guarantee that the kernel integrity monitor is unmodified and runs untampered. When implemented on version 2.6 of the Linux kernel, our rootkit detector was able to detect all publically-known rootkits for this series of the Linux kernel.

An important property of Pioneer is that it enables software-based code attestation [19]. Code attestation allows a trusted entity, known as the *verifier*, to verify the software stack running on another entity, known as the *attestation platform*. The verifier and the attestation platform are usually different physical computing devices. A measurement agent on the attestation platform takes integrity measurements of the platform's software stack and sends them to the verifier. The verifier uses the integrity measurements obtained from the attestation platform to detect modifications in the attestation platform's software stack.

The Trusted Computing Group (TCG) has released standards for secure computing platforms, based on a tamper-resistant chip called the Trusted Platform Module (TPM) [22]. All code is measured before it is loaded and the measurements are stored inside the TPM. In response to an attestation request, the attestation platform sends the load-time measurements to the verifier. The verifier can the load-time measurements to obtain the guarantee of load-time attestation, whereby the verifier obtains a guarantee of what code was loaded into the system memory initially.

The load-time attestation mechanism proposed by the TCG standards has two disadvantages: 1) it requires hardware extensions to the attestation platform in the form of a TPM chip and is hence not suitable for legacy systems, and 2) the mechanism is not field upgradable using software means. It is not possible to update the software running on the TPM using software methods. The only way to update the TPM software is to physically replace the TPM. TPMs are designed this way to prevent an adversary from loading malicious software into the TPM via the update mechanism. However, this also means that whenever the cryptographic primitives used by the TPM are compromised or any vulnerabilities are found in the TPM software, the only way to re-secure already deployed systems is to physically replace their hardware.

The software-based code attestation provided by Pioneer does not require any hardware extensions to the attestation platform. The verifier depends on Pioneer to guarantee the verifiably correct execution of the measurement agent. Pioneer-based code attestation has three main advantages: 1) it can be updated using software methods if the underlying primitives are compromised, 2) it works on legacy systems that lack secure co-processors or other hardware enhancements to protect the measurement agent from a malicious attestation platform, and 3) it provides the property of *run-time attestation*, i.e., the verifier can verify the integrity of software running on the attestation platform at the present time. Run-time attestation provides a stronger guarantee than the TCG-based load-time attestation, since software can be compromised by dynamic attacks, such as buffer overflows, after software is loaded into memory.

The chapter is organized as follows. Section 12.2 describes the problem we address, our assumptions, and attacker model. In Section 12.3, we give an overview of Pioneer. We then describe the design of the verification function and its implementation on the Intel Pentium IV Xeon processor in Sections 12.4 and 12.5, respectively. Section 12.6 describes our kernel rootkit detector. We discuss related work in Section 12.7 and conclude in Section 12.8.

12.2 Problem Definition, Assumptions & Attacker Model

In this section, we describe the problem we address, discuss the assumptions we make, and describe our attacker model.

12.2.1 Problem Definition

We define the problem of *verifiable code execution*, in which the dispatcher wants a guarantee that some arbitrary code has executed untampered on an untrusted external platform, even in the presence of malicious software on the untrusted platform.

The untrusted platform has a self-checking function, called the verification function. The dispatcher invokes the verification function by sending a challenge to the untrusted platform. The verification function returns a checksum to the dispatcher. The dispatcher has a copy of the verification function and can independently verify the checksum. If the checksum returned by the untrusted platform is correct and is returned within the expected time, the dispatcher obtains the guarantee that a dynamic root of trust exists on the untrusted platform. The code in the dynamic root of trust measures the executable, sends the measurement to the dispatcher, and invokes the executable. The executable runs in an untampered execution environment, which was set up as part of instantiating the dynamic root of trust. The dispatcher can verify the measurement since it has a copy of the executable. Taken together, the correctness of the checksum and correctness of the executable measurement provide the guarantee of verifiable code execution to the dispatcher.

Even if malicious software runs on the untrusted platform, it cannot tamper with the execution of the executable. The adversary can perform an active DoS attack and thwart Pioneer from being run at all. However, the adversary cannot cheat by introducing a false negative, where the correct checksum value has been reported within the expected time to the dispatcher, without the correct code executing on the untrusted platform.

12.2.2 Assumptions

We assume that the dispatcher knows the exact hardware configuration of the untrusted platform, including the CPU model, the CPU clock speed, and the memory latency. We also assume that the CPU of the untrusted platform is not overclocked. In addition, the untrusted platform has a single CPU, that does not have support for Symmetric Multi-Threading (SMT). For the x86 architecture, we also assume that the adversary does not generate a System Management Interrupt (SMI) on the untrusted platform during the execution of Pioneer.

We assume the communication channel between the dispatcher and the untrusted platform provides message-origin authentication i.e., the dispatcher is guaranteed that all Pioneer packets it receives originate at the untrusted platform. Also, we assume that the untrusted platform can only communicate with the dispatcher during the time Pioneer runs. Equivalently, the dispatcher can detect the untrusted platform attempting to contact other computing platforms. We make this assumption to eliminate the *proxy attack*, where the untrusted platform asks a faster computing device (proxy), to compute the checksum on its behalf.

Assuming that the untrusted platform has only one wired communication interface, we can provide message-origin authentication and eliminate the proxy attack by physically connecting the untrusted platform to dispatcher with a cable. Also, if the untrusted platform can only communicate over a Local Area Network (LAN), the network administrators can configure the network switches such that any packets sent by the untrusted platform will reach only the dispatcher.

12.2.3 Attacker Model

We assume an adversary who has complete control over the software of the untrusted platform. In other words, the adversary has administrative privileges and can tamper with all software on the untrusted platform including the OS. However, we assume that the adversary does not modify the hardware on the untrusted platform. For example, the adversary does not load malicious firmware onto peripheral devices such as network cards or disk controllers, or replace the CPU with a faster one. In addition, the adversary does not perform DMA-based attacks like scheduling a DMA-write causing a benign peripheral device to overwrite the executable between the time of measurement and time of invocation.

12.3 Pioneer Overview

In this section, we give an overview of the verification function and describe the challenge-response protocol used to set up a dynamic root of trust on the execution platform and to obtain the guarantee of verifiable code execution.

12.3.1 The Verification Function

The verification function is the central component of the Pioneer system. It is responsible for performing an integrity measurement on the executable, setting up an execution environment for the executable that ensures untampered execution, and invoking the executable. As Figure 12.1 shows, the verification function has three parts: a checksum code, a hash function and a send function.

Checksum code. The checksum code computes a checksum over the entire verification function, and sets up an execution environment in which the send function, the hash function and the executable are guaranteed to run untampered by any malicious software on the untrusted platform. The checksum code computes a fingerprint of the verification function, i.e., if even a single byte of the verification function code is different, the checksum will be different with a high probability. Thus, a correct checksum provides a guarantee to the dispatcher that the verification function code is unmodified. However, an adversary could attempt to manipulate the checksum computation to forge the correct checksum value in spite of having modified the verification function. For example, the adversary could detect when the checksum code reads the altered memory locations and redirect the read to other memory locations where the adversary has stored the correct values. To detect such manipulations, we construct the verification function such that if an adversary tries to manipulate the checksum computation, the computation time will noticeably increase. Thus, a

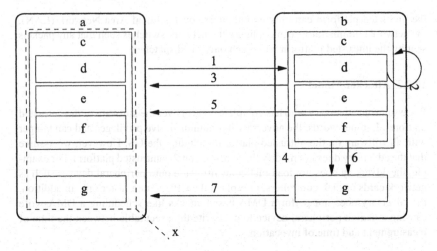

Fig. 12.1. Overview of Pioneer. The numbers represent the temporal ordering of events.

correct checksum obtained within the expected amount of time is a guarantee to the dispatcher that the verification function code on the untrusted platform is unmodified and that there is an environment for untampered execution on the untrusted platform. In other words, the dispatcher obtains the guarantee that there is a dynamic root of trust on the untrusted platform.

Hash function. We use SHA-1 as the hash function to perform the integrity measurement of the executable. Although the collision resistance property of SHA-1 has been compromised, we rely on the second-preimage collision resistance property for which SHA-1 is still considered secure [25]. To achieve this property, we design the hash function so that it computes the hash of the executable as a function of a nonce that is sent by the dispatcher. Thus, the adversary cannot take advantage of the compromised collision resistance property of SHA-1 to create to two different copies of the executable both of which have the same hash value. After the measurement, the hash function invokes the executable.

Send function. The send function returns the checksum and integrity measurement to the dispatcher over the communication link.

12.3.2 The Pioneer Protocol

The dispatcher uses a challenge-response protocol to obtain the guarantee of verifiable code execution on the untrusted platform. The protocol has two steps. First, the dispatcher obtains an assurance that there is a dynamic root of trust on the untrusted platform. Second, the dispatcher uses the dynamic root of trust to obtain the guarantee of verifiable code execution.

1. D : $t_1 \leftarrow$ current time, $nonce \overset{R}{\leftarrow} \{0,1\}^n$
   $D \rightarrow P$: $\langle nonce \rangle$
2. P : $c \leftarrow$ Checksum$(nonce, P)$
3. $P \rightarrow D$: $\langle c \rangle$
   D : $t_2 \leftarrow$ current time
               if $(t_2 - t_1 > \Delta t)$ then exit with failure
               else verify checksum c
4. P : $h \leftarrow$ Hash$(nonce, E)$
5. $P \rightarrow D$: $\langle h \rangle$
   D :   verify measurement result h
6. P :   transfer control to E
7. $E \rightarrow D$: $\langle$result (optional)$\rangle$

Fig. 12.2. The Pioneer protocol. The numbering of events is the same as in Figure 12.1. D is the dispatcher, P the verification function, and E is the executable.

We describe the challenge-response protocol in Figure 12.2. The dispatcher first sends a challenge containing a random nonce to the untrusted platform, initiating the checksum computation of the verification function. The untrusted platform uses the checksum code that is part of the verification function to compute the checksum. The checksum code also sets up an execution environment to ensure that the send function, the hash function and the executable can execute untampered. After computing the checksum, the checksum code invokes the send function to return the checksum to the dispatcher. The dispatcher has a copy of the verification function and can independently verify the checksum. Also, since the dispatcher knows the exact hardware configuration of the untrusted platform, the dispatcher knows the expected time duration of the checksum computation. After the send function returns the checksum to the dispatcher, it invokes the hash function. The hash function measures the executable by computing a hash over it as a function of the dispatcher's nonce and returns the hash of the executable to the dispatcher using the send function. The dispatcher also has a copy of the executable and can independently verify the hash value. The hash function then invokes the executable, which optionally returns the execution result to the dispatcher.

12.4 Design of the Checksum Code

In this section, we discuss the design of the checksum code that is part of the verification function. The design is presented in a CPU-architecture-independent manner. First, we discuss the properties of the checksum code, and explain how we achieve these properties and what attacks these properties can prevent or help detect. Then, we explain how we set up an execution environment in which the hash function, the send function and the executable execute untampered. In Section 12.5, we shall describe how to implement the checksum code on an Intel Pentium IV Xeon processor.

12.4.1 Required Properties of the Checksum Code

The checksum code has to be constructed such that adversarial tampering results in either a wrong checksum or a noticeable time delay. We now describe the required properties of the checksum code and explain how these properties achieve the goals mentioned above.

Time-optimal implementation. Our checksum code needs to be the checksum code sequence with the fastest running time; otherwise the adversary could use a faster implementation of the checksum code and use the time saved to forge the checksum. Unfortunately, it is an open problem to devise a proof of optimality for our checksum function. Promising research directions to achieve a proof of optimality are tools such as Denali [13] or superopt [8] that automatically generate the most optimal code sequence for basic code blocks in a program. However, Denali currently only optimizes simple code that can be represented by assignments, and superopt would not scale to the code size of our checksum function.

To achieve a time-optimal implementation, we use simple instructions such as add and xor that are challenging to implement faster or with fewer operations. Moreover, the checksum code is structured as code blocks such that operations in one code block are dependent on the result of operations in the previous code block. This prevents operation reordering optimizations across code blocks.

Instruction sequencing to eliminate empty issue slots. Most modern CPUs are superscalar, i.e., they issue multiple instructions in every clock cycle. If our checksum code does not have a sufficient number of issuable instructions every clock cycle, then one or more instruction issue slots will remain empty. An adversary could exploit an empty issue slot to execute additional instructions without overhead. To prevent such an attack, we need to arrange the instruction sequence of the checksum code so that the processor issue logic always has a sufficient number of issuable instructions for every clock cycle. Note that we cannot depend solely on the processor out-of-order issue logic for this since it is not guaranteed that the out-of-order issue logic will always be able to find a sufficient number of issuable instructions.

CPU state inputs. The checksum code is self-checksumming, i.e., it computes a checksum over its own instruction sequence. The adversary can modify the checksum code so that instead of checksumming its own instructions, the adversary's checksum code computes a checksum over a correct copy of the instructions that is stored elsewhere in memory. We call this attack a *memory copy attack*. This attack is also mentioned by Wurster et al. in connection with their attack on software tamperproofing [28]. The adversary can perform the memory copy attack in three different ways: 1) as shown in Figure 3(b), the adversary executes an altered checksum function from the correct location in memory, but computes the checksum over a correct copy of the checksum function elsewhere in memory; 2) as shown in Figure 3(c), the adversary does not move the correct checksum code, but executes its modified checksum code from other locations in memory; or 3) the adversary places both the correct checksum code and its modified checksum code in memory locations that are different from the memory locations where the correct checksum code originally resided, as shown in Figure 3(d).

It is obvious from the above description that when the adversary performs a memory copy attack, either the adversary's Program Counter (PC) value or the data pointer value or both will differ from the correct execution. We cause the adversary to suffer an execution time overhead for the memory copy attack by incorporating both the PC and the data pointer value into the checksum. In a memory copy attack, the adversary will be forced to forge one or both of these values in order to generate the correct checksum, leading to an increase in execution time.

Both the PC and the data pointer hold virtual addresses. The verification function is assumed to execute from a range of virtual addresses that is known to the dispatcher. As a result, the dispatcher knows the excepted value of the PC and the data pointer and can compute the checksum independently.

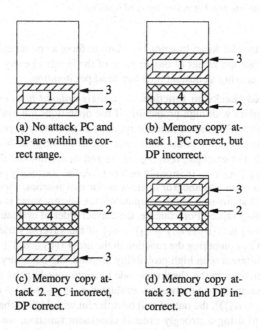

(a) No attack, PC and DP are within the correct range.

(b) Memory copy attack 1. PC correct, but DP incorrect.

(c) Memory copy attack 2. PC incorrect, DP correct.

(d) Memory copy attack 3. PC and DP incorrect.

Fig. 12.3. Memory copy attacks. PC refers to the program counter, DP refers to the data pointer, V.func refers to the verification function, and Mal. func refers to the malicious verification function.

Iterative checksum code. As Figure 12.4 shows, the checksum code consists of three parts; the initialization code, the checksum loop and the epilog code. The most important part is the checksum loop. Each checksum loop reads one memory location of the verification function and updates the running value of the checksum with the memory value read, a pseudo-random value and some CPU state information. If the

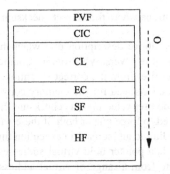

Fig. 12.4. Functional structure of the verification function. The checksum code consists of an initialization code, the checksum loop which computes the checksum, and the epilog code that runs after the checksum loop but before the send function.

adversary alters the checksum function but wants to forge a correct checksum output, it has to manipulate the values of one or more of the inputs in every iteration of the checksum code, causing a constant time overhead per iteration.

Strongly-ordered checksum function. A *strongly-ordered function* is a function whose output differs with high probability if the operations are evaluated in a different order. A strongly-ordered function requires an adversary to perform the same operations on the same data in the same sequence as the original function to obtain the correct result. For example, if a_1, a_2, a_3, a_4 and a_5 are random inputs, the function $a_1 \oplus a_2 + a_3 \oplus a_4 + a_5$ is strongly-ordered. We use a strongly ordered function consisting of alternate add and xor operations for two reasons. First, this prevents parallelization, as at any step of the computation the current value is needed to compute the succeeding values. For example, the correct order of evaluating the function $a_1 \oplus a_2 + a_3 \oplus a_4$ is $(((a_1 \oplus a_2) + a_3) \oplus a_4)$. If the adversary tries to parallelize the computation by computing the function in the order $((a_1 \oplus a_2) + (a_3 \oplus a_4))$, the output will be different with high probability. Second, the adversary cannot change the order of operations in the checksum code to try to speed up the checksum computation. For example, if the adversary evaluates $a_1 \oplus a_2 + a_3 \oplus a_4$ in the order $(a_1 \oplus (a_2 + (a_3 \oplus a_4)))$, the output will be different with high probability.

In addition to using a strongly ordered checksum function, we also rotate the checksum. Thus, the bits of the checksum change their positions from one iteration of the checksum loop to the next, which makes our checksum function immune to the attack against the Genuinity function that we point out in our paper [19].

Small code size. The size of the checksum loop needs to be small for two main reasons. First, the code needs to fit into the processor cache to achieve a fast and deterministic execution time. Second, since the adversary usually has a constant overhead per iteration, the relative overhead increases with a smaller checksum loop.

Low variance of execution time. Code execution time on modern CPUs is nondeterministic for a number of reasons. We want a low variance for the execution time of the checksum code so that the dispatcher can easily find a threshold value for the correct execution time. We leverage three mechanisms to reduce the execution time variance of the checksum code. One, the checksum code executes at the highest privilege CPU privilege level with all maskable interrupts turned off, thus ensuring that no other code can run when the checksum code executes. Two, the checksum code is small enough to fit completely inside the CPU's L1 instruction cache. Also, the memory region containing the verification function is small enough to fit inside the CPU's L1 data cache. Thus, once the CPU caches are warmed up, no more cache misses occur. The time taken to warm up the CPU caches is a small fraction of the total execution time. As a result, the variance in execution time caused by cache misses during the cache warm-up period is small. Three, we sequence the instructions of the checksum code such that a sufficient number of issuable instructions are available at each clock cycle. This eliminates the non-determinism due to out-of-order execution. As we show in our results in Section 12.5.3, the combination of the above three factors leads to a checksum code with very low execution time variance.

Keyed-checksum. To prevent the adversary from pre-computing the checksum before making changes to the verification function, and to prevent the replaying of old checksum values, the checksum needs to depend on a unpredictable challenge sent by the dispatcher. We achieve this in two ways. First, the checksum code uses the challenge to seed a Pseudo-Random Number Generator (PRNG) that generates inputs for computing the checksum. Second, the challenge is also used to initialize the checksum variable to a deterministic yet unpredictable value.

We use a T-function as the PRNG [16]. A T-function is a function from n-bit words to n-bit words that has a single cycle length of 2^n. That is, starting from any n-bit value, the T-function is guaranteed to produce all the other $2^n - 1$ n-bit values before starting to repeat the values. The T-function we use is $x \leftarrow x + (x^2 \vee 5) \mod 2^n$, where $\vee$ is the bitwise-or operator. Since every iteration of the checksum code uses one random number to avoid repetition of values from the T-function, we have to ensure that the number of iterations of the checksum code is less than 2^n when we use an n-bit T-function. We use $n = 64$ in our implementation to avoid repetition.

It would appear that we could use a Message Authentication Code (MAC) function instead of the simple checksum function we use. MAC functions derive their output as a function of their input and a secret key. We do not use a MAC function for two reasons. First, the code of current cryptographic MAC functions is typically large, which is against our goal of a small code size. Also, MAC functions have much stronger properties than what we require. MAC functions are constructed to be resilient to MAC-forgery attacks. In a MAC-forgery attack, the adversary knows a finite number of (data, MAC(data)) tuples, where each MAC value is generated using the same secret key. The task of the adversary is to generate a MAC for a new data item that will be valid under the unknown key. It is clear that we do not require resilience to the MAC forgery attack, as the nonce sent by the Pioneer dispatcher is not a secret but is sent in the clear. We only require that the adversary be unable to pre-compute the checksum or replay old checksum values.

Pseudo-random memory traversal. The adversary can keep a correct copy of any memory locations in the verification function it modifies. Then, at the time the checksum code tries to read one of the modified memory locations, the adversary can redirect the read to the location where the adversary has stored the correct copy. Thus, the adversary's final checksum will be correct. We call this attack the *data substitution attack*. To maximize the adversary's time overhead for the data substitution attack, the checksum code reads the memory region containing the verification function in a pseudo-random pattern. A pseudo-random access pattern prevents the adversary from predicting which memory read(s) will read the modified memory location(s). Thus, the adversary is forced to monitor every memory read by the checksum code. This approach is similar to our earlier work in SWATT [19].

We use the result of the Coupon Collector's Problem to guarantee that the checksum code will read every memory location of the verification function with high probability, despite the pseudo-random memory access pattern. If the size of the verification function is n words, the result of the Coupon Collector's Problem states: if X is the number of memory reads required to read each of the n words at least once, then $Pr[X > cn \ln n] \leq n^{-c+1}$. Thus, after $O(n \ln n)$ memory reads, each memory location is accessed at least once with high probability.

12.4.2 Execution Environment for Untampered Code Execution

We now explain how the checksum code sets up an untampered environment for the hash function, the send function, and the executable.

Execution at highest privilege level with maskable interrupts turned off. All CPUs have an instruction to disable maskable interrupts. Executing this instruction changes the state of the `interrupt enable/disable` bit in the CPU condition codes (flags) register. The `disable-maskable-interrupt` instruction can only be executed by code executing at the highest privilege level. The initialization code, which runs before the checksum loop (see Figure 12.4), executes the `disable-maskable-interrupt` instruction. If the checksum code is executing at the highest privilege level, the instruction execution proceeds normally and the `interrupt enable/disable` flag in the flags register is set to the `disable` state. If the checksum code is executing at lower privilege levels one of two things can happen: 1) the `disablemaskable-interrupts` instruction fails and the status of the `interrupt enable/disable` flag is not set to `disable`, or 2) the `disable-maskable-interrupt` instruction traps into software that runs at the highest privilege level. Case 2 occurs when the checksum code is running inside a virtual machine (VM). Since we assume a legacy computer system where the CPU does not have support for virtualization, the VM must be created using a software-based virtual machine monitor (VMM) such as VMware [24]. The VMM internally maintains a copy of the flags register for each VM. When the VMM gains control as a result of the checksum code executing the `disable-maskable-interrupt` instructions, the VMM changes the state of the `interrupt enable/disable` flag in the copy of the flags register it maintains for the VM and returns control to the VM. This way, the actual CPU flags register remains unmodified.

We incorporate the flags register into the checksum in each iteration of the checksum loop. Note that the adversary cannot replace the flags register with an immediate since the flags register contains status flags, such as the carry and zero flag, whose state changes as a result of arithmetic and logical operations. If the adversary directly tries to run the checksum code at privilege levels lower than the highest privilege level, the final checksum will be wrong since the interrupt enable/disable flag will not be set to the disable state. On the other hand, if the adversary tries to cheat by using a software VMM, then each read of the flags register will trap into the VMM or execute dynamically generated code, thereby increasing the adversary's checksum computation time. In this way, when the dispatcher receives the correct checksum within the expected time, it has the guarantee that the checksum code executed at the highest CPU privilege level with all maskable interrupts turned off. Since the checksum code transfers control to the hash function and the hash function in turn invokes the executable, the dispatcher also obtains the guarantee that both the hash function and executable will run at the highest CPU privilege level with all maskable interrupts turned off.

Replacing exception handlers and non-maskable interrupt handlers. Unlike maskable interrupts, exceptions and non-maskable interrupts cannot be temporarily turned off. To ensure that the hash function and executable will run untampered, we have to guarantee that the exception handlers and the handlers for non-maskable interrupts are non-malicious. We achieve this guarantee by replacing the existing exception handlers and the handlers for non-maskable interrupts with our own handlers in the checksum code. Since both the hash function and the executable operate at the highest privilege level, they should not cause any exceptions. Also, non-maskable interrupts normally indicate catastrophic conditions, such as hardware failures, which are low probability events. Hence, during normal execution of the hash function and the executable, neither non-maskable interrupts nor exceptions should occur. Therefore, we replace the existing exception handlers and handlers for non-maskable interrupts with code that consists only of an *interrupt return* instruction (e.g., iret on x86). Thus, our handler immediately returns control to whatever code was running before the interrupt or exception occurred.

An intriguing problem concerns where in the checksum code we should replace the exception and non-maskable interrupt handlers. We cannot do this in the checksum loop since the instructions that replace the exception and non-maskable interrupt handlers do not affect the value of the checksum. Thus, the adversary can remove these instructions and still compute the correct checksum within the expected time. Also, we cannot place the instructions to replace the exception and non-maskable interrupt handlers in the initialization code, since the adversary can skip these instructions and jump directly into the checksum loop.

We therefore place the instructions that replace the handlers for exceptions and non-maskable interrupts in the epilog code. The epilog code (see Figure 12.4) is executed after the checksum loop is finished. If the checksum is correct and is computed within the expected time, the dispatcher is guaranteed that the epilog code is unmodified, since the checksum is computed over the entire verification function. The adversary can, however, generate a non-maskable interrupt or exception when the epilog code tries to run, thereby gaining control. For example, the adversary can

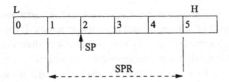

Fig. 12.5. The stack trick. A part of the checksum (6 words long in the figure) is on the stack. The stack pointer is randomly moved to one of the locations between the markers by each iteration of the checksum code. Note that the stack pointer never points to either end of the checksum.

set an execution break-point in the epilog code. The processor will then generate a debug exception when it tries to execute the epilog code. The existing debug exception handler could be controlled by the adversary. This attack can be prevented by making use of the stack to store a part of the checksum. The key insight here is that all CPUs automatically save some state on the stack when an interrupt or exception occurs. If the stack pointer is pointing to the checksum that is on the stack, any interrupt or exception will cause the processor to overwrite the checksum. We ensure that the stack pointer always points to the middle of the checksum on the stack (see Figure 12.5) so that part of the checksum will always be overwritten regardless of whether the stack grows up or down in memory.

Each iteration of the checksum loop randomly picks a word of the stack-based checksum for updating. It does this by moving the stack pointer to a random location within the checksum on the stack, taking care to ensure that the stack pointer is never at either end of the checksum (see Figure 12.5). The new value of the stack pointer is generated using the current value of the checksum and the current value of the stack pointer, thereby preventing the adversary from predicting its value in advance.

The epilog code runs before the send function, which sends the checksum back to the dispatcher. Thereby, a valid piece of checksum is still on the stack when the epilog code executes. Thus, the adversary cannot use a non-maskable interrupt or exception to prevent the epilog code from running without destroying a part of the checksum. Once the epilog code finishes running, all the exception handlers and the handlers for non-maskable interrupts will have been replaced. In this manner, the dispatcher obtains the guarantee that any code that runs as a result of an exception or a non-maskable interrupt will be non-malicious.

12.5 Checksum Code Implementation on the Netburst Microarchitecture

In this section we describe our implementation of the checksum code on an Intel Pentium IV Xeon processor with EM64T extensions. First, we briefly describe the Netburst microarchitecture, which is implemented by all Intel Pentium IV processors, and the EM64T extensions. Next, we describe how we implement the checksum code on the Intel x86 architecture. Section 12.5.3 shows the results of our experi-

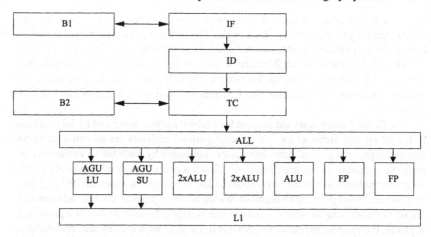

Fig. 12.6. The Intel Netburst Microarchitecture. The execution units are LU: Load Unit; SU: Store Unit; AGU: Address Generation Unit; 2xALU: Double-speed Integer ALUs that execute two µops each per cycle; ALU: Complex Integer ALU; FP: Floating Point, MMX, and SSE unit.

ments measuring the time overhead of the different attacks. Finally, in Section 12.5.4 we discuss some points related to the practical deployment of Pioneer and extensions to the current implementation of Pioneer.

12.5.1 The Netburst Microarchitecture and EM64T Extensions

In this section, we present a simplified overview of the Intel Netburst microarchitecture that is implemented in the Pentium IV family of CPUs. We also describe the EM64T extensions that add support for 64-bit addresses and data to the 32-bit x86 architecture.

Figure 12.6 shows a simplified view of the front-end and execution units in the Netburst architecture. The figure and our subsequent description are based on a description of the Netburst microarchitecture by Boggs et al. [5].

The instruction decoder in Pentium IV CPUs can only decode one instruction every clock cycle. To prevent the instruction decoder from creating a performance bottleneck, the Netburst microarchitecture uses a trace cache instead of a regular L1 instructions cache. The trace cache holds decoded x86 instructions in the form of µops. µops are RISC-style instructions that are generated by the instruction decoder when it decodes the x86 instructions. Every x86 instruction breaks down into one or more dependent µops. The trace cache can hold up to 12000 µops and can issue up to three µops to the execution core per clock cycle. Thus, the Netburst microarchitecture is a 3-way issue superscalar microarchitecture.

The Netburst microarchitecture employs seven execution units. The load and store units have dedicated Arithmetic Logic Units (ALU) called Address Generation

Units (AGU) to generate addresses for memory access. Two double-speed integer ALUs execute two μops every clock cycle. The double speed ALUs handle simple arithmetic operations like add, subtract and logical operations.

The L1-data cache is 16KB in size, 8-way set associative and has a 64 byte line size. The L2 cache is unified (holds both instructions and data). Its size varies depending on the processor family. The L2 cache is 8 way set associative and has a 64 byte line size.

The EM64T extensions add support for a 64-bit address space and 64-bit operands to the 32-bit x86 architecture. The general purpose registers are all extended to 64 bits and eight new general purpose registers are added by the EM64T extensions. In addition, a feature called segmentation[4] allows a process to divide up its data segment into multiple logical address spaces called *segments*. Two special CPU registers (fs and gs) hold pointers to segment descriptors that provide the base address and the size of a segment as well as segment access rights. To refer to data in a particular segment, the process annotates the pointer to the data with the segment register that contains the pointer to the descriptor of the segment. The processor adds the base address of the segment to the pointer to generate the full address of the reference. Thus, fs:0000 would refer to the first byte of the segment whose descriptor is pointed to by fs.

12.5.2 Implementation of Pioneer on x86

We now discuss how we implement the checksum code so that it has all the properties we describe in Section 12.4.1. Then we describe how the checksum code sets up the execution environment described in Section 12.4.2 on the x86 architecture.

Every iteration of the checksum code performs these five actions: 1) deriving the next pseudo-random number from the T-function, 2) reading the memory word for checksum computation, 3) updating the checksum, 4) rotating the checksum using a rotate instruction, and 5) updating some program state such as the data pointer. Except for reading the CPU state and our defense against the memory copy attack, all properties are implemented on the x86 architecture exactly as we describe in Section 12.4.1. Below, we describe the techniques we employ to obtain the CPU state on the x86 architecture. We also describe how we design our defense against the memory copy attacks.

CPU state inputs. The CPU state inputs, namely the Program Counter (PC) and the data pointer, are included in the checksum to detect the three memory copy attacks. On the x86 architecture with EM64T extensions, the PC cannot be used as an operand for any instruction other than the lea instruction. So, if we want to include the value of the PC in the checksum, the fastest way to do it is to use the following two instructions: first, the lea instruction moves the current value of PC into a general purpose register, and next, we incorporate the value in the general purpose register

---

[4] The EM64T extensions to the IA32 architecture support segmentation in a limited way. When running in 64-bit mode, the CPU does not use the segment base values present in segment descriptors pointed to by the cs, ds, ss and es segment registers.

into the checksum. Since the value of the PC is known in advance, the adversary can directly incorporate the corresponding value into the checksum as an immediate. Doing so makes the adversary's checksum computation faster since it does not need the lea instruction. Hence, on the x86 platform we cannot directly include the PC in the checksum.

Instead of directly including the PC in the checksum, we construct the checksum code so that correctness of the checksum depends on executing a sequence of absolute jumps. By including the jump target of each jump into the checksum, we indirectly access the value of the PC.

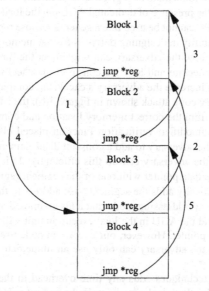

Fig. 12.7. Structure of the checksum code. There are 4 code blocks. Each block is 128 bytes in size. The arrows show one possible sequence of control transfers between the blocks.

As Figure 12.7 shows, we construct the checksum code as a sequence of four code blocks. Each code block generates the absolute address of the entry point of any of the four code blocks using the current value of the checksum as a parameter. Both the code block we are jumping from and the code block we are jumping to incorporate the jump address in the checksum. The last instruction of code block jumps to the absolute address that was generated earlier.

All of the code blocks execute the same set of instructions to update the checksum but have a different ordering of the instructions. Since the checksum function is strongly ordered, the final value of the checksum depends on executing the checksum code blocks in the correct sequence, which is determined by the sequence of jumps between the blocks.

The checksum code blocks are contiguously placed in memory. Each block is 128 bytes in size. The blocks are aligned in memory so that the first instruction of each block is at an address that is a multiple of 128. This simplifies the jump target address generation since the jump targets can be generated by appropriately masking the current value of the checksum.

Memory copy attacks. Memory copy attacks are the most difficult attacks to defend against on the x86 architecture, mainly for of three reasons: 1) the adversary can use segmentation to have the processor automatically add a displacement to the data pointer without incurring a time overhead; 2) the adversary can utilize memory addressing with an immediate or register displacement, without incurring a time overhead because of the presence of dedicated AGUs in the load and the store execution units; and 3) the PC cannot be used like a general purpose register in instructions, which limits our flexibility in designing defenses for the memory copy attacks.

We now describe how the adversary can implement the three memory copy attacks on the x86 architecture and how we construct the checksum code so that the memory copy attacks increase the adversary's checksum computation time.

In the first memory copy attack shown in Figure 3(b), the adversary runs a modified checksum code from the correct memory location and computes the checksum over a copy of the unmodified verification function placed elsewhere in memory. This attack requires the adversary to add a constant displacement to the data pointer. There are two ways the adversary can do this efficiently: 1) it can annotate all instructions that use the data pointer with one of the segment registers, fs or gs, and the processor automatically adds the segment base address to the data pointer, or 2) the adversary can use an addressing mode that adds an immediate or a register value to the data pointer, and the AGU in the load execution unit will add the corresponding value to the data pointer. However, our checksum code uses all sixteen general purpose registers, so the adversary can only use an immediate to displace the data pointer.

Neither of these techniques adds any time overhead to the adversary's checksum computation. Also, both techniques retain the correct value of the data pointer. Thus, this memory copy attack cannot be detected by including the data pointer in the checksum. However, both these techniques increase the instruction length. We leverage this fact in designing our defense against this memory copy attack. The segment register annotation adds one byte to the length of any instruction that accesses memory, whereas addressing with immediate displacement increases the instruction length by the size of the immediate. Thus, in this memory copy attack, the adversary's memory reference instructions increase in length by a minimum of one byte. An instruction that reads memory without a segment register annotation or an immediate displacement is 3 bytes long on the x86 architecture with EM64T extensions. We place an instruction having a memory reference, such as add mem, reg, as the first instruction of each of the four checksum code blocks. In each checksum code block, we construct the jump target address so that, the jump lands with equal probability on either the first instruction of a checksum code block or at an offset of 3 bytes from the start of a code block. In an unmodified code block, the second instruction is at an offset of 3 bytes from the start of the block. When the adversary modifies the code blocks to do a memory copy attack, the second instruction of the block cannot begin before the 4th byte of the block. Thus, 50% of the jumps would land in the middle of the first instruction, causing the processor to generate an illegal opcode exception.

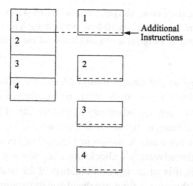

Fig. 12.8. Comparison of the code block lengths in the original verification function and an adversary-modified verification function. The adversary moves its code blocks in memory so that the entry points of its code blocks are at addresses that are a power of two.

To accommodate the longer first instruction, the adversary would move its code blocks farther apart, as Figure 12.8 shows. The adversary can generate its jump target addresses efficiently by aligning its checksum code blocks in memory in the following way. The adversary places its code blocks on 256 byte boundaries and separates its first and second instruction by 8 bytes. Then, the adversary can generate its jump addresses by left-shifting the correct jump address by 1. We incorporate the jump address into the checksum both before and after the jump. So, the adversary has to left-shift the correct jump address by 1 before the jump instruction is executed and restore the correct jump address by right-shifting after the jump is complete. Thus, the adversary's overhead for the first memory copy attack is the execution latency of one left-shift instruction and one right-shift instruction.

In the second memory copy attack shown in Figure 3(c), the adversary keeps the unmodified verification function at the correct memory location, but computes the checksum using a modified checksum code that runs at different memory locations. In this case, the entry points of the adversary's code blocks will be different, so the adversary would have to generate different jump addresses. Since we include the jump addresses in the checksum, the adversary would also have to generate the correct jump addresses. Hence, the adversary's checksum code blocks would be larger than 128 bytes. As before, to accommodate the larger blocks, the adversary would move its code blocks apart and align the entry points at 256 byte boundaries (Figure 12.8). Then, the adversary can generate its jump address by left-shifting the correct jump address and by changing one or more bits in the resulting value using a

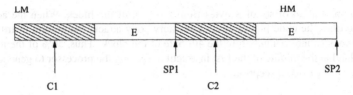

Fig. 12.9. The layout of the stack on an x86 processor with EM64T extensions. Both checksum pieces are 8 bytes long and are aligned on 16-byte boundaries. The empty regions are also 8 bytes long. The stack pointer is assigned at random to one of the two locations SP1 or SP2.

logical operation. To restore the correct jump address, the adversary has to undo the changes either by loading an immediate value or by using a right-shift by 1 and a logical operation. In any case, the adversary's time overhead for this memory copy attack is greater than the time overhead for first memory copy attack.

In the third memory copy attack shown in Figure 3(d), both the unmodified verification function and the adversary's checksum code are not present at the correct memory locations. Thus, this attack is a combination of the first and the second memory copy attacks. The adversary's time overhead for this memory copy attack is the same as the time overhead for the second memory copy attack.

Variable instruction length. The x86 Instruction Set Architecture (ISA) supports variable length instructions. Hence, the adversary can reduce the size of the checksum code blocks by replacing one or more instructions with shorter variants that implement the same operation with the same or shorter latency. The adversary can use the space saved in this manner to implement the memory copy attacks without its code block size exceeding 128 bytes. To prevent this attack, we carefully select the instructions used in the checksum code blocks so that they are the smallest instructions able to perform a given operation with minimum latency.

Execution environment for untampered code execution. In order to get the guarantee of execution at the highest privilege level with maskable interrupts turned off, the checksum code incorporates the CPU flags in the checksum. The flags register on the x86 architecture, `rflags`, can only be accessed if it is pushed onto the stack. Since we use to the stack to hold a part of the checksum, we need to ensure that pushing the `rflags` onto the stack does not overwrite the part of the checksum that is on the stack. Also, a processor with EM64T extensions always pushes the processor state starting at a 16-byte boundary on receiving interrupts or exceptions. Thus, we need to make sure that the checksum pieces on the stack are aligned on 16-byte boundaries so they will be overwritten when an interrupt or exception occurs.

Figure 12.9 shows the stack layout we use for x86 processors with EM64T extensions. Our stack layout has checksum pieces alternating with empty slots. All four elements are eight bytes in size. The checksum code moves the stack pointer so that the stack pointer points either to location SP1 or to location SP2. On the x86 architecture, the stack grows downwards from high addresses to low addresses. To push an item onto the stack, the processor first decrements the stack pointer and then writes the item to the memory location pointed to by the stack pointer. With EM64T extensions, pushes and pops normally operate on 8-byte data. Since the stack pointer is always initialized to either SP1 or to SP2, a push of the rflags register will always write the flags to one of the empty 8-byte regions. If an interrupt or exception were to occur, the processor would push 40 bytes of data onto the stack, thereby overwriting either checksum piece 1 or both checksum pieces.

We keep checksum pieces on the stack to prevent the adversary from getting control through an exception or a non-maskable interrupt. However, the x86 architecture has a special non-maskable interrupt called System Management Interrupt (SMI), which switches the processor into the System Management Mode (SMM). The purpose of SMM is to fix chipset bugs and for hardware control.

The SMI does not save the processor state on the stack. So, it is not possible to prevent the SMI by keeping checksum pieces on the stack. Since the SMI is a special-purpose interrupt, we assume that it never occurs when the verification function runs. During our experiments, we found this assumption to be true all the time. In Section 12.5.4, we discuss how we can extend the current implementation of Pioneer to handle the SMI.

Description of verification function code. Figure 12.10 shows the pseudocode of one code block of the verification function. The block performs six actions: 1) deriving the next pseudo-random value from the T-function; 2) generating the jump address, the stack pointer, and the data pointer using the current value of the checksum, 3) pushing rflags onto the stack, 4) reading a memory location containing the verification function, 5) updating the checksum using the memory read value, previous value of the checksum, the output of the T-function, the rflags register, and the jump address, and 6) rotating the checksum using the rotate instruction.

The checksum is made up of twelve 64-bit pieces, ten in the registers and two on the stack. The checksum code uses all sixteen general purpose registers.

Figure 12.11 shows the assembler code of one block of the verification function. The code shown is not the optimized version but a verbose version to aid readability.

12.5.3 Experiments and Results

Any attack that the adversary uses has to be combined with a memory copy attack because the adversary's checksum code will be different from the correct checksum code. Hence, the memory copy attack is the attack with the lowest overhead. Of the three memory copy attacks, the first has the lowest time overhead for the adversary. Hence, we implemented two versions of the checksum code using x86 assembly: a legitimate version and a malicious version that implements the first memory copy attack (the correct code plus two extra shift instructions).

Experimental setup. The dispatcher is a PC with a 2.2 GHz Intel Pentium IV processor and a 3Com 3c905C network card, running Linux kernel version 2.6.11-8. The untrusted platform is a PC with a 2.8 GHz Intel Pentium IV Xeon processor with EM64T extensions and an Intel 82545GM Gigabit Ethernet Controller, running

```
//Input: y number of iterations of the verification procedure
//Output: Checksum C, (10 segments in registers C₀ to C₉,
//         and 2 on stack C_stk₁, C_stk₂, each being 64 bits)
//Variables: [code_start, code_end] - bounds of memory address under verification
//          daddr - address of current memory access
//          x - value of T function
//          l - counter of iterations
//          rflags - flags register
//          jump_target[1 : 0] - determines which code block to execute
//          temp - temp register used to compute checksum
daddr ← code_start
for l = y to 0 do
  Checksum 1
    //T function updates x where 0 ≤ x ≤ 2ⁿ
    x ← x + (x² ∨ 5) mod 2ⁿ
    //Read rflags and incorporate into daddr
    daddr ← daddr + rflags
    //Read from memory address daddr, calculate checksum.Let C be the checksum vector and j be the current
    index.
    jump_target ← not(jump_target) + loop_ctr ⊕ x
    temp ← x ⊕ C_{j−1} + daddr ⊕ C_j
    if jump_target[1] == 0 and jump_target[0] == 0 then
      C_j ← C_j + mem[daddr + 8] + jump_target
    else
      C_j ← C_j + jump_target
    end if
    C_{j−1} ← C_{j−1} + temp
    C_stk ← C_stk ⊕ jump_target
    C_{j−2} ← C_{j−2} + C_j
    C_{j−3} ← C_{j−3} + C_{j−1}
    C_j ← rotate_right(C_j)
    //Update daddr to perform pseudo-random memory traversal
    daddr ← daddr + x
    //Update rsp and jump_target
    rsp[1] ← C_j[1]
    j ← (j + 1)  mod 11
    jump_target[8 : 7] ← C_j[8 : 7]
    jump_target[1 : 0] ← temp[0], temp[0]
    if jump_target[8 : 7] = 0 then
      goto Checksum 1
    else if jump_target[8 : 7] = 1 then
      goto Checksum 2
    else if jump_target[8 : 7] = 2 then
      goto Checksum 3
    else if jump_target[8 : 7] = 3 then
      goto Checksum 4
    end if
  Checksum 2
  ...
  Checksum 3
  ...
  Checksum 4
  ...
end for
```

Fig. 12.10. Verification Function Pseudocode

Assembly Instruction	Explanation
//Read memory	
add (rbx), r15	*memory read*
sub 1, ecx	decrement loop counter
add rdi, rax	$x \leftarrow (x * x) \ OR \ 5 + x$
//modifies jump_target register rdx *and* rdi	
xor r14, rdi	$rdi \leftarrow rdi \oplus C_{j-1}$
add rcx, rdx	$rdx \leftarrow rdx + loopctr$
add rbx, rdi	$rdi \leftarrow rdi + daddr$
xor rax, rdx	*input x (from T function)*
xor r15, rdi	$rdi \leftarrow rdi \oplus c_j$
//modifies checksum with rdx *and* rdi	
add rdx, r15	*modify checksum C_j*
add rdi, r14	*modify checksum C_{j-1}*
xor rdx, -8(rsp)	*modify checksum on stack*
xor r15, r13	$C_{j-2} \leftarrow C_{j-2} \oplus C_j$
add r14, r12	$C_{j-3} \leftarrow C_{j-3} + C_{j-1}$
rol r15	$r15 \leftarrow rotate[r15]$
//Pseudorandom memory access	
xor rdi, rbx	$daddr \leftarrow daddr \oplus random_bits$
and mask1, ebx	*modify daddr*
or mask2, rbx	*modify daddr*
//Modify stack pointer and target jump address	
xor rdx, rsp	*Modify rsp*
and mask3, esp	*create rsp*
or mask4, rsp	*create rsp*
and 0x180, edx	*jump_target $\leftarrow$ r15*
and 0x1, rdi	$rdi \leftarrow rdi \ AND \ 0x1$
add rdi, rdx	$rdx \leftarrow rdx + rdi$
add rdi, rdi	*shift rdi*
add rdi, rdx	$rdx \leftarrow rdx + rdi$
or mask, rdx	*create jump_target address*
xor rdx, r15	*add jump target address into checksum*
//T function updates x, at rax	
mov rax, rdi	*save value of T function*
imul rax, rax	x = x*x
or 0x5, rax	$x \leftarrow x * x \ OR \ 5$
//Read flags	
pushfq	*push rflags*
add (rsp), rbx	$daddr \leftarrow daddr + rflags$
jmp *rdx	*jump to 1 of the 4 blocks*

Fig. 12.11. Checksum Assembly Code

Linux kernel version 2.6.7. The dispatcher code and the verification function are implemented inside the respective network card interrupt handlers. Implementing code inside the network card interrupt handler enables both the dispatcher and the untrusted platform to receive the Pioneer packets as early as possible. The dispatcher and the untrusted platform are on the same LAN segment.

Empty instruction issue slots. In Section 12.4.1, we mentioned that the checksum code instruction sequence has to be carefully arranged to eliminate empty instruction issue slots. The Netburst Microarchitecture issues μops, which are derived from decoding x86 instructions. Hence, to properly sequence the instructions, we need to know what μops are generated by the instructions we use in the checksum code. This information is not publically available. In the absence of this information, we try to sequence the instructions through trial-and-error. To detect the presence of empty instruction issue slots we place no-op instructions at different places in the code. If there are no empty instruction issue slots, placing no-op instructions should always increase the execution time of the checksum code. We found this assertion to be only partially true in our experiments. There are places in our code where no-op instructions can be placed without increasing the execution time, indicating the presence of empty instruction issue slots.

Determining number of verification function iterations. The adversary can try to minimize the Network Round-Trip Time (RTT) between the untrusted platform and dispatcher. Also, the adversary can pre-load its checksum code and the verification function into the CPU's L1 instruction and data caches respectively to ensure that it does not suffer any cache misses during execution. We prevent the adversary from using the time gained by these two methods to forge the checksum.

The theoretically best adversary has zero RTT and no cache misses, which is a constant gain over the execution time of the correct checksum code. We call this constant time gain as the *adversary time advantage*. However, the time overhead of the adversary's checksum code increases linearly with the number of iterations of the checksum loop. Thus, the dispatcher can ask the untrusted platform to perform a sufficient number of iterations so that the adversary's time overhead is at least greater than the adversary time advantage.

The expression for the number of iterations of the checksum loop to be performed by the untrusted platform can be derived as follows. Let c be the clock speed of the CPU, a be the time advantage of the theoretically best adversary, o be the adversary's overhead per iteration of the checksum loop represented in CPU cycles, and n is the number of iterations. Then $n > \frac{c*a}{o}$ to prevent false negatives[5] in the case of the theoretically best adversary.

Experimental results. To calculate the time advantage of the theoretically best adversary, we need to know the upper bound on the RTT and the time saved by pre-warming the caches. We determine the RTT upper bound by observing the ping latency for different hosts on our LAN segment. This gives us an RTT upper bound

---

[5] A false negative occurs when Pioneer claims that the untrusted platform is uncompromised when the untrusted platform is actually compromised.

of 0.25 ms since all ping latencies are smaller than this value. Also, we calculate the amount of time that cache pre-warming saves the adversary by running the checksum code with and without pre-warming the caches and observing the running times using the CPU's rdtsc instruction. The upper bound on the cache pre-warming time is 0.0016 ms. Therefore, for our experiments we fix the theoretically best adversary's time advantage to be 0.2516 ms. The attack that has the least time overhead is the first memory copy attack, which has an overhead of 0.6 CPU cycles per iteration of the checksum loop. The untrusted platform has a 2.8 GHz CPU. Using these values, we determine the required number of checksum loop iterations to be 1,250,000. To prevent false positives due to RTT variations, we double the number of iterations to 2,500,000.

The dispatcher knows, r, the time taken by the correct checksum code to carry out 2,500,000 iterations. It also knows that the upper bound on the RTT, rtt. Therefore, the dispatcher considers any checksum result that is received after time $r + rtt$ to be late. This threshold is the *adversary detection threshold*.

We place the dispatcher at two different physical locations on our LAN segment. We run our experiments for 2 hours at each location. Every 2 minutes, the dispatcher sends a challenge to the untrusted platform. The untrusted platform returns a checksum computed using the correct checksum code. On receiving the response, the dispatcher sends another challenge. The untrusted platform returns a checksum computed using the adversary's checksum code, in response to this challenge. Both the dispatcher and the untrusted platform measure the time taken to compute the two checksums using the CPU's rdtsc instruction. The time measured on the untrusted platform for the adversary's checksum computation is the checksum computation time of the theoretically best adversary.

Figures 12.12 and 12.13 show the results of our experiments at the two physical locations on the LAN segment. Based on the results, we observe the following points: 1) even the running time of the theoretically best adversary is greater than the Adversary Detection Threshold, yielding a false negative rate of 0%; 2) the checksum computation time shows a very low variance, that we have a fairly deterministic runtime; 3) we observe some false positives (5 out of 60) at location 2, which we can avoid by better estimating the RTT.

We suggest two methods for RTT estimation. First, the dispatcher measures the RTT to the untrusted platform just before it sends the challenge and assumes that the RTT will not significantly increase in the few tens of milliseconds between the time it measures the RTT and the time it receives the checksum packet from the untrusted platform. Second, the dispatcher can take RTT measurements at coarser time granularity, say every few seconds, and use these measurements to update its current value of the RTT.

12.5.4 Discussion

We now discuss virtual-memory-based attacks, issues concerning the practical deployment of Pioneer, and potential extensions to the current implementation of Pioneer to achieve better properties.

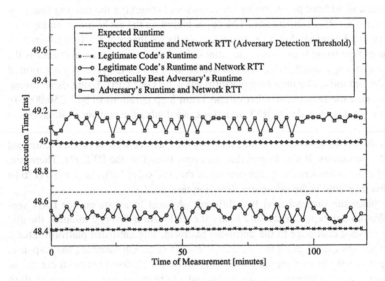

Fig. 12.12. Results from Location 1.

Implementing the verification function as SMM module. The System Management Mode (SMM) is a special operating mode present on all x86 CPUs. Code running in the SMM mode runs at the highest CPU privilege level. The execution environment provided by SMM has the following properties that are useful for implementing Pioneer: 1) all interrupts, including the Non-Maskable Interrupt (NMI) and the System Management Interrupt (SMI), and all exceptions are disabled by the processor, 2) paging and virtual memory are disabled in SMM, which precludes virtual-memory-based attacks, and 3) real-mode style segmentation is used, making it easier to defend against the segmentation-based memory copy attack.

Virtual-memory-based attacks. There are two ways in which the adversary might use virtual memory to attack the verification function: 1) the adversary could create memory protection exceptions by manipulating the page table entries and obtain control through the exception handler, or 2) the adversary could perform a memory copy attack by loading the instruction and data Translation Lookaside Buffer (TLB) entries that correspond to the same virtual address with different physical addresses. Since we use the stack to hold checksum pieces during checksum computation and later replace the exception handlers, the adversary cannot use memory protection exceptions to gain control.

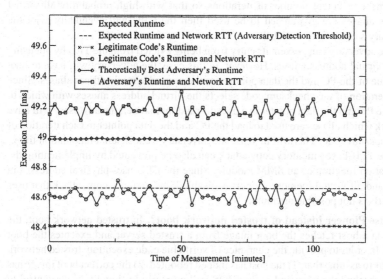

Fig. 12.13. Result from Location 2.

The adversary can, however, use the CPU TLBs to perform a memory copy attack. Wurster et al. discuss how the second attack can be implemented on the Ultra-Sparc processor [28]. Their attack can be adapted to the Intel x86 architecture in the context of Pioneer as follows: 1) the adversary loads the page table entry corresponding to the virtual address of the verification function with the address of the physical page where the adversary keeps an unmodified copy of the verification function, 2) the adversary does data accesses to virtual addresses of the verification function, thereby loading the its mapping into the CPU's D-TLB, and 3) the adversary replaces the page table entry corresponding to the virtual address of the verification function with the address of the physical page where the adversary keeps the modified checksum code is kept. When the CPU starts to execute the adversary's checksum code, it will load its I-TLB entry with the mapping the adversary set up in step 3. Thus, the CPU's I-TLB and D-TLB will have different physical addresses corresponding to the same virtual address and the adversary will be able to perform the memory copy attack.

The current implementation of Pioneer does not defend against this memory copy attack. However, a promising idea to defend against the attack is as follows. We create virtual address aliases to the physical pages contaning the verification function so that the number of aliases is greater than the number of entries in the CPU's TLB.

Each iteration of the checksum code loads the PC and the data pointer with two of the virtual address aliases, selected in a pseudo-random manner. If the checksum loop performs a sufficient number of iterations so that with high probability all virtual address aliases are guaranteed to be used then the CPU will eventually evict the adversary's entry from the TLB.

The adversary can prevent its entry from being evicted from the TLB by not using all the virtual address aliases. However, in this case, the adversary will have to fake the value of the PC and the data pointer for the unused virtual address aliases. Since each iteration of the checksum code selects the virtual address aliases with which to load the PC and the data pointer in a pseudo-random manner, the adversary will have to check which aliases are used to load the PC and the data pointer in each iteration of the checksum code. This will increase the adversary's checksum computation time.

The TLB-based memory copy attack can also be prevented by implementing the verification function as an SMM module. Since the CPU uses physical addresses in SMM and all virtual memory support is disabled, the memory copy attack that uses the TLBs is not possible anymore.

Why use Pioneer instead of trusted network boot?. In trusted network boot, the BIOS on a host fetches the boot image from a trusted server and executes the boot image. In order to provide the guarantee of verifiable code execution, trusted network boot has to assume that: 1) the host has indeed rebooted; 2) the correct boot image has indeed reached the host; and 3) the BIOS will correctly load and transfer control to the boot image. To guarantee that the BIOS cannot be modified by the adversary, the BIOS will have to stored on an immutable storage medium like Read-Only Memory (ROM). This makes it impossible to update the BIOS without physically replacing the ROM, should any vulnerability be discovered in the BIOS code.

Pioneer does not require any code to reside in immutable storage media, thereby making it easy to update. Also, Pioneer provides the property of verifiable code execution without having to reboot the untrusted platform, without having to transfer code over the network and without relying on any unverified software on the untrusted platform to transfer control to the executable.

MMX and SSE instructions. x86 processors provide support for Single Instruction Multiple Data (SIMD) instructions in the form of MMX and SSE technologies [11]. These instructions can simultaneously perform the same operation on multiple data items. This is faster than operating on the data items one at a time. However, the adversary cannot use the MMX or SSE instructions to speed up its checksum code, since we design the checksum code to be non-parallelizable.

Pioneer and TCG. A promising approach for reducing exposure to network RTT and for achieving a trusted channel to the untrusted platform is to leverage a Trusted Platform Module (TPM). The TPM could issue the challenge and time the execution of the checksum code and return the signed result and computation time to the dispatcher. However, this would require that the TPM be an active device, whereas the current generation of TPMs are passive.

Directly computing checksum over the executable. Why do we need a hash function? Why can the checksum code not simply compute the checksum over the executable? While this simpler approach may work in most cases, an adversary could exploit redundancy in the memory image of the executable to perform data-dependent optimizations. A simple example is a executable image that contains a large area initialized to zeros, which allows the adversary to suppress memory reads to that region and also to suppress updating the checksum with the memory value read (in case of add or xor operations).

skinit and senter. AMD's Pacifica technology has an instruction called skinit, which can verifiably transfer control to an executable after measuring it [2]. Intel's LaGrande Technology (LT) has a similar instruction, senter [10]. Both senter and skinit also set up an execution environment in which the executable that is invoked is guaranteed to execute untampered. These instructions can be used to start-up a Virtual Machine Monitor (VMM) or a Secure Kernel (SK). Both instructions rely on the TCG load-time attestation property to guarantee that the SK or the VMM is uncompromised at start-up. Unlike Pioneer, however, neither Pacifica nor LT can be used on legacy computing systems.

Implementing Pioneer on other architectures. We use the x86 architecture as our implementation platform example for the following reasons: 1) since x86 is the most widely deployed architecture today, our implementation of Pioneer on x86 can immediately be used on many legacy systems; and 2) due to requirements of backward compatibility, the x86 is a complex architecture, with a non-orthogonal ISA. Therefore, implementing Pioneer on the x86 architecture is more challenging than implementing it on RISC architectures with more orthogonal instruction sets, such as the MIPS, and the Alpha.

Verifying the timing overhead. Pioneer relies on the execution time of the checksum code. Therefore, the dispatcher has to know ahead of time what the correct checksum computation time should be for the untrusted platform. The checksum computation time depends on the CPU of the untrusted platform. There are two ways by which the dispatcher can find out the correct checksum computation time: 1) if the dispatcher has access to a trusted platform having the same CPU as the untrusted platform, or a CPU simulator for the untrusted platform, it can run experiments to get the correct execution time; or 2) we can publish the correct execution time for different CPUs on a trusted web-site.

12.6 Applications

In this section, we first discuss the types of applications that can leverage Pioneer to achieve security, given the assumptions we make. Then, we describe the kernel rootkit detector, the sample application we have built using Pioneer.

12.6.1 Potential Security Applications

Pioneer can be applied to build security applications that run over networks controlled by a single administrative entity. On such networks, the network administrator could configure the network switches so that an untrusted host can only communicate with the dispatcher during the execution of Pioneer. This provides the property of message-origin-authentication while eliminating proxy attacks. Examples of networks that can be configured in this manner are corporate networks and cluster computing environments. On these networks the network administrator often needs to perform security-critical administrative tasks on untrusted hosts, such as installing security patches or detecting malware like viruses and rootkits. For such applications, the administrator has to obtain the guarantee that the tasks are executed correctly, even in the presence of malicious code on the untrusted host. This guarantee can be obtained through Pioneer.

As an example of how Pioneer could be used, we briefly discuss secure code updates. To verifiably install a code update, we can invoke the program that installs the code update using Pioneer. Pioneer can also be used to measure software on an untrusted host after a update to check if the code update has been successfully installed.

12.6.2 Kernel Rootkit Detection

In this section, we describe how we build a kernel rootkit detector using Pioneer. Our kernel rootkit detector allows a trusted verifier to detect kernel rootkits that may be installed on an external untrusted host without relying on signatures of specific rootkits or on low-level file system scans. Sailer et al. propose to use the load-time attestation guarantees provided by a TPM to detect rootkits when the kernel boots [18]. However, their technique cannot detect rootkits that do not make changes to the disk image of the kernel but only infect the in-memory image. Such rootkits do not survive reboots. Our rootkit detector is capable of detecting both kinds of rootkits. The only rootkit detection technique we are aware of that achieves similar properties to ours is Copilot [17]. However, unlike our rootkit detector, Copilot requires additional hardware in the form of an add-in PCI card to achieve its guarantees. Hence, it cannot be used on systems that do not have this PCI card installed. Also, our rootkit detector runs on the CPU of the untrusted host, making it immune to the dummy kernel attack that we describe in Section 12.7 in the context of Copilot.

Rootkits primer. Rootkits are software installed by an intruder on a host that allow the intruder to gain privileged access to that host, while remaining undetected [17, 29]. Rootkits can be classified into two categories: those that modify the OS kernel, and those that do not. Of the two, the second category of rootkits can be easily detected. These rootkits typically modify system binaries (e.g., ls, ps, and netstat) to hide the intruder's files, processes, network connections, etc. These rootkits can be detected by a kernel that checks the integrity of the system binaries against known good copies, e.g., by computing checksums. There are also tools like Tripwire that can be used to check the integrity of binaries [23]. These tools are invoked from read-only or write-protected media so that the tools do not get compromised.

As kernel rootkits subvert the kernel, we can no longer trust the kernel to detect such rootkits. Therefore, Copilot uses special trusted hardware (a PCI add-on card) to detect kernel rootkits. All rootkit detectors other than Copilot, including AskStrider [26], Carbonite [12] and St. Michael [7], rely on the integrity of one or more parts of the kernel. A sophisticated attacker can circumvent detection by compromising the integrity of the rootkit detector. Recently Wang et al. proposed a method to detect stealth software that try to hide files [27]. Their approach does not rely on the integrity of the kernel; however, it only applies when the stealth software makes modifications to the file system.

Implementation. We implement our rootkit detector on the x86_64 version of the Linux kernel that is part of the Fedora Core 3 Linux distribution. The x86_64 version of the Linux kernel reserves the range of virtual address space above 0xffff800000000000. The code segment of the kernel starts at virtual address 0xffffffff80100000. The kernel text segment contains immutable binary code which remains static throughout its lifetime. Loadable Kernel Modules (LKM) occupy virtual addresses from 0xffffffff88000000 to 0xffffff-fffff00000.

We build our kernel rootkit detector using a Kernel Measurement Agent (KMA). The KMA hashes the kernel image and sends the hash values to the verifier. The verifier uses Pioneer to obtain the guarantee of verifiable code execution of the KMA. Hence, the verifier knows that the hash values it receives from the untrusted host were computed correctly.

The KMA runs on the CPU at the kernel privilege level, i.e., CPL0; hence, it has access to all the kernel resources (e.g., page tables, interrupt descriptor tables, jump tables, etc.), and the processor state, and can execute privileged instructions. The KMA obtains the virtual address ranges of the kernel over which to compute the hashes by reading the *System.map* file. The following symbols are of interest to the KMA: 1) _text and _etext, which indicate the start and the end of the kernel code segment; 2) sys_call_table which is the kernel system call table; and 3) module_list which is a pointer to the linked list of all loadable kernel modules (LKM) currently linked into the kernel. When the Kernel Measurement Agent (KMA) is invoked, it performs the following steps:

1. The KMA hashes the kernel code segment between _text and _etext.
2. The KMA reads kernel version information to check which LKMs have been loaded and hashes all the LKM code.
3. The KMA checks that the function pointers in the system call table only refer to the kernel code segment or to the LKM code. The KMA also verifies that the return address on the stack points back to the kernel/LKM code segment. The return address is the point in the kernel to which control returns after the KMA exits.
4. The KMA returns the following to the verifier: 1) the hash of the kernel code segment; 2) the kernel version information and a list indicating which kernel

modules have been loaded; 3) the hash of all the LKM code; 4) a success/failure indicator stating whether the function pointer check has succeeded.

5. The KMA flushes processor caches, restores the register values, and finally returns to the kernel. The register values and the return address were saved on the stack when the kernel called invoked the Pioneer verification function.

We now explain how the verifier verifies the hash values returned by the untrusted platform. First, because the kernel text is immutable, it suffices for the verifier to compare the hash value of the kernel code segment to the known good hash value for the corresponding kernel version. However, the different hosts may have different LKMs installed, and so the hash value of the LKM code can vary. Therefore, the verifier needs to recompute the hash of the LKM text on the fly according to the list of installed modules reported by the KMA. The hash value reported by the KMA is then compared with the one computed by the verifier.

Experimental results. We implemented our rootkit detector on the Fedora Core 2 Linux distribution, using SHA-1 as the hash function. The rootkit detector ran every 5 seconds and successfully detected adore-ng-0.53, the only publically-known rootkit for the 2.6 version of the Linux kernel.

Table 12.1. Overhead of the Pioneer-based rootkit detector

	Standalone (s)	Rootkit Detect (s)	% Overhead
PostMark	52	52.99	1.9
Bunzip2	21.396	21.713	1.5
Copy Directory	373	385	3.2

We monitor the performance overhead of running our rootkit detector in the background. We use three representative tasks for measurements: PostMark, bunzip2, and copying the entire contents of a directory. The first task, PostMark [3], is a file system benchmark that carries out transactions on small files. As a result, PostMark is a combination of I/O intensive and computationally intensive tasks. We used bunzip2 to to uncompress the Firefox source code, which is a computationally intensive task. Finally, we modeled an I/O intensive task by copying the entire /usr/src/linux directory, which totaled to 1.33 GB, from one harddrive to another. As the table above shows, all three tasks perform reasonably well in the presence of our rootkit detector.

Discussion. As with Copilot, one limitation of our approach is that we do not verify the integrity of data segments or CPU register values. Therefore, the following types of attacks are still possible: 1) attacks that do not modify code segments but rely merely on the injection of malicious data; 2) if the kernel code contains jump/branch instructions whose target address is not read in from the verified jump tables, the jump/branch instructions may jump to some unverified address that contains malicious code. For instance, if the jump address is read from an unverified data segment, we cannot guarantee that the jump will only reach addresses that have been verified.

Also, if jump/branch target addresses are stored temporarily in the general purpose registers, it is possible to jump to an unverified code segment, after the KMA returns to the kernel since the KMA restores the CPU register values. In conclusion, Pioneer limits a kernel rootkit to be placed solely in mutable data segments; it requires any pointer to the rootkit to reside in a mutable data segment as well. These properties are similar to what Copilot achieves.

Our rootkit detection scheme does not provide backward security. A malicious kernel can uninstall itself when it receives a Pioneer challenge, and our Pioneer-based rootkit detector cannot detect bad past events. Backward security can be achieved if we combine our approach with schemes that backtrack intrusions through analyzing system event logs [15].

12.7 Related Work

In this section, we survey related work that addresses the verifiable code execution problem. We also describe the different methods of code attestation proposed in the literature and discuss how the software-based code attestation provided by Pioneer is different from other code attestation techniques.

12.7.1 Verifiable Code Execution

Two techniques, Cerium [6] and BIND [21], have been proposed. These use hardware extensions to the execution platform to provide a remote host with the guarantee of verifiable code execution. Cerium relies on a physically tamper-resistant CPU with an embedded public-private key pair and a μ-kernel that runs from the CPU cache. BIND requires that the execution platform has a TPM chip and CPU architectural enhancements similar to those found in Intel's LaGrande Technology (LT) [10] or AMD's Secure Execution Mode (SEM) [1] and Pacifica technology [2]. Unlike Pioneer, neither Cerium nor BIND can be used on legacy computing platforms. As far as we are aware, Pioneer is the only technique that attempts to provide the verifiable code execution property solely through software techniques.

12.7.2 Code Attestation

Code attestation can be broadly classified into hardware-based and software-based approaches. While the proposed hardware-based attestation techniques work on general purpose computing systems, to the best of our knowledge, there exists no software-based attestation technique for general purpose computing platforms.

Hardware-based code attestation. Sailer et al. describe a load-time attestation technique that relies on the TPM chip standardized by the Trusted Computing Group [18]. Their technique allows a remote verifier to verify what software was loaded into the memory of a platform. However, a malicious peripheral could overwrite code that was just loaded into memory with a DMA-write, thereby breaking the load-time attestation guarantee. Also, as we discussed in Section 12.1, the load-time attestation property provided by the TCG standard is no longer secure since the collision resistance property of SHA-1 has been compromised. Terra uses a Trusted Virtual Machine Monitor (TVMM) to partition a tamper-resistant hardware platform in multiple virtual machines (VM) that are isolated from each other [9]. CPU-based virtualization and protection are used to isolate the TVMM from the VMs and the VMs from each other. Although the authors only discuss load-time attestation using a TPM, Terra is capable of performing run-time attestation on the software stack of any of the VMs by asking the TVMM to take integrity measurements at any time. All the properties provided by Terra are based on the assumption that the TVMM is uncompromised when it is started and that it cannot be compromised subsequently. Terra uses the load-time attestation property provided by TCG to guarantee that the TVMM is uncompromised at start-up. Since this property of TCG is compromised, none of the properties of Terra hold. Even if TCG were capable of providing the load-time attestation property, the TVMM could be compromised at run-time if there are vulnerabilities in its code. In Copilot, Petroni et al. use an add-in card connected to the PCI bus to perform periodic integrity measurements of the in-memory Linux kernel image [17]. These measurements are sent to the trusted verifier through a dedicated side channel. The verifier uses the measurements to detect unauthorized modifications to the kernel memory image. The Copilot PCI card cannot access CPU-based state such as the pointer to the page table and pointers to interrupt and exception handlers. Without access to such CPU state, it is impossible for the PCI card to determine exactly what resides in the memory region that the card measures. The adversary can exploit this lack of knowledge to hide malicious code from the PCI card. For instance, the PCI card assumes that the Linux kernel code begins at virtual address 0xc0000000, since it does not have access to the CPU register that holds the pointer to the page tables. While this assumption is generally true on 32-bit systems based on the Intel x86 processor, the adversary can place a correct kernel image starting at address 0xc0000000 while in fact running a malicious kernel from another memory location. The authors of Copilot were aware of this attack [4]. It is not possible to prevent this attack without access to the CPU state. The kernel rootkit detector we build using Pioneer is able to provide properties equivalent to Copilot without the need for additional hardware. Further, because our rootkit detector has access to the CPU state, it can determine exactly which memory locations contain the kernel code and static data. This ensures that our rootkit detector measures the running kernel and not a correct copy masquerading as a running kernel. Also, if the host running Copilot has an IOMMU, the adversary can re-map the addresses to perform a data substitution attack. When the PCI card tries to read a location in the kernel, the IOMMU automatically redirects the read to a location where the adversary has stored the correct copy.

Software-based attestation. Genuinity is a technique proposed by Kennell and Jamieson that explores the problem of detecting the difference between a simulator-based computer system and an actual computer system [14]. Genuinity relies on the premise that simulator-based program execution is bound to be slower because a simulator has to simulate the CPU architectural state in software, in addition to simulating the program execution. A special checksum function computes a checksum over memory, while incorporating different elements of the architectural state into the checksum. By the above premise, the checksum function should run slower in a simulator than on an actual CPU. While this statement is probably true when the simulator runs on an architecturally different CPU than the one it is simulating, an adversary having an architecturally similar CPU can compute the Genuinity checksum within the alloted time while maintaining all the necessary architectural state in software. As an example, in their implementation on the x86, Kennell and Jamieson propose to use special registers, called Model Specific Registers (MSR), that hold various pieces of the architectural state like the cache and TLB miss count. The MSRs can only be read and written using the special rdmsr and wrmsr instructions. We found that these instructions have a long latency ($\approx$ 300 cycles). An adversary that has an x86 CPU could simulate the MSRs in software and still compute the Genuinity checksum within the alloted time, even if the CPU has a lower clock speed than what the adversary claims. Also, Shankar et al. show weaknesses in the Genuinity approach [20]. SWATT is a technique proposed by Seshadri et al. that performs attestation on embedded devices with simple CPU architectures using a software verification function [19]. Similar to Pioneer, the verification function is constructed so that any attempt to tamper with it will increase its running time. However, SWATT cannot be used in systems with complex CPUs. Also, since SWATT checks the entire memory, its running time becomes prohibitive on systems with large memories.

12.8 Conclusions and Future Work

We present Pioneer, which is a first step towards addressing the problem of verifiable code execution on untrusted legacy computing platforms. The current version of Pioneer leaves open research problems. We need to: 1) deriving a formal proof of the optimality of the checksum code implementation; 2) proving that an adversary cannot use mathematical methods to generate a shorter checksum function that generates the same checksum output when fed with the same input; 3) deriving a checksum function that is largely CPU architecture independent, so that it can be easily ported to different CPU architectures; and 4) increasing the time overhead for different attacks, so that it is harder for an adversary to forge the correct checksum within the expected time. There are also low-level attacks that need to be addressed: 1) the adversary could overclock the processor, making it run faster; 2) malicious peripherals, a malicious CPU in a multi-processor system or a DMA-based write could overwrite the executable code image in memory after it is checked but before it is invoked; and 3) dynamic processor clocking techniques could lead to false positives. We plan to address these open research problems in our future work.

There are also two known issues with the current version of Pioneer: 1) On the x86 architecture with 64-bit extensions, any interrupt and exception handler can be set up to have a dedicated stack. The CPU will unconditionally switch to this stack when it calls the corresponding interrupt or exception handler. This feature can be used to defeat the stack trick used by Pioneer, thereby allowing the attacker to tamper with the execution of the executable by generating an exception. 2) The attacker can run the Pioneer verification function in user space with interrupts turned off while running a malicious operating system kernel in kernel space. The malicious kernel could obtain control through an exception after the checksum code returns the checksum to the verifier. We will address these issues in our future work.

This chapter shows an implementation of Pioneer on an Intel Pentium IV Xeon processor based on the Netburst Microarchitecture. The architectural complexity of Netburst Microarchitecture and the complexity of the x86_64 instruction set architecture make it challenging to design a checksum code that executes slower when the adversary tampers with it in any manner. We design a checksum code that exhausts the issue bandwidth of the Netburst microarchitecture, so that any additional instructions the adversary inserts will require extra cycles to execute.

Pioneer can be used as a new basic building block to build security applications. We have demonstrated one such application, the kernel rootkit detector, and we propose other potential applications. We hope these examples motivate other researchers to embrace Pioneer, extend it, and apply it towards building secure systems.

12.9 Acknowledgments

We gratefully acknowledge support and feedback of, and fruitful discussions with William Arbaugh, Mike Burrows, George Cox, David Durham, David Grawrock, Jon Howell, John Richardson, Dave Riss, Carlos Rozas, Stefan Savage, Emin Gün Sirer, Dawn Song, Jesse Walker, Yi-Min Wang. We would like to thank the anonymous reviewers who reviewed the conference version of this chapter for their helpful comments and suggestions. We also thank Elaine Shi for her help with writing an earlier version of this work.

References

1. * * *. AMD platform for trustworthy computing. In *WinHEC*, Sept. 2003.
2. * * *. *Secure Virtual Machine Architecture Reference Manual*. AMD Corp., May 2005.
3. N. Appliance. Postmark: A new file system benchmark. Available at http://www.netapp.com/techlibrary/3022.html, 2004.
4. W. Arbaugh. Personal communication, May 2005.
5. D. Boggs, A. Baktha, J. Hawkins, D. Marr, J. Miller, P. Roussel, R. Singhal, B. Toll, and K. Venkatraman. The microarchitecture of the Intel Pentium 4 processor on 90nm technology. *Intel Technology Journal*, 8(01), Feb. 2004.
6. B. Chen and R. Morris. Certifying program execution with secure procesors. In *Proceedings of HotOS IX*, 2003.
7. A. Chuvakin. Ups and downs of unix/linux host-based security solutions. *;login: The Magazine of USENIX and SAGE*, 28(2), Apr. 2003.

8. F. S. Foundation. superopt - finds the shortest instruction sequence for a given function. http://www.gnu.org/directory/devel/compilers/superopt.html.

9. T. Garfinkel, B. Pfaff, J. Chow, M. Rosenblum, and D. Boneh. Terra: A virtual machine-based platform for trusted computing. In *In Proceedings of ACM Symposium on Operating Systems Principles (SOSP)*, 2003.

10. Intel Corp. *LaGrande Technology Architectural Overview*, September 2003.

11. Intel Corporation. *IA32 Intel Architecture Software Developer's Manual Vol.1*.

12. K. J. Jones. Loadable Kernel Modules. *;login: The Magazine of USENIX and SAGE*, 26(7), Nov. 2001.

13. R. Joshi, G. Nelson, and K. Randall. Denali: a goal-directed superoptimizer. In *Proceedings of ACM Conference on Programming Language Design and Implementation (PLDI)*, pages 304–314, 2002.

14. R. Kennell and L. Jamieson. Establishing the genuinity of remote computer systems. In *Proceedings of USENIX Security Symposium*, Aug. 2003.

15. S. King and P. Chen. Backtracking intrusions. In *Proceedings of the ACM Symposium on Operating Systems Principles (SOSP)*, pages 223–236, 2003.

16. A. Klimov and A. Shamir. A new class of invertible mappings. In *CHES '02: Revised Papers from the 4th International Workshop on Cryptographic Hardware and Embedded Systems*, pages 470–483, 2003.

17. N. Petroni, T. Fraser, J. Molina, and W. Arbaugh. Copilot - a coprocessor-based kernel runtime integrity monitor. In *Proceedings of USENIX Security Symposium*, pages 179–194, 2004.

18. R. Sailer, X. Zhang, T. Jaeger, and L. van Doorn. Design and implementation of a TCG-based integrity measurement architecture. In *Proceedings of USENIX Security Symposium*, pages 223–238, 2004.

19. A. Seshadri, A. Perrig, L. van Doorn, and P. Khosla. SWATT: Software-based attestation for embedded devices. In *Proceedings of IEEE Symposium on Security and Privacy*, May 2004.

20. U. Shankar, M. Chew, and J. D. Tygar. Side effects are not sufficient to authenticate software. In *Proceedings of USENIX Security Symposium*, pages 89–101, Aug. 2004.

21. E. Shi, A. Perrig, and L. van Doorn. Bind: A fine-grained attestation service for secure distributed systems. In *Proc. of the IEEE Symposium on Security and Privacy*, pages 154–168, 2005.

22. Trusted Computing Group (TCG). https://www.trustedcomputinggroup.org/, 2003.

23. Tripwire. http://sourceforge.net/projects/tripwire/.

24. VMware. http://www.vmware.com/.

25. X. Wang, Y. Yin, and H. Yu. Finding collisions in the full sha-1. In *Proceedings of Crypto*, Aug. 2005.

26. Y. Wang, R. Roussev, C. Verbowski, A. Johnson, and D. Ladd. AskStrider: What has changed on my machine lately? Technical Report MSR-TR-2004-03, Microsoft Research, 2004.

27. Y. Wang, B. Vo, R. Roussev, C. Verbowski, and A. Johnson. Strider GhostBuster: Why it's a bad idea for stealth software to hide files. Technical Report MSR-TR-2004-71, Microsoft Research, 2004.

28. G. Wurster, P. van Oorschot, and A. Somayaji. A generic attack on checksumming-based software tamper resistance. In *Proceedings of IEEE Symposium on Security and Privacy*, May 2005.

29. D. Zovi. Kernel rootkits. http://www.cs.unm.edu/~ghandi/lkr.pdf.

Principles of Secure Information Flow Analysis

Geoffrey Smith

School of Computing and Information Sciences, Florida International University
smithg@cis.fiu.edu

In today's world of the Internet, the World-Wide Web, and Google, information is more accessible than ever before. An unfortunate corollary is that it is harder than ever to protect the privacy of sensitive information. In this chapter, we explore a technique called *secure information flow analysis*.

Suppose that some sensitive information is stored on a computer system. How can we prevent it from being leaked improperly? Probably the first approach that comes to mind is to limit access to the information, either by using some access control mechanism, or else by using encryption. These are important and useful approaches, of course, but they have a fundamental limitation—they can prevent information from being *released*, but they cannot prevent it from being *propagated*. If a program legitimately needs access to a piece of information, how can we be sure that it will not somehow leak the information improperly? Simply *trusting* the program is dangerous. We might try to monitor its output, but the program could easily disguise the information. Furthermore, after-the-fact detection is often too late.

Consider for example a scenario involving e-filing of taxes. I might download a tax preparation program from some vendor to my home computer. I could use the program to prepare my tax return, entering my private financial information. The program might then send my tax return to the IRS electronically, encrypting it first to protect its confidentiality. But the program might also send billing information back to the vendor so that I could be charged for the use of the program. How can I be sure that this billing information does not covertly include my private financial information?

The approach of secure information flow analysis involves performing a *static analysis* of the program with the goal of proving that it will not leak sensitive information. If the program passes the analysis, then it can be executed safely.

This idea has a long history, going back to the pioneering work of the Dennings in the 1970s [9]. It has since been heavily studied, as can be seen from the survey by Sabelfeld and Myers [22], which cites about 150 papers. Our goal here is not to duplicate that survey, but instead to explain the principles underlying secure information flow analysis and to discuss some challenges that have so far prevented secure information flow analysis from being employed much in practice.

13.1 Basic Principles

The starting point in secure information flow analysis is the classification of program variables into different *security levels*. The most basic distinction is to classify some variables as L, meaning low security, public information; and other variables as H, meaning high security, private information. The security goal is to prevent information in H variables from being leaked improperly. Such leaks could take a variety of forms, of course, but certainly we need to prevent information in H variables from flowing to L variables.

More generally, we might want a *lattice* of security levels, and we would wish to ensure that information flows only upwards in the lattice [8]. For example, if $L \leq H$, then we would allow flows from L to L, from H to H, and from L to H, but we would disallow flows from H to L.

Another interesting case involves *integrity* rather than *confidentiality*. If we view some variables as containing possibly *tainted* information, then we may wish to prevent information from such variables from flowing into *untainted* variables, as in Orbæk [19]. We can model this using a lattice with *Untainted* $\leq$ *Tainted*. This idea is also the basis of recent work by Newsome and Song [18] that attempts to detect worms via a dynamic taint analysis.

Let us consider some examples from Denning [9], assuming that `secret` : H and `leak` : L. Clearly illegal is an *explicit flow*:

```
leak = secret;
```

On the other hand, the following should be legal:

```
secret = leak;
```

as should

```
leak = 76318;
```

Also dangerous is an *implicit flow*:

```
if ((secret % 2)==0)
  leak = 0;
else
  leak = 1;
```

This copies the last bit of `secret` to `leak`.

Arrays can lead to subtle information leaks. If array a is initially all 0, then the program

```
a[secret] = 1;
for (int i = 0; i < a.length; i++) {
  if (a[i] == 1)
    leak = i;
}
```

leaks `secret`.

How can we formalize the idea that program c does not leak information from H variables to L variables? In Volpano, Smith, and Irvine [32], the desired security property is formulated as follows:

Definition 1 (Noninterference). *Program c satisfies* noninterference *if, for any memories μ and ν that agree on L variables, the memories produced by running c on μ and on ν also agree on L variables (provided that both runs terminate successfully).*

The name "noninterference" was chosen because of its similarity to a property proposed earlier by Goguen and Meseguer [10]. The idea behind noninterference is that someone observing the final values of L variables cannot conclude anything about the initial values of H variables.

Notice that the noninterference property defined above is applicable only to *deterministic* programs. In later sections, we will consider noninterference properties that are appropriate for nondeterministic programs.

Of course, leaking H information into L variables is not the only way that H information might be leaked. Consider

```
while (secret != 0)
    ;
```

This program loops iff `secret` is nonzero. So an attacker who can observe termination/nontermination can deduce some information about `secret`. Similarly, the running time of a program may depend on H information. Such *timing leaks* are very hard to prevent, because they can exploit low-level implementation details. Consider the following example, adapted from Agat [1].

```
int i, count, xs[4096], ys[4096];

for (count = 0; count < 100000; count++) {
    if (secret != 0)
        for (i = 0; i < 4096; i += 2)
            xs[i]++;
    else
        for (i = 0; i < 4096; i += 2)
            ys[i]++;
    for (i = 0; i < 4096; i += 2)
        xs[i]++;
}
```

At an abstract level, the amount of work done by this program does not seem to depend on the value of `secret`. But, when run on a local Sparc server with a 16K data cache, it takes twice as long when `secret` is 0 as it takes when `secret` is nonzero. (When `secret` is nonzero, the array `xs` can remain in the data cache throughout the program's execution; when `secret` is 0, the data cache holds `xs` and `ys` alternately.)

Because *outside* observations of the running program make it so hard to prevent information leaks, most work on secure information flow addresses only leaks of information from H variables to L variables, as captured by the noninterference property. Focusing on noninterference can also be justified by noting that when we run a program on our own computer (as in the e-tax example above) we may be able to prevent outside observations of its execution.

13.2 Typing Principles

In this section, we describe how *type systems* can be used to ensure noninterference properties. For simplicity, we assume that the only security levels are H and L. We begin by considering a very simple imperative language with the following syntax:

$$
\begin{array}{lll}
(phrases) & p ::= e \mid c \\
(expressions) & e ::= x \mid n \mid e_1 + e_2 \mid \ldots \\
(commands) & c ::= x := e \mid \\
& \quad \textbf{skip} \mid \\
& \quad \textbf{if } e \textbf{ then } c_1 \textbf{ else } c_2 \mid \\
& \quad \textbf{while } e \textbf{ do } c \mid \\
& \quad c_1 ; c_2
\end{array}
$$

Here metavariable x ranges over identifiers and n over integer literals. Integers are the only values; we use 0 for false and nonzero for true.

A program c is executed under a memory μ, which maps identifiers to values. We assume that expressions are total and evaluated atomically, with $\mu(e)$ denoting the value of expression e in memory μ. Execution of commands is given by a standard *structural operational semantics* as in Gunter [11], shown in Figure 13.1. These rules define a transition relation $\longrightarrow$ on *configurations*. A configuration is either a pair (c, μ) or simply a memory μ. In the first case, c is the command yet to be executed; in the second case, the command has terminated, yielding final memory μ. We write $\longrightarrow^*$ for the reflexive, transitive closure of $\longrightarrow$.

Going back to Denning's original work [9], we can identify the following principles:

- First, we *classify* expressions by saying that an expression is H if it contains any H variables; otherwise it is L.
- Next we prevent *explicit flows* by forbidding a H expression from being assigned to a L variable.
- Finally, we prevent *implicit* flows by forbidding a guarded command with a H guard from assigning to L variables.

We can express these classifications and restrictions using a type system. The security types that we need are as follows:

$$
\begin{array}{lll}
(data\ types) & \tau ::= L \mid H \\
(phrase\ types) & \rho ::= \tau \mid \tau\ var \mid \tau\ cmd
\end{array}
$$

(UPDATE)

$$\frac{x \in dom(\mu)}{(x := e, \mu) \longrightarrow \mu[x := \mu(e)]}$$

(NO-OP)

$$(\mathbf{skip}, \mu) \longrightarrow \mu$$

(BRANCH)

$$\frac{\mu(e) \neq 0}{(\mathbf{if}\ e\ \mathbf{then}\ c_1\ \mathbf{else}\ c_2, \mu) \longrightarrow (c_1, \mu)}$$

$$\frac{\mu(e) = 0}{(\mathbf{if}\ e\ \mathbf{then}\ c_1\ \mathbf{else}\ c_2, \mu) \longrightarrow (c_2, \mu)}$$

(LOOP)

$$\frac{\mu(e) = 0}{(\mathbf{while}\ e\ \mathbf{do}\ c, \mu) \longrightarrow \mu}$$

$$\frac{\mu(e) \neq 0}{(\mathbf{while}\ e\ \mathbf{do}\ c, \mu) \longrightarrow (c; \mathbf{while}\ e\ \mathbf{do}\ c, \mu)}$$

(SEQUENCE)

$$\frac{(c_1, \mu) \longrightarrow \mu'}{(c_1; c_2, \mu) \longrightarrow (c_2, \mu')}$$

$$\frac{(c_1, \mu) \longrightarrow (c_1', \mu')}{(c_1; c_2, \mu) \longrightarrow (c_1'; c_2, \mu')}$$

Fig. 13.1. Structural Operational Semantics

The intuition is that an expression e of type τ contains only variables of level τ or lower, and a command c of type τ *cmd* assigns only to variables of level τ or higher.

Next, we need an identifier typing Γ that maps each variable to a type of the form τ *var*, giving its security level. A *typing judgment* has the form $\Gamma \vdash p : \rho$, which can be read as "from identifier typing Γ, it follows that phrase p has type ρ". In addition, it is convenient to have *subtyping judgments* of the form $\rho_1 \subseteq \rho_2$. For instance, we would want H *cmd* $\subseteq L$ *cmd*, because if a command assigns only to variables of level H or higher then, *a fortiori*, it assigns only to variables of level L or higher. The typing rules are shown in Figures 13.2 and 13.3; they first appeared in Volpano, Smith, and Irvine [32].

Programs that are well typed under this type system are guaranteed to satisfy noninterference. First, the following two lemmas show that the type system enforces the intended meanings of expression types and command types:

Lemma 1 (Simple Security). *If* $\Gamma \vdash e : \tau$, *then* e *contains only variables of level* τ *or lower.*

Lemma 2 (Confinement). *If* $\Gamma \vdash c : \tau$ *cmd, then* c *assigns to only to variables of level* τ *or higher.*

Next, we say that memories μ and ν are *L-equivalent*, written $\mu \sim_L \nu$, if μ and ν agree on the values of L variables. Now we can show noninterference:

(R-VAL)
$$\frac{\Gamma(x) = \tau \; var}{\Gamma \vdash x : \tau}$$

(INT)
$$\Gamma \vdash n : L$$

(PLUS)
$$\frac{\Gamma \vdash e_1 : \tau, \;\; \Gamma \vdash e_2 : \tau}{\Gamma \vdash e_1 + e_2 : \tau}$$

(ASSIGN)
$$\frac{\Gamma(x) = \tau \; var, \;\; \Gamma \vdash e : \tau}{\Gamma \vdash x := e : \tau \; cmd}$$

(SKIP)
$$\Gamma \vdash \mathbf{skip} : H \; cmd$$

(IF)
$$\frac{\begin{array}{l}\Gamma \vdash e : \tau \\ \Gamma \vdash c_1 : \tau \; cmd \\ \Gamma \vdash c_2 : \tau \; cmd\end{array}}{\Gamma \vdash \mathbf{if} \; e \; \mathbf{then} \; c_1 \; \mathbf{else} \; c_2 : \tau \; cmd}$$

(WHILE)
$$\frac{\begin{array}{l}\Gamma \vdash e : \tau \\ \Gamma \vdash c : \tau \; cmd\end{array}}{\Gamma \vdash \mathbf{while} \; e \; \mathbf{do} \; c : \tau \; cmd}$$

(COMPOSE)
$$\frac{\begin{array}{l}\Gamma \vdash c_1 : \tau \; cmd \\ \Gamma \vdash c_2 : \tau \; cmd\end{array}}{\Gamma \vdash c_1; c_2 \; : \; \tau \; cmd}$$

Fig. 13.2. Typing rules

(BASE)
$$L \subseteq H$$

(CMD$^-$)
$$\frac{\tau' \subseteq \tau}{\tau \; cmd \subseteq \tau' \; cmd}$$

(REFLEX)
$$\rho \subseteq \rho$$

(TRANS)
$$\frac{\rho_1 \subseteq \rho_2, \;\; \rho_2 \subseteq \rho_3}{\rho_1 \subseteq \rho_3}$$

(SUBSUMP)
$$\frac{\Gamma \vdash p : \rho_1, \;\; \rho_1 \subseteq \rho_2}{\Gamma \vdash p : \rho_2}$$

Fig. 13.3. Subtyping rules

Theorem 1 (Noninterference). *If c is well typed and $\mu \sim_L \nu$ and c runs successfully under both μ and ν, producing final memories μ' and ν', respectively, then $\mu' \sim_L \nu'$.*

Proof. The proof is by induction on the length of the execution $(c, \mu) \longrightarrow \mu'$. We describe two interesting cases:

- Suppose c is an assignment $x := e$. If x is H, then $\mu' \sim_L \nu'$ trivially. And if x is L, then the type system requires that $e : L$, which means that by Simple Security, e contains only L variables. Hence $\mu(e) = \nu(e)$, which means that $\mu' \sim_L \nu'$.
- Suppose c is **while** e **do** c'. If e is L, then by Simple Security $\mu(e) = \nu(e)$, which means that the executions from (**while** e **do** c', μ) and from (**while** e **do** c', ν) begin in the same way; they go either to μ and to ν (if $\mu(e) = \nu(e) = 0$) or to $(c'; \textbf{while } e \textbf{ do } c', \mu)$ and to $(c'; \textbf{while } e \textbf{ do } c', \nu)$ (otherwise). In the former case we are done immediately, and in the latter case the result follows by induction.

  If, instead, e is H, then the type system requires that c' has type H *cmd*. So, by Confinement, c' assigns only to H variables. It follows that $\mu \sim_L \mu'$ and $\nu \sim_L \nu'$, which implies that $\mu' \sim_L nu'$.

The remaining cases are similar.   □

Of course the language that we have considered so far is very small. In the next subsections, we consider a number of extensions to it.

13.2.1 Concurrency

Suppose that we extend our language with multiple threads, under a shared memory. This introduces *nondeterminism*, which makes the noninterference property in Definition 1 inappropriate—now running a program twice under the *same* memory can produce two memories that disagree on the values of L variables.

As a starting point, we might generalize to a *possibilistic noninterference* property that says that changing the initial values of H variables cannot change the *set* of possible final values of L variables:

Definition 2 (Possibilistic Noninterference). *Program c satisfies possibilistic noninterference if, for any memories μ and ν that agree on L variables, if running c on μ can produce final memory μ', then running c on ν can produce a final memory ν' such that μ' and ν' agree on L variables.*

Do the typing rules in Figures 13.2 and 13.3 suffice to ensure possibilistic noninterference? They do not, as is shown by the example in Figure 13.4, which is from Smith and Volpano [28]. The initial values of all variables are 0, except mask, whose value is a power of 2, and secret, whose value is arbitrary. It can be seen that, under any fair scheduler, this program always copies secret to leak. Yet all three threads are well typed provided that secret, trigger0, and trigger1 are H, and leak, maintrigger, and mask are L.

So we need to impose additional restrictions on multi-threaded programs. Before considering such restrictions, however, we must first address the specification of

Thread α:

```
while (mask != 0) {
  while (trigger0 == 0)
    ;
  leak = leak | mask;    // bitwise 'or'
  trigger0 = 0;
  maintrigger = maintrigger+1;
  if (maintrigger == 1)
    trigger1 = 1;
}
```

Thread β:

```
while (mask != 0) {
  while (trigger1 == 0)
    ;
  leak = leak & ~mask;   // bitwise 'and' with
                         //     complement of mask
  trigger1 = 0;
  maintrigger = maintrigger+1;
  if (maintrigger == 1)
    trigger0 = 1;
}
```

Thread γ:

```
while (mask != 0) {
  maintrigger = 0;
  if (secret & mask == 0)
    trigger0 = 1;
  else
    trigger1 = 1;
  while (maintrigger != 2)
    ;
  mask = mask/2;
}
trigger0 = 1;
trigger1 = 1;
```

Fig. 13.4. A multi-threaded program that leaks secret

the *thread scheduler* more carefully. Possibilistic noninterference is sufficient only if we assume a *purely nondeterministic* scheduler, which at each step can choose any thread to run for the next step. Under this model, there is no *likelihood* associated with the memories that can result from running a program—each final memory is simply *possible* or *impossible*. But a real scheduler would inevitably be more predictable. For example, a scheduler might flip coins at each step to choose which thread to run next. Under such a probabilistic scheduler, possibilistic noninterference is insufficient. Consider the following example from McLean [14]. Let the program consist of two threads:

```
leak = secret;
```

and

```
leak = random(100);
```

Assume that `random(100)` returns a random number between 1 and 100 and that the value of `secret` is between 1 and 100. This program satisfies possibilistic noninterference, because the final value of `leak` can be any number between 1 and 100, regardless of the value of `secret`. But, under a probabilistic scheduler that flips a coin to decide which thread to execute first, the value of `leak` will be the value of `secret` with probability 101/200, and each other number between 1 and 100 with probability 1/200. This example motivates a stronger security property, *probabilistic noninterference*, which says that changing the initial values of H variables cannot affect the *joint probability distribution* on the final values of L variables. Further discussion of possibilistic and probabilistic security properties can be found in McLean [15].

We now describe a type system for ensuring probabilistic noninterference in multi-threaded programs. The first such systems (Smith and Volpano [28, 31] and Sabelfeld and Sands [23]) adopted the severe restriction that guards of while-loops must be L. This rules out the program in Figure 13.4 (`trigger0` and `trigger1` are H), but it also makes it hard to write useful programs.

Later, inspired by Honda, Vasconcelos, and Yoshida [12], a better type system was presented by Smith [26, 27]. (Remarkably, almost the same system was developed independently by Boudol and Castellani [5].) This type system allows while-loop guards to contain H variables, but to prevent timing flows it demands that a command whose running time depends on H variables cannot be followed sequentially by an assignment to a L variable. The intuition is that such an assignment to a L variable is dangerous in a multi-threaded setting, because if another thread assigns to the same variable, then the likely *order* in which the assignments occur (and hence the likely final value of the L variable) depends on H information.

The type system uses the following set of types:

$$(\text{data types}) \quad \tau ::= L \mid H$$
$$(\text{phrase types}) \quad \rho ::= \tau \mid \tau \text{ var} \mid \tau_1 \text{ cmd } \tau_2 \mid \tau \text{ cmd } n$$

The new command types have the following intuition:

- A command c is classified as $\tau_1 \text{ cmd } \tau_2$ if it assigns only to variables of type τ_1 (or higher) and its running time depends only on variables of type τ_2 (or lower).
- A command c is classified as $\tau \text{ cmd } n$ if it assigns only to variables of type τ (or higher) and it is guaranteed to terminate in exactly n steps.

The new typing and subtyping rules are presented in Figures 13.5 and 13.6. These rules make use of the lattice *join* and *meet* operations, denoted $\vee$ and $\wedge$,

(R-VAL) $$\frac{\Gamma(x) = \tau\ var}{\Gamma \vdash x : \tau}$$

(INT) $$\Gamma \vdash n : L$$

(PLUS) $$\frac{\Gamma \vdash e_1 : \tau, \quad \Gamma \vdash e_2 : \tau}{\Gamma \vdash e_1 + e_2 : \tau}$$

(ASSIGN) $$\frac{\Gamma(x) = \tau\ var, \quad \Gamma \vdash e : \tau}{\Gamma \vdash x := e : \tau\ cmd\ 1}$$

(SKIP) $$\Gamma \vdash \mathbf{skip} : H\ cmd\ 1$$

(IF) $$\frac{\begin{array}{l}\Gamma \vdash e : \tau \\ \Gamma \vdash c_1 : \tau\ cmd\ n \\ \Gamma \vdash c_2 : \tau\ cmd\ n\end{array}}{\Gamma \vdash \mathbf{if}\ e\ \mathbf{then}\ c_1\ \mathbf{else}\ c_2 : \tau\ cmd\ n+1}$$

$$\frac{\begin{array}{l}\Gamma \vdash e : \tau_1 \\ \tau_1 \subseteq \tau_2 \\ \Gamma \vdash c_1 : \tau_2\ cmd\ \tau_3 \\ \Gamma \vdash c_2 : \tau_2\ cmd\ \tau_3\end{array}}{\Gamma \vdash \mathbf{if}\ e\ \mathbf{then}\ c_1\ \mathbf{else}\ c_2 : \tau_2\ cmd\ \tau_1 \vee \tau_3}$$

(WHILE) $$\frac{\begin{array}{l}\Gamma \vdash e : \tau_1 \\ \tau_1 \subseteq \tau_2 \\ \tau_3 \subseteq \tau_2 \\ \Gamma \vdash c : \tau_2\ cmd\ \tau_3\end{array}}{\Gamma \vdash \mathbf{while}\ e\ \mathbf{do}\ c : \tau_2\ cmd\ \tau_1 \vee \tau_3}$$

(COMPOSE) $$\frac{\begin{array}{l}\Gamma \vdash c_1 : \tau\ cmd\ m \\ \Gamma \vdash c_2 : \tau\ cmd\ n\end{array}}{\Gamma \vdash c_1; c_2 \ :\ \tau\ cmd\ m+n}$$

$$\frac{\begin{array}{l}\Gamma \vdash c_1 : \tau_1\ cmd\ \tau_2 \\ \tau_2 \subseteq \tau_3 \\ \Gamma \vdash c_2 : \tau_3\ cmd\ \tau_4\end{array}}{\Gamma \vdash c_1; c_2 \ :\ \tau_1 \wedge \tau_3\ cmd\ \tau_2 \vee \tau_4}$$

(PROTECT) $$\frac{\begin{array}{l}\Gamma \vdash c : \tau_1\ cmd\ \tau_2 \\ c \text{ contains no } \mathbf{while} \text{ loops}\end{array}}{\Gamma \vdash \mathbf{protect}\ c : \tau_1\ cmd\ 1}$$

Fig. 13.5. Typing rules for multi-threaded programs

$$\text{(BASE)} \qquad L \subseteq H$$

$$\text{(CMD}^-) \qquad \frac{\tau_1' \subseteq \tau_1, \quad \tau_2 \subseteq \tau_2'}{\tau_1 \ cmd \ \tau_2 \subseteq \tau_1' \ cmd \ \tau_2'}$$

$$\frac{\tau' \subseteq \tau}{\tau \ cmd \ n \subseteq \tau' \ cmd \ n}$$

$$\tau \ cmd \ n \subseteq \tau \ cmd \ L$$

$$\text{(REFLEX)} \qquad \rho \subseteq \rho$$

$$\text{(TRANS)} \qquad \frac{\rho_1 \subseteq \rho_2, \quad \rho_2 \subseteq \rho_3}{\rho_1 \subseteq \rho_3}$$

$$\text{(SUBSUMP)} \qquad \frac{\Gamma \vdash p : \rho_1, \quad \rho_1 \subseteq \rho_2}{\Gamma \vdash p : \rho_2}$$

Fig. 13.6. Subtyping rules for multi-threaded programs

respectively. Also, we extend the language with a new command, **protect** c, which runs command c atomically. This is helpful in masking timing variations.

The key idea behind the soundness of this type system is that if a well-typed thread c is run under two L-equivalent memories, then in both runs it makes exactly the same assignments to L variables, *at the same times*. Given this property, we are able to show that well-typed multi-threaded programs satisfy probabilistic non-interference. The proof involves establishing a *weak probabilistic bisimulation*; the details are in Smith [27].

13.2.2 Exceptions

Another language feature that can cause subtle information flows is exceptions. For example, here is a Java program that uses exceptions from out-of-bounds array indices to leak a secret:

```
int secret;
int leak = 0;
int [] a = new int[1];

for (int bit = 0; bit < 30; bit++) {
    try {
        a[1 - (secret >> bit) % 2] = 0;
        leak |= (1 << bit);
    }
    catch (ArrayIndexOutOfBoundsException e) { }
}
```

In this code, bit is L. Here the key is that array a has length 1, so the assignment

```
a[1 - (secret >> bit) % 2] = 0;
```

raises an exception iff the current bit of `secret` is 0. As a result, the assignment

```
leak |= (1 << bit);
```

is executed iff the current bit of `secret` is 1.

How should leaks due to exceptions be prevented? One possibility is to use an approach similar to what was used for concurrency: we can require that a command that might raise exceptions based on the values of H variables must not be followed sequentially by an assignment to L variables. This is the approach taken by Jif [16].

Because this would seem to be quite restrictive in practice, Deng and Smith [6] propose a different approach. If we change the language semantics so that array operations never raise exceptions, then we can type them much more permissively. The idea is to treat commands with out-of-bounds array indices as no-ops that are simply skipped.

Under this approach, we give an array type τ_1 *arr* τ_2 to indicate that its contents have level τ_1 and its length has level τ_2. Then, for example, we can use the following straightforward and permissive typing rule for array assignment:

$$\frac{\Gamma(x) = \tau_1 \ arr \ \tau_2, \ \ \Gamma \vdash e_1 : \tau_1, \ \ \Gamma \vdash e_2 : \tau_1}{\Gamma \vdash x[e_1] := e_2 : \tau_1 \ cmd}$$

The full type system is given in [6].

In contrast, but with the same intent, Flow Caml [25] specifies that an out-of-bounds array index causes the program to *abort*. This also prevents out-of-bounds exceptions from being observed internally, allowing more permissive typing rules.

13.2.3 Other Language Features

Secure information flow analysis can treat larger languages than we have considered here. Notable is the work of Myers [16] and Banerjee and Naumann [3], which treats object-oriented languages, and that of Pottier and Simonet [20] which treats a functional language.

Another useful technology in this context is *type inference*, which frees the programming from having to specify the security levels of all the variables in the program. He or she can specify the levels of just the variables of interest, and have appropriate security levels of all other variables be inferred automatically.

Interestingly, the desire to do type inference is one reason for assuming that the set of security levels forms a lattice, because type inference is NP-complete over an arbitrary partial order. This follows from a result of Pratt and Tiuryn [21]. They show that over the "2-crown" given by

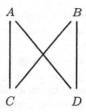

the problem of testing the satisfiability of a set of inequalities between variables (x, y, z, ...) and constants (A, B, C, D) is NP-complete. We can easily reduce the satisfiability problem to the inference problem by mapping a set of inequalities C to a program p such that C is satisfiable iff some choice of security levels for the inferable variables of p makes p well typed. For example, we map

$$\{x \le A, B \le y, x \le y\}$$

to the program

$$a := x; y := b; y := x$$

where a and b are variables of levels A and B, respectively, and x and y are variables whose levels are to be inferred.

In contrast, type inference can be done efficiently over a lattice. Work on type inference for secure information flow includes Volpano and Smith [30], Pottier and Simonet [20], Sun, Banerjee, and Naumann [29], and Deng and Smith [7].

13.3 Challenges

In spite of a great deal of research, secure information flow analysis has had little practical impact so far. (See, for example, Zdancewic's discussion [33].) In this section we discuss some challenges that need to be overcome to make secure information flow analysis more useful in practice.

One obvious concern is that much of the work in the research literature has been theoretical, treating "toy" languages rather than full production languages. While this has surely hindered adoption of this technology somewhat, in fact there are two mature implementations of rich languages with secure information flow analysis, namely Jif [17] and Flow Caml [25]. This fact suggests that the problems largely lie elsewhere.

In exploring this issue further, it seems helpful to distinguish between two different application scenarios: *developing secure software* and *stopping malicious software*. We consider these in turn.

13.3.1 Scenario 1: Developing Secure Software

In this scenario, the idea is to use secure information flow analysis to help in the development of software that satisfies some security goals. Here the analysis serves as a *program development tool*. We could imagine such a tool being used interactively to help the programmer to eliminate improper information leaks. Here, the analysis could be carried out on *source code*.

The static analysis tool would alert the programmer to potential leaks. The programmer could respond to such alerts by rewriting the code as necessary. We also might allow the programmer to insert explicit *declassification statements* (in effect, type casts) to deal with situations where the analysis is overly restrictive. (Such declassification statements are allowed in Jif, for example.) Allowing declassification statements is risky, of course, but it might be reasonable in situations where we can trust that the programmer is not malicious or incompetent.

An example of this scenario can be found in Askarov and Sablefeld [2] which discusses the implementation of a "mental poker" protocol in Jif. The program is about 4500 lines long, and it uses a number of declassification statements, for example to model the intuition that encrypting H information makes it L.

13.3.2 Scenario 2: Stopping Malicious Software

In this scenario, the idea is to use secure information flow analysis as a kind of *filter* to stop malicious software ("malware"). We might imagine analyzing a piece of untrusted downloaded code before executing it, with the goal of guaranteeing its safety.

This scenario is clearly much more challenging than Scenario 1. First of all, we probably would not have access to the source code, requiring us to analyze *binaries*. Analyzing binaries is more difficult than analyzing source code and has not received much attention in the literature, aside from some recent work on analyzing Java bytecodes, such as Barthe and Rezk [4].

A further challenge here is that the analysis would need to be fully automatic, without the possibility of interaction with the programmer. Moreover, declassification statements certainly cannot be blindly accepted in this scenario. If we do allow declassification statements, then it becomes unclear what (if any) security properties are guaranteed.

13.3.3 Flow Policies

In both scenarios we have a key question: what information flow policies do we want? As we have discussed above, secure information flow analysis has focused on enforcing *noninterference*. But noninterference requires absolutely no flow of information. As it turns out, this does not seem to be quite what we want in practice.

A first concern is that "small" information leaks are acceptable in practice. For instance, a password checker certainly must not leak the correct password, but it must allow a user to enter a purported password, which it will either accept or reject. And, of course, rejecting a password leaks some information about the correct password, by eliminating one possibility. Similarly, encrypting some H information would seem to make it L, but there *is* a flow of information from the plaintext to the ciphertext, since the ciphertext depends on the plaintext.

As another example, consider *census data*. *Individual* census data is expected to be private (H) but *aggregate* census data needs to be public (L), since otherwise the census data is useless. But, of course, aggregate data depends on individual data, contrary to what noninterference demands.

Flow policies sometimes involve a *temporal* aspect as well. For example, we might want to release some secret information after receiving a payment for it.

These examples suggest that, in many practical situations, enforcing noninterference on a static lattice of security levels is too heavy-handed. At the same time, it seems difficult to allow "small" information leaks without allowing a malicious program to exploit such loopholes to leak too much.

A major challenge for secure information flow analysis, then, is to develop a good formalism for specifying useful information flow policies that are more flexible than noninterference. The formalism must be general enough for a wide variety of applications, but not too complicated for users to understand. In addition, we must find enforcement mechanisms that can provably ensure that the flow policy is satisfied. Such richer information flow policies and their enforcement are the subject of much current research. One interesting approach is Li and Zdancewic [13], which uses downgrading policies as security levels, so that the security level specifies what must be done to "sanitize" a piece of information. More broadly, the survey by Sabelfeld and Sands [24] gives a useful framework for thinking about recent approaches to declassification.

13.4 Conclusion

Secure information flow analysis has the potential to guarantee strong security properties in computer software. But if it is to become broadly useful, it must better address the security properties that are important in practice.

This work was partially supported by the National Science Foundation under grants CCR-9900951 and HRD-0317692.

References

1. J. Agat. *Type Based Techniques for Covert Channel Elimination and Register Allocation.* PhD thesis, Chalmers University of Technology, Göteborg, Sweden, Dec. 2000.
2. A. Askarov and A. Sabelfeld. Security-typed languages for implementation of cryptographic protocols: A case study. In *Proceedings of the 10th European Symposium on Research in Computer Security (ESORICS 2005)*, pages 197–221, Sept. 2005.
3. A. Banerjee and D. A. Naumann. Secure information flow and pointer confinement in a Java-like language. In *Proceedings 15th IEEE Computer Security Foundations Workshop*, pages 253–267, Cape Breton, Nova Scotia, Canada, June 2002.
4. G. Barthe and T. Rezk. Non-interference for a JVM-like language. In *Proceedings of TLDI'05: 2005 ACM SIGPLAN International Workshop on Types in Language Design and Implementation*, pages 103–112, Jan. 2005.

5. G. Boudol and I. Castellani. Noninterference for concurrent programs and thread systems. *Theoretical Computer Science*, 281(1):109–130, June 2002.

6. Z. Deng and G. Smith. Lenient array operations for practical secure information flow. In *Proceedings 17th IEEE Computer Security Foundations Workshop*, pages 115–124, Pacific Grove, California, June 2004.

7. Z. Deng and G. Smith. Type inference and informative error reporting for secure information flow. In *Proceedings ACMSE 2006: 44th ACM Southeast Conference*, pages 543–548, Melbourne, Florida, Mar. 2006.

8. D. Denning. A lattice model of secure information flow. *Commun. ACM*, 19(5):236–242, 1976.

9. D. Denning and P. Denning. Certification of programs for secure information flow. *Commun. ACM*, 20(7):504–513, 1977.

10. J. Goguen and J. Meseguer. Security policies and security models. In *Proceedings 1982 IEEE Symposium on Security and Privacy*, pages 11–20, Oakland, CA, 1982.

11. C. A. Gunter. *Semantics of Programming Languages*. The MIT Press, 1992.

12. K. Honda, V. Vasconcelos, and N. Yoshida. Secure information flow as typed process behaviour. In *Proceedings 9th European Symposium on Programming*, volume 1782 of *Lecture Notes in Computer Science*, pages 180–199, Apr. 2000.

13. P. Li and S. Zdancewic. Downgrading policies and relaxed noninterference. In *Proceedings 32nd Symposium on Principles of Programming Languages*, pages 158–170, Jan. 2005.

14. J. McLean. Security models and information flow. In *Proceedings 1990 IEEE Symposium on Security and Privacy*, pages 180–187, Oakland, CA, 1990.

15. J. McLean. Security models. In J. Marciniak, editor, *Encyclopedia of Software Engineering*. Wiley Press, 1994.

16. A. Myers. JFlow: Practical mostly-static information flow control. In *Proceedings 26th Symposium on Principles of Programming Languages*, pages 228–241, San Antonio, TX, Jan. 1999.

17. A. C. Myers, S. Chong, N. Nystrom, L. Zheng, and S. Zdancewic. *Jif: Java + information flow*. Cornell University, 2004. Available at http://www.cs.cornell.edu/jif/.

18. J. Newsome and D. Song. Dynamic taint analysis for automatic detection, analysis, and signature generation of exploits on commodity software. In *Proceedings of the 12th Annual Network and Distributed System Security Symposium (NDSS 05)*, Feb. 2005.

19. P. Ørbæk. Can You Trust Your Data? In *Proceedings 1995 Theory and Practice of Software Development Conference*, pages 575–589, Aarhus, Denmark, May 1995. Lecture Notes in Computer Science 915.

20. F. Pottier and V. Simonet. Information flow inference for ML. *ACM Transactions on Programming Languages and Systems*, 25(1):117–158, Jan. 2003.

21. V. Pratt and J. Tiuryn. Satisfiability of inequalities in a poset. *Fundamenta Informaticae*, 28(1–2):165–182, 1996.

22. A. Sabelfeld and A. C. Myers. Language-based information flow security. *IEEE Journal on Selected Areas in Communications*, 21(1):5–19, Jan. 2003.

23. A. Sabelfeld and D. Sands. Probabilistic noninterference for multi-threaded programs. In *Proceedings 13th IEEE Computer Security Foundations Workshop*, pages 200–214, Cambridge, UK, July 2000.

24. A. Sabelfeld and D. Sands. Dimensions and principles of declassification. In *Proceedings 18th IEEE Computer Security Foundations Workshop*, June 2005.

25. V. Simonet. *The Flow Caml System: Documentation and user's manual*. Institut National de Recherche en Informatique et en Automatique, July 2003.

Available at http:// cristal.inria.fr/ ~simonet/ soft/ flowcaml/ manual/ index.html.

26. G. Smith. A new type system for secure information flow. In *Proceedings 14th IEEE Computer Security Foundations Workshop*, pages 115–125, Cape Breton, Nova Scotia, Canada, June 2001.

27. G. Smith. Probabilistic noninterference through weak probabilistic bisimulation. In *Proceedings 16th IEEE Computer Security Foundations Workshop*, pages 3–13, Pacific Grove, California, June 2003.

28. G. Smith and D. Volpano. Secure information flow in a multi-threaded imperative language. In *Proceedings 25th Symposium on Principles of Programming Languages*, pages 355–364, San Diego, CA, Jan. 1998.

29. Q. Sun, A. Banerjee, and D. A. Naumann. Modular and constraint-based information flow inference for an object-oriented language. In *Proc. Eleventh International Static Analysis Symposium (SAS)*, Verona, Italy, Aug. 2004.

30. D. Volpano and G. Smith. A type-based approach to program security. In *Proc. Theory and Practice of Software Development*, volume 1214 of *Lecture Notes in Computer Science*, pages 607–621, Apr. 1997.

31. D. Volpano and G. Smith. Probabilistic noninterference in a concurrent language. *Journal of Computer Security*, 7(2,3):231–253, 1999.

32. D. Volpano, G. Smith, and C. Irvine. A sound type system for secure flow analysis. *Journal of Computer Security*, 4(2,3):167–187, 1996.

33. S. Zdancewic. Challenges for information-flow security. In *Proceedings of the 1st International Workshop on Programming Language Interference and Dependence (PLID'04)*, 2004.

Index